# Missing Lenses

How reading scripture with the
first century church can help us
find our lost identity

# Tom Holland
## with Ann Weaver

Apiary Publishing

# ENDORSMENTS

*Missing Lenses* is an updated version of Dr. Tom Holland's scholarly book, *Contours of Pauline Theology* written for the non-academic reader.

*"Missing Lenses offers non-specialist biblical readers a concisely written, yet amazingly informative text from an evangelical, Reformed perspective concerning a major issue in New Testament Studies: the recovery of the corporate, Hebraic backdrop undergirding earliest Christian thought. Serious Bible study participants from many traditions will enjoy engaging with this volume."*

    — **Florence Morgan Gillman**, University of San Diego, CA USA

*"There is a remarkable thesis being presented here that demands scholarly attention. He has certainly produced a strong argument for a much greater influence of Passover typology than has generally been thought to be the case, and his arguments for the atoning sacrificial understanding of the original Passover sacrifice powerfully support the case argued by J. Jeremias and L. Morris. Dr. Holland has produced a stimulating volume which deserves the most careful scrutiny from New Testament students. It is a remarkably fresh and creative study which makes one re-think familiar passages in new ways."\**

    — The late **Prof. I. Howard Marshall**, Aberdeen University
      Evangelical Quarterly

*"It provides a fresh and useful treatment of Pauline theology, and many of its arguments offer corrections to widespread misunderstandings of Paul."\**

    — **Prof. Anthony C. Thiselton**, Nottingham University
      Expository Times

*"If Tom Holland's conclusions are accepted, then it would mean a radical rethinking in the way we approach some of the well-known passages of Paul's letters."\**

    — **Philip Eveson**, Evangelical Times

*"It is refreshing to read something radically new in such a popular area as Pauline studies. So often what promised new perspectives, new insights, turns out not to be essentially different. Tom Holland's original*

and creative approach to Paul does not fall into this category. I anticipate that if it finds acceptance, the proposals of this book should provide a timely and fruitful alternative to some of the theological emphases that have guided the church for too long."*

> — **Dr. William S. Campbell**, University of Wales, Trinity St. David

"This is certainly radical, and it boldly pushes forward an idea that has not really been discussed in Pauline scholarship."*

> — **Tan Kim Huat**, Trinity Theological Journal

"A welcome and important contribution to the controversial area of Pauline theology."*

> — **Bill James**, Reformation Today

"The strengths of the book are its robust challenge to many scholarly presuppositions and an impetus to new research on Paul's debt to the Old Testament...There is much that is very good and stimulating in this book."

> — **Anthony Bash**, European Journal of Theology

"He has pointed to an interesting and important motif in the OT, in early Judaism and in Paul's theology, which needs to be studied more systematically and in depth. Many of his challenges of recent scholarship on Paul and suggestions of his own are worth pondering."*

> — **Christoph Stenschke**, *Themelios*

"Generally speaking, conservative Reformed criticisms of the new perspective on Paul strike me as lackluster and predictable. That cannot be said, however, of Tom Holland's new book, which is bound to shake loose some long-standing presuppositions in Pauline studies. Holland's book raises enough questions about traditional assumptions to clear the way for groundbreaking research, and his approach does allow for a rigorous reexamination of the degree to which Paul is indebted to texts like Isaiah and the Pentateuch."*

> — **Mark Mattison**, The Paul Page

"The present reviewer, an Old Testament specialist, finds Holland's arguments as largely compelling and would suggest that Holland has re-integrated the faith of Old and New Testaments in a manner that serves effectively to emphasise the unity of Scripture."*

> — **Stephen Dray**, *Evangel*

"It should be compulsory reading for any who feel in any way seduced by the arguments of either liberal or 'New Perspective' theologians on the origins and content of Paul's theology. It presents compelling evidence that Paul's theology was thoroughly rooted in the Old Testament."*
   — **Robert Strivens**, The Banner of Truth

"This is a book to be placed in the hands of serious academics, Jewish or Christian, who are interested in Pauline studies and the relationship between Christianity and Judaism."*
   — **David Bond**, Lausanne Consultation on Jewish Evangelism

"An important and brilliant book. I recommend it to all prospective students of theology to read and study before they go to university."*
   — **Mike Moore**, Christian Witness to Israel

"No one has helped me read and understand St. Paul more than Tom Holland. I find his work to be the near-perfect balance of creative yet careful, original yet faithful. While many talk about theological exegesis—Dr. Holland actually does it, and he does it well."*
   — **Dustin Messer** (www.kuyperian.com)

"In his Contours of Pauline Theology Dr. Holland argues forcefully that the main contours of Paul's thought can only be understood when we understand Paul as an exegete and theologian of the Old Testament, with the hoped-for New Exodus, now fulfilled in Christ, at the centre of his reading strategy. This approach finds corporate and covenantal themes to lie at the very heart of Paul's concerns. In constant critical engagement with the whole range of contemporary scholarship Holland maps out for himself and his readers new ways of understanding Paul and offers new insights into a range of absolutely vital issues from justification to Christology, and new insights into Pauline texts from Romans to Colossians. Challenging, unsettling and infuriating Dr. Holland's tour de force cannot be ignored."*
   — **Dr. Peter Head**, University of Cambridge, UK

   * Quotes refer to Contours of Pauline Theology

# COPYRIGHT

For Ann and Bill Weaver whose love, kindness and encouragement has meant so much.

## PREFACE

**TOM HOLLAND** - I am somewhat surprised that you are reading the introduction to this book! To explain, I need to share the backstory about *Contours of Pauline Theology*, an earlier work of mine on which *Missing Lenses* is based. Although I didn't envision writing a book at the time, it was birthed in seed form when I began to wonder if something was amiss with the way we approached scripture. As a young pastor, I had resisted preaching through Paul's letter to the Romans mainly because of something Dr. Martin Lloyd Jones, who headed the famous Westminster Chapel in London, once said. He advised preachers not to tackle this letter until they understood its meaning. My problem was that I had studied Romans in the Greek text for my final year of undergraduate biblical studies, and still had questions! I knew what scholars said, but they all disagreed with each other on major matters and I wasn't willing to mindlessly repeat a view that had not fully become my own.

After struggling with this dilemma for years, I finally decided I would be dead before I gained such confidence, so in the hot summer of 1976 I began to preach through Romans. I was soon forced to make uncomfortable decisions. As I read various commentaries, what I came to see is that to make a theological point stick, the clear meaning of the Greek text was sometimes bypassed and then accompanied by an unconvincing explanation of why Paul meant something different. The difficulty is that literally everyone in my circles was doing this, even those whom I looked up to theologically.

As I raised these issues with pastoral friends, they were clearly uncomfortable with my questions for which they had no answers. Later, I found out that while recognizing my pastoral and teaching gifts, other leaders opted not to invite me to preach because they were uncertain about my theological positions. Eventually, I had to decide which way to go—was God calling me to advance in my ministry through the invitation to larger, more influential pastorates, or should I remain in relative obscurity as I continued to grapple with what was going on in biblical interpretation? Feeling directed to choose the latter, I decided getting to the bottom of these issues had the potential to benefit the church to a far greater extent than any preaching that I might do.

As I went on to discover, the central problem with so many interpretations was that key biblical passages were often seen as being about the individual when, actually, they carried a corporate meaning. This was true not just in isolated instances, but it reflected the apostles' overall mindset. Their presentation of redemptive history was primarily focused on the community rather than the individual. Of course, the apostles were concerned about the impact of their message on individuals, but that's not where their thinking began. Furthermore, this corporate way of reasoning was not only biblical but was prevalent in the ancient world as well, so the recipients of Paul's letters would naturally have read them in this light. This was reinforced by the thoroughly corporate focus of the Old Testament, the texts to which the apostles continually referred. Given these factors, it became clear that reading the text corporately is essential for a proper understanding of the apostolic message.

At the end of a preaching series in which I explained these discoveries, a fine young man, who was one of my deacons, said, "Tom, you say these ideas are not found in any of the books you have read. Will you write a pamphlet explaining your understanding, so we can reflect on this?" I agreed and some years later when the "pamphlet" reached 220,000 words, my research came to the attention of others. Dr. Eryl Davies, the editor of a theological journal and the principle of the Evangelical Theological College of Wales, (now Union School of Theology) asked me to write an article about my findings. Later, he kindly invited me to join the staff of the college and get a PhD so that I could engage in advanced teaching and supervise other research students. I cannot say enough about what this good and kind man means to me. He put his own reputation at risk to support what he sensed I was trying to do.

In pursuing my studies, I also began to notice something else—the New Testament writers not only looked to the Passover to explain Christ's death, but also drew on other themes from the First Exodus out of Egypt and the promises God gave through the prophets to bring captive Israel back from exile in Babylon. I began to refer to this as the Paschal-New Exodus Paradigm. The challenge was how could I show that reading scripture through this corporate lens was as important as I believed? The model needed further work and testing, so in the following years about half of the two dozen students I supervised used this paradigm to interpret other New Testament texts. It has been thrilling to see the examiners, who awarded degrees to these men but were not familiar with my work, admit they had not previously seen what was now plain to them, even though they had done their own in-depth studies of the texts.

In addition to this supervisory work, I also began writing and publishing my own research. My first book, *Contours of Pauline Theology*, which presented the fruit of my research to the public, was well-received by the academic world as well as the Christian press. Further books followed— *Romans: The Divine Marriage, Hope for the Nations,* and more recently *Tom Wright and the Search for Truth.*

And now we come to this, my latest book. The reason I'm surprised you're reading this preface is that once *Contours* came out, I thought there would be no reason to cover this material again. However, after it was published I had several requests to rewrite *Contours* for the non-academic reader, one of which came from Ann Weaver, an American student who lived in Chattanooga, Tennessee. She had approached me with a question at school and later took the course on Biblical Hermeneutics that I taught. I had to explain that it would be difficult for her to follow my answer unless she first understood how I reasoned and suggested that she read *Contours*. Weeks later, she emailed to say that reading the book was not only transforming her understanding on a number of levels, but her husband Bill's as well. They both asked if I would consider writing a version of *Contours* for the younger generation of American Christians who they thought would benefit from engaging with my work.

My response was cautious. I knew the danger of rushing off a draft, realizing there could be any number of blunders since I was not American and the culture, which is so like the British culture, is also very different. Knowing that Ann had done editorial work for the American Bible Society and having read her thesis and other theological essays, I asked if she would consider doing this project. This was a huge request as, at the time, she was considering whether to study for her own PhD. However, after talking it over with Bill and praying, she felt that rewriting *Contours* was the greater priority. What a sacrifice and a blessing to me! Using all of her skills, she has helped me communicate what I want to say to this generation with a clarity of which I could have only dreamed. Not only has Ann been faithful to what I have written elsewhere, she also repeatedly accepted my editorial control when I feared a suggested illustration or particular wording did not accurately represent my views or personality.

I cannot convey the effort Ann has put into this task. While she could have finished within a year, she took the time to work through every chapter of *Contours* (and my Romans commentary), comparing my arguments with other views, reflecting on more recent scholarship, and asking probing questions. This extensive scrutiny, coupled with the research on the Paschal-New Exodus model conducted by the grad students I have supervised, is what gives me the confidence to claim that I am not offering new or half-baked ideas on these pages; the major concepts in *Missing Lenses* have been thoroughly examined.

I want to record my debt to Ann and her dear husband, Bill, who has also helped with this project by reading, critiquing, editing, proofreading, and formatting. They are examples of servanthood, and the fellowship in the gospel that I have been privileged to share with them has meant so much to me. Our partnership is one that I will forever cherish. To them both, I say a thousand thanks for laboring with me in this task, which I pray will be blessed beyond our wildest dreams to the glory of God.

**ANN WEAVER** - Working on this project has been a labor of love. I met Tom Holland when I was at a pivotal place in my spiritual journey. Although theology is often portrayed as an intellectual exercise that mostly involves the head rather than the heart (which it can be), this has not been my experience. I had already seen the integral connection between truth and love earlier in my life when, as a young believer, I began to process childhood wounds and realized my concepts of God and love were both twisted. It was only in gaining more knowledge about God and the Son whom he sent that my heart became free to love.

Later, the importance of developing a sound biblical theology was driven home in a new, unexpected way when the Holy Laughter Revival (also known as the Toronto Blessing) swept through our church in the mid 90's. This movement, which was characterized by wild laughter, people falling into trances, and being "drunk" in the Spirit, sparked one of the most confusing periods in my Christian life. While some of my friends reported having life-changing encounters with God, critics said it was a counterfeit revival, a claim that I could not easily dismiss given some of the disturbing things I had witnessed. What made it especially challenging is that both those for and against the movement were quoting Jonathan Edwards, pulling conflicting evidence from church history, and picking and choosing scriptures to make their case. Who to believe? This was no small matter as opponents were presenting different, sometimes incompatible pictures of how to know and relate to God. The controversy surrounding the movement was also creating relational tension between friends, family members, and within local churches, as well as the larger body of Christ. Realizing that my heart could not be settled until I knew what was true, I began to sift through the perplexing mix of issues.

Little did I know at the time that I was heading down a long and winding theological road that would eventually lead me to Eifion Evans, author of *The Welsh Revival of 1904*. Taking an interest in the questions I was asking, Eifion became a valued mentor and friend, encouraging me to write about what I was learning. Later, he and other friends suggested I go to graduate school for further training. Searching for a program that meshed with my other responsibilities, Eifion steered me towards a small theological school in Wales where I met Dr. Holland.

My first conversation with Tom occurred as professors and students walked along the fierce, windy cliffs of the Southerndown seacoast in one of our initial "get-to-know-you" sessions. At the time, I was theologically stuck. In my personal studies, I had run across several tangled issues about which theologians disagreed and commentaries were no help in unravelling. These were not peripheral matters but went to the very heart of the gospel and core identity issues that I saw so many people, including myself, wrestle with over the years. After listening to my story, Tom gently suggested that I read his book, *Contours of Pauline Theology*.

My initial reaction, which I did not share with him at the time, is that I could hardly see what a book about Pauline theology had to do with the trail I was following, but as I discovered to my delight, it had everything to do with it! I was deeply encouraged when I saw that Tom had been exploring similar foundational issues but from a different angle and was decades ahead of me in researching the answers. However, as much as I resonated with *Contours*, when he talked to me about writing a more accessible version for the church at large it was not an easy decision. For one thing, it was a detour from my own work. Also, having discussed Tom's main ideas with Reformed friends, I knew that some of his views were likely to meet with pockets of resistance, despite the fact that *Contours* had been well-received by reputable men in the UK. Through these conversations, it became clear to me that taking on this project might also mean swimming upstream. Nevertheless, after weighing the costs, I opted to do it because I believed in the great value of Tom's work, especially given the issues we are facing in this present generation.

One of the reasons the project took so much longer than I originally anticipated is that to write on someone's behalf it is necessary to first enter into their mindset. This was no easy task. Tom's work deals with a range of complex issues that build on one another. Also, since it challenges several traditional ideas often assumed to be "givens," I felt it was important to test his conclusions against other points of view, which required additional research. Furthermore, scholars, who are already familiar with the backdrop of many issues, often speak to one another in shorthand or make references which the non-academic reader may not always understand. This made it necessary to stop at several points to explore additional background information that might be helpful in knowing how best to position a particular issue.

The benefit of this process is that as I engaged with Tom's ideas more deeply, I began to experience a paradigm shift that opened up scripture in new, life-changing ways. Like the examiners Tom mentioned above, I too see things in scripture now that were always there, but I had never seen before. His views also helped to resolve a number of pastoral conundrums that, as I came to learn, were part of our theological inheritance in the West. I can only say that Tom's insights on Romans 7 and the identity of the Wretched Man, which is at the root of so much of our tangled thinking about sin and the human person, are groundbreaking.

Although the ultimate goal was to produce a version of *Contours* that was more user-friendly, there's no getting around it—*Missing Lenses* is still a meaty book that will require some work on the reader's part. But, as I can attest, the effort is well worth it! Having read a wide swath of material from various traditions now, I have no illusions that everyone will agree with all that Dr. Holland says. However, I have remained passionate about this project, mainly because I am convinced that his ideas need to be part of the conversation the contemporary church is having as we seek to better understand our sacred texts and live into our true identity as the one unified body of Christ.

I will be forever grateful for the privilege of working for and with Tom Holland. Throughout this lengthy process he has been incredibly patient, kind and charitable, even when I'm sure I must have driven him almost mad with all my questions! In spite of the fact that he was so much further down the road in thinking through critical issues than I was, he always graciously allowed for open dialogue and had the humility to refine some of his ideas whenever Bill or I suggested the need for further clarification. Tom has modeled all the qualities that I hope to emulate in any future theological discussions, but even more than this, his sacrificial love for Christ and his body has made an indelible mark on my life.

There is no way I will ever be able to express sufficient gratitude to my husband, Bill, who fully entered into this process with me. In addition to his invaluable insights and the practical support he provided on so many different levels, he was there in the dark hours when I felt like I was way in over my head and despaired of ever crossing the finish line. I am not exaggerating when I say this book may not have ever seen the light of day without his help. I also want to say thanks to all of my gracious friends who kindly suffered through the many conversations about Romans 6-8, Augustine, Plato and other thorny matters, and who also forgave my periodic unavailability. Love truly does endure all things. With Tom, I pray that God will use this work in unforeseen ways to advance his purposes so that many others can experience the beauty, wonder, and joy of life in his marvelous kingdom of light.

# CONTENTS

## PART THREE Recovering the Passover Lens

# Shifting Lenses

The world is going through a period of unprecedented change. Some refer to it as a "Cosmic Transition," "a Third or Fourth Awakening," "a New Reformation," "the Dawning of a New World Order," or more dramatically, "the End of the World as We Know It." However, it's labeled or characterized, something BIG is happening.

Thanks to the internet and other advanced technologies, we are experiencing a global interconnectivity on a scale unparalleled in the history of humankind. As journalist Thomas Friedman observed, "We are now connecting all the knowledge centers on the planet together into a single global network."[1] This ongoing process has birthed massive cultural shifts that are sweeping across the world, displacing older political, financial, social, and even national systems and structures that have been sources of common values and identity, while, at the same time, new ones are struggling to emerge.

People often rely on religion to provide stability and meaning, but in these tumultuous times religions are in flux too. As noted by one spiritual leader, "Paradoxically, the world is getting both more and less religious at the same time."[2] On a global scale, secularism, Christianity, and Islam are each growing, colliding, and having a polarizing effect. Yet, due to the cultural exchange of ideas, different religions are also influencing one another, sometimes evolving into new, blended expressions of faith.

Similar dynamics are at work in the West where Christianity has long been the dominant religion.[3] Judeo-Christian values are woven into the very fabric of Western society. In recent decades, however, it has gradually been losing influence at the same time that numerous forms of alternative spirituality have flooded the marketplace. Commenting on evolving spiritual trends, author and religion professor, Stephen Prothero, contends, "It is not that religion is in trouble. It is that religion is morphing into something new."[4] Caught in the middle of these swirling changes, Christianity in the West is experiencing an identity crisis of its own.[5]

For some time now, Christians from various quarters of the church have been engaged in a large, ongoing conversation about how to respond to these turbulent transitions and find our way forward. Long before the extent of this cultural transformation became apparent, a haunting question was already on the discussion table—if Christians are supposed to love one another and live in unity, why can't we all get along? First came the schism between the Eastern and Western church in the eleventh century. Catholics and Protestants split a few centuries later, followed by the seemingly endless divisions in the Protestant world. Today, the church is splintered into thousands of denominations and sects all claiming to be Christian and to follow Jesus!

It would be one thing if these groups were simply expressions of diversity. Many, however, not only disagree with one another about organization, worship and how salvation occurs, but they also teach contradictory doctrine. In fact, so many competing versions of Jesus and his teachings are floating around today that as one spiritual writer puts it, "Jesus is in trouble . . . no matter where you look, a cloud of confusion hangs over the message" he came to deliver.[6] This fractured picture has left many wondering—is it even possible to know who Jesus is?

Since the Bible is one of the primary sources of Christian identity and guidance, it seems that we should be able to turn to it for help in coming to a more unified understanding of Jesus and the Christian life, but that is not as easy as it sounds. While it continues to be a best seller in the West, biblical illiteracy is rampant and even among professing believers, there is no consensus about its role in the Christian life.[7] This is not surprising, as the Bible has taken a series of hits in the last two hundred years that have weakened its influence. Historically, in spite of their differences, those who have professed Christ have generally held a high view of scripture, meaning the Bible was seen as the inspired Word of God and regarded as an authoritative, God-given guide for faith and practice. For centuries, Christians have looked to the Bible as the primary source of knowledge about Jesus and the church's unique identity as a Spirit-breathed community united with him and one another.

Starting in the mid-nineteenth century, however, this high view of scripture began to face serious and consistent challenges that called into question the reliability not only of the content, but also of the very texts themselves. As a result, an attitude of suspicion began to spread regarding the Bible's truthfulness, accuracy, and historical authenticity. Postmodern thought further rocked the boat by disputing the idea that there is any kind of overarching metanarrative that gives meaning to life (which Christians have traditionally claimed scripture provides), or that we can know truth with any degree of certainty. This unsettling turn of events generated a profusion of new controversies, some of which tied into older historic debates. In recent years, sorting through theological issues has become such a complex, confusing endeavor that according to one theologian, it is like going to a "large and somewhat chaotic party."[8]

Combined, these dynamics have made deep inroads into how many relate to the Bible. A good number still believe it is the inspired Word of God, but skepticism towards scripture has continued to rise, especially in the younger generations.[9] A growing perception is that it teaches good ethics, but that men wrote it, not God. Others contend that the Bible is mainly metaphorical or that it contains myths, errors, and contradictions. In the eyes of some, it is a record of the first-century church's experiences but is meant to serve as an example rather than convey timeless truths. Other common assumptions are that it is simply one of several ancient documents that provide wisdom and comfort, or that it is acceptable to choose the parts that are personally meaningful and discard the rest.

Given the confusion surrounding scripture, no wonder many feel disheartened about ever being able to comprehend it. One sincere young woman said it this way, "I feel like I'll have to study for years to figure out what to believe about the Bible itself, and if I don't do that first, how can I be sure what it says is true?"

As challenging as these contemporary trends may be, there is a deeper, foundational problem with how we have viewed scripture that, ironically, helped bring us to this crisis point—I am firmly convinced that we have been reading the Bible through distorted lenses and not just in recent times, but for centuries! I would even go so far as to say this has played a significant role in the declining influence of Christianity in the West and has given rise to some of the theological tensions between the different branches of the church. I know these are BIG statements that will raise eyebrows—and rightly so. We should be suspicious of anyone who makes such bold claims. Nevertheless, I believe there is good reason for saying these things. And also, for proposing that if we are to recover a clear-eyed vision of who we are and where we are headed—both as a collective community of Christ-followers and as individuals—it is essential to reframe the way we read scripture. While this may not resolve all of the challenges we face today, it can help us gain confidence in scripture, see the roots of some of our differences, and recover common ground.

## Reading through Distorted Lenses

The reason I believe reframing is necessary has to do with the two-way relationship between the church and culture. As Christians, we like to think of ourselves as changing the world, but as journalist Andy Crouch points out, the world also "thoroughly changes, shapes, and even determines us."[10]

One of the dynamics we have become keenly aware of in recent years is that our experiences, plus the intricate web of beliefs, ideas, and thoughts we knowingly or unknowingly absorb from previous generations and our surrounding culture, affects the way we perceive, interpret, and apply texts. These influences form the "eyeglasses" or "frame" through which we view the world. This is why, throughout history, people from various cultures and historical periods all bring a different set of hidden biases and presuppositions to the table when reading texts. Consequently, the lenses through which we read and interpret scripture depend a great deal on "where we stand" at the moment.[11] As the authors of *Misreading Scripture with Western Eyes* note, "We instinctively draw from our own cultural context to make sense of what we're reading."[12]

Speaking of the West, I suggest that one of the major reasons there are so many contradictory, inconsistent, and divisive interpretations is that our "eyeglasses" have been shaped by hidden assumptions that are sometimes incompatible with scripture. Our Western view has been colored by presuppositions inherited from our Greek and Roman background, while the Bible is a collection of texts that are rooted primarily in the Jewish culture. Some contend that, for the most part, the Greco-Roman framework was adjusted when necessary throughout church history to ensure alignment with what the Bible revealed. I acknowledge this effort, but after studying the biblical texts and other materials for more than fifty years, I believe certain assumptions that are at odds with scripture have not been fully detected and are still embedded in our lenses. Reading scripture this way is like trying to see through eyeglasses when the prescription is off—everything ends up getting pulled out of focus. This doesn't mean we have to write off all we know and believe about the Bible and its teachings. However, learning to see through Hebraic eyes may require us to make some much needed, and ultimately beneficial adjustments.

## Inverting the Biblical Picture

A major assumption that has been instrumental in shaping our "eyeglasses" has to do with one of the most cherished values in the West—the belief in the primary importance of the individual. As one academic website notes, "No other intellectual tradition has been as intensively (some would say excessively) preoccupied with singling out and defining the individual self than Western philosophy."[13]

Individualism is so deeply ingrained in the West, especially in America, that it is mostly taken for granted. This cultural emphasis can be traced back, in part, to the inscription "know thyself" that was carved over the entrance of Apollo's temple at Delphi, a worship site in ancient Greece.[14] Variations of this theme such as "to know thyself is the beginning of wisdom" and Shakespeare's "to thine own self be true" have become an integral part of our cultural vocabulary. Plato's teachings about the private, inward journey of the soul to find the true self and return to the higher realm of the spirit, modified and embraced by various Christian thought leaders, has also contributed to the Western emphasis on self.[15] In the seventeenth century, Descartes, who is known as the father of modern Western philosophy, further developed the concept of the individual self that has influenced subsequent generations to this day. Others, like Freud, introduced their own variations.

On the positive side, we can easily make a long list of benefits that have come from championing the individual. The downside, however, is that in recent decades, the Western fascination with self began to mutate into hyper-individualism, a troubling form of narcissism that social experts say has now reached epidemic proportions.[16]

Much has already been written about this trend. Not only has it had a detrimental effect on society, but it has also seeped into the church, influencing the way many worship and relate to the larger faith community. Worship songs, prayers, and preaching are often focused on the relationship between the individual and God, with the church being relegated to a supporting role. For all practical purposes, in many areas of the church, the local congregation is seen as a voluntary collection of individuals who come together to "fellowship with other individuals who have a private relationship with God."[17] Consequently, the kind of vibrant kingdom-centered, Spirit-breathed-and-directed and other-oriented community life that is described in scripture has either been limited or lost.

This mentality has also made deep inroads on the way we read scripture. It is being increasingly recognized that because of the inherited emphasis on self, indigenous Westerners tend to read the Bible through a predominantly *individualistic lens.* When I use this phrase, I do not mean that individuals read scripture privately and therefore come up with differing interpretations, although this is definitely a problem in some parts of the church. What I mean is that the New Testament letters are mistakenly read as describing *individual* experience and *personal* morality. Or, said another way, it is commonly assumed that they mainly speak to *me* about *my* relationship with Jesus and teach *me* how to be a better person.

While scripture certainly esteems the individual, the biblical writers, most of whom were Jewish, had a communal mindset in which the self is not an isolated, independent entity, but an integral part of a larger whole. Commenting on individualism in the West, theologian Soong-Chan Rah states "We see that theme, not in scripture but in Western culture." He goes on to explain, "*Scripture actually speaks to the people of God, to the entire church, rather than specific individuals.*"[18] In other words, scripture is primarily focused on the *church's corporate experience* of *God's saving activity* and the *community's response* to this saving event.

Reading scripture through an individualistic lens is like looking through the wrong end of a telescope. Instead of seeing it from a corporate perspective first, and *then* considering the individual's role in relation to the whole, we have turned it the other way around. Consequently, critical aspects of the believing community's central role in God's plan for humanity have been inadvertently pushed into the background. In turn, this has caused both past and present believers to unwittingly misread key texts. As we will see, even many who readily agree that most of the New Testament is addressed to the community have sometimes unknowingly read individualistic assumptions back into scripture.

Although this method of reading scripture prevails in much of academia as well as the church today, such a strategy would have been completely foreign to first-century believers! Rooted in Hebraic thought, the apostles taught that committed believers were to see themselves first and foremost not as independent individuals, but as members of a "holy *nation*, God's special possession." [19] Reflecting this corporate perspective, the New Testament describes the church as a single, unified, organic entity—the new man (humanity), the body of Christ, the bride of Christ, or God's temple made of living stones. Orthodox theologian, John Zizioulas, explains that in the understanding of the primitive church

> Christ was *not conceivable as an individual* but always "in the Spirit," *as a corporate person*, as one who is at the same time many. Likewise, the many were never understood apart from the one, Christ . . . Unlike other nonbiblical forms of spirituality, which could be understood individualistically, *Christian spirituality was ecclesial [congregational] in its nature.*" [20]

He explains that in the biblical view,

> Individualism is incompatible with Christian spirituality . . . When the Spirit blows the result is never to create good individual Christians, but members of a community. *This became fundamental for Christian spirituality in the New Testament and was in direct line with the Old Testament mentality.* [21]

The message the apostles preached was set in context of this larger, communal picture. It is quite amazing to re-read scripture with this corporate perspective in mind and see just how many of the texts we have traditionally regarded as being about "me and Jesus" are, in reality, about God and his people. I will give specific examples of this throughout the book.

## More Hidden Assumptions

In addition to this individualistic approach, our Western lenses have also been shaped by dualistic presuppositions inherited from our Greek background. Early on, the church fathers soundly rejected certain forms of Greek dualism such as the belief that the material world, including the body, is evil and the spiritual realm or the soul is superior. Since God created the material world Christians have generally agreed that it is good, but other dualistic presuppositions about the human person quietly slipped through undetected and were read back into scripture. Consequently, like the culture, Western Christianity been troubled with various, disjointed views of the individual self.

For instance, Plato's idea that the soul is divided into higher and lower parts in tension with one another is reflected in the teaching that Christians have two conflicting natures, or that our hearts are divided into an upper room in which the Spirit lives and a lower room that is corrupt. [22] Although some conjecture the New Testament writers themselves introduced these dualistic ideas, I am convinced that reading scripture through a corporate lens will show they stayed true to the holistic view of the human person characteristic of Old Testament, Hebraic thought, and that dualistic notions about the human person entered into Christian teaching later.

Furthermore, I suggest that a number of other key salvation-related texts have been distorted because they have been interpreted against the individualistic, legalistic backdrop of the Roman law court. In contrast, I contend the predominant context is the covenantal relationship God entered into with his people that scripture describes as a marriage, and that this was made possible by the Passover/Exodus events. In the Western forensic model, sin is defined as a crime and God is depicted as a criminal court judge, when in scripture, he is portrayed as a loving husband who has been betrayed. As we shall see, God does judge, but this role is performed in a relational context as opposed to the impersonal Roman law court. This faulty lens has affected influential teachings about justification, the doctrine of sin, and of Christ's atoning death, issues that have been long-standing sources of debate and division. [23]

In sum, reading scripture through "eyeglasses" colored by Greco-Roman thought has resulted in an over-emphasis on the individual, a diminished understanding of the Christian community, and a fragmented view of the human person. And this in turn, has skewed how we have interpreted key texts, which has contributed to divisions within the body of Christ. It is like the proverbial chicken and egg—by shaping the way we read scripture, the culture has contributed to Western Christianity's identity crisis, and reading scripture through a Greco-Roman framework has unintentionally contributed to some of Western society's current woes.

## How We Got Our Eyeglasses

When and how did our individualistic approach to reading scripture in the West begin? Some contend Martin Luther introduced it during the Reformation and the evangelical movement that blossomed in the early 1700s carried it forward. [24] This is when personal salvation and piety became prominent themes in Western Christianity. No doubt, the emphasis on the individual that occurred in that period was a factor. But actually, the seeds of it can be traced to the second, third, and fourth centuries, when some of the early church fathers unwittingly read into scripture some of the individualistic and dualistic assumptions inherited from their Greek upbringing. At this same time, the Jewish context of scripture characterized by a corporate, holistic mindset was obscured, minimized, or misunderstood.

To be clear, it is not that the believing community completely lost a corporate understanding of the Christian life in this era or any other for that matter; the church has always retained knowledge of her communal life in Christ. It is more that key concepts were individualized or interpreted through a different framework, which muddled the biblical picture. Because all branches of Christianity share the same root system, the entire church—Protestant, Catholic, Anglican, and Orthodox—has been affected by these developments, albeit in different ways and in varying degrees. [25]

After seeing the long-term, detrimental effect of reading scripture through distorted lenses, I believe it is fair to say that in the West, we live in a period similar to medieval times when Aristotle's philosophy controlled biblical interpretation and threatened to choke the life out of the Western church! Enthralled at the time with the philosopher's newly discovered works, theologians placed so much emphasis on reason, logic, systematic thinking, propositional truth, and philosophical intricacies that in its official form, Western Christianity became quite arid and lifeless. As a result, it failed to touch the heart or imagination! Although we are facing a different set of problems today (some of which are rooted in these older issues), I suggest reading scripture with an individualistic, dualistic mindset is causing the church to experience far less than what scripture promises regarding our life together as a Spirit-filled community.

In one way, this is not a new subject. The relationship between Greco-Roman thought and Christian theology has been a topic of ongoing debate for centuries, and the ways individualism and dualism affected the Western church have also been much discussed in recent history. Thankfully, the importance of recovering the biblical emphasis on community is now receiving significant attention as well. Nevertheless, these matters continue to be highly relevant to the church today as there is still much to sort through. We live in exciting times when the entire New Testament is being increasingly recognized as a thoroughly Jewish book, the message of which was shaped primarily by Hebraic, rather than Greco-Roman thought. This is helping us see our sacred texts in fresh, new ways. As the church continues to recover the Jewish backdrop of the New Testament, I predict that we will be shocked to see the degree to which some of the hidden assumptions embedded in our Greco-Roman framework have influenced the way we read scripture and approach the Christian life. While a number of scholars and Christian thought leaders are in the process of seeing this, I suggest that it goes much further than what we previously realized.

## Where I Stand

Given the historic emphasis on having a personal relationship with God in some parts of the church, certain aspects of what I am saying may be concerning to some, so before going any further, I want to make a few things clear about my position.

First, I am in *no way downplaying the need for individual salvation* or the value of private Bible reading, nor am I denying that scripture has personal application. What I am saying is that unless these individual exercises are properly set within the larger corporate context of scripture and the believing community, we will end up with a distorted, diminished view of the faith. There is a vast difference between a healthy biblical view of the individual in which each person is equally valued and seen as uniquely gifted to serve the community, and the Western concept of the autonomous individual who functions as a "self-directing chooser."[26] In my opinion, the way to recover this distinction is to understand scripture's predominantly corporate emphasis *first* and only then reconsider how we, as individuals, are called to respond. This is not taking away from the necessity of personal faith; it is simply saying that the individual's role and experiences need to be understood within this communal framework.

Second, we live in a day and age when so much is changing that old labels often do not reflect the more nuanced positions held by many now. Yet because we all come from some type of heritage that has shaped our thinking to one extent or another, it is a common courtesy to be forthcoming about our backgrounds. To this end, I want to state up front that I am a fairly conservative biblical theologian who is rooted in the evangelical, Reformed tradition. As I see it, a biblical theologian is one who seeks to understand and follow the progressive revelation of scripture by considering the texts in their historical setting and honoring the Bible's own "categories and thought forms."[27] Creeds or later understandings should not control this approach, although I believe biblical theology normally confirms those great statements of faith that were eventually articulated. As far as the Bible is concerned, I am convinced it is inspired by God and presents an amazingly unified grand narrative about his relationship with humankind, both here on earth and in eternity.

Being that I am not exactly the revolutionary type, I have no desire to introduce innovations that may be unnecessarily disturbing to others. However, in keeping with the historic motto, "the church reformed, always being reformed," I also think there are times when all of us, no matter what tradition we hold dear, may find it necessary to humbly re-examine our fundamental presuppositions and adjust even some of our most treasured positions *if it is proved from scripture there is a need to do so.* Because Reformed thought has been so influential in the West, in addition to speaking to matters that affect the entire church, I will also be addressing a number of issues within my own tradition that I believe warrant review in light of the Bible's communal emphasis.

## About the Book

While I believe a fresh exploration of these issues can benefit the global church, my primary focus will be on how reading scripture through a Greco-Roman framework has affected Christianity in the West. I want to show how recovering the Jewish, Old Testament backdrop and two missing lenses—the biblical emphasis on the collective people of God and the Paschal-New Exodus model for interpreting Christ's death—can help us see both scripture and our life together in a new light.

The original purpose of this book was to take the content in my scholarly work, *Contours of Pauline Theology*, and make it more accessible to a wider audience. Along the way, the work was expanded to address issues that needed further clarification and to discuss some of the practical implications of reading scripture from a corporate perspective. In doing this, I also drew on material from my commentary, *Romans: The Divine Marriage*. Parts of *Missing Lenses* may seem familiar to those who have read my scholarly works as in certain instances the same language was used because it expressed exactly what I wanted to say. This book also includes some original material, the bulk of which is found in chapter 9 and the article in Appendix B.

Because I am calling for a reassessment of several long-standing traditional interpretations in *Missing Lenses*, it is both important and necessary to show the reasoning behind the suggested changes, which accounts for the book's length. For ease of reading, it is organized into three parts; each chapter is divided into two to five sub-chapters; and scripture references that would normally be included in the body of a primarily academic work were placed in the endnotes at the back of the book.

Regarding terminology, I am using *the church, body of Christ, the believing community* and *the new covenant community*, synonymously and look to 1 Corinthians 12:12-27 and Ephesians 2:11-22 for the definition. The reason for specifying the new covenant community is to convey the difference between the church and the Old Testament community, which also shared in a covenant relationship with God. The original covenant God made with Israel at Mount Sinai fell apart because as a nation, she repeatedly broke the terms, but God promised to establish a new and better one with his people. Unlike the first covenant that was centered on Moses, the new one is based on Christ as our Savior and Lord, a role that Moses could never fill. It is also inclusive. Rather than being limited to the Jews, the new covenant community is made up of Jews *and* Gentiles (all other people groups) who repent and trust in Jesus for salvation. When I use the phrase *Christian community*, it refers to all of the various denominations, groups and individuals who self-identify as Christian. And in speaking of *believers*, I am referring to those who have actively placed their faith in Christ as Savior and Lord and are committed to following him.

In one more note about terminology, I have chosen to use the term *Yahweh* at times when referring to God in an Old Testament context.

This is a phonetic spelling of the unpronounceable name of YHWH, meaning "I am that I am," which is how God revealed himself to Moses.[28] It is often translated as *the Lord* or *Adonai*. While there is debate about whether or not this name should be used because the Jews have chosen not to speak it out of respect, scripture does not forbid its use. For the purposes of this book, the name Yahweh serves to describe God as he was known by Israel.

## Potential Benefits of a Corporate Reading

I am not suggesting that rediscovering the corporate, Hebraic context of scripture will be a panacea for everything that ails contemporary Christianity. But personally, I believe that learning to read scripture in light of its corporate dimension can go a long way in restoring health, well-being, and unity to the body of Christ.

Christians today desperately need to hear the original meaning of the New Testament texts, a meaning that begins first with God, then the people of God, and *then* the individual. By making this major correction, I believe the church will understand her sacred texts more accurately, interpret her experience of God's grace more clearly, and better identify the roots of some of our doctrinal differences. It will also enable God's people to regain confidence not just in scripture itself, but also that it is not necessary to be a scholar or theologian to understand it!

Furthermore, a corporate reading will set forth a clearer, grander vision of the church—both for her communal life as well as her mission—and assist individuals in discovering a greater sense of identity and purpose. Realizing the emphasis that scripture places on the believing community can inspire individual Christians to find his or her rightful place within this holy nation. In this context, as we sacrificially serve and are served by others, one of the greatest paradoxes of the Christian life has the potential to become a living reality—the less we focus on our own happiness and, instead, increase our focus on pursuing God's kingdom and righteousness *together*, the more we will experience personal satisfaction, liberty, and joy.

Finally, seeing the central role of God's holy community and the corporate, Paschal-New Exodus storyline that unifies scripture can lead us back to a much more balanced and authoritative doctrine of Christian salvation. In turn, this can help us more deeply value not only those within our local churches, but also members of other congregations and denominations as being an integral part of Christ's body.

## Making the Shift

In light of the deep-seated individualism in the West, seeing things from a corporate point of view can be quite challenging. We are so accustomed to reading certain texts in particular ways that viewing them from a different angle can be quite disconcerting, much like adjusting to a new pair of eyeglasses can cause us to feel off balance.

To make this transition, we first need to clear up several faulty ideas that have either undermined confidence in scripture or clouded the biblical picture. We will do this in the next two chapters, and also identify the ancient writings and storyline that had the most influence on Jesus and the authors of the New Testament. This will allow us to gain greater insight into what shaped their thinking and lay the necessary groundwork for seeing scripture through the corporate, Hebraic "eyeglasses" of the first-century church.

# PART ONE

# Recovering the Hebraic Backdrop

CHAPTER 1

# Cleaning the Canvas

The current confusion about who Jesus is and how to interpret the Bible reminds me of a story I once heard about John Ruskin, a nineteenth century poet, artist, and social thinker. On one occasion, Ruskin brought a friend to his studio to show him his latest painting. When he removed the dustcover from the canvas, Ruskin's friend could not make out what the picture was supposed to be. To him, it looked like an incoherent mass of color with no form or obvious subject. Then Ruskin took his palate, squeezed paint onto his board, and before his friend's eyes started to brush it on selected places around the canvas. Slowly, the subject of the painting came to life until finally there was a work of art that he could recognize and admire. It was the absence of those critical details that had robbed the picture of the artist's intended meaning. In the same way, if we miss the meaning of key ideas in the New Testament, all we will see is a conglomeration of unrelated concepts; Jesus and the bigger picture (and yes, I'm convinced there is one) will always evade us.

Fortunately, when it comes to the Bible, we don't have to wait for an artist to come along and add the defining brush strokes. The keys to help us understand scripture have been there all along. Unfortunately, many have been smudged over by layers of cultural biases and assumptions that clash with scripture, such as the ones we saw in the introduction.[1] In addition to the individualistic, dualistic ideas that have shaped the Western mindset over the centuries, modern scholars also introduced a mixed bag of flawed theories that have created immense confusion about the Bible.

For instance, in recent history, claims have been made that

- Paul created Christianity by importing Greek concepts into a Jewish message; Jesus would not have recognized what emerged as being faithful to his teaching.

- The four gospels are riddled with stories and sayings the early church invented to make Jesus's message relevant to the Gentiles.

- Jesus did not think he was God; the early church conspired to give him divine status to prove to the Gentiles that he was superior to pagan gods.

- The Bible is not a revelation from God; it was written by fallible men who were influenced by views in their own times. Therefore, scripture is best seen as a prototype, an example of how the church addressed the issues of their day, not a permanent "guidebook."

- To protect their positions, powerful bishops suppressed equally valid writings that were penned by dissenting Christ-followers at a time when no one orthodox version of Christianity existed.

- As the original writings (which we no longer have) were copied, unnamed writers added their own thoughts.

Any one of these ideas is enough to create serious doubts about the reliability of scripture or our ability to know its meaning. In various combinations, they represent a *colossal*—some say, *insurmountable*—assault on the gospel. If any of these theories are true, then it seems as though the Bible provides us with nothing more than a collage of apparently conflicting data and no way of knowing who Jesus was, or what he and the apostles really taught. Which, in turn, means there is no definitive basis for the Christian faith.

This touches on one of the main reasons why we have so many different Jesus's today. It is one thing to have questions about the Bible—many of us do. However, once the overall integrity of scripture is undermined and people start saying that some parts are valid, and others are not, then Jesus is up for grabs. We can cut and paste scriptures together to create any picture of him that suits us.[2] If this approach is acceptable—and many today seem to think it is—then one designer Jesus is as good as another. It's just a matter of picking the one we each like best.

This method, however, simply does not do justice to the stunning portrayal of Jesus and his work that is actually described in scripture! If we are to recover a more authentic, cohesive rendition of the biblical picture and regain confidence in our sacred texts, then much like those who lovingly restore old paintings that have been discolored by centuries of accumulated dirt and environmental damage, it will be necessary to patiently clear away some of these confusing ideas. Once this is done, then we will begin looking more closely at the biblical storyline that shaped the message of the New Testament.

**THE RECOVERY PROCESS⁋** I'm not going to sort through the different versions of Jesus or address the full spectrum of problems generally associated with biblical interpretation, as a number of books have already been written about these subjects.[3] Rather, my immediate goal is to concentrate on a few pervasive, but erroneous scholarly theories that have an enormous impact on way scripture is read. To this end, I want to show that:

- A good deal of modern New Testament scholarship has been based on flawed assumptions.

- The gospels are faithful records of Jesus's teaching.

- Paul did not depart from the teaching of Jesus. He stayed true to his Jewish roots.

- The early church did not arbitrarily exclude other writings; rather the Old Testament and the original apostolic message served as their guideline when assessing various teachings.

- While it is true that Greek thinking eventually influenced some of the church's teachings, this happened later, after the New Testament was written.

- Far from being a loose collection of unrelated documents, as some claim, the New and Old Testaments are bound together by a grand storyline that centers on Israel's Exodus from Egypt, their return from exile in Babylon, and the nation's hope for a New Exodus. Both Jesus and Paul used this New Exodus model as a unifying framework for the gospel.[4]

I know the mere mention of the word *scholarly* is enough to cause some to say, "well, this part of the discussion is not for me then." Let me encourage you that since several of the theories we shall be discussing have been instrumental in eroding confidence in scripture across the board, this is a critical matter for us all. This is true even for those who tend to be wary of academia or who feel like anything remotely connected with scholarship is either over their heads or irrelevant to everyday life. Scripture was given as a gift to God's people. No matter how grateful we may be for some of the work done by academics, the believing community is still responsible for sifting and weighing their findings. For this reason, it is important not just for leaders, but for all members of the church to be aware of these errors and the way in which they influence our understanding of scripture.

Interestingly, a good number of these errors have come about because scholars made wrong conclusions about the New Testament's cultural setting. So, in the next two chapters we will look at four scholarly errors and consider how we can best determine the New Testament's cultural backdrop.

## Cultural Barriers

If we are honest, reading and understanding scripture is not always as easy as some people make it sound. Since it was written nearly two thousand years ago, the minute we open the pages of the Bible, we are confronted with a number of formidable barriers. Life today is so radically different from life in the first century that it is often difficult for modern day readers to relate to the language, customs, ideas, and illustrations that were commonly understood in Jesus's time.

One major obstacle in comprehending scripture has to do with questions about the cultural background of the New Testament. Similar to our globalized world of today, Jesus and the apostles lived in a multi-cultural society. Although all of the New Testament writers (except Luke) were Jews, in many instances, they were addressing audiences that consisted of both Jews *and* Gentiles (non-Jews). To complicate matters even further, the Gentile world in the first century encompassed a hodgepodge of peoples with disparate beliefs and customs. Greeks, Celts, Babylonians, Italians, Samaritans, Persians, Egyptians, Berbers, and others all co-mingled under the Latin umbrella of the Roman Empire.

Given the multi-cultural setting of the New Testament times, scholars over the centuries have wrestled with a fundamental question—in what cultural context did the authors of the New Testament set their writings? Did they draw their examples and illustrations from the Jewish, Greek, or Latin cultures, or a mixture of all of them? This is a critical issue when it comes to understanding biblical concepts as knowing the cultural context is often key in determining the meaning of a text.[5]

Take the word *football* for instance. In Europe, the term *football* refers to soccer, but in the United States it is an entirely different game that involves either kicking or throwing a ball in the air and running it down the field. So, if a European has a conversation with an American about football, unless they first clarify the term, they will be talking about two very different ballgames. If the goal is to communicate with more than one ethnic group, then the writer will need to either use concepts that are familiar to all or explain the terminology which he or she chooses. This is why knowing the target audience can provide important clues to an author's intended meaning.

Of course, it is possible that culture was not such a big issue for the New Testament writers, for although most were Hebrew they had grown up in a pluralistic Greco-Roman world. Many modern Europeans switch without thought between their own and the American culture. Were the authors of the New Testament doing the same? How do we know which culture they were drawing from when selecting the imagery used in the New Testament?

## Error #1: The Early Church Abandoned Its Jewish Heritage

Undoubtedly, determining the cultural backdrop of scripture involves some thorny issues, so it is perhaps not surprising that even experts can get things wrong sometimes. One error has to do with the claim made by some prominent scholars that the early church sacrificed its Jewish heritage in order to effectively communicate the gospel to the Gentile world. This line of reasoning led these scholars to assume the New Testament evolved through three layers of traditions:

- Stage One. The first layer was based on the Jewish material that came from the life and teaching of Jesus in Palestine

- Stage Two. When the church took its message about Jesus to the Jews scattered throughout the Roman Empire, imagery easily understood in Palestine but meaningless in other parts of the world was dropped. Instead, the church used illustrations that would have been familiar to the dispersed Jews, and Jesus was portrayed as a divine, universally significant figure.

- Stage Three. In proclaiming its message to the Gentiles, the original Jewish message was all but abandoned by the Christian community. As they tried to win the Gentile world, the church used new imagery drawn from the Greco-Roman culture in order to explain the gospel message.

Many New Testament scholars have spent their lives trying to fit the origin of particular biblical texts into one stage or another, often with unsatisfying results. But this practice raises a very important question about how we can know the meaning of scripture: if the New Testament message evolved as the early church responded to changing cultures, then *which culture(s) are we expected to read it against?* If the three-stage theory is true and the gospel message now consists of a mishmash of concepts drawn from the Gentile and Jewish worlds, this question is impossible to answer—we can only guess! Which means there is no way to establish biblical truth. This, in fact is at the core of most modern thinking. Consequently, many lost all hope of discovering a trustworthy biblical message.

The fundamental flaw with this perspective is that the process described above assumes that the core beliefs of the first century church *evolved*. According to this view, the New Testament message is a product of the early church's interaction with Greek philosophy and pagan religions. If this is true, then the Christian message was not a divinely inspired revelation of God through the writings of the Old Testament prophets and the teachings of Jesus. Instead, it is derived from the church's intellectual and spiritual syncretism!

This perspective took root because certain scholars presupposed there was no unique divine revelation, and that all religions were either the products of folklore or a conglomeration of ideas borrowed from other faith systems. These theories struck right at the heart of the traditional understanding of Christian revelation and the authority of the Bible in particular. They not only insinuated scripture originated solely from the human mind, but also that it was not historically reliable. Such claims cannot but shake the foundations of our faith and leave us with the questions like, "Do we have the right Jesus?" and "How can we ever know if we do?"

The current crisis of belief about the Bible in the Western world has come about, in part, because many bought into this idea that the Christian message was progressively altered to accommodate each new audience to which the gospel was taken. The problem, however, is that according to this theory, while supposedly making it easier for the newly evangelized group to accept the gospel, each level or layer progressively made Jesus into something he was not!

Now, if this were a true account of how the New Testament writings developed, then it would follow that the apostles left an example for all future generations of Christians to repeat. That is, whenever the gospel is taken into a new culture, whatever is offensive or unclear to the people being evangelized should be abandoned and ideas from their own cultural should be grafted into the message. Indeed, there are those who now contend that following the early church's lead, contemporary missionaries must rewrite or *contextualize* the gospel using culturally acceptable symbols that help the people they seek to evangelize. The legitimacy of this contextualizing process is so widely accepted that it is hardly ever questioned.

## The Theory Crumbles

Upon closer scrutiny, however, the entire line of reasoning associated with the three-stage theory does not hold up. First, the idea that Christian teaching evolved from a Jewish to a Gentile message has been seriously challenged. New evidence from leading academic institutions around the world suggests the three-stage transition process never took place; rather, the early church stayed true to its Jewish heritage when writing the New Testament.[6] This means there was no radical Hellenistic development of the gospel message in the first-century church. Greek-influenced ideas affected Christian thought later, *after* the New Testament had already been written, when the young church began to engage more with the surrounding culture.

As a result of these new developments, today, there is "virtually unanimous consent . . . [that] Jesus lived as a Jew."[7] In addition, more scholars are recognizing that the New Testament, Paul's letters included, is essentially a collection of Jewish writings. Mark Nanos states that "where New Testament scholarship is concerned, the literature can now be read as Jewish correspondence, written by and for Jews and Gentiles concerned with the Jewish context of their faith in Jesus as the Messiah. Simply put, we can now read the New Testament as a Jewish book."[8]

The evolutionary position is troubling for another reason. If it is true that the New Testament is laced with invented stories and ideas imported from pagan religions, then we can only guess at what Jesus himself actually said. If we don't know what Jesus taught, how can we possibly know whether or not Paul departed from Jesus's teaching? This illustrates the folly of some New Testament research. To argue that we don't have access to the original teaching of Jesus, and then to say that Paul moved away from it and introduced Greek ideas into the gospel is blind prejudice!

Furthermore, there is a much better way of explaining how the apostles communicated the gospel of Jesus. If we comb through the New Testament documents, we will see that rather than adapting the message of Jesus to suit various Gentile audiences, first-century converts were taught the Jewish scriptures. This gave them the key to understanding Jesus's message and work. Exposure to the Old Testament background helped new disciples appreciate the life and teaching of Jesus in all of its Jewish significance.

It is true that Paul quoted a Cretan prophet in Titus 1:12 and referred to pagan literature in the book of Acts.[9] However, if you read the passages for yourself, you will see that references like these did not affect his message. When Paul talked to the philosophers at Athens, he used illustrations known to them in order to find common ground with his listeners. This is simply a good communications practice. Far from altering the content of the gospel, he boldly preached about the resurrection! There is no way he would have done this if he wanted to eliminate anything that might have been offensive to the pagan philosophers as the resurrection challenged one of their most cherished beliefs. Their hope was for the soul to be released from the "prison house" of the body when death occurred. The idea they might live eternally in a body was not only a revolutionary concept, it was repugnant to many Greeks.

## True to the Message

It will help us to realize that the church's earliest teachers were simply not free to shape the apostolic message as they saw fit. Their responsibility was to show how Jesus fulfilled and interpreted the Old Testament—something Jesus himself had taught them to do—and how this applied to the life of the churches, which were made up of both Jews and Gentiles.[10] This is clearly what they did.

Since the first missionaries were Jews, initially, they took their message to the synagogues that were populated not only by Jews who shared their acceptance of the Hebrew Bible, but also by people known as "God-fearers." These were Gentiles who were offended by the corruption of the pagan religions and sought the God of Israel because they respected the high moral standards of Judaism. Although the God-fearing Gentiles attended synagogue services, few actually converted to Judaism mainly because, understandably so, most Gentiles were not keen on being circumcised as adults.

The Jews and the Gentile God-fearers in the synagogues did not need to be taught the Old Testament background—they were already familiar with it. After only a short time of instruction, they were able to understand the message of Jesus almost in its entirety. The Gentile God-fearers enthusiastically welcomed the apostolic message that God accepted them without circumcision. As the apostles explained, a change of heart is what really counted to God, which is what circumcision was intended to symbolize.[11]

This explains how the first-century church not only survived, but also thrived. The apostles were often driven out of the communities where they had preached, leaving behind a handful of believers. Sometimes these Christians had been converted for only a matter of days.[12] How could they subsist without the apostles' help?

The young converts were able to grow in their faith thanks to the Hebrew Bible (Christian Old Testament). These sacred Jewish writings taught them about the Messiah-King and what God planned to do through him. They also gave these fledgling Christians a framework for understanding their past as well as hope to face the future. Contrary to popular theories, the primitive church did not jettison their Jewish heritage or invent stories for the Gentile converts. Rather they endeavored to show how the teachings of Jesus, which were rooted in the Jewish scriptures, were now relevant to the Gentiles and how Christ called Jews and Gentiles together into a new kind of relationship.

Having said all this, it is important to acknowledge there is some validity to the evolutionary model, but it applies to the teaching of the church starting in the second century and beyond, not the primitive community. Hellenism definitely had a decided impact on Christianity, but it happened *after* the New Testament documents were completed and so did not affect their content.

## Error #2: Jewish Literature is an Interpretive Key

While this error is being rectified, scholars are falling into a different trap. Ironically, the discovery of the Dead Sea Scrolls in the 1940's and 50's has led many to believe the key to understanding scripture is now to be found in a collection of ancient extra-biblical Jewish documents, known as *intertestamental* or *Second Temple literature.* This material was written by Jews between the end of the Old Testament and the determination of the final canon of the New (400 BC-200 AD). Since Jesus was a Jew, it is commonly assumed that if we could understand what the Jewish community believed at the time of his birth this would explain the influences that shaped his mindset. Therefore, these extra-biblical writings could help us interpret the New Testament more accurately. Based on this assumption, interest in intertestamental studies has mushroomed!

There is no doubt the church has benefitted from these materials in several ways. For one thing, the texts have been instrumental in causing scholars to recognize the essentially Jewish nature of the New Testament. However, when it comes to relying on intertestamental literature as an indispensable tool for interpreting the New Testament, as many scholars are doing these days, I believe that in the years ahead it will be seen *as another colossal mistake.* I want to emphasize that *I am not dismissing the usefulness of this material*, but I am persuaded that the extent of its relevance for interpreting the New Testament message must be questioned.

A common assumption is that the terminology and themes in this material mean the same thing when used in the New Testament. The problem with this view is that it presupposes these Jewish extra-biblical works all share the same theological outlook and, therefore, the terms have the same meanings. But this is to overlook an absolutely critical point—there were many different theologies within Judaism during the New Testament era. The Dead Sea Scrolls revealed that Judaism was not a homogenous religion; it consisted of numerous groups and subgroups. As is often said, we cannot speak of Judaism but of *Judaisms.*

In reality, these writings represent various Jewish perspectives many of which were distinct from, and in contradiction to, the others. One scholar who has been the most vocal in warning about the complexities of this material says, "What is wrong with the established view is simple. People join together books that do not speak the same language or thought, that refer to distinctive conceptions and doctrines of their own."[13] For instance, he explains that Jews did not share the same expectations concerning the coming Messiah; they had many and sometimes conflicting ideas. Indeed, it appears that Israel did not look for *a* Messiah but for *many* messiahs. Therefore, we cannot assume that whenever the authors of these Jewish writings used the word *messiah*, they had the same meaning in mind.

Nor can we assume that all Jews—Jesus and the apostles included—were aware of all these different strands of thought. It would be like assuming that all Catholics are familiar with Amish beliefs and practices, or that all Pentecostals know the ins and outs of the Westminster Confession. Furthermore, we have very limited samples of the particular traditions from which these various texts come, so there is no way to know if they represent the full theology of that group. There are still more problems with using this material which I describe in my scholarly study, *Contours of Pauline Theology*. Given the complexity of the issues, the use of these texts calls for extreme caution!

## Jesus, Our Martyr

Unfortunately, caution has been thrown to the wind in some cases, and with serious consequences. Let me give you an example of why relying on intertestamental literature as an interpretive key is problematic. Based on the Jewish books of Maccabees 1–4 and other extra-biblical texts, a number of scholars across the theological spectrum contend that both Jesus and the apostle Paul used the Jewish martyr tradition to explain the meaning of what was achieved on the cross. The ideas found in these writings are seen as a plausible way of resolving problems certain theologians have with some of the biblical texts about Christ's sacrificial death.

Different versions of the martyr theory have been proposed.[14] One is that Jesus's death had no atoning value; rather he died as a martyr to provide an example of sacrificing oneself for others. Another is that Jesus saw himself as being one in a long line of Jewish martyrs who gave their lives for the nation of Israel with the expectation that it would contribute to her redemption.[15] Also, a number of parallels between the account of what the martyrs' deaths accomplished in the books of Maccabees 2 and 4, and Paul's description of what Jesus's death achieved are seen as evidence that the apostle's views were shaped by the martyr tradition.[16] At first glance, similarities between the two descriptions do seem striking, but in scripture it is the God sent Messiah King *alone* who saves his people, not Jewish martyrs.

Admittedly, some who embrace martyrdom theology say they still see the atonement as the primary model for Christ's death and do not deny that Jesus and Paul also relied on scripture. However, whether intended or not, martyrdom theology surrenders the great doctrine of the unique substitutionary sufferings of Christ, a teaching that traces back to the early church. No matter how noble or sacrificial his or her death may be, no martyr is a savior in the way that Jesus is. In Maccabean teaching, anyone can add to the pool of merit that is made available to put right Israel's sins. Not only is this completely contrary to the Old Testament model of the atonement that we shall consider later, but it also goes against the grain of the New. As the New Testament writers explain, Christ alone suffered and died to defeat the powers of evil, atone for our sin, rescue those who are willing from the grip of Sin and Death, and bring into existence the one new man, which consists of Jews and Gentiles joined together in Christ's body by the Spirit. Through his death, Jesus also established God's kingdom on earth and inaugurated the new creation in which all things will be restored to the Father. No martyr's death ever accomplished such feats!

Modern scholarship has pressed the martyr model on to the New Testament text in a way that can only be described in academic terms as irresponsible, for the supporting evidence has been poorly scrutinized. In turn, doctrines have been developed from the supposed evidence that portray Jesus as a well-meaning religious leader who is confused over the purpose of his death. For those who are interested, I explore this evidence in depth in my book *Tom Wright and the Search for Truth*.[17] In coming chapters, I will argue for a biblical model centered on the Passover that I believe offers a far more satisfying explanation of Christ's view of what his death would achieve and that is far more persuasive than martyrdom theology. It can also help us sort through some versions of the doctrine of substitutionary atonement that have become quite controversial in recent years.

## A Better Way

These observations about Jewish intertestamental literature are not meant to suggest that we have no way of knowing about the first-century church's mindset. Paul's reliance on the Law and the Prophets shows without a shadow of doubt that the early church depended on the Old Testament writings. Indeed, we know that *all* Jews fed off these scriptures. Every member of the covenant community drank from their streams of warning, comfort, encouragement, and hope. They gathered at least weekly to hear them read and be taught from their pages, and the Psalms were used to express their worship to God. The New Testament is *saturated* with references to these writings.

To treat the Old Testament scripture as though it had little formative influence on the early church, as some (not all) do, and then rely on extra-biblical texts as the key to understanding the New Testament is totally irrational! The New Testament writings were addressed to and circulated among communities outside of Palestine that presumably had little access to most of these extra-biblical works. In contrast, the Old Testament scriptures were influential not only throughout every form of Judaism within the Promised Land, but in every synagogue in the Roman Empire! Furthermore, Paul explicitly says these are the writings that were fulfilled in the person and work of Jesus, the Son of David.[18] The apostles taught from these scriptures, and from the perspective which Jesus himself had imparted to them, not from the dubious views of any particular Palestinian sect.

If we are to see the biblical backdrop more clearly, it is essential to understand the foundational role the Old Testament plays in grounding the New Testament message, so it will be to our benefit to explore this further before going on to the other two scholarly errors.

**THE OLD TESTAMENT CONNECTION¶** I want to say upfront that in considering how the Old and New Testaments relate, I plan to cite scripture. I realize that because of questions about the reliability of the biblical text, its many conflicting interpretations, and the general attitude of suspicion that currently surrounds the Bible, whenever someone uses the phrase "The Bible says" it can trigger a number of guarded reactions. One is "the Bible says according to who?" Another is, "why should I believe what you are saying has any more merit than what anyone else says?" It can also seem like circular reasoning to show the Bible is true by quoting from it., so let me say a few things here.

First, regarding the reliability of the texts themselves, much has been made of the fact that we do not have the original New Testament manuscripts and that there are variants such as spelling errors, inverted phrases, and differences in factual details. For these reasons, some claim we can't trust the Bible. The reality, however, is that most of the textual variations have proved to be minor. Plus, so many early copies of the manuscripts exist that it is possible to accurately identify deviations from the original. Others have already written extensively about these issues so there is no need to go into further detail here.[19] The bottom line is that from an objective, academic standpoint, there is simply no basis for saying we cannot look to the Bible to provide reliable information about Jesus.

Second, as far as circular reasoning is concerned, one of the benefits of postmodernism is that it has leveled the playing field. If, as is claimed, all "facts" are grounded on unprovable, value-based presuppositions, then I can't really prove that the Bible is divinely inspired and true, yet no one can prove that it's not. The fact that knowledge of the Bible is at an all-time low while skepticism is on the rise suggests that many may be wary or disinterested in scripture without actually knowing what's in it. So, whether one has a high or low view of scripture, it would be beneficial to at least consider what the Bible says about itself. This doesn't mean we need to blindly accept whatever it says. Scientist and theologian Alister McGrath, who was a committed atheist because he believed it was "the only worldview that had any intellectual integrity," explains that he eventually embraced

Christianity after carefully considering its claims. Acknowledging that he knew far less about Christianity than he assumed, he realized he had been rejecting a "religious stereotype."[20]

In regard to weighing various interpretations and what I am saying in comparison to the views of others, as we move further into our discussion, I will explain how the early church tested the many competing "truth claims" they encountered in the first century and how we can do the same.

## Nothing New

One of the first observations I want to make is that controversy about scripture is nothing new. Even before the New Testament was written, Jesus chastised religious leaders for mishandling the Old Testament texts and failing to recognize him as the one of whom the Jewish writings testified.[21] He also warned that false christs and prophets would rise up and try to deceive his followers by twisting scripture and performing false signs and wonders.[22] Other New Testament writers issued the same types of warnings.[23] Admonitions to stay true to "sound doctrine" (biblical teaching) and to watch out for false leaders and their distorted messages run all throughout the New Testament.[24]

This tells us several important things. First, it indicates a message had been deposited in the church from the *earliest days* that Jesus's followers were supposed to know, understand, and guard.[25] In fact, Paul said not to listen to *anyone*—including *himself* or even an angel—who taught anything contrary to the message that had been already delivered to the church by Jesus and the twelve apostles.[26] From this we learn that Paul was no maverick or innovator. He not only saw his message as being consistent with Jesus's teaching, he also expected his own words to be weighed against this already established norm.

The statement I'm about to make may seem a little obvious but given current cultural trends it is worth saying—this also shows that before any dogma was ever formulated or creed written, a body of teaching existed which was regarded as being "true" and other messages that did not line up with this truth were seen as "false." In other words, it was not only possible to distinguish between truth and error, but it was also the church's responsibility to do so.

This counters the claim there were no "orthodox" views in the early church or that heresy was a later invention. Even though the word *heresy* itself was not used until later and was also misused at different points in history, Jesus himself made a distinction between true and false teachings and teachers. It also refutes the idea that early leaders arbitrarily rejected other writings that were circulating at the time. If other documents or truth claims were challenged, it was most often because they did not square up with their given plumb line—the Old Testament and the apostolic message based on the teachings of Jesus.[27] An example of this is when Paul commended the Bereans for eagerly "receiving the word" from him and then "examining the scriptures daily to see whether these things were so."[28] Since the New Testament had not yet been fully written or identified as a sacred canon, clearly, this is a reference to the Old Testament, which served as a plumb line for the primitive Christian community.

## The New Grounded in the Old

This leads to one of the main points I want to make—the Old and New Testaments are inextricably bound to one another. In fact, the entire New Testament is *packed* with quotes, expressions, and allusions taken from the ancient Jewish scripture. By some counts, Jesus himself referred to the Old Testament at least 400 times![29] He studied it when he was young, read it in the synagogues, preached from it in the marketplace, quoted it when he withstood Satan's temptations in the wilderness, used it to explain who he was, and relied on it when telling his followers about his upcoming death.

Between the time of his resurrection and ascension, Jesus appeared to some of his disciples and, starting with Moses and the prophets, told them all the things concerning himself and the kingdom of God that were found in the scriptures.[30] Throughout his lifetime, he made it clear that his purpose was not to set aside, but to *fulfill* what was written in scripture. The fact that Jesus quoted the ancient texts so extensively indicates he saw it as being a trustworthy document. And because his message and ministry activities were rooted in the Old Testament, it could be used to verify what he was saying. The apostles depended heavily on the Old Testament as well. If you cut out every text that is somehow connected with the sacred Jewish texts, not much of the New Testament would be left!

And these were not random references—they were linked to a storyline. I'll explain this in more detail later, but there is clear evidence that in the days before Jesus was born, the hope of another national exodus is what sustained Israel through the hardships that came with being a conquered people. They were looking for a powerful leader, a messiah, to rise up and rescue them from the oppressive rule of alien powers much like Moses did when he led Israel out of Egypt during the First Exodus. This expectation was fueled by a number of yet-to-be-fulfilled prophetic promises that were found mainly in Isaiah, but also in some of the other prophetic writings as well. Although the word *exodus* (departure) is specifically used only once in relation to Jesus, as we shall see, not only did he and John the Baptist understand their own ministries in the light of a New Exodus, but this theme also had profound influence on the New Testament writers.[31]

## Paul's Roots

This is true of Paul as well. Contrary to those who say he Hellenized the gospel when he proclaimed Christ to the Gentiles, I contend that if you listen to Paul very carefully, there is only *one source* that dominates his thinking—it is the Old Testament and its message that drives him as he declares the coming of the hope of Israel and its implications for the nations. The letters to the churches in Galatia and Rome alone show us this is not the mind of a multi-cultural Hellenist; it is the mind of a devout Jew who has understood that the covenant promises made to Abraham have been fulfilled in Jesus Christ.

Immersed in the prophetic stream of expectations of a New Exodus, many of Paul's major doctrines can be found in embryonic form in the book of Isaiah. He not only quoted from this prophet more times than all the other Old Testament prophets put together, but he used Isaiah's writings as the skeleton of his gospel. Far from taking a casual, off-the-cuff approach to his letter to the Romans as some today claim, Paul arranged quotations from the book of Isaiah in such a way as to outline the history of salvation from the fall of man to the eventual establishment of the messianic kingdom. He then built his argument around these quotations.

The full import of this fact is only appreciated when the quotations are listed in the order they are used and read in the same sequence. What it shows is that if the letter to the Romans was laid out on one continuous sheet of the parchment used in those days, and the citations from Isaiah were raised out of the text and suspended at their point of use, those texts, in that order, would summarize salvation history.[32] There is no way such a pattern could be anything but intentional! I've included an outline of these scriptures in Appendix A at the end of the book.

Furthermore, Paul himself makes the centerpiece of his message abundantly clear—his aim is to preach Christ crucified, which he says is a "stumbling block to the Jews, and foolishness to the Gentiles."[33] The teaching that Christ suffered and died on the cross, which is the very foundation of Christianity, was not in line with Jewish expectations of a national deliverer. This is why they wanted him to prove himself by performing signs. Nor was it compatible with Greek philosophy, which prized the pursuit of wisdom through human means. As we will discover, in numerous instances where scholars claim to see examples of how Greek or Roman concepts penetrated Paul's teachings, many of them can either be traced back to the Old Testament, or they stem from the implications of Christ's teachings and work.

## A Message for All

The way Jesus and the apostles relied on the Old Testament when declaring his mission and purpose also clearly shows they believed their listeners—the poor and illiterate as well as the educated—would understand what the references meant. This was a realistic expectation because most Jews, as well as the earliest "God-fearing" Gentile converts, learned scripture either from the Jewish leaders when they attended synagogue or from their parents at home.

Because their audience was familiar with the background story, the New Testament writers did not have to spell out the meaning of everything they said. The quotes and allusions Jesus and the apostles used would have had the same effect as if a speaker today used the phrase "May the Force be with you" to illustrate a point. Not only would most contemporary audiences know this was from the movie *Star Wars* and what it meant, but it would also immediately call to mind the movie's content, including the story and images of Luke Skywalker, light-saber duels, Han Solo, Princess Leia, star-fighters, Darth Vader, and the fierce battle between the little band of freedom fighters and the powerful evil empire. It is this larger context that gives the phrase meaning.

In the same way, Jesus's audiences knew what it meant when he stood up in his hometown synagogue and quoted Isaiah 61:1-2, saying:

> The Spirit of the Sovereign Lord is on me,
>   because the Lord has anointed me
>     to proclaim good news to the poor.
> He has sent me to bind up the brokenhearted,
>   to proclaim freedom for the captives
> and release from darkness for the prisoners,
>   to proclaim the year of the Lord's favor.

Because they knew the Old Testament storyline this verse evoked, when Jesus said, "Today this scripture is fulfilled in your hearing," they understood that he was declaring himself to be the Anointed One, the Son of David, the Messiah-King who was coming to deliver Israel from her oppressors and rule over the nations.[34] Jesus was saying the Messianic Kingdom had come. This is why some took offense—how could the one they watched grow up and later practice his father's trade presume to be the long-awaited Christ, the nation's deliverer?

I saw the power of understanding these allusions firsthand when I lectured once to Christian leaders in communist Romania who had no libraries apart from their Bible. On one occasion I said, "I want to talk to you about a covenant with death." To my amazement they all instantly opened their Bibles and without me telling them to do so, turned to Isaiah 28. After a few moments of reading they broke into a heated debate. I watched this for about five minutes and then, slowly they began to nod and smile at each other as the din subsided. I told my translator what I wanted to say, and he replied, "Oh, that's okay—they have just discussed that!" All I had to do was mention an obscure Old Testament text and they quickly connected it to the historical and theological significance of the passage quoted. In turn, they immediately used this information to interpret the meaning of the passage as quoted in the New Testament.[35] Their intimate knowledge of the Old Testament gave them a rich backdrop for effectively interpreting the New.

It is critical to realize that Jesus and the apostles didn't simply draw from the Old Testament to illustrate a point here and there, but on a deep and fundamental level *it actually shaped the very message they proclaimed.* In this way, rather than seeing the New Testament as a separate, stand-alone document that *replaces* the ancient Jewish scriptures, it would be far more helpful—and, I might add, more accurate—to regard the New Testament as the final chapter of the Old, to see that together, they form one continuous narrative. Anyone who has ever skipped ahead to read the end of an exciting story will understand the importance of this point. While it is possible to get a general idea of how everything comes out by flipping to the final pages, many things don't make sense without knowing all that led up to it. The same is true with the New Testament—it is almost impossible to fully grasp what it means unless we're familiar with the earlier part of the story.

## An Inseparable Bond

Disregard for the Old Testament backdrop is one of the major reasons why so many today have trouble understanding the Bible and why we have so many different understandings of key texts. Just imagine what kind of answers you would get if you asked a group of people who have never seen or heard of *Star Wars* to explain the meanings of the phrase, "May the Force be with you." Without understanding the larger context of the movie, it is certain that few, if any, "interpretations" would be accurate. Likewise, think of what would happen if we cut the New Testament loose from its Old Testament moorings, zeroed in on various passages, and then asked people "now what does this mean to you?" There's no end to the creative interpretations that could be generated if all of us were free to come up with our own idea of what the texts meant and who we think Jesus was or is!

It would be one thing if it were only inexperienced believers who fell into this error, but it's astonishing how even some otherwise fine scholars have failed to take into account the significant connection between the two testaments. As a result of overlooking the inseparable bond, they ended up devising theological systems that were attractive initially, but later fell apart because they were built on faulty foundations.[36]

One of the reasons I am bringing this up is because I want to encourage you that contrary to what many believe these days, you do not have to be a scholar or theologian to understand scripture. Nor do you need to be an "expert" in order to assess modern day theories about the New Testament or spot false messiahs. We have the same resources the primitive church did when they first heard the apostolic message—the Old Testament, the Holy Spirit, and the Christian community.

Granted, as contemporary readers, we have to deal with some challenges in understanding scripture that first-century believers didn't face as a result of the two-thousand-year cultural gap between our world and theirs. And there are issues related to the continuity and discontinuity of what, in the Old Testament, applies to the Christian new covenant community and what doesn't, which the early church had to sort through. But still, the reality is that like the first-century believers, even today, we can test the veracity of the New Testament message (and other ancient extra-biblical documents as well) by seeing how it lines up with key elements of the Old.

At first glance, this may not seem like great news—many today find the Old Testament hard to comprehend or irrelevant—but once it is understood how the Jewish story and corporate mindset, and God's promises to Israel regarding a New Exodus serve as the framework for the New Testament, then all of scripture begins to make more sense, and actually, becomes simpler to understand.

Now that we have identified the Jewish, Old Testament backdrop for the new, we need to address two other major scholarly errors that have also blurred the biblical picture and then we will take a closer look at our Jewish roots.

CHAPTER 2

# Gaps and Gaffes

Some of the failed attempts at cross-cultural advertising can be pretty funny. Like when Kentucky Fried Chicken opened stores in China and their well-known slogan "finger lickin' good" was interpreted as "eat your fingers off." Or when an Italian campaign for "Schweppes Tonic Water" became one for "Schweppes Toilet Water." We can laugh, but these gaffes point to a more serious problem that comes up whenever we attempt to communicate across cultural lines—somehow, concepts that are clearly understood in one language do not always transfer well into another. (Just try telling a British joke to an American!)

Concepts do not always transfer well over the years either—even within one particular culture, words and their meanings can change over time. Some evolutions take place gradually, but others happen so quickly that a "communications gap" of sorts can develop between one generation and the next. To express new ideas and values, the younger generation sometimes infuses old words with new meanings or coins new terms, both of which can be confusing to older people. An example is the word *bad* in our day. Previously, it always meant *undesirable, evil,* or *defective.* However, in popular youth slang, it now also means *cool, good,* or as one younger man phrased it "wicked sweet" (whatever that means!). Twenty years ago, no one had heard of *going viral* or the term *glocal,* which is a combination of *global* and *local.*[1] And the word *gay* has a completely different connotation today than it did in previous generations.

Customs and beliefs can change rapidly as well. How many in the older generation understand the new custom of "hooking-up" that's the latest evolution of "dating"? Conversely, how many young people understand what it means to "go courting," which was the formal dating practice in our grandparents' generation? If these types of language barriers, communications gaps and evolving customs can make it difficult for ethnic groups and even different generations who are living at the same time to relate to one another, think of the immense chasm that exists between modern society and the New Testament world!

## Missing Lenses

In wrestling with some of these language problems, scholars made a couple of serious gaffes that have created great confusion when it comes to reading scripture. After looking at these errors, we'll see how they muddled the meaning of a key Hebrew term, *ebed* (servant) that is frequently rendered as *doulos* in the Greek New Testament and *slave* or *servant* in English translations. Recovering the Old Testament context for this term will illustrate why reading against a Hebraic rather than Greco-Roman cultural backdrop is critical when it comes to knowing our true identity in Christ.

**MORE FLAWED ASSUMPTIONS¶** In the last chapter, we looked at two scholarly theories related to the Jewish culture that have clouded the biblical picture. The next error I want to discuss has to do with the influence of the Greek culture on scripture and Christian thought.

## Error #3: Knowledge of the Greek Culture Is Essential for Interpreting Scripture

Because New Testament documents were written in Koine Greek, the common language used in the Roman world, for centuries scholars assumed the Hellenistic culture played a significant role in shaping the teachings of Jesus and the apostles, especially Paul.

This idea was further reinforced by modern scholars who claim that in Jesus's day, Judaism was already far more influenced by the Greek culture (Hellenized) than previously thought. Since the lines between the two cultures were porous, they say, it is impossible to make a clear distinction between them, which is why it cannot be said that Jesus, the twelve apostles or Paul had a purely Jewish mindset.[2] The implication of this line of thinking is that Paul was not solely responsible for Hellenizing the gospel as some scholars theorized—it was set in a mixed context of the Jewish and Greek cultures from the very beginning. For this reason, it is argued, we should give up "using any form of the Judaism/Hellenism divide as an interpretive lens" and look to both cultures for insights into the meaning of the New Testament.[3]

In light of this long-standing perception, it was commonly believed that a thorough grounding in the Greek classics, philosophy, and the Greco-Roman culture was necessary preparation for studying the New Testament and theology. Most New Testament scholars in previous generations followed this well-tried and little questioned route into theology. Those who had this classical training were seen as being imminently qualified to analyze and interpret scriptures since they had a broad understanding of the Hellenistic world, its thought patterns and vocabulary. Few realized this method was seriously flawed, but it was.

## Greek Language, Jewish Concepts

What many theologians failed to take into account is that although New Testament writers used a Greek vocabulary, *the words had a different meaning within the Jewish community*. While the words themselves were Greek, the concepts were derived from the Jewish scripture.

To explain, we need to go back several hundred years before Christ to when the Jews were conquered by the Babylonians and forced into exile (587–582 B.C.). Although a few Jews eventually returned to their homeland after being released from captivity, many remained scattered throughout various parts of the Middle East. Later, when the Greeks became the new world rulers, the dispersed Jews who lived in this new Hellenistic world were in serious danger of losing touch with their heritage. Since many of these Jews were more familiar with Greek than with the Hebrew language, a group of Jewish elders translated the Jewish scriptures (what Christians refer to as the Old Testament) into Greek. Known as the Septuagint or the LXX, this Greek version of the Jewish scriptures was widely respected in ancient times. In fact, Jesus, the apostles, and the early church fathers all used this translation.

What needs to be understood about the LXX is that Jewish elders poured Hebrew theological meaning into the text of this Greek translation to produce a *language with a unique semantic range*. The alphabet and vocabulary were Greek, but conceptually, it was still Hebraic in its *essential meaning and mindset*. Judaism bequeathed this special language to the infant church as she interpreted and proclaimed the message of the prophets.

When Jesus and the first century church leaders read the LXX, they did not need to turn to a secular Greek dictionary for help in deciphering words and concepts—they naturally understood them in light of their Hebrew meaning learned in the synagogues. Thus, when the authors of the New Testament drafted the gospels and their letters, they preserved their Hebraic heritage by transferring the Jewish Old Testament mindset into the Greek New Testament writings. Evidence of this process can be found simply by looking at how often Jesus and the apostles quoted the LXX in their teachings. Clearly, this was foundational to their thinking!

## Same Words, Different Mindset

The understanding that a person's mindset may differ from the language he or she uses is critical to this discussion. At one conference I attended, a lecturer from an internationally famous university dismissed the argument I am making about Paul's Jewish mindset as being ridiculous, saying I had "shot myself in the foot because it was obvious that Paul wrote in Greek."[4] It is easy to understand why someone would make such a remark, but this criticism is missing a vitally important point—a person or people can use the language and images of another culture without buying into its belief system or adopting its mindset.

To illustrate this point, in the West there are millions of people who have settled as immigrants from all parts of the world. Among them is a large Muslim population. The second generation has adapted to their parents' new home of choice remarkably well. Not only do many speak perfect English, but also, some have gone through the West's best universities and have a thorough understanding of the Western way of life. They use the West's legal and financial systems and also its technology, but that does not mean they have embraced Western religious values. In fact, most would be horrified if it were suggested they had become Westerners because of this training. As far as their beliefs and religious practices are concerned, they may use the English language, but many remain as committed to their original heritage as they would have been had they never immigrated.

In light of this dynamic, if we want to know where an immigrant population is in terms of being assimilated into the host culture, we have to go beyond their words and listen to them very carefully in order to evaluate what underlying beliefs are motivating their actions. Rather than automatically assuming the first-century church's belief system was Hellenized because they used the Greek language, we need to carefully investigate the documents they wrote and the sacred texts they used in order to understand the worldview that shaped their lives.

Seen from this perspective, the classical method of training for biblical studies is fundamentally flawed. Yes, the Jews were living in a Hellenized culture, and some may have even adopted Hellenistic ideas and customs as certain documents show, but this does not automatically mean all Jews took on a Greek mindset. As we have seen and will continue to explore, the New Testament writers drew their understanding primarily from the Old Testament rather than the surrounding culture. Much of the existing theological literature demonstrates confusion on this point. This is evidenced in the way that even those today who fully acknowledge the New Testament's dependency on the Old Testament, nevertheless, still emphasize the Hellenistic cultural and literary background on which they presuppose the text draws.[5]

## Greek Philosophy and Christian Theology

While we're on this subject, I want to briefly touch on one other sensitive matter related to this error and that is the relationship between philosophy and theology. According to the authors of *Philosophy for Understanding Theology*, "the two main sources of Christian theology are the Bible and Hellenic culture, especially Greek philosophy."[6] In fact, in their opinion, the relationship between the two is so intertwined that "when people call for purging Greek philosophy from Christian theology, unless they are referring to specific ideas or concepts, they are really calling for the end of the discipline of theology itself, though they may not realize it."[7] As they explain, "Christian theology is *inherently Hellenic* because it could not exist as a discipline without the kind of intellectual curiosity that was unique to ancient Greece."[8]

In light of all we have discussed so far, the idea that Greek philosophy is *essential* to Christian theology should give us reason to stop and think: if the Bible is a Jewish book inspired by the God of Israel who elected to work through the Jewish people to reach the other nations, and if it is written by Jewish men and their companions about a Jewish Messiah who came to fulfill the Jewish Old Testament scriptures, then is Greek philosophy truly *indispensable* to Christian theology? Of course, I have already stated my position: I am firmly persuaded that one of the reasons Christian theology has been so complicated, confusing, divisive, and even misguided at times is that inadvertently, hidden Greek philosophical presuppositions have been read into scripture. The result has been that many of our theologies have been shaped by Greek, rather than biblical categories of thought.

In raising this issue, I want to be clear that I am not denying there is a place for *interacting* with Greek thought. As others have pointed out, the dialogue between the two has proven to be beneficial at times so there is definitely room for certain types of Christian theologies to engage with philosophy.[9] Also, some knowledge of classical philosophy is necessary in order to understand the historical development of Christian doctrine. However, I don't see this approach as applying to biblical theology, which has to do with the way we read the original texts. As we will continue to see, whenever we read the Bible itself through a Greek philosophical framework, whether intentionally or not, we are super-imposing one system of thought over another that is incompatible in several fundamental ways.[10]

The point I want to make is that before we can interpret and apply scripture within the church, constructively engage with the church fathers, develop effective theologies, or enter into a productive dialogue with any cultural group, including our own, we first need to make sure that we have a sound biblical theology. What this means is that a clear understanding of the apostolic message must be the bedrock of our thinking; it is the divine baseline that can help us see if we are drifting off into error. And in order to have an accurate view of the biblical message, we first need to approach scripture as a Jewish book and read the New Testament as though it is the final chapter of the Old. While there is an appropriate place for discourse with Greek philosophy and other academic disciplines, extra-biblical frameworks *must not be allowed to form the grid through which we read and interpret scripture.*

## Shifting Trends

As a result of the greater recognition of the Jewishness of scripture and the integral connection between the Old and New Testaments, the traditional reliance on Greek thought is beginning to shift. Theologian Jurgen Moltmann observed, "We stand today in a remarkable period of transition. On the one side the hellenistically structured form of the Christian faith is ebbing . . . On the other side the Christian faith is experiencing what I would like to call a Hebraic wave.'"[11] While encouraging, this process is by no means complete. We are still discovering how Hellenistic ideas have shaped our mindset, interpretations, and theological writings—both historic and contemporary. Since it's important not to over-react and throw the baby out with the bathwater, it will take time to sift through this mixture.

## Error #4: Overlooking Language Morphs

In addition to the faulty assumption that using Greek language meant Greek concepts influenced the New Testament writers, another simple scholarly mistake has to do with the way languages morph over time. Until recently, many scholars saw no problem with relying on *etymology*, the study of word origins, as a key in understanding the meaning of biblical terms. Experts who study ancient texts and languages would tell us what the root definition of a word was. It was then naively assumed the word's original meaning had transferred across the centuries and still applied to whatever text in which it occurred.

It does not take a trained linguist to know, however, that when societies evolve, the meanings of words and the ideas they contain can also change. As we saw earlier in the example of *bad*, a word can take on a new meaning within a generation. Thus, to go back and look at just the original definition is of little help in understanding what a word may mean to subsequent generations. What determines the meaning of a word in any given document is not only how it was defined originally, but also how it was understood by the generation that produced that particular text. If we simply take the original definition of a word and apply it across the board to all uses of that term, we run the risk of reading an alien meaning back into the text. Ultimately, the only way to know a word's intended meaning is by carefully reflecting on how it was used both within its immediate and its wider context.

To better understand why this is critical when reading ancient manuscripts like the Bible, let's look at the English word *nice* that, while not in scripture, has been around for a while. Although *nice* commonly means *kind* or *agreeable* today, it comes from a Latin word that originally meant *ignorant*.[12] As you can see, the meaning changed completely over the years! If, as contemporary readers, we saw the sentence, "I met some nice people today" in an older document—say, in a letter written in the 1600's— what would it mean?

Given current usage, we might interpret it as *pleasant* or *amiable* when actually, the author may have meant, "I met some uneducated people today." In this case, not only would we have misunderstood the sentence, but we would have also read a meaning back into the text that the author never intended! Even if we looked at the root definition, it wouldn't necessarily settle the issue. How would we know whether the old or new definition applied? The only way to understand what the author meant is to search the context for clues. This is one of the reasons why the backdrop against which we read scripture is so incredibly important.

**CONFUSED IDENTITIES: SLAVE OR SERVANT¶** To see the practical impact of these two language-related errors, let's take a close look now at Paul's use of the Greek word *doulos*. This term was often used to translate the Hebrew Old Testament word *ebed (servant)* into Greek for the LXX and has several different connotations. The New Testament writers used *doulos* to describe various people who were engaged in some form of service. In some English versions, it's simply rendered as *servant* and in others it is translated as *slave, bondservant,* or *bond slave*. These latter terms refer to someone who is not free, but who is wholly owned and controlled by another and in some cases, purchased like livestock. But depending on the context, they can also refer to someone who has willingly and completely surrendered to another power. Later, the idea that *doulos* involved some form of slavery became commonly accepted because that is what it was in Greco-Roman culture, which, as we have seen, was thought to have influenced New Testament thought.

Whether *doulos* should be translated as *servant* or *slave* is not just a technical matter. Some who believe that *doulos* usually means slave claim this interpretation is the key to fully realizing our identities in Christ! They contend that translating *doulos* as *servant* instead of *slave* obscures the vital truth that "Scripture's prevailing description of the Christian's relationship to Jesus Christ is the slave/master relation."[13] According to one influential leader and author, the difference is that "servants are *hired*; slaves are *owned*...The concept of servanthood contains some level of self-autonomy and personal rights. Slaves, on the other hand, have no freedom, autonomy, or rights."[14] He goes on to explain that, "As Christians, we have been *bought with a price*. We *belong to Christ*. We are part of a people for *His own possession*... to be a Christian is to be Christ's *slave*."[15]

This influential view is based on three assumptions: 1) that when Jesus and the apostles used the word *doulos* to describe his followers, it usually meant slave as opposed to servant; 2) it meant slave in the Greco-Roman sense of the word; and 3) the phrases "we have been bought at a price" and "we are a people for His own possession" refer to the master-slave relationship.

I suggest, however, that such a view ignores the broader range of meanings the word had in ancient cultures, and also directly contradicts the defining relationship between God and his people as described throughout the biblical narrative. As we shall see, *doulos* takes on a much different, liberating, and noble hue when read against a corporate, Hebraic backdrop. As will become clear, the definition of *doulos* as slave in the classic Greek or Roman sense falls far short of the magnificent meaning that it had to Paul and the other New Testament writers whose thinking was shaped by the Old Testament.

Seeing *doulos* in a Jewish context can lead us to a clearer understanding of our individual standing with Christ. As we'll discover, Christians are not slaves groveling in abasement with no rights or privileges; as Christ's bride and co-heirs, we have a much more dignified relationship with God. It will also shed light on our corporate identity as those who are united with Christ, the suffering Servant, and called to a common mission. For some, this discussion may seem a bit detailed—and I can only say that it is—but I believe gaining greater insight into this key term will make pressing through this next section worthwhile.

## From Beloved Servant to Slave

The first step in retrieving the full, rich meaning of *doulos* in the New Testament is to see what the corresponding Old Testament word *ebed (servant)* meant to the Hebrews. A good place to start is with the writings of Isaiah, for as we saw in the last chapter, his prophecies clearly determined Paul's theology of salvation. For Isaiah, the central figure in his message of hope was someone known as the servant (*ebed*) of the Lord. By means of his suffering, this servant was to be a source of Israel's salvation in that through his willing death, he would justify many, meaning he would make the way for them to be reconciled to God.[16]

For the Old Testament Jews, the identity of the servant was somewhat of a mystery. Based on Isaiah's description, in some ways it sounded like the servant was the promised Messiah. However, they were looking for a powerful leader who could defeat their enemies, not a Messiah who would suffer and die, which is what Isaiah predicted would happen to the servant. It made no sense. If this servant was the Messiah sent to rescue Israel from its oppressors why would Yahweh allow him to be crushed? How could his death bring about national deliverance? Since the nation's destiny was bound up with the Messiah's, what, if anything, did this suffering Servant have to do with the Israel's future?

Isaiah's understanding of this mysterious figure is especially important because out of all the Old Testament writers, he was the one who had the most insight about how this servant related to Israel's divine assignment to be a light to the nations. The messianic figure was not the only one who was referred to by Yahweh as "my servant"; this title was applied to Israel as well.[17] Together, both the servant and his people had a role to play in bringing salvation to the nations and, paradoxically, it involved humble service rather than world domination. One scholar noted that in contrast to the abstract philosophical notions of a lofty deity that was beyond knowing, Isaiah "seems to have given *living embodiment* to his understanding of *Israel's call to be God's servant (ebed) in the world.*"[18]

In other words, in Isaiah's view, God was not an intellectual concept or an idea to be discussed like mathematics. Nor, in contrast to Platonic ideas, was he a transcendent, static entity that existed apart from the material world. Although he is indeed incomprehensible on one level, the reality of Yahweh's goodness and his kind intentions towards humanity were also meant to be *visibly demonstrated*, to be *actively shown* to the world through the actions of this suffering servant leader and his people, the nation of Israel.

## The Morphing Meaning of *Ebed*

To grasp the significance of this potent imagery it is important to understand what the word *ebed* (servant) meant when Isaiah used it, and then see how it evolved and influenced the New Testament writers.

*Stage One: The Hebraic Old Testament meaning of* ebed. In the Hebrew culture, *ebed* was a title that applied to a wide range of people who provide a service whether given freely or out of obligation. The nation of Israel is referred to as *ebed*, as are prophets, priests, the Messiah, kings appointed by God and kings used by God to accomplish his purpose. An *ebed* could also be a counselor, advisor, one who attended people of position, or a domestic servant. Or an *ebed* could be a free person wholly devoted to serving another, someone who was voluntarily sold into service to repay a debt, or a person forced into service by circumstance. The latter were slaves in every sense of the word, such as prisoners of war serving a household or convicted criminals paying the penalty for their crime.

While an *ebed* served in a subordinate relationship to another as master, whether to God or man, it's important to note that did not always refer to someone with absolute and total dominion over another like a slave owner; it might have simply meant a person who, for whatever reasons, the servant chose or was obliged to obey. This could have been because he or she worked for another person or because the one in authority had a superior legal, civic, religious or social status. Or, going back to the Star Wars analogy, it may have been similar to Luke Skywalker's apprentice relationship with Yoda, his Jedi Master. In this sense, a master was a respected mentor or authority figure. The point is that it did not always mean a slave owner. Because this one word had such a wide range of connotations, the *meaning of ebed had to be derived from the context.*

*Stage Two: The Greek Old Testament (LXX) meaning.* Now here is where the picture starts to get confused. When the Hebrew Bible was translated into the Greek LXX, there was no consistency among the Jewish scholars when they were deciding on which Greek word to use for a particular type of *ebed*. The two main Greek words available were *doulos* and *pais*. The problem is they had similar meanings; both were used generally as a title for anyone who was subordinate to another. In the LXX,

- *Pais* carried the connotation of a child but was also used on a wider scale to refer to servants in general, slaves, individual prophets, domestic servants, or to Israel (in such a way as to remind her of her unworthiness).

- *Doulos* was also used to refer to servants, slaves, prophets, domestic servants, or the nation of Israel.

There was no rhyme or reason for why one word was used over the other—the translators appear to have used *doulos* and *pais* arbitrarily. Again, the meaning of either term could only be determined by paying attention to the context.

*Stage Three: The Greek New Testament.* When the New Testament was written in Koine Greek, both words continued to have an equally wide range of connotations, but there were some differences:

- *Pais* often referred to adolescents, child servants or child slaves, but was also used for bondwomen, Jesus, Israel, and David.

- *Doulos*, on the other hand, was used for servants and slaves in general, bondservants or domestic help, but also for a prophet, for Christians, and even for Christ himself

It is important to keep in mind that *doulos*, which the New Testament writers used more frequently, had more than one meaning, so there was not one single all-purpose definition.

*Stage Four: Translations of the Greek New Testament.* The next layer of confusion came about when the Greek New Testament was translated into other languages. Up through the mid-1800's, *doulos* was interpreted as *servant* or sometimes *bondservant* in most English Bibles. That began to change in the nineteenth century, as with increasing frequency, various translations began to render *doulos* as *slave*. We don't have time to look at the full story of how and why some translators started favoring *slave* at this time. Suffice to say, the varying choices between *servant*, *bondservant*, and *slave* presented a challenge to the reader. Also, by translating *servant* and *slave* as though the meanings primarily fall into two distinct, black-and-white categories— either a free *servant* with rights and privileges or *slave* with no freedom or rights—the more nuanced shades of meaning of *ebed* and *doulos* that were embedded in the ancient texts were obscured.

We have already observed that *doulos* is frequently seen as referring to a slave because, according to some, that's how the term was most often understood in the Greco-Roman culture. Those who prefer this interpretation have, in turn, assumed that Paul's concept of *doulos* was based on the Roman idea of slavery. A second assumption naturally seemed to follow. Because the same Greek word, *doulos*, was used in both the LXX and the New Testament, the logical inference is that *it must have the same meaning in both texts*. As the thinking goes, since Paul understood the term to mean slave in the New Testament, this is what the Old Testament concept of *doulos* (ebed*)* must have also meant. In this way, the Greco-Roman notion of slavery has sometimes been read back into the Jewish scriptures.

## Disposable Tool versus Beloved Servant

There is a serious problem with this entire line of reasoning, however. For one thing, whether Israel ever experienced slavery among her own people in the same sense as the classical Greek or Roman way is a point of dispute. In the Greco-Roman world, what we refer to today as slaves were on the very lowest rung of the social ladder. In fact, they were often regarded as almost non-humans, to be used and discarded at will. However, although it can be interpreted as slave in certain contexts, in Hebrew usage *ebed* also had a much nobler connotation and was often used as a term of courtesy and respect.

To explain the Hebrew mindset, in the ancient Jewish world, whoever was King had absolute power and functioned as a master who ruled over the nation. Consequently, *ebed* was used to describe the King's subjects, especially the officials and soldiers who willingly broke off other social bonds in order to serve him. Far from being seen as the dregs of society, the King's *ebeds*, his servants, were esteemed and treated with respect. Moreover, ancient Hebrews tended to relate to God in the same way they related to their earthly sovereign. In context of this relationship, *ebed* was often used as "a title for pious men and was applied to Abraham, Moses, Joshua or David, and finally to the mysterious servant of Yahweh."[19] These godly leaders were certainly not slaves in the classic Greco-Roman sense. Although they regarded Yahweh as their Lord and Master, they *willingly* chose to love, obey, and serve him.

This is not to discount the fact that slaves—meaning those who became the property of another—did exist in Israel, but slavery was not practiced in the same way as in the Greco-Roman culture. Sometimes, prisoners of war were used as slaves, and any Israelite could choose to become a slave. If a Jewish man or woman was unable to pay a debt, they could sell themselves into slavery to raise funds, but this was only a temporary state—all slaves of Jewish descent were to be released and restored to their own properties during the year of Jubilee. In comparing the Semitic form of slavery with Greco-Roman practices, scholars have pointed out that slavery in the Jewish world was far more controlled and humane than the dehumanized form that was common in the Roman Empire.

## A Covenant Relationship

While this insight may be helpful, it still doesn't go far enough in giving us a complete picture of the Jewish understanding of *ebed*. The problem is that it fails to make the critical distinction between a Hebrew slave who is sold and becomes the possession of another versus what it means to be Yahweh's *ebed* (servant) in context of a covenant relationship with him.

Covenant, not slavery, is the key concept in understanding Israel's relationship to Yahweh. Going back to the time of Abraham, the Lord promised that his offspring would become a great nation, and through his seed all the nations of the earth would be blessed. Yahweh then formalized this promise by entering into an eternal, binding agreement, a covenant with Abraham that extended down the line to his descendants.

This covenant was far greater than any kind of slave purchase—it was the beginning of a committed relationship between God and the soon-to-be-established nation of Israel, the nation that would, in turn, birth the Messiah, the suffering Servant. Yahweh, as the benevolent initiator of the covenant, promised to love and care for Abraham and his descendants; as grateful recipients of his goodness, Israel promised to love and be faithful to him in return. In this way, even though God was master in that he ruled over all, it was far more than a one-sided, top-down, "I own you" slave relationship—it was more like a marriage. In fact, in the Old Testament God referred to Israel as his wife and used the term *adultery* whenever Israel was unfaithful to him by worshipping other gods. As we will see later, phrases like "we are bought at a price" and "a people for God's own possession" are best understood in context of the church's covenant relationship with God. They reflect the Old Testament custom of purchasing a bride, not Greco-Roman slave imagery!

In keeping his commitment to Israel, Yahweh chose leaders to serve as his representatives and also to represent the people to him. Whenever a King took the throne in Israel, it was to be solely because he had been elected, called and appointed to that office by God and not for any other reason. As Yahweh's *ebed*, his chosen servant, the King was charged with faithfully executing the covenant God had made with Israel. He was to rule over the nation in righteousness, to administer justice, to protect, care for, and watch over the people—not to dominate, control, or enslave them. By extension, the King's ministers were Yahweh's servants as well in that they were charged with helping the King fulfill the purposes of the covenant.

Abraham, Moses, Joshua, David and all of the faithful prophets, priests, and kings of the Old Testament were *willing* servants of the covenant, *ebeds* who looked out for God's best interests as well as the nation's. (Some of the leaders, of course, did not serve God faithfully.) Far from regarding them as talking tools that just did what they were told, God often revealed his plans and purposes to them and listened when they interceded for the nation. He even related to Abraham, Moses, and Jeremiah as friends.[20] In this way, to be Yahweh's *ebed*, his servant was a very high calling.

To fail to see this is to miss the whole point of being Yahweh's *ebed* (servant). In social terms it would be equivalent to seeing little difference between the role of a professional housekeeper and that of a traditional homemaker in Western society today. A housekeeper is hired to do what she or he is told, but a homemaker is in a covenant relationship with a marriage partner and therefore, has a different status and motivation for managing the household. Because of the marriage contract, the homemaker has ownership in the family estate and serves not only for the sake of the marriage, but also for the well-being of the entire family. Although both may serve in similar capacities, there is a significant difference between being a hired housekeeper and a homemaker who is in a covenantal marriage relationship. Furthermore, a loving husband would never refer to his covenant partner as *slave*. Let's circle back now and see how all of this sheds light on why translating *doulos* as slave falls dismally short of the meaning Paul had in mind.

**THE CORPORATE SERVANT**¶ Most of the New Testament writers use the term *doulos*, but it's especially prevalent in Paul's thought. He repeatedly uses it to refer not only to himself, but also applies it to fellow Christians. Some scholars believe that Paul's notion of *doulos* reflects a hybrid or "modified" classical view of slavery. The theory is that his usage was based on the Greco-Roman concept, but following the Hebraic tradition, he elevated and dignified the term. Assigning this kind of mixed meaning to Paul's use of *doulos*, however, is not only confusing, it is also problematic.

First, if *slave* is the correct interpretation for *doulos*, when Paul used this term in reference to himself, was he claiming that he was enslaved to Christ, that he had no rights and was forced to serve Christ against his own will? If so, then how could he look forward to a reward or payment for his labor? Why should he expect "a crown of life"? The Greco-Roman slave concept totally precludes such a possibility.[21]

Furthermore, if he did indeed see himself as being a slave in the classical Greek sense, then it seems to contradict what he says in Romans 6. In the NIV translation of this passage, he asks the believers in Rome, "Don't you know that *when you offer yourselves to someone to obey him as slaves,* you are slaves to the one you obey—whether you are slaves to sin, which leads to death, or obedience, which leads to righteousness."[22] Some translations use the word *servant* rather than *slave*. As you can see, the slaves (or servants) mentioned here have a choice—they are not dragged against their will into slavery by one master or another; rather they decide for themselves whom they want to serve. And they serve willingly, not by force. In fact, whenever *doulos* or its verbal form *douleuo* is used in the New Testament, it suggests *willing* service. The ability to choose one's degree of service is not a factor in any type of slavery.

Some have argued this is a reference to the Old Testament practice of bond slavery in which a slave chooses to stay with his master when the year of Jubilee arrives. In this practice, the slave makes a free decision to have his ear bored and become the lifetime possession of his master.[23] However, this perspective also fails to resolve the problem.

For one thing, it moves between Hellenistic and Hebraic concepts of slavery without any indication as to which practice is being followed in which part of the illustration. In the classic Greco-Roman sense, Israel was never in slavery to Yahweh. After he liberated the Hebrews from forced servitude in Egypt, he didn't "re-enslave" them when Moses led the children of Israel to Mt. Sinai—rather, he entered into a covenant agreement with them. The Old Testament practice of becoming a bond slave is simply not an accurate reflection of Israel's covenant relationship with Yahweh nor does it do justice to the Hebraic understanding of *ebed* that informed Paul.

Also, the basic meaning of *doulos* in the Greco-Roman understanding is that of one captured or born as a slave. Either way, it was a lifelong position. Under the controlled form of slavery in the Old Testament, only those outside of Israel—those who were either conquered in war or purchased as bondmen or bondwomen (along with their children)—could become permanent slaves. As we saw earlier, while Israelites were permitted to sell themselves into temporary service to recover from debt, they were to be released, along with all they owned, in the year of Jubilee.

Furthermore, in Romans 8, Paul goes on to describe our adoption, our status as *sons* of God who now cry out, "Abba Father." Taking this into consideration, some scholars continue to argue for the slave model in which a slave was adopted into the family and so became a son. But this interpretation raises all sorts of problems. First, if the believer has already become a son or daughter, how can he or she still be described as a slave? Also, the New Testament makes it clear that Christians are sons and daughters of God because they have received the Spirit. Such a notion has no parallel in Greco-Roman culture, but it runs all throughout the Old Testament. The king was given the Spirit to enable him to fulfill the role of an *ebed* (servant) to which he was called and Israel, God's son, was given the Spirit to guide them.[24] To say that we are slaves, willing or not, and sons at the same time is not only confusing, but it blocks us from seeing and fully appreciating the incredibly high calling God has given to his people.

## Paul, the Servant of God

So how does Paul understand the title *doulos*? What did he mean when he applied the word to himself? As Paul's biographer and one who was deeply influenced by Paul himself, several clues can be found in Luke's writings. Since Luke was Greek, if Paul was introducing Hellenistic concepts into the gospel it would seem that of all people, he would be most likely to make note of this development. Yet, as he records it, Paul's message was firmly rooted in Hebrew theology. Luke saw Paul's calling as mirroring his Master's. And Paul's Master—Jesus—fulfilled the Old Testament expectation of the ideal suffering Servant, the *ebed*, described by Isaiah.

Luke's picture of Paul as the servant in the Hebraic theological sense is no coincidence; it reflects Paul's own description of his apostolic ministry. Like the Old Testament prophets, Paul saw himself as being called from birth to serve God. Just as the ancient prophets saw themselves as servants of the old covenant, Paul regards the apostles as ministers of the new covenant. And like the servants of old, he is compelled to serve not because he is forced to, but out of love for his Master.[25]

The content of Paul's message is also linked to Isaiah's prophecy regarding the suffering servant. Paul's statement that "in Christ all will be made alive" through his death and resurrection in 1 Corinthians echoes Romans 5:12-19, a passage accepted by some scholars as referring to Isaiah 53.[26] This is the chapter in which the suffering servant is described. That Paul is referring to Isaiah's prophecy is borne out by his discussion of the new creation that is brought about by Christ's representative death.[27] This is the very theme found in Isaiah's writings, for the prophet also speaks of all things being made new in context of the new covenant that's established by the servant's death. Thus, Paul sees his ministry as being to proclaim the fulfillment of all that Isaiah had predicted.

This fact is further supported by perhaps one of the most significant passages of 2 Corinthians. In chapter 6, Paul describes the sufferings he has endured as a result of his apostolic work by quoting from Isaiah's Servant Songs and concludes with another quotation from the Songs.[28] Admittedly Paul does not call himself a *doulos* in this passage, but this reinforces the point I've made earlier. All terms are governed by their context and in this particular instance, the fact that Paul sees himself as a servant is underscored by his quotes from the Servant Songs.[29] This chapter clearly shows that Paul believed he was called to be a servant of the new covenant, just as Moses, Isaiah, and

Israel herself were the servants of the old covenant. In the same way the prophets addressed Israel and appealed for fidelity, so Paul is appealing to the church at Corinth to be faithful to God. And Paul's credentials for making this appeal are that he is fulfilling all that the suffering servants, the *ebeds* of old, endured in their ministry to Israel.

## The Church as the *Doulos* of God

Now here comes a central question—does Paul see himself in line with the Old Testament suffering servants because he is an apostle or because he is a Christian? The importance of this issue cannot be overstated. If Paul suffered as a result of being an apostle, then it follows that his experience of suffering is uniquely limited to the apostolic office and does not apply to all Christians in general.

However, if Paul suffered because he was a Christian, it means that all believers are called to this same realm of suffering. If this is the case, then it further demonstrates why the term *doulos* should not be equated with slavery, but rather with *the covenant figure of the servant mentioned in the Old Testament.* The implications of this are profound as far as our identity and purpose are concerned. To be Yahweh's *ebeds*, his esteemed servants of the covenant, not only involves carrying responsibilities, but it also comes with privileges that far exceed those of a slave!

At this point, we can see why it is so important to read scripture through a corporate, Hebraic lens. There is no doubt about where Paul stood—he never regarded his sufferings as being unique. They were part of the sufferings to which the corporate servant—the body of Christ, the entire church—was called. When he went on tour to encourage the fledgling churches, he warned believers that they must enter the kingdom of God through much suffering.[30] In fact, echoing Peter's teaching, he presupposed the inevitability, if not the necessity, of suffering as a result of being God's servant.[31]

For Paul and the apostles, this suffering was not something to be merely endured; it was actually a part of God's will. While the church's suffering was not vicarious like Christ's, it was essentially the same kind of suffering as that which Christ experienced during his ministry. Because of this, Paul frequently linked his own suffering and that of other believers with Christ's. In his view, to be God's servants meant being rejected by those who insisted on remaining in darkness.[32]

Paul did not believe Christians who suffered for Jesus were called to do so in isolation, however, for the believer is part of Christ's body, and Jesus is the head. This corporate reality was revealed to Paul during his road to Damascus experience, when Christ said, "I am Jesus whom you are persecuting."[33] In harming Christ's followers, Paul was harming Christ himself. Reflecting this realization, Paul taught the Corinthians to have a corporate view of suffering; since believers are members of Christ's body, we are all in this together. As he stated, each part of the body "should have equal concern for each other. If one part suffers, every part suffers with it; if one part is honored, every part rejoices with it."[34]

For Paul, suffering is not merely a sign of being part of the kingdom of God; it is a means by which we mature spiritually and become prepared for the glory and splendor of Christ's appearing. This parallels the theme of Isaiah who saw Israel's suffering as a necessary part of bringing in the Messianic Kingdom.[35] First, Paul tells the Roman Christians that they should rejoice in sufferings because it produces perseverance, which, in turn, births character and hope. Then he says, "Now if we are children, then we are heirs—heirs of God and co-heirs with Christ if indeed we share in his sufferings in order that we may also share in his glory. I consider that our present sufferings are not worth comparing with the glory that will be revealed in us."[36]

## In Solidarity with Christ

There is a deep significance in the New Testament passages that speak of the suffering of believers. Fulfilling what Isaiah foreshadowed, in solidarity with Christ, her head, and grafted into the Jewish root, the church is called to be the suffering servant who is a light to the nations. Since space doesn't allow for a full discussion of all the ways Paul and the apostles saw the church's sufferings as being linked to those of the servant figure in Isaiah, I want to sum up a couple of key points.

First, in his writings, Paul draws parallels between the sufferings of ancient Israel and the New Testament church. The faithful Jews suffered as they journeyed from their exile in Babylon to their inheritance in Zion. Similarly, the pilgrim church now endures tribulations as she anticipates the day when her journey will finally be completed at Christ's return and she is presented before God's throne.

The suffering Old Testament exiles proclaimed the good news of their deliverance as they returned to their place of promise. In like fashion, the suffering church is called to share the good news of her salvation as she journeys towards her promised home. In this way, Paul sees the Old Testament Exodus events, both the original Exodus from Egypt and the Second Exodus—Israel's return from exile in Babylon—as a prototype for the New Exodus theme that undergirds the New Testament (which we'll discuss in more detail in the next chapter).

Second, Paul's faithful use of Isaiah's writings as a structure for his own theology of salvation is a strong indicator that he also remained true to Isaiah's concept of servanthood. The prophet's work is characterized by a threefold use of the term—he applies it to the Messiah, the prophets, and Israel. There is no doubt that Paul followed this same mold when he used the term *doulos* to describe Christ, the apostles, and the church.

Although we have only just scratched the surface when it comes to this incredible subject, by now we've seen enough to conclude that the traditional Greco-Roman context in which *doulos* is normally set is simply not adequate when it comes to interpreting how this term is applied to Christians![37] Seeing *doulos* in its Hebraic setting, however, allows us to unlock the many remarkable, but previously hidden theological implications that surround its use. In light of our discoveries, I believe it can be safely said that neither Paul nor any other Christian is a slave of Christ but is an esteemed servant with all of the dignity and privileges that such a calling carries!

Let me make one final note before we leave this subject. It is important to remember that context determines the meaning of a word and that one definition can't necessarily be applied across the board to every use of a word. In talking about the relationship between Satan and unredeemed humanity, it is appropriate to translate *doulos* as *slave*. Why? In this context, it is a parallel to the slavery Israel experienced while in Egypt. In the same way that Israel was enslaved to Pharaoh, in our unredeemed state we were enslaved to Satan. However, as we saw earlier, when Yahweh delivered Israel from Pharaoh, he did not re-enslave them, rather they entered into a committed, covenant relationship. Therefore, when applied to redeemed humanity in Christ, *doulos* is better translated as *servant* for all of the reasons we just discussed.

## An Exciting Recovery

Having gone through this exercise, it is quite astonishing to step back and realize how a faulty understanding of just this one word—*doulos*—has deprived the contemporary church of so much when it comes to realizing her true identity, calling, and mission. This is only one of several examples of how Greco-Roman concepts have determined the way the New Testament is read.

As the book progresses, we will see other instances as well. Think of the riches that might be unearthed if we make a concentrated effort to free ourselves from the unrecognized presuppositions that have entombed Paul in a Greco-Roman prison! This is a challenge for all believers, whether Catholic, Orthodox, or Anglican, Reformed, Charismatic, or non-denominational. My hope is that seeing this example of how previously unrecognized Old Testament theology breaks out of the New Testament text will give us confidence and also an appetite for exploring other strands of Old Testament theology in Paul's writings.

I realize that at this stage, it may seem like I've been misleading. Earlier, I said there was no need to be a scholar or theologian to understand scripture, and then I went down a fairly complicated trail that required a certain degree of skill to navigate. But I would like to offer some encouragement at this point. One of the goals of this chapter is to demonstrate how scholarly errors are responsible, in part, for making scripture more difficult to understand than it needs to be. It is my contention that the more we learn to recognize some of these mistaken notions, and to read the New Testament against a Hebraic, rather than Greco-Roman backdrop, the simpler it will become to understand the Bible.

## Clearing the Way

Now that we've cleared away some of these faulty assumptions and seen the Old Testament backdrop for the New, we are ready to start exploring the corporate, Hebraic framework that unifies scripture! And we'll begin by looking at our family history.

CHAPTER 3

# Our Family Story

There's a big drive these days to learn about family history. In fact, according to one source, genealogy is the second most researched topic online.[1] In explaining why it was important to him to know his ancestry, one friend said, "Basically, I'm a product of everything that went before me so knowing the past provides clues about who I am." This touches on why genealogy has become such a popular pastime. It addresses some of the fundamental questions men and women have asked throughout the ages—Where do I come from? Why am I here? Where am I going? An article on one web site notes, "Genealogy helps satisfy a deep need to understand how we fit into the broader world around us . . . it is important because ultimately it lies at the heart of the human condition."[2] In this way, genealogy has a lot in common with religion—both seek to answer similar questions and for mostly the same reasons.

Christians actually have two family stories—one derived from our birth parents, and another that became ours when we were adopted into God's family. Just as knowing our natural family's story can shed light on who we are, understanding our spiritual family history can satisfy critical questions about our identities and help us see our place in God's unfolding plan. Not only does this allow us to realize a greater sense of purpose and meaning, but also having an awareness of the narrative in which all believers share can foster unity by showing our common heritage.

The reality is that as Christians, our family story is inseparably intertwined with Israel's history—in fact, our spiritual lineage can be traced all the way back to Abraham. This is not some kind of mildly interesting historical fact to tuck away in the back of our minds; it has very real and practical implications for our lives, both now and in the future. In order to gain insight into our root system and how it relates to us today, what I want to do now is briefly look at Israel's history and God's promises to redeem his people that are recorded in the Old Testament. Since the Jews were expectantly waiting for the Messiah to come and fulfill these promises, this will go a long way in helping us understand Jesus, his mission, and the New Testament message. We will also identify the outlines of the narrative that frames and unifies scripture. In addition to allowing us to see our own identities more clearly, becoming acquainted with this context will give us an indispensable tool for assessing some of the confusing teachings about Jesus and the Christian life that are swirling about today.

Since I want to stay focused on the big picture, I do not plan to go into much detail. I mainly want to provide a broad, bird's eye view of the storyline so we can identify key themes, figures, and events, and then see how they serve as scaffolding for the New Testament message. Even if you are already familiar with the story, I encourage you to keep reading, as this brief overview will lay the groundwork for our upcoming discussion about scripture's corporate framework and our identity as God's people.

**THE JEWISH STORY, OUR STORY¶** The Jews claim to have a unique history that traces back to the covenant that God made with one man.

*Father Abraham.* As recorded in the Old Testament, the story of the Jewish people started when the only true and living God, the Creator of all things, chose a man named Abram, later renamed Abraham, and made some astounding promises to him. Yahweh said he would:

- Bless Abraham and make him into a great nation.

- Give Abraham and his offspring the land of Canaan for his inheritance.

- Make him the father of many nations; through him, all the peoples on earth would be blessed.

- Give Abraham and his wife, Sarah, a son and heir through whom these promises would come to pass.

He also predicted that at some point in the future, Abraham's descendants would be strangers in a foreign land, enslaved and oppressed for 400 years, after which Yahweh would deliver them. Abram believed God's promises, even though he would not live to see all of them come true. Pleased with his response, God then formalized these promises by making a permanent covenant with Abraham.[3] To seal the covenant, Yahweh asked Abraham and his offspring to be circumcised as an outward sign of their commitment.

Known as the Abrahamic covenant, this agreement is foundational in that it is the basis of all that happened to Abraham and his descendants. The Old Testament tells the story of the Hebrews, Abraham's physical descendants, leading up to Christ; the New Testament reveals that now Abraham's offspring is no longer limited to one ethnic groups—it consists of all those who, by faith, believe and trust God is making good on his covenant promises through Abraham's descendant, Jesus, Jews and Gentiles alike.[4] This shows that even though God singled out Israel to be his special people at the time, she was not chosen so she could glory in her special privileges. Rather, God's intention was to work through Israel to bless the other nations.

From the very beginning, Yahweh's long-range redemptive plan was to include the Gentiles.

There were a lot of bumps in the road, however, in realizing these grand promises. After numerous trials and setbacks, Abraham and his family eventually settled in the Promised Land of Canaan and prospered, but as with all families, they faced difficult times. A major setback came hundreds of years later when the family, which was very large by now, had to migrate to Egypt to survive a famine that was ravaging Canaan. At first, they got along well with the Egyptians and life was comfortable. However, as time went by, the government of the land changed and took a hard line against immigrants. Threatened by the size and strength of the Hebrew people, the Egyptians ferociously persecuted the Hebrews and forced them to work as slaves just as Yahweh had predicted when he entered into the covenant with Abraham. To weaken them as a people, the new Pharaoh even went so far as to have all the male Hebrew babies put to death at birth.

*Moses.* At this point in history, another great Jewish figure came on the scene—Moses. When he was born, his mother hid him from Pharaoh's executioners. His life was spared when an Egyptian princess found him and adopted him as her son, making him part of the royal family. Eventually, as an adult, he transferred his allegiance to his own people and had to flee for his life when he killed an Egyptian who was mistreating a Hebrew slave. After forty years in exile, God called him to return to Egypt and lead his people to freedom. Pharaoh did everything possible to keep them from leaving. Finally, Moses warned that if he did not let God's people go, then the firstborn son and even the animals of all the families in Egypt would be struck dead. Pharaoh ignored the warning.

*Passover.* God carried through on his word. The firstborn of the Hebrews were protected, however, because they obeyed the instructions God gave them through Moses. Taking the blood of a slain lamb, they smeared it on the doorposts of their homes and stayed indoors. That night the angel of death came through the land of Egypt and killed the firstborn males, both humans and animals. Wherever the angel saw the blood of the lamb, he passed over the home. This was the night of the Passover and the beginning of Israel's Exodus from Egypt. It is the greatest event in Jewish history and central to their identity as a people—some even regard it as *the* event of human history—which is why it is celebrated even to this day.[5]

*The First Exodus.* The story of the Exodus is well known. After suffering through ten horrific plagues Pharaoh finally relented and released the Hebrews. Moses led the Jews across the Red Sea and out of Egypt. They camped at the foot of Mount Sinai where God made another binding agreement with the Jewish people that Christians refer to as the old covenant. In the same way that vows are exchanged in a marriage ceremony, Yahweh promised to be faithful to the Israelites, and in return, they pledged to be faithful to him. The Old Testament goes on to describe God as being a husband to Israel and to depict the nation as his bride, his wife. When they entered into the covenant agreement, God made it clear that if Israel was unfaithful and started "flirting" with other gods, he would see it as adultery and put her away if she persisted.

It looked like a promising start, but instead of immediately returning to Canaan, the land of their ancestors, and repossessing the land, the Israelites ended up wandering in the wilderness for forty years because they refused to trust God and kept disobeying him. Eventually, the unbelieving generation passed away and the Jews finally settled in the Promised Land, but their history continued to have highs and lows.

*King David.* Rather than being content and rejoicing in all that God had done for them after they entered the Promised Land, the Jews began to envy the surrounding nations. Thinking the nations were successful because they had kings, the Jews asked God to give them one as well. Reluctantly, he honored their wishes and Israel became a monarchy. Their first king was Saul. He was succeeded by another important figure in Jewish history—King David. Even though flawed as a leader through an act of moral failure, the Bible presents David as a man whose heart was set on God. Under his leadership, the nation became secure and prosperous.

Despite this, David did not get to do the one thing that was near and dear to his heart—he was not allowed to build a temple for God to dwell in. This is because he was a military commander who had blood on his hands. However, David's desire pleased God. So, God promised that instead of allowing David to build a house for him, he would build a house for David and the family of David would become the Jewish royal dynasty. God assured David that one of his descendants would always rule over the people. This is known as the Davidic covenant.

*Solomon.* David's son, Solomon took the throne after David and with God's permission, constructed the magnificent temple David had longed to build for Yahweh. Tragically, however, Solomon was not the king the nation needed. Although he was known for his wisdom, he did not apply it to his own life. He demanded far too much tax from the people in order to finance fabulous building projects. Worse still, he ignored God's clear instructions to the Israelites not to marry foreign wives. God had issued this command to make sure gods from other nations did not gain a foothold in Israel and lead the nation into spiritual adultery.

Unfortunately, this is exactly what happened when Solomon's foreign wives brought their entourages along with them. Soon there were thousands of foreigners living in Jerusalem as part of the extended royal family. It wasn't long before the Israelites began worshipping the alien deities these newcomers brought with them. Instead of remaining devoted to the one true God, they began practicing paganism, the very thing they suffered so much to overcome after their time in Egypt. And all of this took place in the very temple of Israel's God.

*Decline and Division.* Once the Israelites began worshipping foreign gods, it wasn't long before they also embraced the lifestyles of the surrounding nations. In imitating them, the Jewish people broke the other moral commands God had given them. Immorality led to infighting and schisms. Before long, the nation divided under two kings. As Israel's national life continued to decline, God sent prophets to warn her about the consequences of infidelity. Some kings paid attention, but for the most part, Israel's rulers refused to listen, and the divided nation slid downward into further moral chaos.

*Captivity.* After repeatedly sending prophets to warn Israel over a lengthy period of time, God eventually acted against his people just as he said he would if she became involved with other gods. First, the Assyrians invaded the ten tribes in the northern kingdom that had broken off and gone their own way. Its cities were destroyed, and the people were taken into exile. Later, the Babylonians warred against Judah, the two of the original twelve tribes that had remained faithful to the house of David. They destroyed Judah's town and villages. They also laid siege to the capital, Jerusalem, and eventually overthrew it. The Babylonians destroyed the entire city, including the sacred temple Solomon had built for Yahweh. Members of the royal family were either put to death or taken into captivity along with almost the entire population. It was the beginning of one of the darkest periods of ancient Israel's history.

## The Promise of Restoration

*Sorrow and Hope.* God warned the Israelites over and over again that he would divorce them if they continued to commit adultery with foreign gods, but they wouldn't listen. Finally, he kept his word—the Babylonians invaded the land and Jerusalem, the capital city, was totally destroyed. The conquerors carried off all who were suitable into exile and left the weak and sick behind. Israel never thought God would actually judge them, but he did! Understandably, the morale of the nation collapsed. They saw the exile as God's punishment for their sins and found it difficult to believe there could ever be a fresh start. But a new beginning is the very thing God's prophets promised Israel when she was in exile. In spite of the downfall of the royal family, they predicted one of David's descendants would be raised up who would:

- Deliver the people from captivity back to the Promised Land (Isa. 11:11).

- Be anointed with the Spirit of the Lord for this task (Isa. 61:1-2).

- Lead the people through the wilderness (Hos. 2:14).

- The prophets also said it would just like when the Jews left Egypt—it would be another exodus.

*A Second Exodus.* The prophets had a great deal to say about this Second Exodus and how it would parallel the first one. They prophesied:

- The pilgrimage through the desert would be under the protection of the Holy Spirit just as the pilgrimage from Egypt had been (Isa. 44:3).

- There would be miracles like when they came out of Egypt. Even the desert itself would be transformed as nature shared in the re-creation of the nation (Isa. 55:13).

- A prince who comes from David's line would establish a new covenant with Israel (Isa. 9:6-7).

- Although all males who came out of Egypt during the First Exodus had to be circumcised physically as a sign of fidelity, in the new covenant, the people's hearts would be circumcised; God promised to give his people a new heart and to put his Spirit within them (Jer. 31:31-44; Ezek. 36:25-27).

- The return from exile would be their return to Eden (Isa. 51:3).

- Once the people journeyed back to Jerusalem, they would build a magnificent temple that would be dedicated by the promised descendant of David (Ezek. 44-45).

- All the nations of the world could come to this temple to worship Israel's God (Isa. 2:1-5).[6]

- The Lord would come into his temple and be with his people (Isa. 4:2-6).

- And finally, the wedding between God and his people would be celebrated with a great cosmic banquet (Isa. 54:1-8).

*Unfulfilled Promises.* Israel's release from captivity and return from exile is recorded in the books of Ezra, Nehemiah, and the Minor Prophets such as Haggai, Zechariah, and Malachi. What these books show is that Israel's return from Babylon back to the Promised Land fell far short of what the prophets had described. Even though some of the people returned to Jerusalem and attempted to rebuild the temple, it was a poor, pathetic version of the original one Solomon spared no cost to build and that the Babylonians had destroyed. They were constantly looking for the promised descendant of King David to come and restore the nation, but he never showed up. Rather than being the leader of the world as promised, Israel continued to be under the control of other nations. For four hundred years—from the time of their return from exile until the birth of Christ—they groaned in their sense of failure, guilt and disappointment.

*In Between Times.* During this time period, the Jews saw no significant change in their circumstances. They longed to be restored to the former greatness experienced under David's rule, but they were as far from God as they had ever been for he had not fulfilled all of his promises. They couldn't accept that their punishment was over until they had complete freedom from foreign oppressors. The writings of the Jews in this era, which as noted earlier are collectively referred to as intertestamental or Second Temple literature, clearly shows the status of their faith—they continued to cling to the hope that God would yet fulfill the promises he had made to them through the prophets. The scriptures surveyed above became their light throughout the long dark years of shame under the domination of the Greeks and then the Romans.

Ancient documents such as the *Dead Sea Scrolls*, the writings of Josephus, some of the apocryphal texts, and Rabbinic texts all show the Jews in this era were expectantly waiting for the descendant of David, the Messiah to come and make good on the promises spoken by the prophets. Since there were different sects within Judaism during the intertestamental period, ideas varied about the Messiah, who he was, and what would happen when he came. Nevertheless, a common thread regarding a New Exodus and the restoration of Israel runs throughout these writings. The Old Testament, along with this literature, clearly shows that a strong and abiding hope for a New Exodus is what sustained Israel through her suffering in the centuries before Jesus came.[7]

*A New Exodus.* We are ready to follow the storyline into the New Testament now. As we do, it is important to keep in mind the way the exodus theme evolves in scripture. If we fail to appreciate the development of this motif and how the New Testament writers build on it, we will miss important markers than can help us decipher the meaning of key terms and passages. As we saw,

- The First Exodus is about Israel's deliverance from bondage in Egypt, crossing the Red Sea into a new life, and the first covenant God made with the nation at Mt. Sinai when he promised to be her God and she vowed to be his people.

- The Second Exodus has to do with the promises Yahweh made to Israel after he "divorced" her because of her blatant, ongoing unfaithfulness and sent her into exile.[8] This exodus event has to do with Israel's redemption from captivity in Babylon, her pilgrimage back to the Promised Land, and God's intention to enter into a new covenant relationship with her that would supersede the one she violated earlier. Although the term, Second Exodus is never used in the New Testament, it is clearly foundational to the apostles' understanding of the gospel. In many instances, references to justification, a significant salvation-related term in both the Old and New Testaments, are set against the backdrop of Second Exodus promises, especially in Isaiah. In this setting, justification is a corporate term that refers to Israel's return from exile and her restored marital relationship with God.

- New Exodus theology refers to how the New Testament writers take themes associated with the First Exodus along with Second Exodus promises that were unrealized in the Old Testament era and show how they point to and are fulfilled in the life, death, and resurrection of Jesus, the Son of David.

What unifies these exodus events is the theme of the divine marriage, which runs all throughout scripture. In each instance, God's intention was to deliver his people from bondage to their oppressors and bring them back to himself so that he could enter (or re-enter) into a covenant relationship with them which scripture describes as a marriage. Looking back to the First Exodus, the prophets refer to the establishment of the old covenant at Mount Sinai as the time when Israel became Yahweh's wife. In the Second Exodus, after Israel served her time in exile, God delivered Israel's remnant community (the smaller group that was willing to return to Zion) from captivity. He brought her back to him with the promise that he would renew his covenant relationship with her and restore her inheritance. And in a New Exodus, Jesus, our Passover, restores the covenant relationship with God that Adam and Eve violated in the garden. Through his death, he rescues those who are willing from Satan, inaugurates a new covenant, and betroths the church as his bride. This New Exodus is to culminate in the marriage supper of the Lamb that will take place at the end of the ages.

Another common point is that each exodus event was initiated by a Passover sacrifice. The First Exodus began with the death of the paschal lamb; as we shall see, Passover imagery was heavily associated with the Second Exodus; and Jesus's death as our Paschal Lamb launched a New Exodus. We will talk about why a Passover sacrifice was necessary before an exodus event could take place later. This connection with a Passover sacrifice is why, in some cases, I will use the phrase *Paschal-New Exodus* when referring to this theme.

Again, while the term *New Exodus* is never explicitly mentioned in the New Testament, the concept is certainly there. In scripture, Christ is called the Lamb of God, and at the Last Supper he described his death in terms of the Passover. This connects Christ's life and death to the First Exodus event. The New Testament writers also show how the prophets' expectations that were related to the Second Exodus pointed to something much greater in Christ than Israel's national deliverance alone.

For instance, the prophets looked for Israel's restoration to the Promised Land, but as the New Testament writers explained, these predictions were looking forward to the kingdom Jesus came to establish and will fully reveal when he comes again. They also foresaw the establishment of a new covenant, which occurred through Christ but was not for Israel alone—the Gentiles were also invited to become members of the new covenant community by believing in Jesus. And while the prophets looked for Israel to rebuild a literal temple, the apostles taught the birth of the church, made up of believing Jews and believing Gentiles, fulfilled this Second Exodus promise. The collective church is now God's living temple. So, in the New Testament understanding, the actual fulfillment of these promises in Christ is not identical with the predictions made by the Old Testament prophets— rather, they were types and shadows that have to do with a grander, more expansive spiritual reality.

An important point to keep in mind regarding New Exodus theology is that while Jesus fulfilled the Old Testament prophecies, he also enlarged the church's understanding by bringing new revelation about the kingdom, his rule, and God's unfolding plan. This is why Jewish intertestamental literature is of little help when determining what the primitive church believed. Although these writings show that in general the Jewish people were expecting a Messiah who would lead a New Exodus, Jesus challenged popular expectations and defined his own role in a unique way. To bring the specific views of different Jewish sects that existed at this time into the Christian understanding would obscure Christ's own distinctive message.

## The New Exodus in the New Testament

Here's the question we need to answer as we begin talking about Christ's work—did the expectation of a New Exodus have a *significant* influence on the New Testament writers? Evidence suggests the answer is a resounding "yes!" In fact, it is not going too far to say the longing to see God fulfill the Old Testament promises of a New Exodus that culminates in the divine marriage forms the backdrop for the entire New Testament.

In looking at the Gospels, a number of scholars believe a New Exodus pattern runs all through the Gospel of Mark.[9] They claim to have identified the presence of highly developed theological insights that could be triggered by the Old Testament texts. As we have seen, the mere quotation of a short text had the effect of alerting the reader to the Old Testament passage from which it had been taken. In this way, these references had a far greater significance for the first readers of the New Testament than is normal today.

For instance, in chapter four, Mark includes a quote from Isaiah about how some will harden their hearts when the kingdom of God comes.[10] Reading the original quotation from Isaiah in context, the prophet speaks of a king who would be rejected and how judgment will follow as a result of this hardness.[11] This echoes the story of the First Exodus when the Egyptians hardened their hearts against Moses, the deliverer God sent to lead his people out of captivity and establish a new nation. The same pattern was repeated again in the way many in the nation of Israel hardened themselves to Jesus. There are a number of other allusions that tie into the idea of a New Exodus in the Gospel of Mark.[12]

Furthermore, all the Gospels open with John the Baptist saying that he is "the voice of one crying in the wilderness, 'Prepare the way of the Lord.'"[13] The importance of this text is clear in that it is one of the few passages preserved in all four Gospels. John the Baptist used these words from Isaiah's prophecy to announce that the long-awaited descendant of David was coming to fulfill God's promises. As mentioned previously, when Jesus stood up in the synagogue, he too quoted a passage from Isaiah about how the Spirit of the Lord would be upon the deliverer God sent to preach the good news to the poor, and then he applied this text to himself. In doing this, he was claiming to be the son of David, the promised King who had come to bring freedom from captivity.

The fact that both John the Baptist and Jesus began their ministries by quoting Isaiah is very significant, as both passages are based on prophetic promises of the Messiah and of a New Exodus that had not yet been fulfilled. By using these texts, they were declaring that the end times salvation predicted by Isaiah was at long last breaking into human history! The Baptist confirmed this understanding when he sent messengers to ask Jesus if he was the Christ. Jesus replied by pointing to the signs that Isaiah said would accompany the New Exodus when it finally happened— "The blind receive sight, the lame walk, those who have leprosy are cleansed, the deaf hear, the dead are raised, and the good news is proclaimed to the poor."[14] Clearly, both John the Baptist and Jesus set their ministries in the context of Isaiah's prediction of the New Exodus.

This connection was also apparent at Jesus's baptism when the voice from heaven said, "This is my beloved son, in whom I am well pleased."[15] This is widely recognized as a reference to Isaiah's prophecy about the mysterious servant figure who would deliver Israel from captivity. In this statement, God was identifying Jesus as the Servant who would bring about the New Exodus and justify the many.[16] Indeed, on the mount of Transfiguration, a key incident in the Gospels, Jesus talked with Moses and Elijah about "his coming *exodus*," not the much weaker rendering *departure* as in the NIV translation.[17]

The New Exodus theme was also clearly stressed when Jesus took his disciples to the upper room to have their last supper together in in connection with the Passover. There can be no doubt that he wanted his death to be understood as a paschal (Passover) meal. As the Lamb of God, his death was for his followers and the means of their redemption. Without it, there would be no exodus, no deliverance, no divine marriage for them.[18] The New Exodus theme is apparent in other New Testament texts as well.[19]

## A New Leader

Another set of commonly shared expectations related to the New Exodus was Israel's hope of a new national deliverer like Moses. However, while sharing some of the characteristics of Moses, the figure who would lead a New Exodus was not to be from the tribe of Levi as Moses was, but from the tribe of Judah. As noted above, the Jews were looking for none other than the promised descendant of David whom Yahweh declared would have an everlasting throne. Many scholars contend that Matthew's Gospel shows Jesus is the second Moses, but this misses the fact that Moses is rarely mentioned in association with

Jesus, whereas David is repeatedly linked to him. This is important because although Moses was a national leader, he was never a king. Matthew definitely has an exodus structure, but it is not a new Moses who is God's instrument for setting the people free; it is the royal son of David as predicted by the prophets.

Seeing how Jesus fulfilled the promises relating to the predicted Messiah-King from the House of David is crucial for appreciating the first century church's understanding of the person and work of her Savior. It is no coincidence the gospel writers record that when the leaders of Israel brought charges against Jesus, the accusation that led to his crucifixion had to do with his claims to kingship.[20] Nor is it a mere coincidence that Jesus denied plans to rule over an earthly kingdom while asserting his intent to establish a spiritual one.[21]

What's interesting is that the New Testament authors could have chosen from a range of related titles to describe who Jesus was that would have also been meaningful to the first century believers. The way they relied so heavily on the title, son of David, is telling as the prophetic significance would have been clear to any Jewish believer. The fact that Jesus died with the inscription "the King of the Jews" above his head at Passover spoke of the Davidic prince who would offer the Paschal (Passover) sacrifices described by prophet Ezekiel.[22] Though meant derisively by those who mocked Jesus, it pointed to his divine assignment to establish an eternal kingdom into which his subjects were to be incorporated.

The New Exodus storyline is not only present in the Gospel narratives where Jesus is continually honored as the long-awaited descendant of David, but it is also in the early church's preaching as recorded in Acts. The reference to raising the tent of David in Acts 15 is particularly significant.[23] This reveals that the primitive church saw Jesus as taking the role of the Davidic King and that all aspects of the covenant God made with David were being fulfilled in him. Jesus was the suffering Servant, the Son of David, the Messiah-King who came to bring about the New Exodus and establish a new kingdom with all of its resultant blessings. As a result, the Gentiles could now be freely welcomed into the new covenant community, whereas, previously they had been excluded!

It is also thrilling to discover that a number of other themes related to the New Exodus run all throughout the New Testament. These include the new covenant, circumcision of the heart, the gift of the Spirit, the pilgrimage of God's people, the return to Eden, the end times temple, the conversion of the nations, their inclusion into the covenant community, and the marriage of Jesus and his bride, the church, at the end of the ages. These are all further examples of Old Testament expectations that overflow into the aspirations and understanding of the first-century church.

Behind these widely-recognized motifs, there is a whole substructure of allusions in the New Testament that ties into them. As we shall continue to see, once the New Exodus paradigm is identified, this scaffolding lights up with a clarity that is quite compelling! With the New Exodus backdrop in place, the grand storyline that links the Old Testament to the New emerges and the whole Bible begins to make more sense!

**PAUL AND A NEW EXODUS¶** While expectations of a New Exodus may have heavily influenced those who wrote the four Gospels, what about Paul? Was his theology also shaped by this same set of expectations? Were his writings consistent in this way with Jesus and the other gospel writers? Or did he depart from the Old Testament framework they used and, as many have charged, introduce a mix of ideas lifted from Gnosticism, Hellenism, the Romans, or extra-biblical Jewish sources? Did he invent a new religion? How can we know for sure?

As stated previously, I believe it can be amply proved that Paul's teachings are firmly rooted in the ancient Jewish scriptures and that he saw himself as standing in line with the Old Testament prophets, Jesus, and the twelve apostles. In the following chapters, we will be exploring some of his teachings in more depth as the idea that Paul imported foreign ideas into the gospel has created enormous confusion when it comes to interpreting the New Testament. Seeing how New Exodus themes permeate Paul's writings will not only shed amazing light on several controversial passages, but it can also increase our confidence regarding the consistency and reliability of the New Testament message.

## Salvation and the Two Communities

Before we dive into some of Paul's teachings, I want to mention an important consideration about determining the overall theological context of his writings, a critical step for understanding his mindset. It is not enough to rummage through Paul's letters and gather related texts on a subject to understand his views on a particular matter. Although commonly done, the circumstances of each individual letter need to determine how it is read and how a subject is understood.

If we take Paul's teachings on a specific issue out of the context of a particular letter, lump them all together and give every statement equal weight, then we may end up with a distorted picture of his theology. In order to discern some of the main concerns that shaped Paul's thinking, it is important then to distinguish between primary issues that affected the church at large and secondary matters that may have mainly affected a particular congregation.[24]

Looking at the primitive church across the board, some of the major problems Paul sought to address had to do with conflicts between Jewish and Gentile members regarding the necessity of circumcision, the role of Mosaic law, the perceived superiority of one group over another, and boasting as to who had greater faith. These all tie into a larger issue that is foundational to Paul's theology of salvation—the new relationship between the Jews and Gentiles in the end times covenant community. Paul was zealous for Jewish and Gentile believers alike to know that in Christ, the two groups were united, and all members had equal status. Because all had received the Spirit and were now in Christ, the law was no longer a barrier between them as it once had been. In God's eyes, one group was not better than the other; believing Jews and believing Gentiles were now in the same family and shared the same family history!

Paul was deeply concerned that if conflict between the two communities continued to escalate, the young church would split. In his mind, there was a real danger the umbilical cord might be cut, and the Christian Gentile church would permanently separate from its Jewish "Christian" mother. For Paul, this would have been disastrous as in his understanding there is only one body and only one Lord who deals with all on the same grounds of grace. If the body of Christ divided into Jewish and Gentile factions, it would undermine the very heart of the gospel.

In his letter to the Romans, considered by many to be Paul's *magnum opus* that we are preparing to look at next, it is apparent the apostle was addressing the common problems the wider church was facing. This gives weight to the arguments he is making in the letter. The first eleven chapters are about the condition of *all* people and their need for salvation, first the Gentiles then the Jews, showing God's response to their plight. Paul recounts how through Abraham, God chose the Jews to be his people *before* they were circumcised. So again, reasons Paul, God is following the same path in accepting uncircumcised Gentiles. In other words, Paul is stressing the biblical evidence that the Gentiles are being brought into the covenant in exactly the same way as the Jews had been—by faith. To drive the point home, he spells out how God chose Abraham, their representative and father, *before* he was circumcised.

Now here is where the New Exodus model comes into play. Paul regularly makes the point in his letters that the redemption the Jews experienced when God rescued them from Pharaoh's iron grip was only a type of the salvation that was going to be accomplished in the last days.[25] The First Exodus pointed ahead to a far greater act of redemption. In Paul's perspective, it was folly for the Jews to claim superiority because of their deliverance from Egypt that led to the establishment of the old covenant, and not to appreciate it was a mere shadow of the greater salvation to come that all believers now shared through Christ. For this reason, Paul told the Jews they were not to see themselves as being superior to the Gentiles. He explains that by faith, the believing Gentiles are children of the promise God made to Abraham, and for this reason, they too are descendants of Abraham.[26]

In turn, Paul warned the Gentiles not to be conceited or arrogant towards the Jewish people or to disdain the church's rich root system it inherited from the Jews. He explains that although some of the Jewish "branches were broken off" because of unbelief, they could be grafted into the tree once again. He made it clear that God still had a plan for his ancient people.[27]

A careful reading of the letter to the Romans shows Paul was not merely explaining the path to personal salvation. Rather, he was trying to keep the two communities together, so they could bear common witness to the Lord who had saved them. As he points out, from the very beginning God's intention was to bring both groups into the end times new covenant community. It was only as Jewish and Gentile converts accepted each other and lived as one new man (new humanity) that the nations would take note of what God was doing in Christ. Together, they were to be living evidence that God was reconciling enemies not only to himself but to one another as well. For all of these reasons, unity between Jewish and Gentile Christians was vital to Paul's mission. The larger context of the Pauline letters shows him laboring, and also paying an extremely high cost, to maintain this united relationship between the two communities.[28]

## The Corporate Setting of Paul's Letters

In attempting to understand Paul's perspective, we also need to be careful that he is not inadvertently isolated from the corporate mindset that is foundational to the whole Old Testament. It is all too easy to forget that Paul was a devout Jew long before he responded to the claims of Jesus to be the Messiah. After he believed in Jesus, he neither deliberately nor subconsciously rejected his heritage. One of the features of that heritage was to gather to hear the scriptures read to the congregation in the synagogue. The significance of Paul's synagogue experience was that it controlled the way he heard the Jewish scriptures. Listening to them corporately was not a distorting influence, mainly because the messages of the prophets were rarely delivered to individuals. Rather, they were mostly spoken to the covenant people collectively. The gathered congregation was, therefore, the ideal setting to deliver the word that God was speaking to each generation of his covenant people.

Paul follows the same principle in his letters. He expects the believers to gather together to hear them read. Indeed, the possibility of individuals having their own private copy of scripture could hardly have crossed his mind, as this is a blessing that in historical terms, believers have only recently enjoyed. Writing long before printing presses were invented, the apostle intended his letters to be read out loud within context of the believing community and his arguments were, therefore, constructed with this setting in mind.

This is why interpreting letters written to the churches as though they were directed to individuals seriously distorts the content. This may sound startling to us today given our emphasis on personal salvation, but *the letters are not about what God has done or is doing for the individual Christian.* They are about what God has done or is doing for his new covenant people, the church. Therefore, it is not permissible, despite the widespread practice, to read the details as though they describe the experience of the solitary believer. Such an approach not only makes too much of the individual, it makes too little of the new covenant community.

To those who may argue this risks losing the individual perspective of the New Testament, I can only ask, "What is meant by individual perspective?" As mentioned earlier, Western individualism is not the same as biblical individuality. It goes without saying that both the Old and New Testaments clearly recognize the responsibility of individuals to apply the Word of God to their own lives. But that is not individualism as normally understood in our times. The biblical perspective is that every person is a member of a community and that membership determines the individual's self-identity.

The Old Testament prophets reminded Israel of the unique relationship that existed between Yahweh and the nation. They called her, and by implication each individual Jew, to live in a way that reflected who they were as God's people. Paul followed the same pattern. He constantly reminded the church of her high calling and appealed to her to live as the new covenant community in the world. At times, he spoke to specific groups of people such as masters and slaves, spelling out the ramifications of what he said for their daily lives. Very occasionally, he even spoke to individuals, but by far, he addressed his letters to the church at large. If we lose sight of this, then scripture can be used to endorse all manner of individualistic understandings and behaviors. We'll see examples of this in the following chapters.

In insisting that Paul's letters are written to the church, I am not saying anything new. Most commentators point out the same thing. Unfortunately, the practice of reading scripture as though it is addressed to the individual is such an ingrained habit in some traditions that it is easy to slip into this mindset without even realizing it. So, what I want to do as we look more closely at some of Paul's major teachings is to keep the corporate perspective to the forefront of our thinking.

## Initiation into the New Covenant Community

We need to address one more point before moving on. If the claims I am making about the corporate nature of Paul's letters are correct, then they inevitably raise questions about how to become a member of the body of Christ. This is unavoidable because, as we will see, many of the passages that have been commonly seen as referring to the individual salvation experience actually have to do with the historical creation of the new covenant community. So where does the individual fit into this scheme?

This is a serious question. Those who believe in universal salvation would have no problem with the idea of reading scripture corporately. In fact, they would enthusiastically accept it because they believe Christ's death applies to all people, and, therefore, all will be saved. Such euphoria is unfounded, however, as Paul insists there is a fundamental division in the human race, but it is no longer between Jews and Gentiles—it is now between those who are in Adam (unredeemed humanity) and those who are in Christ (redeemed humanity). It is true, of course, that *in Christ*, there are no ultimate divisions based on status, race, or gender, but it is abusing Paul's arguments to claim this applies to all of humanity. To ignore the fundamental premise so clearly found in Paul's theology that humankind consists of two separate communities under two respective heads—Jesus or Satan—is to destroy the very basis of his arguments. If this basic division is ignored when developing a doctrine of salvation, then it is not an accurate reflection of Paul's teaching.

No matter what stance we may take on these issues, one thing is certain—the early church saw the need for personal repentance and faith. There is no suggestion that men and women automatically benefit from Christ's death as God calls all people everywhere to repent and believe.[29] Any argument for the early church's understanding of the corporate nature of the letters must respect this basic tenet, which is clearly expressed in her evangelistic ministry.

## Towards a Corporate Reading

So far, we've seen that the New Testament writers depended not only on Isaiah but also on the Old Testament as a whole when framing their message and I have repeatedly suggested that Paul followed the same pattern. If we want to understand Paul, then it is important to take his commitment to the ancient Jewish texts seriously, especially in regard to the New Exodus paradigm.

I believe it can be shown that his doctrinal system fits perfectly into this model and also that it resolves many of the difficulties with Pauline theology that many have traditionally assumed to exist. This perspective allows him to claim that his gospel is according to the scriptures and that it is the fulfillment of the prophetic promises God has made to his people. Again, I am arguing that Paul was not the innovator of a new religion. Instead, he was a faithful ambassador who conscientiously delivered his Master's message to the Gentiles.

Let's go on now to look at some of the challenging passages in Paul's letters and see how reading them corporately against the backdrop of the New Exodus paradigm can bring the biblical picture into sharper focus and also help resolve longstanding interpretive problems.

# PART TWO

# Recovering the Corporate Lens

CHAPTER 4

# Salvation Incorporated

In the late '60s, British scientist and inventor, Dr. James Lovelock, advanced a theory suggesting the organic and inorganic elements of the Earth function together as a single, living organism. Dr. Lovelock theorized that much like the human body, the planet regulates itself by automatically adjusting elements such as temperature, atmosphere, saline in the ocean, and other factors in order to maintain conditions suitable for life. Because it seemed to operate like a living entity, he personified the planetary organism by naming it Gaia (GUY-uh) after the Greek Goddess of the Earth. Although the theory itself is now regarded as flawed, as one scientist observed, the concept "helped to stimulate many new ideas about the Earth and to champion a holistic approach to studying it."[1]

While not a new idea—how the one and the many relate has been debated for centuries—the interdependence of life is receiving fresh attention as globalization progresses. Increasingly linked by new technologies, international trade, the need to share limited resources, and other common concerns, people around the globe are becoming acutely aware that what happens in one part of the world has the potential to affect everyone else on the planet. As Martin Luther King, Jr. once observed, "We are caught in an inescapable network of mutuality tied in a single garment of destiny. Whatever affects one directly affects all indirectly."[2]

This reality has long been recognized in scripture. In an illustration that's used over 30 times in the New Testament, individuals in the universal church are portrayed as comprising one unified organism— the body of Christ.[3] Individual believers are likened to various body parts such as a hand, a foot, or an eye that are joined to one another and to Jesus Christ, who is the head. Each member has a critical role to play in the proper functioning of the church and no individual can live independently of the others. All are necessary for building up of Christ's body in love.

While this and some other corporate concepts are widely recognized, as I have been saying, I believe a strong case can be made that others which are equally important have been pushed to the background in the West, largely as a result of reading scripture through an individualistic lens. This is especially true when it comes to salvation-related themes. Clearly, in the Old Testament, the Exodus—which was a defining event for the nation of Israel—was not for the individual Jew, but for the Jewish people as a nation. Although the individual benefitted, it was essentially a corporate event. As we have seen, even today the Jews look back to the Exodus as the time when their national identity was established and celebrate the Passover in remembrance of how Yahweh delivered them collectively from slavery and death.

Likewise, I believe the same can be said about salvation in the New Testament—while individuals may enjoy the redemptive benefits of Christ's death, historically, as described by Paul and the rest of the New Testament writers, it has to do with the corporate salvation of God's people. Paralleling the First Exodus, through his death Christ, the Lamb of God and our Passover, inaugurated a New Exodus to lead his people out of bondage to Sin and Death, and into a new kingdom of light. As noted previously, in scripture, this Spirit-birthed community is referred to in singular, corporate terms as the new man (new humanity), the body of Christ, God's temple, a holy nation, and the bride of Christ.

Again, I am not discounting the importance of personal repentance and faith. Rather, I'm saying that in order to fully appreciate the biblical picture of salvation, it is necessary to see this larger corporate context *first* and then set the individual's experience within it. As we shall see, recovering this corporate perspective has immense practical implications for how we live out the Christian life. What I want to do next is to explore some of the corporate themes in scripture that have been brushed out or obscured by reading through individualistic, dualistic lenses. To do this, we'll consider how key texts that have been traditionally interpreted as applying to the individual are, in reality, primarily about the new covenant community.

**CONSISTENTLY CORPORATE¶** The first passage I want to zero in on is Romans 5–8. No doubt, this will lead us into challenging waters as for centuries, scholars and leaders have disagreed about how to interpret these chapters, but it is critical to tackle them for several reasons. Historically, Romans 5–8 has been a foundational text when framing views of salvation, the human person, and the individual Christian's relationship with sin. It is not an exaggeration to say that most theologies regarding the nature of the human person and the Christian life can be traced back to this section of scripture in one way or another.

One of the things I hope to show is that much of the controversy and confusion surrounding these chapters stem from an inconsistent reading—while some parts are clearly recognized as referring to corporate realities, others are read as applying primarily to the individual. I contend that given the overall context of Romans, there is no justification for flipping back and forth—these passages should be read consistently from a corporate perspective first before making individual application.

In exploring the corporate themes that, in my opinion, should control how these chapters are read, we will first look at the confusion caused by individualistic interpretations of chapters 6 and 7. This will clear the way for us to better see Paul's description of two great entities, two parallel cosmic bodies that encompass all of humanity— the body of Christ headed by Jesus and the body of Sin headed by Satan. I want to show how recovering a corporate view of the body of Sin can help unravel a number of perplexing problems in Romans 5–8 and also in I Corinthians 6, another knotty text. Next, we'll see in more depth how this view of the body of Sin ties into Paul's understanding of corporate baptism and why this framework may challenge some of our traditional concepts of sin, the human person, and other aspects of the Christian life. (I will explain why I am capitalizing the body of Sin momentarily.)

Once the discussion of Romans 5–8 is complete, in subsequent chapters, we will circle back to Romans 3 and consider the corporate dimensions of three other significant salvation-related themes—God's righteousness, atonement, and justification—that have been distorted by individualistic readings. We will also explore how recovering this corporate setting shines a different light on the controversial subject of God's wrath. What I want to show is that seeing Christ's work on the cross in context of the corporate, New Exodus storyline can help unify some of the conflicting atonement theories that have previously divided the church.

I realize some of the things I am saying may fly in the face of what has been taught in certain circles. This is why I want to carefully lay out my thinking step by step as it will let you to see how I reached the conclusions I did. Even if it seems novel at first, I hope you will hear me out and search the scriptures to see if what I'm saying has merit. Again, exploring these matters will require us to navigate through some challenging twists and turns, so I want to encourage you keep your Bible close at hand. In fact, I suggest that you stop and read Romans 5–8 so that it can be fresh in your mind as we go along.

In these next chapters about Romans 5–8, I will be doing something a little unusual regarding the Bible translation I have chosen to use. Unless otherwise indicated, I will be quoting primarily from the older 1984 version of the NIV. There are several reasons for doing this. First, the NIV translation has both shaped and been shaped by an influential stream of thought regarding sin and human nature. It is also popular. Written in modern English for contemporary audiences, more than 450 million copies are in print. Although some of the language was revised in 2011, many copies of the 1984 NIV are still in circulation so this version continues to have influence. Looking at the older edition first, and then comparing some of the differences between the newer version of the NIV and other Bible translations will allow us to pinpoint some of the problems created by reading through an individualistic lens. In the rest of the book, I will be quoting primarily from the 2011 NIV.

## Conundrums and Convolutions

When I was a young pastor and preaching through the book of Romans for the first time, I got through the first five chapters reasonably well. Up to that point, my approach was simply to study what others said about the text, distill their insights, and make them accessible to the congregation so it wasn't all that hard. But I hit a wall when I got to chapter 6. The more I compared what the commentators said with the texts themselves, the more unsettled I became. I realized it was not so much that they disagreed among themselves, which they did, but that I found myself disagreeing with them! I must admit I was distinctly uncomfortable with the idea of being at odds with thought leaders that I respected and admired. Nevertheless, I could not stop the flow of questions that kept coming to mind as I continued to dig into the chapter.

The initial problem I encountered had to do with differing opinions over what Paul understood to happen with baptism in 6:1-4. Elsewhere, Paul says, "we were all baptized by one Spirit into one body."[4] Reading these verses in Romans in light of this text, did Paul see the Spirit as being given to the individual for *the first time* in baptism or was the Spirit *already present* in the believer and now uniting the one being baptized with Christ? This was important as it affected what was taught about Christian experience, especially in regard to how and when individuals are saved and receive the Holy Spirit. At the time, my view reflected my Baptist background. However, as I began to look more closely at the event Paul described as our "baptism into death," I had a growing suspicion that something was missing with the traditional perspectives, mine included.[5]

I was also uneasy with the commonly accepted interpretation of Romans 6:6-7 that says,

> For we know that our old self was crucified with him so that the body of sin might be done away with, that we should no longer be slaves to sin—because anyone who has died has been *freed* from sin.[6]

In my mind, commentaries on this passage were problematic for a couple of reasons. First, I was concerned with the cavalier way in which commentators played around with the language in verse 7. When translated directly from the Greek, it says, "anyone who has died has been *justified* from sin." Almost all translators backed away from this, however, and agreed that Paul did not intend to say *justified* but *freed*. I'll explain why many took this position and why it matters later, but here is what struck me at the time. Paul uses this Greek word for justification sixteen times, and *not once* has it ever been suggested it meant anything other than *justified* in these other texts, but in this one instance, it was translated differently. Again, this led me to suspect that somehow, commentators from a wide range of theological traditions could be missing the point of what Paul was saying.

My uneasiness with some of the traditional interpretations grew as I delved into another problem I ran into with Romans 6:6. What is the *body of sin* and how did it relate to *the old self?* Were both terms referring to our physical bodies or something else? In what way were we once slaves to the *body of sin*? And whatever it was, how exactly was it "done away with?" I had struggled with this text long before getting my seminary degree and it continued to trouble me as a pastor because I could see that how *the body of sin* was understood had a real, practical effect on the way people viewed themselves, their standing with God, and the way they lived out their faith. Most expositors follow the individualistic interpretation in saying the *body of sin* is either the human body or the sin that continues to reside within the believer after conversion. This can easily create the impression that the human person is intrinsically sinful. I could see that when sensitive souls failed at times in their struggle with sin, a cloud of self-doubt and loathing would descend on them, causing them to question their faith and experience of Christ's salvation.

Because the exact phrase, *the body of sin,* is used only here in this verse, there was no other passage to directly compare it to, and again, the commentaries offered little help. Not surprisingly, scholars disagreed about what it meant, plus the interpretations many offered created even more conundrums. I'll come back to the subjects of baptism and justification in later chapters, but for now my aim is to focus on the meaning of this mysterious little phrase, *the body of sin.* I want to start here for one primary reason—as I discovered, it proved to be an unexpected key in unlocking the corporate framework that lay behind much of the New Testament.

## The Body of Sin

To understand some of the traditional interpretations of the *body of sin* we need to jump ahead to Romans 7 for a moment and here's where things start to get tangled. Believing it is the same thing as the *body of death* mentioned in Romans 7:24, many commentators looked to this passage for clues to what *the body of sin* means in chapter 6. In 7:7-25, Paul describes a Wretched Man who wants to do what is right but is a prisoner of the sin that lives within him. Torn and tortured, he cries out to be rescued from this *body of death*. Paul says,

So, I find this law at work: When I want to do good, evil is right there in me. For in my inner being I delight in God's law; but I see another law at work in the members of my body, waging war against the law of my mind and making me a prisoner of the law of sin at work within my members. What a wretched man I am! Who will rescue me from this *body of death*?[7]

This text has puzzled Western Christians for centuries. Who exactly is the mysterious Wretched Man that Paul is describing? Since Paul deliberately switched from using the plural "we" earlier in the chapter to the singular "I" in these verses and also shifted from past tense to present tense, the prevailing interpretations have understandably been based on an individualistic reading. Many assumed Paul was offering an autobiographical account of his own struggle with sin. For those who take this position, the big question is not about the Wretched Man's identity, but whether Paul was talking about himself *before* or *after* his conversion experience.[8]

From the second to the fourth century, the dominant view in the church was that Paul was using himself as an example of the *unregenerate* person who was convicted of sin by means of God's law but did not yet know freedom in Christ.[9] Augustine, one of the foundational fathers in the West, saw it differently; he reasoned that Paul was talking about the *regenerate* Christian's ongoing battle with indwelling sin. While the Eastern Church continued to hold to the first view, Augustine's new interpretation heavily influenced the West from the fifth century on, yet not all have agreed with him. In fact, the church has never reached consensus on how to interpret Romans 7 mainly because, as we'll see, reading this passage as though Paul was talking about himself solely as an individual is problematic for a number of reasons.[10]

The point I want to make at the moment is that because the *body of death* in Romans 7 was most often interpreted as having to do with the individual, when Romans 6:6 was read against this backdrop, *the old self* (man) and the *body of sin* were also often seen as being about the individual. As a result, while most traditional views agreed chapter 5 is about two collective bodies of people—redeemed and unredeemed humanity—it was also generally believed that Paul switched from this corporate perspective and started talking about the individual in chapter 6.

As I continued to ask questions and read, however, an alternative but lesser known perspective caught my attention. In recent years, a number of scholars have suggested that because of Paul's Jewish heritage and mindset, Romans 6–8 make far better sense when also seen as being set within a communal rather than individualistic framework.[11] Not only did chapter 5 have to do with two larger corporate entities, but also his entire letter is addressing the relationship between two people groups—Jewish and Gentile Christians. Furthermore, Paul did not speak in first person until later in chapter 7, so what would be his rationale for switching to an individualistic emphasis at the beginning of chapter 6 as was commonly believed?

Scholars in this group also pointed out that collective solidarity is foundational to a Semitic worldview.[12] Given Paul's Jewish heritage, these scholars suggested it is highly unlikely that he would have been talking about himself as an example of the individual believer in Romans 7. Regarding why he switched from "we" in the beginning verses to "I" in the rest of Romans 7, they observed that in Hebraic and other ancient collectivist cultures, using the individual's voice to represent the experience of the community was a common literary device. In fact, in the Hebrew way of thinking, the individual "could pass back and forth from the thought of himself to the thought of the community, and from the thought of the community to himself."[13] Marvin Wilson observes that

> Central to the Hebraic concept of community is the idea of corporate personality. This concept means that the individual was always thought of in the collective (family, tribe, nation) and the collective in the individual. This corporate solidarity was reinforced by the fact that the entire community (past ancestors and future members) was viewed as one personality, "a living whole, a single animated mass of blood, flesh, and bones."[14]

There are numerous examples of this in scripture. For instance, in describing Israel's distress at God's discipline the prophet Jeremiah says, "Woe is *me*, because of my injury. *My* wound is incurable."[15] Here, Jeremiah is speaking as a representative of the entire nation. The Servant Songs in Isaiah 42–53 also use this technique. As I point out in my commentary on the book of Romans, most scholars now agree the Songs reflect a corporate relationship between an individual and the community of which he is the head or part. In the Songs, it is extremely difficult to know exactly who is speaking, the status of the speaker, and if he is talking about himself or someone else.[16] A similar example is found Psalm 69. At first, David is confessing his own struggles, but as the psalm progresses it is challenging to discern whether he is speaking of his experience or the nation's. What David says at the end of the chapter in verses 34-36 seems to merge with a description of Israel's return to Zion. Other texts also show it was common to use the personal pronoun to denote the nation of Israel.[17]

The idea of an individual representing a community is not only found in scripture, but in other forms of literature as well. The epic story of the hero, Beowulf, is a good example. Standing in for his people, he volunteers himself to fight Grendel, Grendel's mother, and later, a dragon. Representing his allies in one part of the story and his people in another, Beowulf triumphs over evil on behalf of all. The dynamic in which one represents the many occurs in real life as well, even in the twenty-first century. For instance, when athletes from a particular country win an Olympic event the whole nation is credited with the victory. Another example is when the ruler, president, or other official of a country speaks for the entire nation and enters into treaties that are binding on all citizens of a particular country.

Based on these and other reasons, some scholars contend that in his description of the Wretched Man, Paul was either acting out the role of humankind in its bondage to sin or representing the Jewish nation as it grappled with the reality of living under the Mosaic law. In either case, this perspective moves from an individualistic to a corporate understanding. (I will present another corporate view in the following chapter.) F.F. Bruce observes that reading Romans 5–8 through a corporate lens reveals,

> This "body of sin" is more than an individual affair, it is rather that old solidarity of sin and death which all share "in Adam," but which has been broken by the death of Christ with a view to the creation of the new solidarity of righteousness and life of which believers are made part "in Christ."[18]

Cambridge theologian T.W. Manson reached a similar conclusion when he wrote his commentary on this verse. Manson states,

> It is perhaps better to regard "the body of sin" as the opposite of "the body of Christ." *It is the mass of unredeemed humanity in*

*bondage to the evil power.* Every conversion means that the body of sin loses a member and the body of Christ gains one.[19]

Because I am now convinced this view is accurate, from this point forward, whenever I am using the body of sin to refer to a corporate entity headed by Satan, I will label it as the *body of Sin*, with a capital "S." When using it in the traditional, individualistic sense, I will use the term *body of sin*, with a lower case "s."

## Individualistic Readings

Before exploring this corporate perspective of the body of Sin further, I would like to briefly review two popular individualistic interpretations of Romans 6 and 7. It is important to do this for several reasons. First, these views have had immense influence in the West, so it is to our benefit to understand the scriptural rationale behind them. This will give us greater insight into the conundrums that result from individualistic readings. Second, although both views agree that Paul is using himself as an example of the individual believer's personal struggle with indwelling evil *after* conversion, they differ when it comes to defining the *body of sin*. I believe it will be helpful to our discussion to see why they reached different conclusions. And finally, by exploring the possibility that Romans 5–8 is all set within a corporate context we will see the New Exodus themes that framed Paul's thinking begin to light up in new and exciting ways. Let's take a brief look now at these two common individualistic interpretations.

*View A: The body of sin=sin in the physical body.* This view maintains *the members of my body* and *the body of death* mentioned in Romans 7:22-23 both refer to the individual's physical body. You can see why it would be easy to reach this conclusion. Paul says, "for in my inner being I delight in God's law; but I see another law at work in *the members of my body*, waging war against *the law of my mind* and making me a prisoner of the *law of sin at work within my members.*" When read as though describing Paul's personal experience as an individual believer, at first glance, it does indeed sound like he is saying sin is lodged within his physical body, creating a battle between his body and mind.

Consequently, when read back into Romans 6:6, some have concluded the *body of sin* that Paul speaks of describes the sin that resides within and corrupts the individual's "mortal frame," to use an older term. To summarize this interpretation:

- Although the body is good because God created it, sin remains within the believer's body after conversion.

- The phrase *members of my body* is seen as referring to the individual's body parts such as a hand, arm, eye, head, etc.

- The individual's sin that dominates the body and the mind that loves God's law is locked into permanent conflict until the believer dies.

- Although we have been freed from the power of sin and it no longer controls us, since it continues to live in our bodies, we will never be fully free from sin's presence this side of heaven.

*View B: The body of sin=the complex of sinful desires that live within the regenerate individual's being, often referred to as a sinful nature.* In this view, the problem is not the physical body; rather in Romans 7, the Wretched Man's trouble is the *flesh* or as the 1984 NIV interprets it, his *sinful nature*. In verse 18, Paul says "For I know that nothing good lives in me, that is, in my *sinful nature.*" And 7:25 reads, "So then I myself in my mind am a slave to God's law, but in the *sinful nature* a slave to the law of sin." In Greek, the term the NIV translates as *sinful nature* is *sarx*, which is often rendered in English as *flesh*. While *sarx* (flesh) can mean the physical body, those who hold View B contend that in this context, it refers to a powerful complex or body of sinful desires living within a believer even after regeneration that produces death. Hence the Wretched man's cry, "who will rescue me from this *body of death*?" takes on an individualistic definition which is then read back into the *body of sin* in Romans 6:6.

Based on this line of thought, some teach that like Jekyll and Hyde, individual Christians have two natures—an evil, sinful nature, referred to as *old self* or *old man,* and a new nature, also called the *new self* or *new man* that is given to us when we accept Christ. The old self is also frequently referred to as the fleshly or carnal nature. Thus, the instruction in Romans 8:13 to "put to death the misdeeds of the body" is taken to mean that we are to kill or subjugate the fleshly, sinful nature that remains within the individual believer even after being made new in Christ. Note that in this view,

- The old self, the old man, the body of sin, and the body of death are synonyms for the sinful, fleshly, carnal nature that lives within the individual believer. The terms are often used interchangeably.

- Sin is located within the individual's inner being not the physical body.

- The permanent conflict Christians experience is inside the individual, between two natures—the believer's old fleshly, sinful nature that remains even after conversion and the new nature given by the Spirit—rather than between the body and the mind as framed in View A.

The 2011 NIV adjusted the language in 7:23 to say, "but I see another law at work *in me*" rather than "I see another law at work *in the members of my body*," which downplays the idea that the body itself is sinful. And *the body of sin* and *the body of death* in Romans 6:6 and 7:24 were changed to "the body *ruled by* sin" and "this body *that is subject to* death," which again minimizes the idea that the physical body is sinful. Even with these changes, however, the focus is still on the individual.

## Tangled Terminology

Both of these views were problematic to me for several reasons. First, scholars could not seem to agree on the definition of terms, making it difficult to determine what exactly Paul means in Romans 6 and 7. As we noted above, both individualistic interpretations agreed in seeing the *old self* and the *body of sin* as having to do with the individual believer. However, they disagreed about how Paul used *soma* (body) and *sarx* (flesh). In some contexts, *soma* (body) can be translated as *flesh* and defined as the physical body. But *soma* has other meanings as well; it can also refer to the whole person, or a collection of desires or thoughts similar to a body of work. This explains why the terms *the body of sin* and *body of death* are sometimes seen as referring to the physical body (view A) and sometimes to a complex of sinful desires living within the individual (view B).

Adding another layer of confusion, *sarx* (flesh) also has different meanings depending on the context and consequently, has been translated inconsistently. Like *soma*, it too might refer to the physical body. However, in the Old Testament setting that shaped Paul's mindset, the concept of *flesh* could also be used to describe collective humankind, the whole person, or a covenant relationship like marriage in which "the two shall become one flesh." It could also simply mean human frailty or weakness, or the corporate realm or domain of humanity.[20]

Unfortunately, what made things even more complicated is that in a well-intentioned effort to help the reader distinguish between the various meanings, the NIV translators chose to interpret *flesh* (sarx) as *sinful nature* in select instances. The problem is that not only does this block out other possible meanings of the term *flesh*, but it also creates the false impression that in and of itself the flesh is sinful, a view which is more in keeping with Greek rather than Hebraic thought.

It is critical to note here that in Jewish thinking, *flesh* (sarx) is morally neutral—it is neither innately good nor bad, which is why the Hebrews did not associate flesh with being sinful, inferior, or evil like some of the Greeks did. For example, one of the new covenant promises the Jews looked forward to is that God said he would replace Israel's heart of stone with a heart of *flesh*.[21] In this context, *flesh* conveys an awareness of our creaturely limitations and dependence on God, and so has more of a positive connotation.[22]

If you read through Romans 5–8, you can see why this all becomes so problematic. When Paul uses the terms *body* (soma) or *flesh* (sarx) in these chapters, what exactly is he talking about? The physical body, an ethereal force or complex of sinful desires that lives within and controls us, the whole person, a corporate entity like the body of Christ, a covenant relationship as in becoming one flesh, or the realm of unredeemed humankind? If we're not clear on how these words are used in each particular context, we can easily misunderstand what Paul is saying and the whole passage becomes a jumble. To give you an example, in the New King James version, Romans 8: 8-9 reads,

> So then, those who are *in the flesh* (sarx) cannot please God. However, *you are not in the flesh* but in the Spirit, if indeed the Spirit of God dwells in you.

Compare this to the 1984 NIV that says,

> Those *controlled by the sinful nature* (sarx) cannot please God. You, however, are controlled not *by the sinful nature* but by the Spirit."

Can you see the confusion? What does it mean to be "in the flesh?" In the New King James rendering, surely it cannot be the physical body. The verse says, "You are not in the flesh" but obviously, we are still very much "in our bodies" so that doesn't fit. Also, it sounds like flesh is a condition or place of some kind that we lived in formerly—we *were* "in the flesh" at one point, but *now* we are "in the Spirit." This seems to reflect the idea that *flesh* refers to a realm or a domain.

However, by translating *flesh* (sarx) as *sinful nature*, the 1984 NIV conveyed the idea that the flesh is some kind of malevolent force that lives inside the individual believer and vies with the Spirit to control us. In an attempt to clarify, the language was partially revised in the 2011 NIV. Although *flesh* is still translated as *sinful nature* in Paul's description of the Wretched Man in Romans 7:18 and 25, in the new edition of the NIV, Romans 7:5 and 8:8-9 now read, "those who are in *the realm of the flesh* cannot please God." In my opinion, although the NIV translators made a welcome effort to adjust the language, they did not go far enough in clearing up the confusion and in fact, intensified it in some ways. Translating *flesh* as *sinful nature* in the passage about the Wretched Man and as *a realm* in other verses that precede and follow it makes it even more challenging to determine what exactly it means to be "in the flesh."[23]

## Paradox or Contradiction?

Not only was the terminology confusing, but for me, one of the most obvious problems with the individualistic readings is that in Romans 6, Christians are described as being set free from sin in some real and fundamental way. Yet, in Romans 7 Paul portrays the Wretched Man as someone who is both unspiritual (carnal, fleshly) and enslaved to sin.[24]

This raises even more difficult questions. If the Wretched Man is a description of a believer, as Augustine thought was the case, how can we be freed from sin and still be a prisoner at the same time? Also, if Paul were indeed talking about his present experience as an individual regenerate, Spirit-filled believer in union with Christ, would he actually describe himself as being carnal or unspiritual? This seems contrary to other passages in which he specifically says he preaches in the Spirit's power and that "we [those preaching] speak, not in words taught us by human wisdom but in words taught by the Spirit, expressing spiritual truths in spiritual words."[25]

In commenting on this apparent dilemma, some teachers agreed it was difficult to understand how both could be true. Many tried to get around the problem by saying it is a paradox that must be accepted. Others pointed out, however, that to say Christians are free from sin and captive to it at the same time is not a paradox—it is a straightforward contradiction.[26] In attempting to deal with this conundrum, commentators who held to an individualistic interpretation often came up with a number of convoluted explanations that, in my mind, were difficult to reconcile with other scriptures.

I won't go into much detail as you can search the web to see some of the various interpretations for yourself.[27] But to give you a taste, here are a few of the common teachings that are based on an inconsistent reading of Romans 6 and 7. In explaining how we can be free from sin and captive to it at the same time, some maintain that:

- "Even though a man is saved by divine grace, he is not wholly cleansed from the corruption of his heart . . . you may rest assured that the heart is never other than it originally was; the evil nature is still evil . . . sin is within us, and therefore it has great power over us."[28]

- "While an entirely new nature is imparted at regeneration, the old one is not removed, nor is it even improved or refined. The old nature, the "flesh," indwelling sin, remains in the Christian to the end of his earthly life, and is a constant source of grief to him."[29]

- Like Jekyll and Hyde, we have two selves that are at war with one another.[30]

- We have only one nature, but sin remains in our flesh. "More than just forcing its way from the outside powerfully on our flesh, it [sin] forces its way on our flesh, as it were, from within us—from within the very flesh. It is very close; in fact, it is our being . . . it is a part of what you are." [31]

- "Our problem is not just that we sin every now and then; our problem is that we are soaked in sin, are born into it, and are never completely free from its presence this side of glory."[32]

- We have new hearts, but "evil continues to dwell within. We engage in a lifelong struggle to identify where evil lurks in our hearts and to tear it out by the roots. Even while we seek after godliness, there is a part of us that yearns to return to our former master and to cast off all traces of God's presence in our lives."[33]

- Even on our best of days, we are divided, doing what we don't want to do and failing to do what we know is right (Rom. 7:18-19). Because of the fall, "we are hardwired toward evil . . . We are, as Luther reminded us, *simul justus et peccator*, 'at the same time justified and sinner.' Likewise, the church is at the same time the bride of Christ and the Lord's harlot."[34]

- The individual soul is a dwelling place with an upper and a lower room. The lower room where our natural self thrives is filled only with evil passions, while the upper room is the new self that Christ gives to all who ask.[35]

Several additional texts are sometimes quoted to support this conflicted picture of the regenerate believer. One is Jeremiah 17:9, "the heart is deceitful above all things, and desperately sick; who can understand it?" Even though the new covenant promise is that God's people will have a new heart and other passages speak of the heart in either neutral or positive terms, this Old Testament verse is often quoted to prove Christians still have wicked hearts.[36] Another is Galatians 5:16-18. This text, which says the flesh is opposed to the Spirit, is also seen as speaking about the individual and frequently interpreted as describing a war *within* the believer. In this reading, the flesh is defined as our internal, ego-driven, "old-man centered desires" that is in permanent enmity with God's Spirit who also dwells within the individual Christian.[37] Paul's statements that he was the worst of sinners and that he buffets his body to make it his slave, and the apostle John's contention that "if we claim to be without sin, we deceive ourselves and the truth is not in us" are also cited to prove that Christians have a sinful nature.[38]

One of the major arguments used to support this view of the divided believer is personal experience. As many point out, in their struggle with sin most believers can identify with the Wretched Man's cry that he delights in God's law in his inner being, but over and over again he does the very thing he doesn't want to do. Surely, it is argued, this proves the ongoing presence of sin and evil within the individual regenerate believer. Many Christians have claimed, in fact, they found great relief in this reading of Romans 7 because it offered an explanation as to why they continue to sin after being freed from sin through Christ as taught in Romans 6:6.

**THE CONFLICTED SELF**¶ These teachings were not new to me—I had heard many of them over the course of my Christian life. But the deeper I went into Romans 5–8, the more I struggled to reconcile these views with statements Paul made in other places. For instance, in stark contrast to the despairing cry of the Wretched Man, Paul boldly told the Corinthians that his conscience was clear. As the New King James translation puts it, he said, "I do not even judge myself. For I know of nothing against myself."[39] In this text, he was not saying this let him off the hook, only that he trusted God to judge him when and if he sinned. This does not sound like a man who saw himself as sinning every hour or who was continually trying to root evil out of his inner being.

Also, later in his letter to the Romans, rather than telling God's people how sinful they were, Paul said he was convinced they were "*full of goodness*, filled with all knowledge, and able also to admonish one another."[40] Furthermore in context, when Paul says he is the worst of sinners, he also mentions that he was once a "blasphemer and a persecutor and a violent man," who acted in "ignorance and unbelief."[41] Based on this, some scholars contend Paul was referring to the time he persecuted the church *before* he met Christ on the road to Damascus, not to his present condition as a believer. And in regard to Paul buffeting his body, the setting of this verse is that of a runner who is disciplining himself in order to complete a race. While this passage shows Paul exercising self-control, so he can reach the finish line, this is simply not proof of an indwelling sin nature.

What I also noticed is that, while Paul certainly does not deny the fact that Christians can and do sin, nowhere does he refer to fellow believers as "sinners." Even when he is writing to a congregation to address sin and error in their midst, he still calls them saints, meaning holy ones. In fact, in each of his letters Paul goes to great lengths to show the marvelous reality of the church's new identity in Christ. According to Paul, having shared in his death and resurrection, the body of Christ is now cleansed, made holy, and set apart to serve God. He emphasizes our freedom in Christ, our new identities as adopted sons and daughters and servants of the most high God, our place in the new creation, and all the spiritual blessings that are now ours in Christ. In light of these truths, he calls believers to walk in a manner worthy of their high calling. When he addresses the matter of sin, he says to put it away because it is no longer consistent with who we are as God's holy people.[42]

When some of the individualistic interpretations based on Romans 7 are combined with other selected texts that are also often read through an individualistic lens, a different and puzzling picture emerges. It would seem as though Paul is teaching that Christians are now strange hybrid creatures, a conflicted mixture of darkness and light who love God but are inherently double-minded and adulterous. Although scripture says the old man has been crucified with Christ and is dead, somehow the old man is still alive within us so that at one and the same time individual believers have:

- A wicked heart and a new heart.

- A sinful nature and a new nature.

- A corrupt, darkened mind and the mind of Christ.

Furthermore, it is said that believers are:

- Cleansed by the blood of the Lamb, but permanently stained by sin.

- Freed from sin, but still prisoner to it.

- No longer in the flesh, but the flesh is in us.

- Full of goodness and full of sin.

- Saints (God's friends) and sinners (God's enemies).

- Perpetually torn between two masters.

The questions continued to mount up. If we are permanently corrupt, then how can the Spirit, who is holy and cannot co-exist with darkness, also live within us?[43] Is there some kind of dividing wall that separates our sinful self and our new Christ-like self that both live within us? How can we follow the exhortation to be holy like God if we have evil, deceitful hearts that will never change in this lifetime?[44] Furthermore, scripture says a double-minded man should expect to receive nothing from God, but if we are by nature perpetually torn between two masters, then aren't we inherently and inescapably double-minded?[45]

This conflicted picture of the individual leads to fundamental identity questions. Who are we? Saints, sinners, or saints who sometimes sin? Or like Jekyll and Hyde, do we have split personalities that are constantly at war with one another? Since, in circular fashion, our beliefs affect our actions and vice-versa, this one issue alone has enormous implications for how we live out the Christian life.

As I continued to look at the texts and commentaries, I could not escape the conclusion that something about this picture did not add up. I would never deny that Christians struggle with sin—I will speak to this more later—but at the same time, to say that we are still prisoners to it, that Christians have a permanent sin nature, or that Christ's own body is inherently corrupt and divided within itself seemed at odds with other clear statements about what Christ accomplished on the cross.

## Does Paul Go Greek?

When I began to pin down my unease, what troubled me was not only the contradictions—or the paradoxes depending on which position you take—but the inescapable dualism that springs from the individualistic readings. While technically maintaining the body is good, View A, which sees sin as permanently residing in the physical frame, is dangerously close to portraying the body as being sinful, a perspective that scripture does not support and which the church has emphatically denied. And View B, which holds that we have two natures, makes it sound like we have split personalities, an evil self and a good self that are at war with one another. Both of these types of dualism run contrary to Hebraic thought which sees the human person as a unified whole.

Furthermore, View B's individualistic interpretation of putting to death the misdeeds of the body that Paul talks about in Romans 8 can easily promote the idea that the primary goal of the Christian life is for the individual to experience victory over sin so that he or she can achieve personal moral perfection. (As we will see later, Romans 8 is set within a corporate context.) Indeed, this is how some define sanctification—to be holy or perfect like God means striving to overcome all personal sin that remains within the individual believer. Of course, many teachers who hold View B rush on to say that we can never be perfect in our lifetime because, by nature, we are sinners. What a discouraging no-win scenario!

As a pastor, I saw the practical and devastating implications this individualistic view had on those who wanted to please God. For one thing, it caused many sincere believers to feel like there was something shameful about their bodies or sinful about normal human needs and desires for food, rest, sex, etc. Also, to say that we should root out or kill our sin, but at the same time teach we have an innate sin nature that "can never be removed or improved," puts Christians in an impossible bind. In fact, one pastor says he visited a woman in a psychiatric ward who had a nervous breakdown because she had diligently tried to consider herself dead to sin as scripture instructs but felt like she continually failed.[46] I can only say that in many ways, the individualistic readings actually set believers up for failure. How can we ever put away sin if an old, evil self remains within us that is inherently sinful?[47] The best we can hope to do is control the old self, but we can never completely "put it off" as in this view it is an integral, permanent part of us.

If the individualistic readings of Romans 6 and 7 are correct, then I could certainly understand why some believe Paul introduced Hellenistic concepts into Christian thought! In both views, Paul appears to be presenting a dualistic view of the human person in which the mind and body are separate and pitted against one another, a perspective more in keeping with Greek philosophy, particularly Plato, than with a Hebraic mindset.

While Plato did not think the body was evil as some other Greeks did, he believed it was inferior because it was part of the unstable, untrustworthy material world. In his conflicted framework, the body was beautiful, but it also served as a "prison house" for the divine and, therefore, superior soul; it was something to be escaped. And, as noted earlier, he also believed the soul was divided into parts that were often at odds with one another.

In contrast, the Hebrews had a positive view of physical creation, the body included. The Old Testament taught that because God created the material world, it was good. Furthermore, the Jews held a holistic, unified concept of the human person. In the Hebrew mindset, "a human being was a dynamic body-soul unity, called to serve God his Creator passionately, with his whole being, within the physical world."[48] Far from seeing the body as an obstacle to the soul, in the biblical view of salvation, God sent his Son to take on bodily form and live among us here on the earth. When Christ returns, like him, our bodies will be resurrected and transformed.

So here is the question: would Paul, who describes himself as a Hebrew of Hebrews and sees himself as being in line with the Old Testament prophets, Jesus, and the twelve apostles, do a complete about face and introduce a dualistic Greek view of the human person into his theology? As a Hebrew, would he really portray the individual's body and the spirit as being at war with one another? Or present a view in which the soul or inner being of a person is divided into two parts that are in permanent conflict, as some believe he does in Romans 7 and Galatians 5?

Many of the commentators I read who defended either of the individualistic interpretations were well aware their views bordered on Platonic dualism and tried to explain their way around it. In my opinion, however, none of the explanations were satisfying and in fact, created even more interpretive difficulties.

## The Old Self, New Self

One more matter underscored the problem with reading Romans 6 and 7 through an individualistic lens—the definition of the *old self* mentioned in 6:6. I want to look at this matter closely because this is when I clearly saw the problem of shifting between a corporate and individualistic reading. I noticed that while the NIV and other translations mentioned the *old self,* a number of others used the phrase the *old man.* Whether rendered *old self* or *old man,* as we saw earlier, in the individualistic readings this term is seen as having to do with sin residing *within* the individual believer in one way or another.

In cross-referencing other passages that talked about the *old self* or *old man* however, I made several interesting discoveries. First, the Greek word for *man* is *anthropos.* Although it is often translated in masculine terms, actually, it is a gender-neutral word that means *human* or *person.* If you look at how Paul uses *anthropos* in Romans 5, he is contrasting unredeemed humanity in Adam with redeemed humanity in Christ. In this context, man (*anthropos*) is not just referring to two individuals—Adam and Christ—but it is also describing *collective solidarities.* Most scholars agree that Paul is talking about two communities that have two respective heads—Adam or Christ. When read from the perspective of Romans 5, a common assumption is that the term *old man/self* in 6:6 refers to the old, ungodly life the Roman believers lived *before* their conversion when they were "in Adam."

But here is where the shift comes in. Rather than starting from Romans 5 and continuing to read Romans 6 within a corporate framework, as we have seen, Romans 6:6 and Paul's description of the Wretched Man in Romans 7 have often been interpreted through an individualistic lens. Believing the *body of death* and *the body of sin* both refer to sin that continues to permanently reside within the individual believer's body or being, some translators opted to render *anthropos* as *self*.

You can see the problem straightaway—this translation makes it sound like the *old self* (old man) refers to the individual rather than unredeemed humanity in Adam that Paul had just spoken of in Romans 5. Such an interpretation raises red flags for a couple of reasons. First, as mentioned previously, there is absolutely no textual justification for shifting from a corporate to an individualistic reading when moving from chapter 5 to chapter 6. And second, translating *anthropos* as *old self* closes the door to other linguistically legitimate shades of meaning.

As I continued exploring this matter, what jumped out at me is that in other texts where *old anthropos* (man, self) is used in direct contrast to *new anthropos* (man, self) these terms referred to a *community*, not the individual self. For instance, in Colossians 3:9-12 (NIV), Paul writes,

> Do not lie to each other, since you have taken off your *old self* (anthropos) with its practices and have put on the *new self* (anthropos), which is being renewed in knowledge in the image of its Creator. Here there is no Greek or Jew, circumcised or uncircumcised, barbarian, Scythian, slave or free, but Christ is all, and is in all. Therefore, as God's chosen people, holy and dearly loved, clothe yourselves with compassion.

Clearly, in this context, the new *anthropos* refers to a community or realm, not the individual. Paul is talking to all of the saints in Colossae together and saying, "Here in this *new anthropos* (humanity), here in this Spirit-breathed community of holy people, there is neither Greek nor Jew, slave or freeman, etc." He is contrasting the community's old identity and ways of relating to others in their former life with their new identity and ways of relating with one another now that they are in Christ.

There is no question the *new anthropos* has a corporate meaning in Ephesians 2:14-16. Interestingly, in this text the 1984 NIV uses the term *man* instead of *self*. Speaking of the relationship between the Jews and Gentiles, Paul says,

> For he [Christ] himself is our peace, who has made the two one and has destroyed the barrier, the dividing wall of hostility by abolishing in the flesh the law with its commandments and regulation. His purpose was to create in himself *one new man* (anthropos) out of the two, thus making peace, and in this *one body* to reconcile both of them to God through the cross.

In this passage, the *new man* refers to a corporate entity consisting of Jews and Gentiles who are now united into one body, with Christ as its head. Clearly, the *new man* is not referring to a spiritual nature that lives within an individual—it is describing the church, the collective body of Christ.[49]

It is quite fascinating then to see that just a couple of chapters later, the NIV, and other translations as well, choose to use the terminology of *old self, new self*, which again creates the impression that Paul is talking about the individual.[50] In 4:22-24, he tells the Ephesians,

> You were taught with regard to your *former way of life*, to put off your *old self* which is being corrupted by its deceitful desires; to be made new in the attitude of your minds; and to put on the *new self* created to be like God in true righteousness and holiness.

Reading these verses in context of the entire chapter, however, shows this passage has a corporate setting. For one thing, *your* is plural; Paul is speaking to the community of saints rather than the individual. Teaching that believers are all members of one body and one spirit, Paul gives instructions about how Christians are to relate to one another now that they are part of this new humanity, this new man. In this context, Paul straightforwardly defines the *old self* (anthropos)—it refers to the *old way of life* the Ephesians practiced *before* becoming members of the new man, the body of Christ that he describes in Ephesians 2. He is contrasting life in the old humanity with life in the new humanity. While putting off this old life may involve a personal battle to learn new ways, what Paul is describing here is simply not about the individual's internal struggle between two opposing natures.

If the corporate reading is correct, and the terms *old man* and *new man* refer to two bodies of people—unredeemed humanity in Adam versus redeemed humanity in Christ—then it is reasonable to conclude this is also the context that frames Paul's use of the term *old anthropos* (man, self) in 6:6. He is simply continuing the corporate argument he began in chapter 5. This, in turn, suggests the *body of sin* also has a corporate meaning, which has implications for interpreting the *body of death* in Romans 7 as well.

Which all leads to the next question that came up in my mind: could the old man, the body of Sin be a parallel to the new man, the body of Christ? As I mentioned earlier, this was the conclusion other scholars had come to, and in my own study I was seeing the validity of this position. It is consistent with a technique used in Hebrew prose known as parallelism where an idea is repeated using a different but corresponding word. By knowing the meaning of one, you can get the meaning of the other that shadows, or is a parallel, to it. Since we know what the *old* and *new man* are from Ephesians and Colossians, we can see what the body of Sin is in Romans 6:6 because the old man is a parallel concept.

This, however, sparked more questions. If Romans 5 and 6:6 are both describing corporate realities, then what about the verses sandwiched in between that talk about our baptism into Christ's death? Traditionally, this has been seen as referring to the individual's baptism into Christ and often linked with water baptism, even though water is not mentioned. But could this text have a corporate meaning as well?

## Glimpses of the Corporate Picture

This is when I began to see the possibility of New Exodus themes bubbling up in Paul's letter to the Romans. Collectively, the Jews "died" to the reign of Pharaoh through their deliverance on the night of Passover. Their captivity to Egypt's tyrannical ruler ended when Moses finally led them across the Red Sea to freedom and he became the recognized head of the nation. Paul refers to this as their "baptism into Moses."[51] All Jews look back to that event as the defining moment of their identity as a people.

Was there any dependence on this model when Paul spoke of Christians dying to sin through Christ, our Passover?[52] Was Paul teaching that as a result of sharing in Christ's death, God's people were freed from Satan and the corporate body of Sin, the old man (unredeemed humanity) all at the same time, just as the Israelites were freed from Pharaoh and Egypt in one event? Is this when the new covenant church, the body of Christ, was formed and baptized into Christ as its head just like Israel was baptized into Moses? And if this corporate, New Exodus storyline was indeed the backdrop of Romans, did it have any bearing on the identity of the mysterious Wretched Man? These questions could only be answered by going deeper into Romans 7, one of the most challenging and controversial passages in the New Testament. This is where we need to go next.

## The Storyline in Brief

In preparation for this part of our discussion, it will be helpful to briefly sum up Romans 1-6, so we can see the flow of Paul's corporate arguments and set the context for Romans 7. In the first three chapters, Paul shows why all of humankind needs a savior. Both Gentiles and Jews have turned away from God, violated his commands, and have come under Sin/Satan's rule. Having sinned against the Holy One, Satan has the legal right to hold humanity captive in the kingdom of darkness, and the law is powerless to free anyone. Paul then draws on Paschal-New Exodus imagery to portray the great work of salvation God has accomplished for humanity through Christ's sacrificial death.

In chapter four, the apostle shows now that Christ has come, Jews and Gentiles alike are justified (made right with God) and accepted into the new covenant community on the same basis—by faith in the saving work God has done through the death and resurrection of his beloved Son, Jesus. In chapter five, Paul sees the justification of God's people to be the first step of their journey back into his presence in the new creation. On pilgrimage like Israel during the exodus events, they will endure hardships and sufferings before arriving and the end goal of their salvation, but God's great love will sustain them.

In 5:12, Paul reflects on this momentous redemptive event by recounting the story of how Adam, humanity's representative head, and his offspring first came to be taken captive by Sin/Satan. In keeping with the Semitic understanding of the solidarity of humankind, Paul explains that all of humanity was alienated from God because of Adam's disobedience in the garden. In contrast, Paul describes Jesus as the "last Adam" who, through his obedience, died to reverse the effects of Adam's actions and make the way for all who are willing to be reconciled to God through faith in Christ.[53] Consequently, all of humankind now resides in one of two communities—the old man, unredeemed humanity "in Adam" headed by Sin/Satan, or the new man, redeemed humanity headed by Christ. Individually, a person is a member of either one or the other but never both.

In the beginning of chapter 6, Paul shows how the freedom and solidarity the new covenant community now enjoys with Christ came about. This occurred when the Spirit baptized all believers of every generation—past, present, and those who will come to him in the future—into union with Jesus as he was dying on the cross. Through this one-time historic event, the Spirit formed one unified corporate body with Christ as its representative head. Sharing in Christ's death and resurrection, together, the members of this new body died to the law that bound them to Satan, thereby ending the bondage to Sin and Death that began in the garden.

As we'll see later, this understanding is dictated by the type Paul gives in 1 Corinthians 10:1-6, where he describes how the entire Jewish nation, including all individuals in all generations, was united with Moses, their representative head, in the First Exodus event. This is when Israel was collectively freed from slavery, so they could enter into a covenant relationship with Yahweh.

Delivered from Sin and Death (Satan) and made alive to God, Paul then urges the local Roman church to live collectively as God's servant, just as Israel was urged to do after her redemption from Egypt. In light of this holy calling, Paul charges the new covenant community not to allow sin/Sin to reign in its body. This is not a reference to the physical body of the individual believer or to an ethereal sin nature, but to the entire church in Rome. In this corporate context, when Paul uses the word *members*, he is not calling for individuals to control their body parts as the individualistic readings often frame it. Rather, he is making a broader appeal for the collective body of Christ, of which individuals are members, to maintain its purity and freedom, explaining that the only reward for serving Sin (Satan) is death when Christ came to give them the free gift of eternal life.

This sets the stage for Romans 7 in which Paul shows in more detail why is was necessary for believers to die together with Christ. Referring to the collective new covenant community in its previous state as the Wretched Man, he describes their tormented existence when members were formerly imprisoned in the body of Death under Sin/Satan's rule. Filled with rejoicing, in chapter 8 Paul contrasts this with the life and liberty the Spirit-filled community now enjoys in Christ.

As we move forward with our discussion, I want to add one more note about terminology. In addition to capitalizing the *body of Sin* in certain instances, I am also doing so with the word *Sin*. The reason is to distinguish between the two types of sin that run through the New Testament. I am using Sin with an upper case "S" to describe the malevolent power that humanity became subjected to when Adam deliberately disobeyed God. In scripture, this power is also personified as a being known as Satan, the serpent, or the devil, so sometimes I will use Sin/Satan as an alternative term.[54] When discussing the sinful acts that we commit, whether as individuals or a group, I will use sin with a lower case "s." And when speaking of both types of sin together, I will refer to sin/Sin. As we will see throughout our discussion, Paul was consistent in distinguishing between these two aspects of sin. I am simply using this language as a discussion aid, as not being clear about difference has created a great deal confusion on a theological and practical level. Let's go on to Romans 7 now.

# CHAPTER 5

# A Deadly Marriage

Everything looked perfect on the outside—Martin, a successful, charming, handsome man was married to the beautiful Laura. They had a stunning house by the ocean, lovely candlelit dinners at night, and were the envy of all their friends. But in the movie, *Sleeping with the Enemy*, all was not as it seemed. Behind closed doors, Martin was cruel and abusive. He controlled every aspect of Laura's life and if she did not live up to his meticulous standards, Martin became physically violent. Desperate to be free from her oppressive husband but fearing for her life if she openly tried to get away, Laura devised a clever plan. Although she was afraid of deep water, secretly, she took swimming lessons, went out on a boat, and deliberately staged a fall overboard. Leading everyone to believe she had drowned, Laura swam to shore, where she took a bus to a distant city and established a new life far away from her husband.

Of course, there's more to the story. Putting things together, Martin tracked her down and there was quite a scene. So as not to give away too much, I'll only say that the marriage was over for good. But I am bringing up the introductory plot because the basic idea of Laura "dying'" to her old marriage in order to start a new life is a clear picture of the reality Paul is describing in the opening verses of Romans 7.

Paul uses the analogy of marriage to show how a woman is legally bound to her husband as long as he lives; if she tries to remarry while he is alive, she becomes an adulteress. But if her husband dies, the woman is released from the law of marriage and free to remarry. Paul, however, is not using this analogy to describe the circumstances of the individual believer. Rather, he is showing how, together and at the same time, the entire new covenant community died to the law that bound her to another so that she could become Christ's bride!

Since verses 1-6 play such a critical role in understanding the rest of the chapter, let's look at this text more closely. Quoting from the 1984 NIV, it says:

> Do you not know brothers—for I am speaking to men who know
> the law—that the law has authority over a man only as long as he

lives? For example, by law a married woman is bound to her husband as long as he is alive, but if her husband dies, she is released from the law of marriage. So then, if she marries another man while her husband is still alive, she is called an adulteress. But if her husband dies, she is released from the law and is not an adulteress, even though she marries another man.

So, my brothers, you also died to the law through the body of Christ that you might belong to another, to him who was raised from the dead, in order that we might bear fruit to God. For when we were controlled by the sinful nature [2011 NIV: *For when we were in the realm of the flesh*], the sinful passions aroused the by the law were at work in our bodies, so that we bore fruit for death. But now, by dying to what once bound us, we have been released from the law so that we serve in the new way of the Spirit and not in the old way of the written code.

What is this law that believers died to through the body of Christ, to whom or what did it bind us, and why did we need to be released from it in order to rightfully belong to Jesus? What does this marital imagery have to do with the passage that follows about the mysterious Wretched Man who loves God's law but at the same time is a prisoner to the law of sin? And how does this all shed light on the meaning of *the body of Sin* in Romans 6:6? These are the questions we want to explore next.

**HUMANITY'S HUSBAND¶** To unravel these mysteries, we need to carefully consider the overall context of Romans 7, patiently taking the time to sort through a number of foundational concepts that undergird this passage as we go along. Starting with 7:1-6, there are several reasons why I believe it can be said with confidence that Paul is continuing to write from a corporate perspective. For one thing, he is still using the plural "we" at this point and for another, it makes good sense to view these verses as the conclusion to chapter 6, which also has a corporate setting.

In chapter 7, Paul is beginning to review how Sin/Satan's authority over the body of Christ came to an end. Scholars have puzzled over why he uses the illustration of marriage in the opening verses. One thought is that Paul was moving into a discussion about the church's relationship to the Mosaic law and wanted to use it to demonstrate principles that were true of all law. For others, the marriage illustration seems random, as it is not immediately apparent how it relates to Paul's arguments in the previous chapter or to the description of the Wretched Man that follows, which seems to be about the relationship between sin and the law. In reading it through a corporate lens, however, the problem became clear—the context of this illustration had not been fully appreciated. If Paul was indeed using the corporate, covenantal New Exodus model as a framework for explaining salvation, then the illustration of marriage makes perfect sense.

All throughout scripture, marriage is one of the main analogies used to describe God's relationship with his people. We will look at the biblical support for this in a moment, but scripture indicates that going back to the garden Adam, humankind's representative head, was in a covenant relationship with Yahweh before he betrayed God and turned to Satan. Moving forward to the First Exodus, Yahweh redeemed Israel from bondage to Pharaoh and Egypt's gods, so she could become his bride at Mt. Sinai. Israel, however, violated the covenant love that Yahweh lavished upon her by turning to other gods as lovers.[1] Repeatedly warned by the prophets about the consequences of playing the harlot, an unrepentant Israel was eventually sent into exile.[2] Looking ahead to a Second Exodus, Yahweh promised to redeem Israel from captivity in Babylon, bring her back to the Promised Land, and restore the marital relationship by entering into a new covenant with her.[3]

Paul uses this same imagery of bride-purchase to describe Christ's work as the redeemer who came to rescue his bride from captivity to Sin/Satan in the New Exodus. Other New Testament writers describe the church's relationship to God in terms of marriage as well.[4] And in the final pages of the New Testament, Christ returns for his bride, an event that is celebrated with the wedding supper of the Lamb.[5]

This is another reason why I believe Romans 7:1-6 has a corporate context. In scripture, the individual is *never* spoken of as being the bride of Christ; it is *always* a reference to the church.[6] If we take Paul's illustration out of its corporate setting and try to apply it to the individual, we are certain to end up with very confused and totally unsatisfying interpretations. What Paul wants to show in 7:1-6 is that having died with Christ to the law of sin and death that bound us to a covenant relationship with Sin/Satan, the believing community has entered into a new existence. Because Sin/Satan, the old husband in Paul's illustration, no longer has legal authority over God's people, Christ could take the newly formed church as his bride without being charged with adultery. Furthermore, now that the body of Christ has been forgiven, reconciled to God, and lives under grace, Satan can no longer use God's law against believers in any way.

## Breaking the Covenant

This brings us to a side of the fall that is not generally recognized, but is key to understanding New Testament thought, particularly in Romans 5–8. As mentioned previously, in the West, our view of salvation is often set within a forensic or legal framework. Set against the backdrop of the Roman criminal court, God's role as Lawgiver and Judge is emphasized and sin is seen as breaking God's law, a crime that requires punishment.

As the basic story goes in this model, having been deceived by Satan's lies, Adam and Eve disobeyed God's command not to eat from the tree of the knowledge of good and evil. Since God said that disobedience would lead to death, Adam and his offspring were condemned and cast out of the garden as punishment. In rebellion against God, humankind continued to sin against him. However, as an act of love and mercy, God sent his son Jesus to pay the penalty for our crimes and satisfy the Father's wrath towards sin by taking the punishment we deserved. This enabled us to be legally pardoned, forgiven, and declared righteous, making the way for our individual relationship with God to be restored.

While there are some elements of truth in this model, what it misses is the corporate, covenantal, and more relational understanding of humanity's marriage relationship with God that framed the biblical picture from the very beginning. It is commonly understood that Yahweh became like a husband to Israel when the old covenant was inaugurated at Mt. Sinai. And it's clear that the church's betrothal to Christ took place when the new covenant was established through his death and resurrection. There is reason to believe, however, that God regarded himself as *humanity's* husband going all the way back to the garden. In the writings of the prophet Hosea, Yahweh comments on Israel's unfaithfulness to him, saying, *"Like Adam, they have broken the covenant*—they were unfaithful to me there . . . I have seen a horrible thing in the house of Israel. There Ephraim [one of the tribes of Israel] is given to prostitution and Israel is defiled."[7] In other words, Yahweh saw Adam as having done the same thing he now sees Israel doing— violating their covenant with him and committing adultery with other gods.

What this text shows is that from God's point of view, he and Adam were in a covenant relationship comparable to the one he would later have with Israel. In other words, Yahweh was not only Adam and Eve's loving Creator, but he also functioned as a husband who cared for them and, as such, had the right to expect their love and fidelity. Seen from this angle, when Adam and Eve believed the serpent's lies in the garden and followed him instead of Yahweh, they willingly chose to put themselves under Satan's control and protection. Essentially, they betrayed Yahweh and took another as their god-husband. As a result, Adam's covenant relationship with God was broken and Satan assumed Yahweh's role, only rather than offering greater status and fulfillment as promised, the evil one proved to be an abusive spouse.

Unfortunately, as Paul sees it, there was no way for Adam to back out of the relationship. Although Sin/Satan tricked Adam and Eve into entering into this unholy alliance, nonetheless, the evil one had a legal right to hold them to it because the law of marriage Paul described in 7:1-4 made it binding.[8] Since in God's eyes a marriage covenant is permanent and can only end through the death of one of the parties,

God's own law had to affirm Satan's right to claim authority over Adam and his offspring since they willingly submitted themselves to him. Legally and relationally bound to Satan, humanity came under the law of its new husband, which Paul calls the law of sin and death. Separated from God, the source of life and light, and now under Sin's authority, Adam and his offspring became captives in Satan's dark kingdom.

Thus, the fall was not simply a matter of disobeying an impersonal command or rule; relationally, it was an act of spiritual adultery for which Adam was judged. Because he took another as his god, he was expelled from the garden and God's presence in the same way that Israel was to later suffer expulsion from the Promised Land and Yahweh's presence because she pursued other gods.

## Supporting Evidence

The idea that God functioned as a husband to Adam and Eve, and humanity came into a binding covenant relationship with Sin/Satan as a result of Adam's infidelity may seem novel to many Westerners. However, several important strands of evidence support this view. First, while it is not specifically spelled out in Genesis that Adam and Eve were in a covenant relationship with Yahweh as husband, in scripture it is not unusual to learn more about significant concepts and events after the fact.

For instance, the understanding that Israel was seen as becoming Yahweh's wife at Mt. Sinai was introduced long after he and Israel entered into their covenant agreement. In fact, the prophet Hosea, who lived many centuries later, was the first biblical writer to explicitly frame the First Exodus as a marriage with Yahweh wooing Israel. As a number of texts clearly show, the covenant-making event Hosea describes reads like a wedding ceremony.[9] Few would disagree that based on the writings of Hosea and the prophets who came after him, the divine marriage became a central and widely accepted theme in scripture. If Hosea is the one who provided this key to understanding the exodus event hundreds of years after the fact, then he can also give us the key to unlocking the covenantal framework of Yahweh as humanity's husband in Eden.

Furthermore, the concept of entering into a covenant with other gods is explicitly stated in the Old Testament. This is seen in Yahweh's instructions to Israel when he was preparing to bring her into the

Promised Land. Warning the Jews about the dangers of intermingling with the various people groups they would encounter along the way, Yahweh told Israel "*do not make a covenant with them or their gods. Do not let them live in your land, or they will cause you to sin against me, because the worship of their gods will certainly be a snare to you.*"[10] While the doctrine of the divine marriage was not overtly stated until Hosea provided insight into this theme, the Lord's statement indicates that even in Israel's earliest tradition, it was understood that worshipping other gods meant the people were rejecting Yahweh and replacing him with another. The end result is that God's people became the possession of whatever god seduced the nation into covenant disloyalty.

Unfortunately, Israel did not follow Yahweh's instructions and repeatedly pursued other gods.[11] Expressing righteous jealousy, Yahweh condemned her for acting like a whore, "like a woman unfaithful to her husband," when she worshipped the deities of the surrounding nations.[12] Interestingly, in scripture, the only legitimate form of jealousy has to do with the unfaithfulness of a spouse.[13] This illuminates the significance of Yahweh's claims that he is jealous when it comes to Israel.

Also supporting this view, we have seen that Sin is often personified as Satan, who, in the New Testament, is depicted as the god of this world. In Genesis, it was the serpent—a communicative *being* also described as Satan, the evil one, the dragon, the father of lies, and the devil—who seduced Adam and Eve, enticing them to betray Yahweh and follow him.[14]

In referring to this event, Paul says Sin, not *sins* entered the garden.[15] It's not splitting hairs to make this distinction. When Paul speaks of Sin in Romans chapters 5-6, although he refers to personal transgressions at times, the main emphasis is on Satan, the one who instigated all wrongdoing. Paul portrays Sin as a ruler or master to whom all the members of Christ's body were once enslaved and shows God and Sin as being in opposition to one another. In reminding members of the new covenant community they are to use their freedom to serve God and not Sin, Paul goes on to say, "*For Sin shall not be your master, because you are not under law but under grace.*"[16] At the end of chapter 6 Paul describes Sin as paying a wage—death—and in Romans 7:8, he depicts Sin as an entity that entices or seduces. Noting that Paul uses sin and Satan synonymously in some cases, N.T. Wright observes that in the apostle's writings, "'sin' refers not just to individual human acts of 'sin' . . . 'Sin' takes on a malevolent life of its own, exercising power over persons and communities."[17]

Echoing Romans 6, in other New Testament texts, it is Satan who is depicted as a master or ruler and the one who tempts. Described as the god of this age who controls the world, Satan is referred to as a "the prince of the power of the air, of the spirit that is now working in the sons of disobedience."[18] Through lies and deceit, he has blinded the minds of the unbelieving so "they cannot see the light of the gospel of the glory of Christ."[19] As the writer of Hebrews reveals, the evil one enslaves humanity through the power of death.[20] Since God said the consequence of sin is death and all have sinned, Satan has the legal right to hold men and women captive in the kingdom of darkness. Though Christ disarmed him on the cross and conquered death in order to free his people, Satan still holds this power over those who are not in Christ.[21]

In an example that shows why this is true, even if a man fights another and wins, that does not give him the legal right to take his wife. In the same way, even though Christ fought Satan and won, that did not give him the right to take the evil one's "bride" (unredeemed humanity) who is legally bound to him. Rather, Christ's victory benefits those who want to leave the old relationship with Sin and who, by faith, died with Jesus to the law that once gave Satan authority over the members of the covenant community.

## A Covenant with Death

It is one thing to see Sin/Satan, who is also referred to as Death, as a ruler or god, but is there any New Testament support for the idea that unredeemed humanity is in a binding *covenant* relationship with him as husband? I believe there is.

Isaiah 28 was well known to the early church. Paul refers to 28:11-13 in his letter to the Corinthians and Isaiah 28:16 is quoted in the New Testament more than any other Old Testament text to speak of the covenant Yahweh would establish through his Servant. Often referred to as the "stone passage," in this text God promises to "lay a stone in Zion, a tested stone, a precious cornerstone for a sure foundation." This verse is the basis for the New Testament descriptions of Christ as the cornerstone of the church.[22]

In between and following these two texts are specific references to Israel making a "covenant with death."[23] Since New Testament writers quoted both passages from Isaiah 28 without introduction or explanation, it is reasonable to assume the early church would have been familiar with the term "covenant of death" as well. Reading verses 14 to 18, this passage, which is directed to the leaders of Israel, says,

> Therefore, hear the word of the Lord, you scoffers who rule this people in Jerusalem. You boast, "We have entered into a *covenant with death*, with the graves we have made an agreement. When an overwhelming scourge sweeps by, it cannot touch us, for we have made lies our refuge and falsehood our hiding place."
>
> So, this is what the Sovereign Lord says: "See, I lay a stone in Zion, a tested stone, a precious cornerstone for a sure foundation; the one who trusts will never be dismayed. I will make justice the measuring line and righteousness the plumb line; hail will sweep away your refuge, the lie, and water will overflow your hiding place. Your *covenant with death will be annulled*; your agreement with the grave will not stand.

In context, this covenant with death referred to the alliance the Jews made with the Egyptians because they were afraid of invasion. Instead of relying on Yahweh for protection, as they saw it, the best way to avoid this was to enter into a pact with a stronger nation who would guarantee their security. In order to forge this alliance, Israel had to accept the patronage of the Egyptians' gods, including Isis, god of death. In seeking Egypt's protection, Israel entered into a covenant with death.

The fact that one of the synonyms for Satan is Death lends support to the idea that Adam entered into a covenant relationship with Satan (Death) when he turned to him as god-husband instead of Yahweh.[24] While some may wonder if Paul's original readers would have put all this together, again, I can only say that my Romanian friends, with whom I spent some time, were steeped in the Old Testament and made these connections about the covenant with death all on their own during one of our sessions.[25] I am confident the early church did the same.

## Transposing Corporate Categories

This gives us further insight into the framework that undergirds Paul's thinking. For the apostle, there is no difficulty in transposing corporate categories that are central to Israel in the Old Testament into the universal picture of the New Testament. The First and Second Exodus are types of the New Exodus led by Christ. In the Old Testament, Israel was Yahweh's bride; in the New, the church is the bride of Christ.

Rather than being divided into Jews and Gentiles, humanity now consists of those who are in Adam and those who are in Christ. To be in Adam is to be in solidarity with unredeemed humanity, the body of Sin also referred to at times as the old man, the body of flesh or body of Death.[26] Having usurped Adam's role as head of humanity, Satan heads this community. On the other hand, to be in Christ is to be in solidarity with redeemed humanity, the body of Christ, the new man, the church. Jesus heads this Spirit-filled community.

In seeing things this way, Paul is not inventing a new and different Christian message. These corporate concepts simply redefine Old Testament categories, so they are no longer nationalistic references to Jews or Gentiles but apply to the two great divisions of humankind spoken of in the New Testament—those in the kingdom of light ruled by Christ, and those in the kingdom of darkness ruled by Sin/Satan.

Reading Paul's arguments in Romans 5–8 against this backdrop helps us see that in the apostle's view, all of humanity came under Sin's authority when Adam entered into an alliance with Satan in the garden. In the same way that Israel made a covenant of death with the gods of Egypt, Adam formed a deadly covenant relationship with Sin/Satan by looking to him as god-husband rather than Yahweh. Since he was the representative head of humankind, this alliance was also binding on his offspring in the same way that an agreement made by a head of state is binding on subsequent generations. Now, like a ruthless husband who demands loyalty by right of the marital relationship, Satan oppresses and abuses the human race that is still in Adam.

This cosmic, corporate backdrop also helps us better understand Christ's great work of salvation—he came to rescue his bride from Sin's dark rule, destroy the works of the evil one, and establish a new kingdom in which all will be restored to the Father. Again, I am not negating the need for personal repentance, but in order to comprehend the full wonder of our salvation, and also to grasp God's mission and our role in it, it is important to see our lives in context of this greater picture.

## Out with the Old, In with the New

Against this backdrop, we can hear the corporate, covenantal, New Exodus themes that frame Paul's mindset coming through in 7:1-6. Because the body of Christ died with him to the law of sin and death that once bound us to Sin/Satan, our old husband, the risen Christ could rightfully take the raised "widow" unto himself. In doing this, Christ fulfilled the role of the Old Testament redeemer who was tasked with rescuing relatives who were in trouble, danger, or need. One of the redeemer's responsibilities was to marry the childless widow of his near kinsman in order to provide care and protection. This is illustrated in the Old Testament story of Ruth, a young impoverished widow, and Boaz, the relative who married her, thereby becoming her kinsman-redeemer.[27] Although Christ is never called the redeemer in the New Testament, his work is certainly described in terms that are modeled on this Old Testament figure.[28]

This redemptive-marital imagery is also apparent in 7:4-5. Paul states that because the body of Christ now belongs to Jesus, our new husband, we are to bear "fruit to God." In contrast, he observes that when we used to live in the flesh (in Adam) under the rule of our old husband, Sin/Satan, we "bore fruit for death."

The reference to bearing "fruit for God" echoes Yahweh's command to Adam to be fruitful and replenish the earth. In Genesis, the original context of the concept of bearing fruit was marital.[29] While it has the same marital connotation in this setting, following his pattern of spiritualizing Old Testament truths, Paul's call to bear fruit for God is not about replenishing the natural order but is about the new creation. The church is called to enlarge the family of God, not through physical procreation but through the proclamation of the life-giving gospel. As the church lives under the law (covenant authority) of Christ, she fulfills the command to be fruitful and replenish the earth. This fruitfulness is the natural consequence of the outflow of love for her redeemer husband.

Paul shows why members of the new covenant community bore fruit for death in their former lives—under Satan's rule the law stirred up sinful passions within them to turn against God. Just as he did in the garden, Satan takes the divine law that is meant to bring life and protect humanity from evil and twists it to insinuate that God is withholding something good from his people. In keeping with his rebellious nature, Sin/Satan arouses the sinful desire to go against whatever God says. He then further deceives by suggesting we can get away with it when he knows full well that sin separates us from God, the source of life, and brings shame, guilt, and condemnation.

But there is another way the law can arouse sinful passions among those who live in the flesh—Satan tempts some to embrace a false form of religion. Not all can be induced to rebel overtly, so for those in Adam who want to follow God, he entices them to treat the law as a set of rules and regulations that can be kept through self-effort. While giving the appearance of true religion, this approach produces pride, self-righteousness, and self-sufficiency—all of which God opposes. Furthermore, it kills life by turning their relationship with God into an external duty dedicated to keeping the letter of the law instead of one that is based on love, freely given from the heart. Whether it is through law breaking or law keeping, the only "fruit" that can come from being in union with Sin/Satan is death because that is his very nature.

In verse 6, Paul teaches that having died with Christ to the law, the new covenant community was raised with him into a new order. As he explains, by dying to what "once bound us," the body of Christ has been "released from the law so that we serve in the new way of the Spirit, and not in the old way of the written code." Paul is not appealing to the Romans believers to die. He is saying they, with all other believers, have *already* died. His focus is on the event he has described earlier in Romans 6:1-6 and 7:1-6—their death with Christ as a result of the union created with him by the Spirit. This is the historic, spiritual reality of which Paul says the church is part. God's wedding gift is the Spirit, who will help the church live in newness of life. Here, Paul begins the argument that he will develop more fully in chapter 8.

Paul realizes, however, that before going on to talk about the community's new life in the Spirit, he first needs to address the relationship between God's law and sin/Sin, a critical subject given the young church's struggle with knowing how to relate to the Mosaic law now that Christ has come. In light of his discussion in verses 1-6, Paul anticipates the question he is sure will come up—if God's law is what bound humanity to Sin/Satan and also brings knowledge of sin/Sin, is the law itself sinful? To address this issue, he assumes the persona of the Wretched Man, whom I will argue is a corporate entity, *not* Paul as an individual, and steps back to look at the role of the law in salvation history. We are ready now to move into 7:7–8:4, the controversial passage about the Wretched Man. It would be good to read this passage in your Bible before we go on.

**TWO SIDES OF THE LAW¶** We need to take our time with this part of the conversation as things can get confusing very quickly. In addition to the problem of determining the Wretched Man's identity, another complicating factor is Paul's discussion of the law. He refers to some kind of law thirty-three times in Romans 7:1–8:4! Although it is commonly assumed Paul is mainly talking about the Mosaic law in this text because of his reference to the written code in 7:6, this is not a given as he mentions a number of other laws—the law of marriage that spans various cultures, the law believers died to in Christ, the law that "when I want to do good, evil is right there with me," "the law of my mind," and "the law of sin" the Wretched man sees at work in his members. He also talks about the law of sin and death and the law of the Spirit of life. While some of these references relate to the Mosaic law, as we'll see others have to do with laws that were at work long *before* Moses received the law at Mt. Sinai, some of which involve general principles that apply to all of humankind.

Given the various references, the question is what does Paul mean when he says in verse 6 that the body of Christ has been released from "*the* law"? Adding another layer of confusion, some also contend that two distinct and opposing laws are at work in this passage—God's law and the law of sin. This view is based on the Wretched Man's statement, "For in my inner being I delight in God's law; but I see *another law* at work in the members of my body, waging war against the *law of my mind* and making me a prisoner *to the law of sin*."[30] What exactly is this "other law" which imprisons the Wretched Man? And if it is not God's law, then how did this law come to have authority over the Wretched Man? As you can see, deciphering what Paul is teaching about the law in this text is no easy matter.

## The Law Through Jewish Eyes

In sorting through this, it will be immensely helpful to first understand the Hebraic perspective of God's law and how it differs from the Western view. We have already established that the authors of the New Testament wrote in Greek but retained their Hebrew mindset so seeing the law through Jewish eyes will provide greater insight into what Paul is saying in his discussion of the Wretched Man.

In the New Testament, the Greek word for law is *nomos*, a general, all-purpose term that refers to any law whatsoever be it a custom, precept, command, or established rule. Given our Greco-Roman background, in the West, we tend to view the law *(nomos)* as an impersonal system of rules, regulations, and edicts instituted by society for controlling actions, by force when necessary. I say *impersonal* as in theory, the law is expected to be objective rather than subjective, and it tends to be institutional in that it is enforced through a system of law courts, governments, and other authoritative entities. In most cases, there is not a personal relationship between the lawgivers and those subjected to the law.

In the Hebraic culture, however, God, not society, is the primary source of their governing law so it is seen as having divine authority. It is also highly relational and personal in that it operates within the context of God's relationship with humankind, and more specifically with his people. An expression of his very nature, God's law is rooted and grounded in love. When asked which commandment in the law is greatest, Jesus said, "Love the Lord God with all your heart, with all your soul, and with all your mind" and "Love your neighbor as yourself." He then explained that the whole law of Moses and the teachings of the prophets depend on these two commandments.[31] Seen in this light, sin is not simply a matter of breaking an impersonal rule or law—it violates our relationship with God and others. This helps explain why God hates sin. It is directly opposed to his nature and brings destruction and death rather than life. If God is love, then sin might be described as that which is "unlove."

The relational nature of God's law can be seen in the very definition of *torah,* the Hebrew word that means *instruction* or *teaching* and that is often translated as *law.* Much more than a set of rules, in the Jewish understanding, the Torah is God's teachings to his children to show them the way of life.[32] The Torah came from the Creator to his creation and then, per his instruction, it was to be passed on through the teaching of religious instructors or parents to the next generation with the aim of bringing the young to maturity. Echoing this understanding, in Galatians, Paul portrays the Mosaic law given to the Jews as "a *guardian*" that provided guidance and protection until Christ came.[33] Other translations use the term *trainer, schoolmaster* or *tutor.*

One of the metaphors for Torah is light. Its purpose is to teach humankind the heart of God and how to walk in his righteousness, his light, which is his very character. In the book of Isaiah God says, "Give attention to me, my people, and give ear to me, my nation; for a law will go out from me, and I will set my justice for a light to the peoples."[34] Viewing the law primarily as a set of rules that leads to punishment when broken, as many do in the West, leaves no room for the positive teaching aspects of Torah that give life, strengthen, build up, equip, and encourage.

Another relational function of Torah is to guard God's people from harm and preserve their covenant relationship with him. For instance, in the garden, the command God spoke to Adam and Eve was meant to protect them from experiencing evil, not to restrict them from something good. Later, Yahweh gave Israel the Mosaic law as a wedding gift that, in addition to establishing a just and holy society, was intended to teach them how to love him and honor their covenant relationship with him. Moses explained that being faithful to God would bring the community into blessings and life, while pursuing other gods or going their own way would only lead to trouble and death.[35]

## The Scope of Torah

Pinning down exactly what the term *Torah* means can be challenging, as it is a broad, comprehensive category that encompasses a number of informal principles, stories, and teachings as well as specific commandments. In the context of Judaic history, the Torah is the whole body of Jewish teachings, instructions, and practice, and "is the axis around which the whole of Judaism revolves."[36] It includes the Pentateuch, the first five books of the Old Testament God gave to Moses, as well as the writings of the psalmists and the prophets. It also includes the oral Torah, which are the spoken teachings of Moses and the elaborations of the written Torah that were passed down from generation to generation. Some of these additional teachings were recorded in a supplementary book called the Talmud.

The Torah is more than this, however. It is also embedded in the ongoing narrative of the Jewish people from Genesis to the end of the twenty-four books that comprise the Hebrew Bible. Torah incorporates the story of how Israel came into being as a nation, her covenant with

Yahweh, and the ups and downs of that relationship. In this way, the narrative itself provides instruction.

It is important for our purposes to underscore the fact that in the Jewish oral tradition, it is said that Yahweh's Torah existed before the foundation of the world, and "was to God, when he created the world, what the plan is to an architect when he erects a building."[37] In other words, the Torah is God's "blueprint" or order for his creation. It is God's wisdom that governs the way the world works through natural laws such as the law of gravity and other principles of life common to all. Examples include the law of reciprocity expressed in axioms such as "you reap what you sow," "you will be judged as you judge others," and "those who live by the sword, die by the sword," etc.[38] These natural laws and principles can be observed and known by all of humankind, even by those who have no interest in God.

This understanding of Torah is reflected in Romans 1 where Paul says, "For since the creation of the world God's invisible qualities—his eternal power and divine nature—have been clearly seen, being understood from what has been made so that men are without excuse" if they refuse to acknowledge him as God.[39] This is a description of God's Torah that was visible to all and inscribed on the consciences of all of humankind *before* the written Mosaic law was given to the Jews.

## The Two Sides of the law

Here is where different perspectives of the law enter the picture. For the most part, the Jews had a positive view of the Mosaic law, seeing it as a gift from Yahweh. However, as a nation, Israel had mixed experiences with it. At times, the Jews failed to honor its relational nature, approaching it as an external set of rules and regulations instead, which displeased God. In the book of Isaiah, the Lord speaks of Israel's waywardness and says, "These people come near to me with their mouth and honor me with their lips, but their hearts are far from me. Their worship of me is made up only of rules taught by men."[40]

Jesus quoted this exact verse when speaking to the Pharisees, the religious leaders of his day, because they had reduced the Mosaic law to a system of rules and regulations based on human traditions while neglecting the greater matters of love and justice.[41] As taught by the Pharisees, the Mosaic law made demands the people could not meet, making it a burden to some rather than a source of life.[42] Although he was always careful to honor God's written word, Jesus frequently defied the meticulous rules the religious leaders had added to it.[43] Distressed that they were misrepresenting God and had become stumbling blocks to others who were trying to enter the kingdom, Jesus indicted the Pharisees for their loveless, legalistic approach to God's written instructions.[44] He actually went so far as to refer to them as children of the devil because they opposed him and with their emphasis on law keeping instead of love, prevented others from entering God's kingdom.[45]

Coming back to Romans 7 now, what Paul has come to see is that there are two sides to God's law. On the one hand, it was intended to bless, instruct, protect, guide, and reveal divine truth, showing what was necessary in order to have a right relationship with a holy God. But Paul teaches that the law also has a downside in that it condemns all who sin. Ironically, Paul sees this ministry of death as also being glorious because it exposes the true nature of Sin, who works in the dark through cunning, lies, and deceit. It also reveals the true condition of the human heart. In the garden, Sin/Satan seduced Adam by persuading him he could be equal to God; as a result, he sinned against his Creator.

One of the benefits of Mosaic law is that it exposed the folly of this lie.[46] Israel's inability to keep the law showed the Jews, and also the rest of the world by example, that humanity was under the power of something far greater than itself, and that no amount of self-effort or law-keeping could free anyone from Sin's rule. In this way, the law humbles by revealing humankind's need for a savior, and for a God who is greater than us and more powerful than Sin/Satan. The condemning role of the law also shows the depths of God's love—no matter how much humanity sins, God's grace is greater still, which is why he sent his Son to atone for sin and rescue all those who long to be free from Sin's rule.

## From Law to Grace

Knowing this background is helpful in understanding Romans 7 for several reasons. First, it provides further insight into the issues that Paul has been addressing in his letter to the Romans. Although the Jews held the Mosaic law in high regard and saw it as being central to their national identity, they were not able to live up to it. Throughout their history, Israel had either broken their covenant with Yahweh by overtly pursuing other gods or had kept the letter of the law religiously while failing to honor its true intent. Although many of the Jews were looking for a Messiah who would free them from the oppression of the surrounding nations, as Paul pointed out, they had a much greater problem—Israel repeatedly fell short of her high calling to faithfully love and serve Yahweh; like the Gentiles, she too was in Adam, bound to Satan by the law of sin and death and in need of a savior.

Paul also wants to make another point clear in his letter to the Romans. While the Mosaic law was a gift to Israel and served God's purposes in exposing and condemning sin, members of the new covenant community are not required to keep the written rules, rites, and ordinances that governed Israel's national life in the old order as these were fulfilled in Christ.[47] This is not to say the body of Christ is lawless. In Christ, believers are called to walk by the Spirit and follow the higher law of love that not only meets the basic moral standards of the written Torah, but also far exceeds the letter of the law.[48]

Second, this background shows there are times when Paul may have a more comprehensive view of the Torah in mind that might include references to the Mosaic law but is not limited to it. I suggest this is the case in Romans 7. Circling back now to 7:1-6 and Paul's statement that believers have been released from the law, it is important to remember that in keeping with the flow of his corporate argument, Paul is not speaking of the Mosaic law alone. This can be stated with certainty because in verse 4, he is talking about the law that *all* believers have been released from in Christ. The Gentiles, however, were never under the Mosaic law; only the Jewish believers were.

Rather, in chapter 7, Paul is starting from the garden and looking at the whole scope of human history. He is describing the body of Christ's former relationship to the law when its members were in Adam and under Sin/Satan's authority to show how the old order has passed away and the new has come through Christ. This transition occurred when members of the new covenant community died together with Christ to the law of sin and death (the law of the husband) that had bound all of humanity to Sin/Satan. The written code mentioned in 7:6, which is most often seen as a reference to the Mosaic law, is part of the old order that has passed away, but it is not all that Paul has in mind.

The body of Christ's relationship to the law is a critical issue because as Paul explained in his letter to the Corinthians, the power of Sin/Satan is in the law.[49] Not only did the evil one use God's command (law) to take authority over humanity in the garden, but Satan also uses the law to arouse sinful desires that when acted on, bring condemnation and death. In the new order, however, Paul points out that having died to the law of sin and death with Christ, Sin is no longer our master (husband) because we now live under grace. Furthermore, because Jesus made atonement for sin, our past transgressions have been forgiven and when we sin in the future, the apostle John teaches that God is faithful and just to forgive us if we confess.[50] For these reasons, God's law does not condemn those who are in Christ. In other words, *since Satan can no longer use the law against us, he has no power over the body of Christ!*

The more comprehensive view of the Torah described above also shows that some of the laws Paul mentions in Romans 7 may not be formal laws such as those written down in the Mosaic law, but general principles that simply reflect the way life works. For instance, when Paul says, "the wages of sin is death" in 6:23, this is not necessarily part of a codified legal system; rather, it communicates the universal principle or "law of life" that what we "earn" when we serve Sin as master instead of God is death. Since God is the source of life and all blessings, it only makes sense that if our relationship with him is broken because we have chosen to serve Sin/Satan instead, we will experience death. Another example is the Wretched Man's reference to the "law of my mind" in 7:25. This is not a written law; rather he is describing the way his mind works—mentally, he agrees that God's law is true, but as a member of the body of Death which Satan rules, he is powerless to act on it.

Finally, this background helps us see the fine line Paul had to walk in helping the Christian community know how to relate to the God's law in the new covenant era. Since God is the source of the law, no wonder some of the Jewish believers struggled with the idea that Sin/Satan used God's good command to ensnare humanity in the garden or that Christians were not required to submit to the Mosaic law's rules and ordinances such as circumcision. Paul's concern, however, was not just to pacify the Jews or prevent the Judaizers from persuading new believers to come under the Mosaic law; he also needed to make sure that Gentile believers did not swing too far the other way and become caught up in an anti-law movement that would negate God's moral teachings. This would have left the believers in Rome exposed to the very corruption from which they had been redeemed.[51]

## Is the Law Sin?

In addressing the relationship between the law and sin/Sin in Romans 7, part of Paul's argument that follows is to reject the idea that God's law is sinful, one that would have been abhorrent to any Jew. His aim in the rest of the chapter, however, is not to write an apology for the law, nor is he digressing from his main argument about life in Adam versus life in Christ. In describing the Wretched Man's struggle, Paul's aim is to show how the law functioned when the members of the new covenant community were still under Sin/Satan's authority; he then contrasts this with the freedom the body of Christ now enjoys in her new life in the Spirit.

Applying all that he has written from Romans 5:12 to 7:1-6, Paul switches to the first person "I" in verse 7 as he continues the discussion, leading many to believe he is talking about his personal experience when he describes the Wretched Man. However, as mentioned earlier, my contention is that Paul was using a literary device to describe the experience of a larger, corporate entity. We have come to the point now where we need to stop and consider who or what the Wretched Man represents as this will shed light on what Paul is saying about the law and its role in the old order.

**THE ELUSIVE WRETCHED MAN¶** In the previous chapter, we saw
there are different opinions regarding the identity of the Wretched Man
in 7:7–8-4. Two traditional views maintain that Paul is speaking of his
personal experience either before or after conversion, while two others
contend the Wretched Man is a corporate entity, possibly Israel under
the law or humankind in Adam. The problem is that while each of these
views has points in its favor, none of them fully resolve the
conundrums associated with this text. What I want to do is briefly
review the drawbacks of each and then describe a fifth view that I
believe honors the corporate arguments Paul has been making since
chapter 5, and that also satisfies some of the difficulties with the other
theories.

## Is the Wretched Man the Individual Christian?

We have already looked at some of the problems with the
individual-istic interpretations of the Wretched Man that maintain Paul
is describing either his own pre-or-post conversion experience. Those
in the post-conversion camp point out that Paul cannot be recounting
his pre-conversion experience because an unregenerate person would
not take pleasure in God's law as the Wretched Man does. On the other
hand, those with a pre-conversion view say that if he is describing his
experience as regenerate believer, he is contradicting himself. In
chapter 6, Paul has already said that because we died with Christ, we
are free from sin. However, in chapter 7, the Wretched Man describes
himself as prisoner to the law of sin, trapped in "this body that is
subject to death" with sin living in him. And then in chapter 8, Paul says
once again that he has been freed from the law of sin and death and is
now a member of the body of Christ in which the Holy Spirit dwells.

Both of these views are very confusing and inevitably result in one
running in circles to make sense of it all! We have seen that most
attempts to resolve this conundrum have either ended up dangerously
close to suggesting Paul embraced some form of dualism, which is
contrary to his holistic Hebraic mindset. Or it is said this is a paradox
that must be accepted, which simply sidesteps the issue. But there are
other difficulties as well.

For one thing, some of what Paul says in this passage is at odds with statements he makes about his attitude towards the law in other places. Although the Wretched Man delights in God's law, he also sees it as condemning him because the sin at work in his members impels him to live in a way that is contrary to the law. In other texts, however, Paul expresses a much more positive view of the law and its demands as well as his ability to keep than the Wretched man does. In Philippians, he describes his pre-Christian legal status as faultless, and in Galatians he says that he advanced in Judaism beyond many of his contemporaries, being zealous for the traditions of his fathers.[52] Given this, it is highly unlikely that seeing the law as condemning him or lamenting about his failure to obey it, as the Wretched Man does, would reflect Paul's own experience with the law.[53] In saying this, I am not siding with those who argue the law did not trouble Paul at all, but I contend this came later as he began to understand Christ's person and work more fully.

Scholars also point out Paul makes a statement that cannot be part of his personal experience with the Mosaic law. He says, "*Once I was alive apart from the law*; but when the commandment came, sin sprang to life and I died."[54] The fact is there never was a time when Paul lived apart from the Mosaic law. Born into a devout Jewish home, he would have known something of the law from his childhood, and it would have been the greatest influence on his life as he grew to adulthood.

Some argue what Paul meant is that although he grew up under the Mosaic law he had not yet experienced a sense of conviction and personal guilt that comes when the Spirit works through it to produce repentance. The contention is that through the Spirit, the commandment not to covet came to him in a new way; his eyes were opened to see how demanding the law's requirements were and how impossible it is for anyone to live up to them. As a result, "sin came alive," and Paul "died" when he realized the depths of his sinfulness. The problem is this suggests that sin did not really exist before the Mosaic law was given to Israel or before it is personally applied by the Spirit. The implication is there is no real guilt for those who have not been exposed to the Mosaic law. I can only say that if sin doesn't exist until the law is made known or applied, then it is far better for people to be left in ignorance!

The bigger obstacle to accepting this position, however, is that it is not aligned with the rest of scripture, which says that sin/Sin is alive and real even when there is no law that specifically defines it. This reality is proven by the fact that between the time Adam first sinned and when the Mosaic law was given at Sinai, everyone still experienced death. Although others did not sin in the same way as Adam, nevertheless, humans still died because the alliance Adam made with evil one in the garden had brought them under the authority of Sin and Death.[55] This shows the existence of sin/Sin did not depend on the Mosaic law. What Paul wants to get across is that God's law itself is good. It did not bring sin/Sin into existence; it simply defines, exposes and increases the sin that is already there.[56]

The greater problem with this entire line of thinking, however, is that it is still highly individualistic. In this view, Paul is describing his personal battle with sin. But again, given that he has been speaking of corporate realities up to this point, it is unlikely he would have shifted midstream to talk about the individual believer's experience, whether pre- or post-conversion.

## Is the Wretched Man the Jewish Nation?

Another possibility is that Paul is representing the Jewish people when he speaks as the Wretched Man. Those who argue for this position say the command "you shall not covet" that gave Sin the opportunity to spring into life and "kill" the Wretched Man was not established until the ten commandments were given to the nation of Israel.[57] As the reasoning goes, sin entered the picture when God issued the Mosaic law at Mt. Sinai to ratify Israel's covenant relationship with him. What should have been the climax of the salvation event—Israel's journey to Sinai to meet with God—was disastrous. This is when Israel was to become Yahweh's bride but instead of entering the fullness of life, she came under the sentence of death because she was unfaithful to God. The Mosaic law, which was God's marital gift to her, should have sealed her relationship with Yahweh, but because she committed spiritual adultery by worshipping Egypt's gods (the golden calf), it did the very opposite—it condemned her and excluded her from her great calling. Like the Wretched Man, Israel delighted in God's law and wanted to do what was good, but continually failed.

Although it has some points in its favor, this interpretation of the Wretched Man is not appealing for two reasons. First, the claim that the command "you shall not covet" was issued when the Mosaic law was established does not hold up. It was the very essence of God's instructions to Adam not to eat from the tree of the knowledge of good and evil. In this command, God was telling Adam that as a creature, he must not covet God's infinite wisdom and knowledge. Satan's cunning argument that Adam and Eve could be wise like God is what seduced them into eating the fruit. The reality is that sin/Sin had already entered the picture long before the Mosaic law was given.

Second, the idea that the Mosaic law could sentence Israel to condemnation in this way was not part of Jewish understanding. As we have seen, most Jews generally had a positive view of the law, seeing it as a source of privilege and life, not condemnation and death. Although the Mosaic law had become a burden to some under the Pharisee's leadership, Judaism as a whole simply did not have the type of tortured conflict with the law that the Wretched Man voices.

## Is the Wretched Man Unredeemed Humanity?

The fourth view is that in verse 7, Paul is taking on the representative role of Adam and acting out the experience of unredeemed humanity under Satan's rule. Of the four views, I believe this one makes the most sense given the corporate arguments Paul has been making since 5:12.

The problem, however, is the Wretched Man makes statements that are contrary to the attitudes Paul ascribes to unredeemed humanity in Romans 1. The Wretched Man delights in God's ways and wants to do what's right, but as a whole, in Romans 1 unredeemed humanity suppresses the truth, refuses to honor God as God, and pursues wickedness. Rather than being in agony because of their sin, they actually revel in it and approve of others who do so as well.

## So, Who is the Wretched Man?

Here is the fifth view that I am proposing. I suggest the Wretched Man represents a *sub-group* of unredeemed humanity in Adam whose members span the ages.[58] Collectively, this group agreed with God's law in their inner being however it had been revealed them—be it through God's wisdom and principles expressed in creation, inherited knowledge passed down from Adam, the written Mosaic law, stories about Yahweh that circulated in other nations, preaching, testimony, or scripture. Nevertheless, in spite of their desire to obey God wholeheartedly, they were trapped in the body of Sin by the law of sin and death along with the rest of humanity.

Sometimes referred to in scripture as Yahweh's "remnant," "a band of survivors," or the "other sheep" Jesus mentioned, this group consists of all those in Adam—past, present, and also the future—who looked or will look to God in faith to keep his promises.[59] In short, I believe the Wretched Man represents the body of Christ in its *former* life in Adam, *before* its members were united with Christ by the Spirit and died with him to the law of sin and death that bound humanity to Sin/Satan. This collective group consists of those in whom the Spirit of God is effectively working; they agree that God's laws and ways are good and see their sinful state that separates them from their creator but have come to realize they cannot free themselves from their abusive captor.

Scripture shows this sub-group is not limited to those who knew the Mosaic law. It includes all who believed God *before* Mount Sinai— men and women like Abel, Enoch, Noah, Abraham, Sarah, Isaac, Jacob, Joseph and Moses—as well as those who came *after* Mt. Sinai. In addition to the faithful in Israel, we read of Gentiles like Rahab and her family, Ruth, Cornelius, the Ethiopian eunuch, and Lydia. No doubt, there were countless others like them whose names have been lost to history but known to God.

These were the ones who, though temporarily under Sin's rule, were like Abraham in *"longing for a better country—a heavenly one,"* a city whose builder and architect is God.[60] They were strangers and pilgrims on the earth who walked by faith in whatever light they had while waiting for God's promises to come to pass. The Wretched Man, who laments because he is being held captive in the body of death, also represents those *after* Christ whose hearts are inclined to God but have not yet heard the gospel and come to faith in Christ. In short, he expresses the collective heart cry of all those throughout the ages who long for God but have not yet found freedom from Sin/Satan.

How is it possible to be in Adam under Sin's authority, yet delight in God's law, principles, and wisdom at the same time? The story of Daniel in the Old Testament serves as an example. Daniel lived in the day when Yahweh finally allowed Israel to be taken captive by the Babylonians as a judgment for committing spiritual adultery with other gods. Even though Daniel was faithful himself, nevertheless, as a Jew who was in solidarity with Israel, he too was carried off into exile along with everyone else who had broken covenant with Yahweh. Enslaved and bound to a foreign king who worshipped other gods, Daniel and other like-minded Jews continued to love and honor Yahweh. Although many other Israelites were assimilated into the culture, those who were part of this faithful remnant longed for redemption, so they could return home to Jerusalem and freely worship Yahweh. Likewise, Paul refers to certain Gentiles who have the law of God written in their hearts and instinctively do the things of the law, even though they are still under Sin's authority.[61]

Let's look now at the Wretched Man's testimony to see if the view I am proposing holds up. As we move into this part of the discussion, let me remind you that when Paul talks about the law in Romans 7:7-25, he has the greater, more expansive view of the law in mind. While this may include references to the Mosaic law that was given to the Jews, as we will see, he also goes back to the garden and speaks about God's laws and principles that apply to all of humankind in Adam.

**THE WRETCHED MAN'S STORY¶** We learned from our earlier discussion that in many societies, but especially the Hebrew culture, the one is often used to represent the many. Taking this approach, in verse 7, Paul begins to use the personal pronoun "I" to represent this sub-group in Adam, with different voices breaking through as the Wretched Man tells his story. As we consider this much-debated passage, I want to suggest the corporate, covenantal paradigm we discussed earlier is the key to not only understanding Romans 5:12–7:6, but this text as well.

Looking at the overall flow of the chapter, Paul is continuing the arguments about life in Adam versus life in Christ that he started in Romans 5. As we've seen, in the first part of chapter 7, Paul shows how collectively, members of the body of Christ died with him to the law of sin and death so they could become his rightful bride. Then in 7:7-13 the apostle takes on the role of the Wretched Man and circles back to the garden to wrestle with how Sin/Satan used God's good and holy law to take authority over him and produce death. Having come under Satan's rule, in 7:14-25 the Wretched Man goes on to describe what life is like in the flesh, the body of Sin and Death where he is held prisoner to the law of sin (the law of the husband) that now controls his existence.

As he moves into 8:1-4, Paul addresses members of the new covenant community and speaks to them of their new life in the Spirit. Having once identified with the Wretched Man, Paul now exults that through Christ Jesus, the law of the Spirit of life has set the believing community free from the law of sin and death that formerly yoked them to Satan! After this, Paul goes on to show the contrast between the church's old life in the flesh (unredeemed humanity) under Satan's control, and its new life in the Spirit under her new husband's covenantal authority.

Reflecting on 7:7-8:4 in more detail now, in verse 7 Paul, as the Wretched Man, speaks first with the voice of Adam and begins to refute the idea that the law is somehow sinful because Sin/Satan used it for evil purposes. The Wretched Man's first argument is that God's law is good because it has made him know what sin/Sin is. The law's purpose is to prevent sin not promote it. As an example, Paul brings up the command that says, "you shall not covet," which harkens back to the garden when Satan enticed Adam to covet knowledge that is reserved only for God. This spoken command was meant to shield Adam and Eve from evil and death, not to limit them or withhold good things.

There is no suggestion on Paul's part that God's law itself stirs up sin or creates an appetite for it. In fact, it is the very opposite—his law is in direct conflict with sin/Sin. As a reflection of God's character, the law defines sin and offers protection. God's commands are like light and reveals what is hidden in the darkness. No, God's law is not the problem, the Wretched Man reasons; the problem lies in the "heart" (condition) of humankind.

There's a good possibility that when the Wretched Man says, "I would not have known what sin was except through the law," Paul is not thinking of sinful acts but of Sin as an entity, which would be in line with his personification of Sin/Satan in other places. The word *known* here refers to experiential rather than intellectual knowledge. In fact, both the Hebrew and the Greek words for *know* are regularly used to describe the intimacy of the marriage relationship. Since Paul used marriage to demonstrate how the law functioned in binding the Wretched Man (now the body of Christ), to Sin/Satan, who is the old husband described in 7:1-6, references to Sin in this passage are likely to have this same connotation. In context of this covenant relationship, the law did not merely give a correct "academic" understanding of sin/Sin; humans intimately experience the law's power and authority through its condemning role. The light of the law exposed the full horror of Sin's abusive, controlling nature. Although Satan sometimes "masquerades as an angel of light," he is a liar and a murderer who is bent on destroying everything that God loves.[62]

## Sin Gets a Foothold

In 7:8-13, Paul describes how Sin used God's command in the garden to gain a foothold over humanity and bring death. Explaining that Sin is powerless (dead) without the law, the Wretched Man testifies that in the very beginning he was "alive." Initially, no law had been given, so Sin had no way to gain power over him. However, when God told Adam not to eat from the tree of the knowledge of good and evil, Sin/Satan saw his opportunity and like a predator waiting to attack and kill, "sprang into life." Using the command to stir up covetous desires to be like God, Satan convinced Adam and Eve that Yahweh lied when he said they would die if they ate the tree's fruit. He enticed them to disobey and follow him instead. When they did so, their covenant relationship with Yahweh was broken and Satan assumed God's functional role. As a result, he became humankind's master (husband) and Adam "died" to all for which God had created him, eventually experiencing physical death.

The weakness of the law is that it was powerless to change the covenant relationship that Adam, humanity's representative head, had entered into with Sin/Satan. In fact, as we saw in the illustration of marriage Paul used earlier, since Adam joined himself to Sin/Satan by choice God's law actually confirmed it, as the law must uphold the rights of both partners. Once Adam betrayed Yahweh and entered into a covenant relationship with Satan, even the evil one could appeal to God's holy law for his exclusive rights to humankind. The weakness of the civil law is also evident in that while it creates a marriage in legal terms, it is utterly helpless to change a bad marriage and make it good.

In verse 13, the Wretched Man, still speaking in Adam's voice, soundly rejects the idea that the law itself is sinful because it produced death in him. No, he says, God's law is good in that it shows how exceedingly sinful sin/Sin really is! Paul makes this point because he hears Adam (fallen humanity) questioning the purpose of the commandment in the garden, reasoning that he sinned because God's command not to eat from the tree of the knowledge of good and evil made it seem so appealing! In other words, with this line of thinking, Adam could insist that he was innocent and blame God's command instead because it presented him with temptation.

Knowing this thought would have been blasphemy for any first century Jew who esteemed God's law, but at the same time identifying with Adam's argument, Paul as the Wretched Man struggles with the way God's commands stir up sin. He realizes the law's negative effect is in stark contrast with its intrinsic goodness. The Wretched Man reasons the law has to be good because it comes from God.; it does what it does precisely because it is holy and true. He sees that God's law excites sin/Sin because it confronts and accuses it.[63] However, the law does not make man sinful; rather, it exposes him to be so. This shows the other side of the law—although it is good, it produces death because it reveals and condemns sin.

144

## Sold to Sin

In 7:14, the Wretched man moves from talking about how Sin used God's good law to take humanity captive in the garden and begins describing how it functions now that he's under Sin/Satan's covenantal authority. Though echoes of Adam's experience can still be heard, this is where other voices begin to break through in the story.

In addition to the fact that it is holy, righteous, and good, the Wretched Man recognizes God's law is also spiritual. However, he sees that he is now "unspiritual, sold as a slave to Sin." After his relationship with God was severed, he begins to realize one of the consequences of selling out to Sin/Satan was not only a gradual physical death, but he also "died" spiritually. No longer connected to the Creator, who is Spirit and reveals the way of life, he is now a mere "natural man" who is unable to receive the things of the Spirit.[64] Cut off from the source of life, humankind in Adam became like a dead man walking.

The statement about being sold as a slave to Sin is what connects the Wretched Man to the illustration of marriage Paul uses in 7:1-6. The terminology of being bought and sold, which is often found in Paul's writings, is normally seen to reflect his use of slave imagery. It is regarded as a natural extension of the analogy of being a *doulos*, a "slave" of Christ. I have questioned this understanding of *doulos*, however, pointing out that the context, not the original meaning, must decide Paul's intended meaning.

I have argued that the proper setting of the language of being bought and sold is the divine marriage imagery of the Old Testament. In this context, Israel was saved and redeemed ("bought") to be Yahweh's bride, not his slave. Although the Lord redeemed Israel from bondage in Egypt, the relationship went disastrously wrong when his bride willingly became the possession of other gods. Essentially, Israel repeated Adam's error and gave herself to Sin/Satan, the one who is ultimately at work under the guise of false gods. Taken into captivity by the Babylonians, Yahweh once again moved to redeem his bride after her allotted time of exile. This bride-purchase context—so common in the ancient Near East—is also the setting for Paul's statement in I Corinthians 6:20 that we have been "bought at a price." (We will look at this more in the next chapter.)

On one level, it could be said a form of "slavery" is involved in that Adam gave himself along with his offspring to the evil one when he willingly entered into a covenant relationship with Satan. Bound to him by law, Sin took on the role of an abusive master (husband). Unfortunately, as we have seen previously, confusing this marital language with Hellenistic slave imagery has masked the richer Old Testament picture that depicts God as redeeming his people so they could become his bride.

## Sin Takes Over

In 7:15-20, the Wretched Man considers his conflicted life now that he's under Sin/Satan's rule. He does not understand himself. Instead of doing what he wants to do, he keeps doing what he hates. He reasons that if he ends up doing what he does not want to do, this means he must agree that God's law is good. But if that is the case, then why then doesn't he do the good he wants to do and follow God's life-giving commands and precepts? Since he wants to do what is right, but cannot carry it out, he concludes that nothing good lives in him, that is, in his life apart from God. But even worse, it dawns on him that if he keeps doing what he does not want to do, he is not free. To his horror, he sees that because his members—those of Adam's offspring who collectively make up Wretched Man—belong to the body of Death (body of Sin), Sin is now living within him and has taken control!

At this point, the Wretched Man realizes he has been duped. Going back to the garden, Sin/Satan had convinced him that God's command was *not* good, that it was holding him back by preventing him from having the same knowledge as God. However, instead of finding freedom, meaning, and fulfillment by going against God as Satan promised, the Wretched Man found himself dragged down into shame, disgrace, and self-hatred. He discovers that everything Satan said is an empty lie. The command the Wretched Man had rejected in the garden was not meant to limit him, as Satan had claimed, but to protect his liberty. While offering deity, the evil one has delivered nothing but despair and hopelessness. Although the Wretched Man hates what he is doing and longs to live according to God's design, the disturbing reality is that he is powerless to change because Sin is now in charge.

Whether speaking of Adam, Israel, or Paul, this is the experience of all who are drawn to God and his goodness but are still part of the old man (unredeemed humanity) headed by Sin/Satan. While some in Adam long to live as God instructed, there is something that overpowers humanity in its corporate, as well as individual, existence. No matter how strenuous and urgent the struggle to be free, humankind under the power of Satan is helpless to alter its condition. Acknowledging this, as the Wretched Man does, is actually the first step towards receiving the grace of God, which leads to freedom.

## Resident Evil

What does the Wretched mean when he says, "it is sin living in me" that is compelling him to do what he doesn't want to do?[65] How can sin live in him if the Wretched Man represents a corporate entity? Interpreted individualistically, this text has been the basis for the widely accepted doctrine that maintains sin is biologically inherited. In this view, ever since Adam and Eve disobeyed, indwelling sin has permanently tainted human nature, the believer's included, and is passed on to the next generation through the sex act.[66]

For many, this version of original sin is supported by the Wretched Man's next statement that "nothing good lives in me, that is, in my *sinful nature* (flesh)." Translating *flesh* as *sinful nature*, as the NIV does, leads the reader in the direction of believing that when Paul refers to the flesh here, he is thinking of an inherited human nature that lives *within* the individual. Together, these interpretations have been used to support the dualistic notions that believers have two natures—one that is fleshly or carnal and another that is spiritual—or that the individual's body is somehow tainted because it hosts and transmits sin. I have argued these ideas are pagan, Hellenistic intrusions into Paul's Hebraic mindset and ought to have no place in biblical thinking. Humanity's sinfulness is not biological; it is covenantal. All who are born are in Adam and chose to remain there, rejecting the last Adam, Jesus Christ, and his saving work, are under the covenant headship of Sin/Satan.

Paul's statements do not have the same dualistic connotations when read through a holistic, corporate lens. In this view, when the Wretched Man speaks of "sin living in me" and that "nothing good lives in me, that is in my flesh," Paul is not referring to a sin nature that lives inside the individual or to the physical body; rather, he is describing unredeemed humanity's condition under Satan's rule.[67] In this context, *flesh* is a corporate concept that refers to the old man, the body of Sin headed by Satan. To be in the flesh is to be in Adam (unredeemed humanity). I contend that in keeping with Paul's arguments since

Romans 5:12, the text should be read with the Old Testament Hebraic outlook in mind, in which the one and the many merge into an almost indistinguishable relationship with the head or king figure. Bound together with the evil one into a fallen, federal existence, Sin/Satan lives in the midst of unredeemed humanity (the flesh), producing sin and death.

The Wretched man sees that since the garden, Sin has been controlling humankind, of whom he is a part, in the most terrible way. The fruit of living in the flesh under Sin's rule is "sexual immorality, impurity, and debauchery; idolatry and witchcraft; hatred, discord, jealousy, fits of rage, selfish ambition, dissensions, factions, and envy; drunkenness, orgies, and the like."[68] Broken families, adultery, murder, slavery, violence, theft, and greed also mar humanity's existence. Not limited to sinful acts committed by individuals, Sin also inspires systemic injustice within groups or nations such as wars, poverty, corrupt economic policies that favor the rich over the poor, or occasions when one nation or ethnic group subjugates another. Even humankind's greatest achievements—be it in education, the arts, the law, politics, commerce, religion, psychology, ethics, etc.—have been twisted by Sin in one way or another, as has God's law which is intrinsically holy. Distressed by the Sin's power over humankind, the Wretched Man yearns for the restoration of paradise where he was free to live as God intended, but he doesn't know how to return to that state now that Adam's offspring is under Sin's authority.

Thus, in looking at the world under Sin's reign, the Wretched Man comes to see there is a power that dominates humanity that cannot be mastered. This does not negate his responsibility, but as humbling as it may be to admit, the Wretched Man concedes there is an evil force at work in the midst of humanity in Adam that is greater and stronger than he. When he struggled with the role and nature of God's law earlier, Paul, as the Wretched Man, acknowledged its intrinsic goodness. Now, in his struggle with his current state, he sees Sin's intrinsic evil and how he uses God's law for harmful purposes. Paul is not only arguing that humankind is weak and powerless; he is making the case for the reality of evil, which is personified in Satan. The evil one has deceived humanity, bringing it into a condition from which it cannot escape on its own.

Let me say here that we can only speculate on the problem of evil. While the Bible gives us certain parameters for our thinking, it does not try to give us a neat and tidy answer that meets the probing demands of the philosopher. Not all truth can be reduced to a rational formula. How can humans that are created in God's image be capable of sin? This seems like an impossible quandary to solve. All we do know is that humans had to be able to choose to sin if they were to have free will and be responsible before God. Indeed, this freedom is an essential part of what it means to be made in God's image.

## Sin's Prisoner

Trying to understand himself, in 7:21-25 the Wretched Man discovers there is a troubling law at work within him: "when I want to do good, evil is right there with me." He is not speaking about a formal law or commandment, but a principle or authority that ties back to the illustration of marriage Paul used earlier in the chapter. Having entered into a legally binding relationship with Sin/Satan through Adam's actions, humankind is like a married woman who, after the wedding, discovers that her once charming husband is an abuser who controls her every action.

The problem is there is no one to call upon who can legally interfere because God's own law—the law of marriage that Satan usurped—protects the relationship. Consequently, apart from death, there is no way for the Wretched Man to break free from the evil one's control. In corporate solidarity with unredeemed humanity ruled by Sin/Satan, evil permeates his entire existence.[69] It is always right there with him, in him, impelling him to act in ways that are contrary to his conscience.

The Wretched Man, representing the collective sub-group in Adam whose hearts are inclined towards God, laments because in his inner being he truly delights in God's law. In his mind, he agrees that Gods ways are true and right, but to his dismay, he sees "*another law* at work in the members of my body, waging war against the law of my mind." The terrible truth strikes home—although he fully acknowledges that God's ways are right, he is trapped in the body of Sin along with the rest of unredeemed humanity, imprisoned by the law of sin with no way to escape. Hence, his plaintive cry, "What a Wretched Man I am! Who will rescue me from this body of Death?" Summing up his hopeless condition, he once again acknowledges that in his mind he wants to serve God, but "in the sinful nature" (the *flesh* in other translations) he is "a slave to the law of sin (Sin)."

Again, these verses should be read through a corporate rather than an individualistic lens or we will end up with a form of dualism that sees the human person's mind and body as somehow being pitted against one another. In keeping with the flow of his corporate arguments, I suggest that when Paul uses the term *inner being* in verse 22, he is talking about the collective mindset of the sub-group in Adam that the Wretched Man represents. And in speaking of the "members of my body" in verse 23, the Wretched Man is referring to the individuals who belong to the corporate body of Sin of which he is a part, not the individual's physical body parts.

This too is consistent with our previous discussion regarding the way Paul uses the term *members* in Romans 6, 1 Corinthians 6:15 and 1 Corinthians 12. I also suggest that *sarx* is best interpreted as *flesh*, which, in this particular context, refers to *unredeemed humanity in Adam*, not to *a sinful nature* that lives within the individual. Paul is looking at humankind's collective condition and seeing that all the members of unredeemed humanity that make up the body of Sin headed by Satan, the Wretched Man included, are prisoners to the law of sin.

## Another Law

Which brings us to a question that we framed earlier—when Paul as the Wretched Man speaks of "another law" that is at work in his members and is contrary to God's law, what is it? Is it the same as or different than the law of sin? And what exactly is the law of sin? At this point, we have laid the necessary groundwork for understanding this. Looking at the context, "another law" refers to the principle of evil at work within the corporate body of Sin and Death that impels the Wretched Man to live in a way that violates God's law. Seen in this light, the law of sin simply refers to Satan's authority or rule over unredeemed humanity. What the Wretched Man is describing in this text is a horrible catch-22. Sin, who controls the corporate body of flesh (unredeemed humanity), provokes him to go against the law even though he does not want to, and since the consequences of sin is death, God's law condemns him when he sins, which further strengthens Satan's grip on him.

Although God's law was meant to be a source of light and life, this dynamic shows that it functions in a different way for those who are living in the flesh. The essence of God's law, later spelled out for the Jews in the Torah, had been planted in the heart of the human family from the beginning, and so operated as a safeguard to protect humankind from the father of lies. This law is holy and good, but now, because of the fall, it condemns! It could be said that in its role of condemning sin, God's law wars against the fallen will of man. In a similar way, the civil law protects but also condemns. The Wretched Man's testimony reflects Paul's understanding that all of humankind is "shut up under Sin," bound to the evil one as a result of their disobedience so that God could show mercy through Christ to all who believe in his promises by faith.[70]

## Liberated!

Despair turns into relief and exultation in Romans 8 as the Wretched Man realizes that, in Christ, he no longer stands condemned. As Paul says to the new covenant community, "the law of the Spirit of life in Christ Jesus has set you free from the law of sin and death."[71] The opening two verses of chapter 8 are the conclusion to chapter 7 and not the start of a new section. Continuing to speak of the corporate deliverance of God's people, Paul begins tying up the theme he introduced in 5 where he showed that through the sin of the one man Adam, judgment and condemnation came to all. Now, he is providing further insight into how God's gracious gift of justification came to his people through the sacrifice of the last Adam, Jesus Christ. To reverse the effects of Adam's actions, God sent his Son to do what the law and humankind were powerless to do—save his people from Sin and Death.

We have already seen that the law was helpless to change humanity's condition in the same way that it is helpless to change a marriage that goes wrong. The law cannot change the heart. All it can do is ratify and protect the relationships it recognizes. So once Adam, humankind's representative, chose to enter into a covenant relationship with Sin/Satan, the law had to acknowledge it. Legally, death was the only way out. Furthermore, there was no way we could free ourselves from this deadly union with Sin/Satan. Because all sinned, all were condemned by God's law, reinforcing Sin and Death's right to hold humanity prisoner. Therefore, since God is just and keeps his word, before he could liberate his people from the kingdom of darkness, Jesus first had to satisfy "the righteous requirement" of God's law that rightfully condemned us and bound humanity to Sin and Death.

To accomplish this, God the Son willingly stepped out of glory and taking on human form entered into humanity's sinful existence. Sharing in our humanity but not our sin, Jesus, as the new covenant community's representative head, defeated and condemned Satan through his work on the cross. United with him in his death by the Spirit, when Jesus died, all the members of the Wretched Man died with him to the law of sin and death (the law of marriage) that bound them to Sin and were raised with him as the body of Christ, the new man. Additionally, Jesus became a sin offering and died on behalf of his people to meet the demand of the law that says the consequence for sin is death. Standing in for humanity and bearing our collective sin, Jesus atoned for our transgressions so that all who turned to him in repentance and faith could be released from condemnation, forgiven, washed clean, and reconciled with God.

Because Jesus was sinless and fulfilled the law's requirement, Sin and Death had no legal claim on him or the new covenant community who exists in solidarity with him. Consequently, the Spirit of life rightfully brought Jesus and his people back from the dead and into a new life. Rising from the grave and leading captives in his train, Jesus inaugurated the New Exodus that freed the Wretched Man from Satan's power and control.[72] Born again as the new man (humanity) through the death and resurrection of Christ, God's people are now free to love and serve him in the Spirit on their pilgrim journey to the Promised Land.

## Reframing the Gospel

This discussion brings up an important point that pertains to how we frame the gospel. When Paul speaks in Romans 8:4 of meeting "the requirement of the law," the prevailing view is that he is saying Jesus met the penal demands of the law. This goes back to the traditional Western forensic and mainly individualistic framework for explaining the gospel that we looked at earlier. We saw that according to this model, by sinning against God, we, as individuals, have committed crimes that deserve the death penalty. Standing in for us, Jesus was punished on our behalf so that we could be legally pardoned for our crimes, forgiven, and declared righteous.

Again, while being pardoned, delivered from death, and forgiven is part of the picture, Paul, I would claim, is continuing to rely primarily on the corporate, covenantal New Exodus framework, not the Roman law court model. Reading against this backdrop, he is saying that the death of Christ has ended the former relationship with Sin/Satan to which his people were legally bound, and he did this in a way that perfectly satisfied the law. This freed God's people from the law of sin and death, which enabled the believing community to enter into a new relationship with Christ. Paul is basically repeating what he said in Romans 6:7, that those who have died with Christ are justified from Sin. No charge of adultery can be made against the covenant community's restored relationship with God as the requirement of the law that once bound us to Satan has been met in the representative, covenant-annulling death of Christ. This is a mostly unrecognized but vitally important aspect of what the death of Christ has achieved.

Distinct echoes of the First Exodus in 8:1-4 further support the idea that Paul is writing with this covenantal framework in mind. The Hebrews in Egypt were under a death threat in two ways—they were under condemnation for worshipping Egypt's gods and Pharaoh was determined to crush them out of existence.[73] If God was to intervene, he had to deal with them in righteousness, addressing their sin first before moving to save them from Pharaoh.

This is why the Passover had to take place at the beginning of the First Exodus. When the LORD passed through the land, he came in judgment to punish the sins of all who lived in Egypt. The firstborn of the Jews were spared from God's judgment because each family obeyed the command to slay a lamb and smear its blood on the doorpost and the lintel as a vicarious sacrifice.[74] Thus, as a result of the exodus event, the Jews could say they were no longer living in condemnation in two distinct ways—the fear of Yahweh's judgment was ended at the Passover when the lambs were slain in place of the firstborn who represented the family, and Pharaoh no longer had the power to harm or destroy them since they were under God's protection.

In keeping with the covenantal, New Exodus theme, Paul sees Christ's death as a sin offering; it is the Paschal sacrifice through which God has delivered his people.[75] Like the deliverance of the Jews from Egypt, God's rescue through Jesus was double-edged. First, there was deliverance from God's judgment, which the Righteous One must pass at some point on all who violate his holy law of love. And there was deliverance from Sin/Satan, who was determined from the beginning to destroy God's people. Thus, the deliverance of the Jews during the exodus was truly a type of that which Christ came to secure for the new covenant community. As we have seen, the original Passover also took place so that Yahweh could take Israel as his bride. That is the purpose of Christ's death as well. In these ways, Paul brings together themes from the Passover and the sacrificial system instituted by Moses to explain the full significance of Jesus's crucifixion. (Although most scholars deny any atoning significance in the Passover, as I will show later this is because significant Old Testament evidence has not been fully considered.)

The Messiah's death alone is the foundation for the believing community's new existence, for in fulfilling the requirement of the law and freeing his people from Sin/Satan, he made it possible for his people to be reconciled to God. In this new era, God bestows the Spirit on the church and the promises Yahweh made through the prophets are now realized: "For no matter how many promises God has made, they are 'Yes' in Christ. And so, through him the 'Amen' is spoken by us to the glory of God."[76] This deliverance does not benefit everyone. It is only for those who are in Christ. Those who choose to stay in the kingdom of darkness are still under the condemnation and judgment that applies to all who are in Adam.

We have come to the end of our discussion of the Wretched Man. In the view that I have presented, he represents a sub-group of unredeemed humanity in Adam whose hearts were drawn to God but were trapped in the body of Sin headed by Sin/Satan. Collectively baptized into Christ's death by the Spirit and dying with him to the law of sin and death (the law of the husband) that formerly bound them to Satan, the members of this group were born-again as the new man (new humanity), the body of Christ, who now lives in the kingdom of light.

We do not have time to look at the rest of Romans 8 in detail. However, I would like to briefly review what it looks like when it is read through a corporate lens, as individualistic interpretations of key concepts in this chapter have created the same type of confusion associated with Romans 7.

**NEW HUSBAND, NEW COMMUNITY, NEW LIFE¶** After showing how the body of Christ was released from the law of the old husband, Sin/Satan, Paul describes the believing community's new existence and future glory. Now that she is betrothed to Jesus, the new covenant community is under the law of the Spirit, which is the law of life in Christ. In a state of transition, as the church waits for her redemption to be made complete and for the consummation of her wedding to her Redeemer, the Spirit represents the groom and acts as the bride's custodian. The Holy Spirit is charged with leading the covenant community to glory for the final revelation of Christ's love toward his people.

The law of the Spirit is the law of Christ in that the Spirit has authority to guide, protect, teach, and prepare the bride for presentation before her groom, the Son of God. This too reflects the exodus paradigm—whether the Egyptian or Babylonian exodus—for the Spirit was active in both, having the same purpose of bringing God's people into their inheritance and preparing them for the end times marriage at which time they will fully experience God's love.[77]

To show the difference between the body of Christ's former life and her new one, in Romans 8:5-13, Paul contrasts life in the flesh (unredeemed humanity) versus life in the Spirit. In this passage, he is comparing two communities, not two internal natures that co-exist within the individual believer. Also, he is continuing to talk primarily about humanity's condition, not sinful acts committed by the individual.

In speaking about those whose minds are set on the flesh, he is describing the carnal mindset or value system of all who are in Adam under the headship of Satan. Those who live in the realm of the flesh are not thinking of God or what he wants. In fact, collectively, the members of this community are hostile to God. Not only do they refuse to submit to God's law, but they couldn't even if they wanted to because Sin controls their existence. For these reasons, it is impossible for those in the flesh to please God.

In contrast, those who have been redeemed and now live in the realm of the Spirit desire to do what is asked of them because they want to be ready when their Bridegroom comes. Secure in the knowledge they are no longer in the flesh (unredeemed humanity) because the Spirit dwells in their midst, the new covenant community is filled with life and peace even in the midst of difficulties, waiting in trust and hope for the end times completion of their marriage to the Lamb.[78]

While in this in-between existence that is sometimes referred to as the "already not yet," Paul explains in Romans 8:10 that because "Christ is in you, [plural]" meaning the community, even though "your body is subject to death because of sin," the Spirit gives life. In this context, the phrase "your body" is not a reference to the individual. Literally translated as "*the* body," Paul is speaking of the corporate solidarity the Roman believers have in Christ. In saying "the body is subject to death because of sin," the apostle is not suggesting the body of Christ is corrupt or that the physical bodies of its members are condemned because they are sinful. Rather, he is saying that, although the body of Christ has been redeemed and made alive to God in the Spirit, as far their physical existence is concerned believers are still living in the realm of fallen humanity; they are part of creation, which was subjected to frustration as a result of Adams actions.[79] As a result, their individual bodies will decay along with the rest of creation and eventually die. Paul encourages the church in Rome that just as the Spirit raised Jesus from the dead, so the Spirit will also give life to their mortal bodies, as a corporate body and as individuals, at the end of the age when all is made new.[80]

In summing up his comparison of the two communities, Paul tells the Roman believers that if they keep living as they did while in the flesh (unredeemed humanity), the church at Rome will die. The community will come under judgment and her "candlestick" or witness will be removed. We see an example of this danger in scripture when the church at Ephesus was warned to repent in the book of Revelation.[81] In some cases, backslidden members of congregations might even die physically, as happened in Corinth.[82]

In verse 13, the apostle tells the Romans, however, that if they put to death "the misdeeds of the body" with the help of the Spirit they will live. Again, in context, this is not about the individual's physical body but rather about their body life as a community. As he does in some of his other letters, Paul is instructing the church at Rome to put off the ways of life they learned while in the flesh and to put on the new.[83] This echoes Moses's warning to the Jews regarding two paths the Israelites could follow: the way of life and the way of death. Moses urged the nation to choose life.

## Suffering and Future Glory

Similarly, Paul encourages the pilgrim church to press forward and not turn back to their formers lives in fear as some of the children of Israel wanted to do on their way to the Promised Land. Although they may face hostility and persecution, the Spirit is there to provide guidance and to continually assure them of their true identity as sons and daughters who are under the care and protection of God, their Father. As co-heirs with Christ, the community will suffer with Jesus while in this present existence, but it is not to be compared with the glory that will be revealed when the new creation is unveiled, the redemption of our bodies is complete, and the adopted sons of God take their rightful place. In the meantime, the Spirit helps the community in its present weakness by interceding on our behalf when we do not know how to pray.

The church can take comfort that even in the midst of persecution, difficulties and danger, God is working through all of life's circumstances to accomplish his purposes in the lives of those who love him. Paul is thinking corporately here. He explains that in his foreknowledge, God predestined his people to be conformed into the image of Christ, so that Jesus would be the firstborn of many brothers. While it is true that God knew all who would be his from eternity, in the Old Testament "foreknowledge" is a covenantal concept having to do with the election of a nation rather than the individual.[84] God's promise is that having called the new covenant community to himself, he will also justify and glorify his people, meaning he will bring them out from slavery to Sin and into his presence in the New Jerusalem.

While the individual will be changed in this process, this is a microcosm of the greater transformation that involves the entire church. It is the new man, the corporate body of Christ that, having been rescued from the kingdom of darkness, will be made into the likeness of Christ. As the church journeys towards her final destination, she can be assured that because she has been justified and is now in Christ, nothing—no danger, hardship, persecution, famine, humiliation, or power, not even death itself—can separate her from "the love of God that is in Christ Jesus our Lord."[85]

Of course, I am barely scratching the surface when it comes to seeing the rich corporate, covenantal Old Testament backdrop for Romans 8. If you are interested in exploring this further, I invite you to read the verse-by-verse discussion of this chapter in the commentary I have written on Romans.[86] This ends our use of the 1984 NIV which has allowed us to see how shifting back and forth from a corporate to an individualistic reading affects key texts in Romans 5-8. Going forward, unless otherwise noted, I will reference the more recent 2011 version of the NIV.

## Questions about sin, Sin, and the body of Sin

If the interpretive framework and the corporate view of the Wretched Man I am offering are accepted, by extension, this means it will be necessary to reconsider some of our traditional thinking and teaching about the nature of Christian spirituality, the human person, and sin/Sin that is based on an individualistic reading of Romans 7 and other texts. I address aspects of Augustine's view of sin in appendix B, but a full exploration of these subjects is beyond the scope of this book, so this will need to take place in subsequent conversations. At the moment, we need to finish our discussion about the body of Sin. Based on Paul's arguments in Romans 5–8, I have suggested this is not a reference to the individual's physical body, but is a corporate entity or realm headed by Satan, also known in some contexts as the body of flesh, the body of death, and the kingdom of darkness that parallels body of Christ. Before settling on this position, however, we need to see if this concept is found in other places in scripture, and if it can shed light on any other difficult passages. To this end, I want to look at some additional texts that provide further support for the view I am proposing.

CHAPTER 6

# The Universal Prostitute

The Ugandans loved him at first. When Idi Amin stepped into power in the early 70's he was charming, mingled freely with the common people, and seemed to be informal and flexible. He also assured Ugandans that he would return power to the civilians. It wasn't long after he took office, however, before Amin's dark side surfaced. Not only did he superintend the slaughter of somewhere between 100,000 to 500,000 people in an effort to exert absolute control over the nation, he spent millions to maintain a royal lifestyle while his people suffered. Enamored with position and power, some of his preferred titles were "The Lord of All the Beasts of the Earth and Fishes of the Sea," "Conqueror of the British Empire in Africa in General and Uganda in Particular," and "Uncrowned King of Scotland." He was also busy in the bedroom; Amin had 5 wives, over 30 mistresses, and somewhere between 45 and 50 children.

It would be one thing if Idi Admin were an anomaly, but he is only one leader among many in recent history who succumbed to the corrupting influences of money, sex, and power. From Hitler to Stalin to Pol Pot, numerous tyrants, intoxicated with power, are responsible for the death of millions in the twentieth century. In other arenas, greedy corporate leaders at companies like Enron bilked millions from trusting stakeholders, a situation that produced long term ripple effects, and Wall Street financiers provoked a global financial crisis that harmed untold numbers of people. Plus, a seemingly endless parade of political leaders, sports figures, and celebrities has been embroiled in sex scandals.[1]

It is not just leaders and famous people who have fallen under the spell of this seductive trio of temptations. Employee theft, the global drug trade and human trafficking are all multi-billion dollar a year enterprises.[2] Sadly, religion has also been susceptible to the allure of these worldly enticements. From sexual impropriety among leaders to televangelists who live luxurious lifestyles to the significant use of porn by professing Christians, moral scandal has rocked the church as well.[3] All of this is nothing new of course. Examples of greed, flagrant sexual immorality, and devastating abuses of power litter the pages of our history books. Even scripture describes how one of the wisest men who ever lived—Solomon—was led astray by the seductive influence of money, sex, and power.

Noting its pervasive influence, author Barbara Kellerman observes that corruption is "like a virus that easily insinuates itself . . . no place is immune: not churches or charities, not banking or biotech, not small towns or large cities, not North America or South America, or, for that matter, any other place on the planet."[4]

In the last two chapters, we have been looking at the *body of Sin* mentioned in Romans 6:6 and seeing how reading scripture through a corporate lens sheds new light on the meaning of this phrase. Traditionally, it has been interpreted as the individual's body tainted by sin or a complex of evil desires living within the individual, believers included. We have seen, however, there is good reason to believe the body of Sin is a corporate entity that parallels the body of Christ, and that all who are outside of Christ are members of this fleshly community headed by Satan, who is the personification of evil. Although he no longer has control over those who are in Christ, nevertheless, Sin/Satan's presence permeates the world and he actively seeks to seduce, deceive, corrupt, oppress, and destroy the body of Christ. Identifying these two communities helped us work through several long-standing problems in Romans 5–8.

What I want to show next is how a covenantal, corporate understanding of the body of Sin and the body of Christ can help resolve difficulties in another problematic passage—1 Corinthians 6:12-20. Most often read through an individualistic lens, this text is frequently quoted to warn believers against the dangers of sexual immorality, particularly intimacy with a prostitute. Viewed from this perspective, Paul tells the Corinthian believers that purity is important because "Your bodies are temples of the Holy Spirit," and that "You are not your own; you were bought at a price." The temple Paul speaks of is commonly seen as referring to the individual's body; the prostitute mentioned is normally thought to be an individual person; and the phrase "you were bought at a price" is often interpreted against the individualistic backdrop of Greek slavery. It is important to consider this passage carefully, as not only is it a critical text when it comes to understanding our communal identity and the biblical view of the human person, but if the traditional interpretations are correct then they are a clear challenge to the corporate view of the body of Sin I have been proposing.

I believe it can be proven, however, that in keeping with the New Exodus framework we have been exploring, Paul's text is directed primarily to the community and set against the covenantal backdrop of the marriage between God and his people, not Greek slavery. Consistent with this context, I propose that the ancient practice of paying a bride price is a more accurate motif for interpreting the phrase "you were bought at a price" than is Greek slavery.

I also contend the apostle had something far greater in mind than an individual prostitute when he exhorted the Corinthians to remain pure and faithful to Christ. Rather, I suggest he was referring to a personified corporate entity that has seduced kings and peoples into committing immorality with her throughout the ages—none other than the mysterious Prostitute of Babylon described in Revelation 17. As we shall see, this Prostitute represents unredeemed humanity under Satan's control and is another name for the body of Sin.

When viewed in this larger corporate framework, the point Paul wants to make to the Corinthians is that tolerating ongoing immorality in their midst is not only dangerous to individual members, it can also corrupt the entire body of Christ. He wants them to understand that engaging in illicit sexual immorality of this type carries with it all the implications of being in a covenant relationship with Satan!

At first glance, this may seem like another one of those interesting-but-irrelevant subjects best left to theologians. However, understanding this text from a corporate perspective can have a significant practical bearing on how we relate to Christ and one another in context of the new covenant community.

**A TROUBLING UNION¶** Looking first at the context of 1 Corinthians so we can see what was on Paul's mind, the apostle is writing to address several problems that were surfacing in the church at Corinth. The spirit of the world was creeping into the community. Some of the members were quarreling and forming factions around their favorite teachers. Enamored with the pursuit of wisdom and seeing themselves as being endowed with superior knowledge because the Spirit was at work in their midst, a number had also embraced faulty, inflated ideas about Christian spirituality.

In light of this, Paul was concerned that the Corinthians' understanding of the gospel was in danger of being corrupted by a form of Hellenistic dualism. Believing they lived on a higher spiritual plane because of the gifts of the Spirit that were at work in their midst, they tended to look down on the material world, including the physical body. As a result, a mentality had taken root among the Corinthians that what they did with their bodies was of little consequence. This had given rise to errors such as denying the place of sexual relations within marriage and the future resurrection of the body.[5] Another is that they were tolerating sexual immorality in their midst.[6] It was also causing some members to feel like they were superior to others.

In chapter 5, Paul begins addressing a situation that was frowned upon even among the pagans—a professing believer is sleeping with his father's wife. This particular sin was expressly forbidden in the Old Testament, but even worse, the relationship was more than a one-night stand—the couple was living together as husband and wife.[7] The apostle expresses dismay not only because the Corinthians were allowing it to continue, they were proud of it! In contrast, Paul is so grieved by the matter that he wants the Corinthians to expel the man from the fellowship. In Paul's vocabulary, he should be "handed over to Satan" so that "his flesh may be destroyed and his spirit saved on the day of the Lord." As Paul sees it, the man's eternal well-being was at stake and it was the fellowship's responsibility to help him by taking redemptive action.[8]

But Paul has another reason for wanting the community to exercise this type of discipline. Because the body of Christ is an organic, inter-related whole, the apostle wants the Corinthians to take action for the congregation's sake as well as the man's. He explains it is critical to maintain the purity of the church because "a little yeast leavens the whole batch of dough," meaning that if they tolerate blatant sin among their members, the whole body can be corrupted. Paul's appeal for purity is based on the fact that Jesus, our Passover Lamb, has been sacrificed on the church's behalf so that the corporate body of Christ could be cleansed from sin, set apart as holy for God, and enter into a new covenant relationship with him.[9] We can hear the strong paschal, New Exodus framework of Paul's argument coming through here.

Throughout chapters 5 and 6, the apostle makes it clear he is only interested in addressing the man, who is a professing believer, not the woman. Since she is not part of the body, in his view, it is God's business to judge those outside the church. However, the church *is* to judge members who are practicing ongoing immorality in their midst, and Paul lays down principles for dealing with improprieties. They are told not to take their problems before the secular court, for this will bring disgrace to the church's testimony as a whole. Rather, they are to deal with the matter themselves, and are qualified to do so in that they have been appointed to ultimately judge both men and angels at the end of the ages.[10] Pointing out that the wicked will not inherit the kingdom of God, Paul tells them to address various forms of flagrant sin in their community and live in keeping with their high calling.

## A Knotty Text

This brings us to the text we are considering. In 6:12, Paul begins to address one of the main theological rationales the Corinthians were using to justify the immoral behavior occurring among them. As they see it, since believers are no longer under the law, they are free to do anything they like with their bodies. If everything is permissible and the food one eats has no moral significance, then why should sexual conduct matter, especially since the physical body will be destroyed anyway?

In Paul's understanding, however, there is a distinct difference between food and the sexual experience. While food pertains to the individual, sexual union, engaged in its appointed way, is designed to seal relationships and permanently bind people to one another within the context of marriage. Such unions are part of the larger community. They are living units that strengthen the body of Christ and represent the covenant relationship between Jesus and the church. When sex is misused and that which is meant to stay bonded gets pulled apart, the body of Christ is weakened, making it more vulnerable to sin/Sin. Furthermore, God is misrepresented and dishonored.

In verse 13, Paul begins to explain that because they are one in Christ, what members of the new covenant community do with their bodies matters a great deal when it comes to immorality, particularly sexual immorality. Speaking from a Hebraic perspective that regards the human person as an integrated whole, the apostle wants the Corinthians to understand they are not only united with Christ spiritually, but collectively their *bodies* are joined not only to him but to one another as well. Addressing the entire community, Paul says,

> The body, however, is not meant for sexual immorality *[porneia]* but for the Lord, and the Lord for the body. By his power God raised the Lord from the dead, and he will raise us also. Do you not know that your bodies are members of Christ himself? Shall I then take the members of Christ and unite them with a prostitute? Never! Do you not know that he who unites himself with a prostitute is one with her in body? For it is said, "The two will become one flesh." But whoever is united with the Lord is one with him in spirit.

> Flee from sexual immorality *[porneia]*. All other sins a person commits are outside the body, but whoever sins sexually, sins against their own body. Do you not know that your bodies are temples of the Holy Spirit, who is in you, whom you have received from God? You are not your own; you were bought at a price. Therefore, honor God with your bodies.[11]

Reading this passage through a predominantly individualistic lens has overshadowed key corporate themes and given rise to several conundrums that have stumped interpreters. One has to do with Paul's statement that "the Lord is for the body." What exactly does this mean if he is speaking in terms of the individual? Also, some claim Paul is saying that a person becomes "one flesh" with an individual prostitute through sexual intercourse. This is puzzling as it would mean the immoral Christian is "one" with both Christ and a whore. In Paul's mind, however, is it even possible to be "one" with two partners at the same time, especially if one of them is Jesus?

Teachers and scholars have also puzzled over what Paul means when he says some sins are "outside of body," but *porneia* (variously interpreted as *immorality, sexual immorality,* or *fornication*) is "against their own body."[12] Since sins such as drunkenness, addictions and the like also affect the individual's body, why does Paul single out *porneia* in this way? Adding another layer of perplexity is that, in scripture, the temple is *always* a corporate term. If Paul were talking primarily about the individual when he says *porneia* is against one's own body, what is the purpose of bringing in the corporate concept of the temple?

Also problematic is the idea of reading Paul's statement that "you are not your own; you were bought at a price" against the backdrop of Greek slavery. A widely-accepted perspective is that when Paul speaks of being bought at a price in this text, he had an individualistic practice known as *sacral manumission* in mind that allowed a slave to purchase his or her freedom in order to serve a god instead of a human master. As I will show momentarily, not only is this model riddled with difficulties, it obscures the corporate, New Exodus, wedding-related theme that I suggest is woven into the entire letter and frames this passage.

## Corporate Body Language

Many factors point to a corporate rather than individualistic setting for this text. First, there is reason to believe a good deal of the body-related language is primarily about the corporate body of Christ and that issues having to do with the individual's body are set within this larger context. Regarding Paul's statement that the body is meant for the Lord and the Lord for the body, while it is difficult to ascertain whether this is referring to the individual's body or the body of Christ, Paul's entire argument in this text is corporate, which provides a major clue to his meaning. Of course, Christ does have a claim on each believer's body. However, Paul's point is that because we are in solidarity with Christ and one another, what individuals do with their bodies affects others, which means that in the apostle's mind the bigger picture has to do with the corporate body of Christ.

Paul's observation that the body is meant for the Lord and the Lord for the body, which is puzzling if read primarily through an individualistic lens, makes perfect sense when read corporately. As Paul explains to the Ephesians in 5:31-33, when scripture refers to the two becoming one flesh, this is not only speaking of the marriage between a man and woman, but also about the relationship between

Christ and the church. To be clear, in this context becoming "one flesh" is not referring to sexual intimacy; rather it describes the new alliance that is formed when a man leaves his father and mother and holds fast to his wife. They are united in one covenant relationship, one body, forming one unit.

Similarly, Paul is talking about the marriage covenant that exists between Christ and his people. Just as husbands are to love and care for their wives as they would their own bodies, Christ, our husband and head of the church, feeds and cares for his body, his bride. In return, the church is to respect and love him with her entire being. In this way, the body of Christ is meant for the Lord and the Lord for the body of Christ. This does not negate application to the individual—what each person does with his or her body matters—but simply recovers the proper emphasis on the larger corporate body and the individual's relationship to it.

Seen in this light, one scholar observes there is a strong possibility that in verse 18 when Paul states, "all other sins a person commits are outside the body, but whoever sins sexually, sins against their own body," the word *body (soma)* refers primarily to the body of Christ rather than the body of the offending person.[13] He argues that in this context, sinning against the body is sinning against the body of Christ, the church.[14]

Some object to this view, saying the Corinthians would not have understood it this way since Paul did not explain the concept of the corporate body of Christ until later in chapters 12–14. Upon closer examination, however, this argument does not hold up. The book of Acts shows that Paul was aware of the corporate solidarity that existed between Christ and his body from the outset of his ministry. In his initial encounter with Christ on the road to Damascus, Jesus asked Paul, "Why do you persecute me?"[15] In saying this, Jesus made it clear that in persecuting Christians, Paul was persecuting him. Surely, it cannot be maintained that a Hebrew as astute as Paul and who already had a collectivist mindset gave no further thought to the concept of solidarity between Christ and his people until it emerged in I Corinthians 12–14.

Also, Paul started speaking in corporate terms from the very beginning of 1 Corinthians. This is seen in his greeting to the church where he refers to the solidarity of believers everywhere and his plea for maintaining unity in chapter 1.[16] It also comes through in his reference to the church as being a singular field or building and God's temple in chapter 3, and his consistent use of the plural you, meaning the corporate "you all."[17] Furthermore, in 6:15 Paul refers to the Corinthians as being *members (limbs and organs)* of Christ. In this verse, he is using the term in the same way that he does in Romans 6 and 7, and 1 Corinthians 12—he is describing individuals who are members of the corporate body of Christ rather than the individual's body parts.

It is hard to believe that Paul would have introduced a major new concept in chapter 6 with no explanation when one of his main reasons for writing these verses was to warn the Corinthians that ongoing immorality could sever them from Christ's body! Paul's disciplined logic and giftedness as a communicator are widely acclaimed. To accept that he built one of his main arguments around a concept that was not commonly understood is incompatible with his reputation.

Paul uses corporate body language before chapter 12 in other places as well. In 10:17 Paul writes, "Because there is one loaf, we, who are many, are *one body*, for we all partake of one loaf." The use of *soma* (body) here is undeniably referring to the church, not the individual. And in 11:27-34, he gives instructions about corporate communion and clearly expects his readers to understand his meaning.

Another argument that supports claims the Corinthians had a corporate understanding of the body is that the bride/bridegroom analogy, from which some believe the concept derived, had already existed within Judaism for centuries. As we saw previously, the idea that Israel was God's wife—a single, corporate body—can be traced back to the prophets in the eighth century before Christ. When Paul wrote 2 Corinthians, he fully expected them to understand that he had a similar corporate concept in mind when he said, "I am jealous for you with a godly jealousy. I promised you to one husband, to Christ, so that I might present you as *a pure virgin* to him."[18] This is evident by the fact that he offers no further explanation when he makes the statement. Paraphrased in light of the grammar he uses, Paul is saying, "I am jealous over *you all individually* with a godly jealousy. I have promised *you all* to one husband, to Christ, so that I may present *you as a people* to be his virgin bride (singular)." Taken all together, evidence points to the fact that the Corinthians had a corporate view of the body of Christ very early on.

Before going on, let me say there is an aspect of Paul's statement "whoever sins sexually, sins against their own body" that *does* apply to the individual. Paul is disquieted about the man sleeping with his father's wife and it is obviously true that the offender is sinning against his own body by using it in an unholy manner. But at the same time, there is a wider framework than the individual that should not be missed. Paul's concern is not only for the man's body, but also for the greater body of Christ, of which the offender is a part. I will speak more about this later.

## Corporate Marriage Theme

Another reason for believing 1 Corinthians 6:12-20 has a corporate setting is that it's full of marital imagery, which, as we saw in our discussion of Romans 7:1-6, is about the church rather than the individual. We have already identified the corporate, New Exodus theme that runs throughout the New Testament. This was reflected in Paul's remark about betrothing the Corinthians to Christ, their one husband, in 2 Corinthians. In the text we are considering, Paul uses language that echoes these same Hebraic motifs— "the Lord for the body . . . one flesh . . . he who unites himself to the Lord." The apostle is not appealing to readers who are owned as slaves in these verses, but to people who are related at a much deeper level, as those who belong to a marriage partner.

This marital theme becomes even more apparent if we see Paul's reference to the temple in context of Hebraic thought. First, I want to argue that in 6:19 when Paul says, "do you not know that your bodies are temples of the Holy Spirit who is in you," *body* and *temple* are both corporate terms.[19] Traditionally, the apostle's statement is taken to mean the individual believer's body is the dwelling place of the Holy Spirit. The 2011 NIV contributes to this perception by translating verse 19 to read, "your *bodies* (plural) are *temples* (plural) of the Holy Spirit." This creates the impression that Paul is saying each believer's body is a self-contained "mini-temple," which implies there are multiple temples instead of one.

The problem with this individualistic interpretation is that in looking more closely at the grammar, *your* is plural whereas *soma (body)* is singular. Paul also couples *the*, a definite article, with *temple*, a singular noun. Paraphrasing with these grammatical considerations in mind, I suggest a more accurate translation of verse 19 goes like this— "this greater body (of Christ) that *you all* are a member of is *the* temple

168

of the Holy Spirit." In support of this reading, the traditional, individualistic interpretation of *temple* is also contrary to the way New Testament writers typically use the term. Elsewhere, it is *always* applied to the church, never to the individual.[20] This comes through loud and clear in 1 Peter 2:5, where the apostle portrays each believer as a single living stone that is being built together with others to form a spiritual house (singular). The only occasion *temple* is used in connection with the individual is when it refers to Christ's own body.[21]

Here is how this relates to the corporate marital theme. All throughout the New Testament, the temple, which is the place of worship, is coupled with a wedding or bride figure. This link suggests the church's true worship will be attained when her marriage relationship is fully realized at the wedding supper of the Lamb.[22] The idea that a connection between the temple and bride exists in Paul's mind is supported by the fact that the Hebrew word for bride is *kallah*, meaning "the complete" or "perfect one." It is likely this concept is behind what Paul says in 1 Corinthians 13:

> For we know in part and we prophesy in part, but when *completeness* comes, what is in part disappears. When I was a child, I talked like a child, I thought like a child, I reasoned like a child. When I became a man, I put the ways of childhood behind me. For now we see only a reflection as in a mirror; then *we shall see face to face*. Now I *know in part*; then I shall *know fully*, even as I am *fully known*.[23]

In scripture, the term *know* is repeatedly used in connection with the marriage relationship. In context of the surrounding chapters, the theme of these verses in 1 Corinthians 13, which seem to speak of *perfection* or *completion* associated with the marriage relationship, is worship. In the old covenant system, the temple is where worship took place.[24] It is the same in the New Testament. However, as we have seen, in the new covenant era, the temple is not a literal building, but the body of Christ.

The connection between the bride, the temple, and worship is clearly visible in 2 Corinthians. Observing that the new covenant community is the living temple of God, the apostle Paul draws on marital imagery when he tells them not to be yoked together with unbelievers. In explaining why, he asks what does wickedness and righteousness, light and darkness, Christ and Belial (Satan), the believer and unbeliever, the temple of God and idols have in common? Given their opposing natures, how can they be in harmony?[25] Paul, speaking in solidarity with the Corinthians, says that in light of God's promises to live in the midst of his people, his living temple, it is vital to "purify ourselves from everything that contaminates body and spirit, perfecting holiness out of reverence for God."[26]

The passages immediately before and after 1 Corinthians 6:12-20 also attest to the corporate, marital context of these verses. Beginning in 5:2, Paul is dealing with sexual immorality, but not all kinds. He is specifically addressing the case of incest in which a member of the body of Christ is uniting himself with a woman who is not a member of Christ's body. If the corporate understanding of the body of Sin I have presented is correct, then in Paul's framework the illicit relationship does not just affect the man, but the physical union threatens to corrupt the entire church, a thought that horrifies the apostle. Again, this is marital imagery. Then, right after Paul says we have been "bought at a price" in 6:20, he goes on to deal with pastoral problems related to marriage in chapter 7. As we shall see, given the marital backdrop of the text and the adjoining context, to introduce an individualistic slave purchase concept here is to insert something that is not directly relevant. Paul's admonitions address issues of marriage, not slavery.

## The Old Testament Connection

What makes the case for a corporate, covenantal backdrop even stronger are the Old Testament themes that undergird the entire letter. Going back to 1 Corinthians 5:7, Christ's death is clearly interpreted as a paschal (Passover) sacrifice parallel to the one God provided for the nation of Israel. Furthermore, Paul's remark to the Corinthians in chapter 6 that "you were washed, you were sanctified, you were justified in the name of the Lord Jesus Christ" is seen by many to be baptism language that applies to the church as a whole rather than individual believers.[27] If so, then it anticipates Paul's reference to Israel's corporate "baptism into Moses" in chapter 10.[28] (I'll speak more about corporate baptism in the next chapter.) Again, this Passover and corporate baptism imagery connects back to the First Exodus, which culminated in the marriage of Yahweh and his people on Mt. Sinai.

The Old Testament marital language and imagery continues in 1 Corinthians 7 where, similar to Ephesians 5, Paul uses the marriage relationship to make a point about Christ and the church. He had just taught that the body is for the Lord, and the Lord for the body," and also that the body, both corporately and individually, belongs to Christ, the church's husband. Reflecting these same principles, in chapter 7 the apostle tells husbands and wives their bodies do not belong to themselves alone, but to one another.[29] And the language of unbelieving spouses and children being sanctified makes no sense outside of the covenantal marriage imagery of the Old Testament.[30] In the old covenant system, the Jews were to welcome uncircumcised Gentiles who wanted to live among them as long as they respected their laws. These Gentiles experienced the benefits of living within the household of faith even though they were not of it. Likewise, unsaved spouses and the children of believers whose hearts have not yet been circumcised in Christ benefit from being with the community of faith through their connection with a believing marriage partner or parents who are in a covenant relationship with Christ.

Paul goes on from this point to emphasize the consequences of communal infidelity to God that coincide with Israel's experiences. In chapter 8, he addresses the serious issue of eating food sacrificed to idols, the very thing Israel did in Exodus 32 when she engaged in harlotry by worshipping idols and came under the covenant curse for her unfaithfulness.[31] Paul continues this theme in I Corinthians 10 and 11 where he warns the community about what happened when the nation of Israel indulged in collective immorality—many experienced death.[32]

Chapters 12–14 are about worship that is connected to the temple and the bride, corporate themes drawn from the Old Testament. 1 Corinthians 15, the passage about the resurrection of the body leading to the marriage supper of the Lamb, also has a corporate context that ties into the Old Testament. Suggestions are this links back to Ezekiel 37 and the prophecy of the dry bones, which foretold the time when Israel would be resurrected as a nation.

Clearly, the new covenant community is at the heart of Paul's discussion, which is why it is only natural for him to express his concern for the faltering people of God at Corinth against the backdrop of Israel's history. The texts he gathers from the Old Testament follow the story of Israel's redemption and then her subsequent fall from grace. Paul's focus in 6:12-20, therefore, is much wider than an individual's behavior, important as that may be. Paul's greater concern is how this behavior—the man sleeping with his father's wife and other forms of unaddressed immorality—putrefies the body of Christ and brings judgment into the new covenant community. Again, all of this points to Paul's consistency in relying on Hebraic thought.[33]

**THE BRIDE PRICE¶** The question now is, what are we to make of Paul's statement to the Corinthians that "you have been bought at a price?" It certainly sounds like the apostle had a Greek slavery model in mind as he was writing! This brings us to a difficult subject. The whole idea of *payment* or *ransom*—what is often referred to as "purchase language"—is a concept that theologians have wrestled with for centuries. Why did Jesus have to pay a price to purchase us and to whom was the payment made? God? Satan? Someone or something else? Scripture does not really spell it out.

One view is Christ's death was a ransom paid to God to satisfy his holiness that had been offended by sin. As this line of thinking goes, since the penalty or price for sinning against him is death, we owed God a debt that we could not repay, so, in his love, God sent Christ to pay it on our behalf. A number of scholars insist, however, that no business transaction took place between Jesus and the Father as that would mean God's own people were in bondage to him in the same way scripture says we were captive to Sin. The idea that Jesus had to pay Satan is equally controversial. How is it possible for God to owe anything to Satan, who is an outlaw? Another view is that the price was not paid to God or Satan but was a matter of satisfying justice. Others contend that Paul's statement in 6:20 does not necessarily require us to speculate about *to* whom a price might be paid; rather, the emphasis is on the costly act of the new owner to whom we now contractually belong.[34]

A slave model raises other questions. Did Jesus redeem us from captivity to sin/Sin, so we could become his beloved slaves? While some teach this is indeed the case, as I showed earlier, this masks the key concept that together, the Messiah-King and his people are called to be God's willing Servant (singular) to the nations.[35] By no stretch of the imagination could Jesus, the Messiah with whom the church is united as one, be seen as God's slave. Such slave imagery is also at odds with the theme of the divine marriage—nowhere in scripture is a wife called to be her husband's slave.

In spite of these numerous difficulties with purchase language, one scholar admonishes that, nevertheless, care must be taken to make sure the "objective character of what is . . . called 'to redeem,' 'ransom,' etc., is not compromised."[36]

Many have favored the slavery model for interpreting purchase language because no alternative has been apparent. However, there is a better explanation that is far more consistent with the theme of the divine marriage that runs throughout scripture—the ancient practice of paying a bride price to obtain a wife. This maintains the biblical integrity of the purchase concept while resolving inherent difficulties with the slave model. Additionally, the "objective character" of ransom is perfectly preserved when the concept of annulling the covenant with Sin/Satan through Christ's representative death is incorporated into our view of redemption. In considering this perspective, I want to look at Jewish wedding customs first, and then compare this with certain practices for freeing slaves that some scholars suggest is the backdrop for Paul's purchase language. This will help us weigh which model makes the best sense of our text.

## Ancient Marriage

We have already seen how the old and new covenants were essentially corporate marriage contracts between God and his people. Now we want to look at how marriages were established in the Hebraic tradition, so we can see how the practice of paying a bride price functions. The ancient Jewish approach to marriage is different than the modern wedding ceremonies we are familiar with in the West. For one thing, marriages were often arranged and took place in two different stages. First came the betrothal when the couple entered into a legally binding contract. However, the bride and groom continued to live apart until the second stage when a public celebration took place and the marriage was consummated, sometimes a year or more (in some cases, many years) after they were betrothed.[37]

In the ancient tradition, it was common for the father of the groom to select a bride for his son. Once the father or his representative found someone he believed was a suitable partner and the woman's father agreed, many times with the bride's consent, discussions began about the specifics of the contract.[38] Interestingly, the reason the couple's fathers conducted the negotiations is because in ancient days, "marriage was not an agreement between two individuals, but between two families."[39] In its earliest form, a verbal agreement was sufficient for sealing the arrangement, but as the tradition evolved, a formal legal contract detailing with the provisions and conditions of the marriage was drawn up and signed. The groom promised to support his wife and give himself for her. He also paid a negotiated price to the father as part of the betrothal process, and the wife and her family agreed to provide a dowry.[40]

We need to be careful not to read our modern sensibilities back into scripture. Although contemporary Westerners may see this process as treating women like commodities to be bought and sold, actually the bride price, which was viewed as a gift to the bride's family, was ultimately meant to benefit the woman herself. It changed the woman's status by freeing her from being a dependent in her parent's household, and in some instances, it served as insurance if her husband divorced her. While the practice may have been abused at times, in the Hebraic culture, the original intent behind the bride price was honorable and meant to reflect the woman's value.

Abraham's effort to find a wife for Isaac is an example of how bride purchase was practiced in ancient times. When Abraham's chief servant, who represented him in the betrothal process, found Rebekah and arranged the marriage with her father, he lavished costly gifts on her as well as her family. This gave Rebekah her own wealth.[41] Another example is when Jacob, Isaac's son, worked for Rachel's father for seven years so that she could become his bride. In this case, the bride price was paid in the form of labor rather than money.[42]

## Paying the Price

Several indicators suggest Paul drew on this model when using purchase language. Just as context and theological associations helped us settle the meaning of *doulos* (servant vs. slave), the idea of bride purchase can also be examined in the same way. In his writings, Paul clearly makes a connection between marriage and the price Christ paid to redeem his people. In his classic description of the marriage relationship, Paul says to the Ephesians,

> Wives, submit yourselves to your own husbands as you do to the Lord. For the husband is the head of the wife as Christ is the head of the church, his body, of which he is the Savior. Now as the church submits to Christ, so also wives should submit to their husbands in everything.

175

Husbands, love your wives, just as Christ loved the church and gave himself up for her to make her holy, cleansing her by the washing with water through the word, and to present her to himself as a radiant church, without stain or wrinkle or any other blemish, but holy and blameless.[43]

This reflects the Jewish betrothal process in which the groom promises to give himself for his bride. The practice of bride purchase is further reinforced in Paul's address to the Ephesian elders in the book of Acts. In exhorting them to be faithful to their calling, he said, "Be shepherds *of the church* of God which *he bought with his own blood.*"[44] This is in keeping with what he said to the Ephesians about Christ giving himself for his bride in the text above and is also similar to Paul's language in 1 Corinthians 6:20 in which Paul tells the Corinthians, "you were bought at a price." As we have seen, this text is also full of marital language. Based on these passages, it is clear that Jesus paid a high price—in this case, his life—to secure the church as his bride.

This context also shows that Paul's purchase language is corporate. For one thing, he uses the collective plural pronoun *you,* meaning *you all,* when he tells the Corinthians, "you were bought at a price." In scripture, the price is always paid for the church, not the lone individual. Furthermore, when Paul mentions the church's redemption early in the letter to the Ephesians, he is echoing the story of Israel's corporate redemption from Egypt.[45] Just as Israel became Yahweh's wife after he redeemed her from captivity, the church's destiny is to become Christ's bride.[46]

Others have noted this Old Testament framework for purchase language as well. According to one scholar, Paul's remark about being "bought at a price" echoes Jesus's statement that he came "to give his life a ransom for many."[47] Linking this to Israel's history, another scholar claims the idea of paying a "ransom for many" operates within the Passover scheme, a paradigm Paul uses in 1 Corinthians 5 to explain the significance of Christ's death.[48] If these observations are correct, and the New Exodus theme forms the context of 1 Corinthian 6, this connects the purchase language in 6:20 with the Passover, the very event when Yahweh redeemed Israel to be his bride!

This also sheds additional light on the phrase Paul uses in 6:16 that "The two shall become flesh." Not only does this reflect the matrimonial language used in Genesis, but it also relates to the corporate marital imagery that is a part of the Passover/First Exodus motif. In the same way Israel was regarded as a single, corporate body that entered into a covenant relationship with Yahweh, Paul sees the church as one body that is united to Christ, her husband.[49]

## The Problem with Slave Purchase

We have already seen a number of problems with using Greek slavery in general as a backdrop for interpreting key New Testament texts. Let's look more closely now at the long-accepted idea that Paul had a specific slave purchase practice known as sacral manumission in mind when he told the Corinthians they had been "bought at a price." Sacral manumission is not a familiar concept to us today, but in the ancient Near East it was a way that that slaves could buy their freedom. This practice allowed a slave to pay a sum of money into the treasury of the local temple and through this means the god of that temple "purchased" him. The slave was freed from his old master because, technically, he became the property of the temple god.

Based on this model, the harlot or prostitute mentioned in 1 Corinthians 6:15 has sometimes been interpreted in context of temple prostitution, a practice associated with some pagan religions. Those who hold this position suggest Paul is saying that since Christ bought the Corinthians with a price and they are now his property, they are not to sleep with the temple prostitutes that serve other gods.

The view that Paul had sacral manumission in mind when he used purchase language is problematic for several reasons. First, would Paul really have used such a morally confusing argument? For the liberated slave, the new ownership was merely a technical arrangement that had no transformative effect on his life. His moral status did not change—he had no more religious responsibilities than he did before he became the property of his new master—and he was no more devoted to the god who now owned him than one who was born free. In short, he continued to live as other men lived.

If Paul were indeed using sacral manumission as a backdrop for his argument, he would have ended up reinforcing the very concepts he was trying to remove. The Corinthians could have easily concluded that redemption meant belonging to Christ was only a technical formality and they were free to live as they pleased. This would *encourage* rather than discourage them to live in a way that had no relation to the price paid for them. By using this model, Paul would have endorsed the Corinthians lax attitude towards the sin in their midst when in reality, he was trying to correct it.

The second problem is that using such a model would have created theological confusion. For Paul, humans have absolutely no part in their redemption; it is entirely a gift given by a sovereign God. An illustration in which the whole drift is based on a person paying for one's own release to a pagan god is totally contrary to Paul's theology of redemption. The idea of sacral manumission takes the initiative completely out of God's hands and puts it entirely into the human sphere. This line of thought simply cannot be attributed to Paul. I can only say that if Paul were indeed using sacral manumission as his interpretive backdrop, then by his own arguments he would have done more serious damage to his gospel than any of his opponents were ever able to do! Others have noted additional problems with sacral manumission model as well.[50]

I want to make one more point while we are on this subject. In addition to the fact that sacral manumission falls short as a model for purchase language, there is another reason why, in all likelihood, Paul did not have temple prostitution in mind when he expressed concern about the Corinthians uniting themselves with a harlot. Contrary to the common assumption that it was widespread at that time, recent scholarly evidence shows that sacred prostitution was not practiced in Corinth in Paul's day, so it would have had no relevance to the Corinthians![51]

## Paying the Bride Price

Looking now at purchase language in context of the corporate, covenantal, New Exodus setting that I propose frames Paul's thinking, Christ gave his life to rescue (redeem, ransom) his bride from Sin/Satan. We saw why Jesus's death was necessary in our discussion of Romans 7. When Adam and Eve betrayed Yahweh and formed an adulterous alliance with Satan, all of humanity ended up becoming ensnared in a legally binding covenant with the evil one. It is not that Jesus had to pay Satan in order to redeem his bride; rather, it was necessary for Jesus to satisfy the requirement of the law, so his people could rightfully be released from the covenant with death that yoked us to our old husband.[52] As we saw, the only legal way out was the death of one of the parties. In a breathtaking plan, the Spirit took all those who looked to God in faith throughout the ages—past, present, and future— and united them with Christ as he hung on the cross on our behalf. Dying with him to the law that formerly bound us to Sin/Satan, and resurrected with Christ as his newly formed body, the new covenant community was free to marry another. In union with Christ, our new husband, the church now belongs to him.

Far from being regarded as slaves, the New Testament portrays the church as Jesus's beloved *bride* who willingly submits to her betrothed husband and who is treated with all the dignity and respect of a co-heir. I must say that not only does the Greek slavery model fail to do justice to the concept of the divine marriage that is woven throughout scripture from beginning to end, but it also presents a distorted picture of the church's relationship with Christ. Unfortunately, the traditional reading has controlled how the corporate marriage language in 1 Corinthians 6:12-20 is often interpreted. The individualistic Greek slavery model has masked the Hebraic concept of the bride price.

What also obscures the corporate marital imagery is that Paul's remark about becoming one flesh with a prostitute is often seen as either referring either to a temple prostitute, the woman with whom the professing believer was sleeping, or church members who were being intimate with prostitutes. The problem with these individualistic views is that at the end of the text, Paul uses temple imagery, which, as noted above, is always closely connected to the theme of the church in her role as the bride of Christ. This predominantly corporate picture suggests Paul may have something larger in mind than an individual person when he talks about the dangers of being united with a prostitute. This is what we want to consider next.

**THE MYSTERIOUS PROSTITUTE¶** We have come to an intriguing question—if not an individual person then who or what is the prostitute Paul refers to in 6:15-16? Are there any factors that, if introduced, would help us have a more complete picture of what was in Paul's mind? I believe so. The corporate context provides critical clues. First, I do not agree with those who believe the prostitute figure and the woman in the immoral relationship are one and the same for reasons I will explain in a moment. I do believe, however, that the issue Paul is addressing in chapter 6 stems from the case of incest in chapter 5. The apostle wants to show how the Corinthians' arrogant attitude towards this illicit affair and other forms of immorality in their midst endangers the entire congregation. Because of their solidarity with Christ and one another, when members of the body of Christ unite themselves with members of body of Sin (which, as we will see, is also called the Great Prostitute in Revelation 17) in this manner, it opens the door to Sin/Satan's corrupting influence. But what makes this type of sexual immorality especially troubling is that also brings God and Satan into a mutual covenant relationship through the actions of their subjects who represent them. This explains Paul's strong reaction to the situation.

One clue that Paul has a larger, corporate understanding of the Prostitute (Harlot) in mind comes from his use of the word *members*. As we saw earlier, Paul always uses this term to denote the relationship of the individual believer to the body of Christ.[53] He never uses it to describe an individual's body parts nor is it ever used to speak of a man being a member of a woman or vice versa. It is about corporate relatedness. In 1 Corinthians 6:15, Paul has a strong reaction to the idea of *members* of Christ being united with *members* of a harlot.[54] If Paul's language is to be allowed any reasonable degree of consistency, then I suggest the prostitute figure in the passage does not refer to an individual person, but to *a society* called the Harlot.[55] As one scholar points out in his comments on this text,

> If whole individual bodies belong to Christ as his limbs [members], then he [Jesus] must be more than an individual body. It is true that in the very same verse, Paul asks the indignant question: "Shall I then take away the limbs [members] of Christ and make them

180

limbs [members] of a harlot? Which, if we pressed the analogy would have to imply that a harlot too, had more than an individual body [but was] made up of a plurality of persons."[56]

Just as the phrase, *the body of Sin,* is used only once in scripture, the language in this passage that implies believers could potentially become members of a society known as the Harlot is also unique. But the idea behind it is surely not. Looking at New Testament examples, in 1 Corinthians 5 Paul told the Corinthians to discipline the man sleeping with his father's wife by delivering him over to Satan, the one who heads the body of Sin. In another text, Paul tells of how two false teachers, Hymenaeus and Alexander, were handed "over to Satan to be taught not to blaspheme."[57] In this situation, the two men were put outside of the body of Christ and into the community of unredeemed humanity that is under Satan's authority, which I argued in the last chapter is the body of Sin.

Similar imagery is found in Revelation 2 where Jesus warns the church at Thyatira what will happen to the immoral woman, Jezebel, who is operating in their midst, and those who partner with her in acts of harlotry.[58] He says, "So I will cast her on a bed of suffering, and I will make those who commit adultery with her suffer intensely, unless they repent of her ways." The specific behaviors referred to in this text are sexual immorality and also eating food sacrificed to idols, the very issues Paul addresses in 1 Corinthians 5 and 6, and also in 8 and 10. His meaning is clear—the false prophetess and her followers who continue to participate in these adulterous acts will be separated from the body of Christ. Set outside of the new covenant community and into the body of Sin, they will come under Satan's rule, which will lead to suffering.

As we can see, the concept of handing a renegade believer over to Satan is very clearly taught in both Paul's letters and the rest of the New Testament. The language of taking unrepentant members of the body Christ and making them members of a society known as the Harlot is nothing more than a different way of saying the same thing. This shows that in referring to the Prostitute in I Corinthians 6:15, Paul is not using some kind of imaginary analogy so that he can emphasize the scandal of an individual Christian having an incestuous relationship or sex with a literal prostitute, as some have suggested. Rather, in regard to the Prostitute, he is describing an alternative corporate spiritual reality and relating it to the discipline that those within the church community would experience if they continued to commit spiritual adultery—be it through sexual sin or other immoral behaviors—now that they belonged to Christ.

Identifying the Prostitute as a community explains how Paul can use the same language to describe the Harlot's relationship with her members that he uses to describe the relationship between Christ and members of his body. In 6:16-17, the apostle says, "Do you not know that he who unites himself with a prostitute is one with her in body? For it is said, 'The two will become one flesh.' But whoever is united with the Lord is one with him in Spirit." Paul uses similar imagery in Ephesians 5 where he writes, "for we are members of his [Christ's] body. 'For this reason a man will leave his father and mother and be united to his wife, and the two will become one flesh.' This is a profound mystery—but I am talking about Christ and the church."[59]

In both passages, we have parallel expressions that clearly relate to one another. Paul uses marital language to show that individuals have a covenantal relationship with either Christ or the Prostitute—they are members of one corporate body or another. Paul's answer to whether or not it is possible to be one with these two partners at the same time is a resounding NO! The choice is to be united with Christ *or* the Harlot (the body of Sin), as it is impossible to be a member of both communities.

## Corporate Prostitution

It is possible to reason, however, that Paul has a physical union in mind when he speaks of becoming one with a prostitute. Surely this is evidence, one might say, that he is warning the Corinthians to stay away from prostitutes. My answer is "Yes, it is a physical union, but no, it does not necessarily mean that Paul is thinking primarily about a literal prostitute."[60]

Paul's doctrine of the church is not just spiritual; it also incorporates the physical. As he says in I Corinthians 6:15, "Your *bodies* are members of Christ himself." As a Hebrew who has a holistic view of the human person, Paul cannot separate people's spirits from their bodies. For this reason, he sees the church as possessing a physical dimension. Without this, the relationship between Christ and his people would be incomplete. Paul is perfectly consistent in explaining that the final act of redemption is to transform the believer's body.[61] In this way, he never abandons the essentially Hebraic nature of his thinking. Paul assigns an importance to the physical body that a Greek mind could never accept. This is why he insists that what believers do with their bodies matters, especially in the area of sexual relations. Because of our union with Christ and one another, sexual sin not a private matter—as Paul points out, it is spiritually significant to the rest of the community when a member of the body of Christ engages in an unholy physical union with a member of the body of Sin.

Recovering a corporate view of the Prostitute provides greater insight into Paul's understanding of the term *porneia* used in verses 13 and 18. Variously interpreted as *sexual immorality, immorality,* or *fornication*, it is often used in reference to the sexual misconduct of an individual. In Hebraic thought, however, it also has a corporate application that encompasses, but also involves far more than sexual immorality. The Hebrew word for the Greek *porneia* is *zenut,* which means *fornication* or *harlotry.* Also translated as *prostitution, whoredom, adultery,* and *unfaithfulness,* it has to do with "a wide register of sexual behavior and relations outside the framework of legitimate marriage"; it conveys the idea of "cohabitation in forbidden degrees."[62] While certainly carrying sexual overtones, in its wider scope, *harlotry* or *fornication* is also used in the Old Testament to describe Israel's unfaithfulness in embracing the values, mindsets, and practices of other nations or gods that Yahweh said were off limits for his covenant people.

The prophets provide a vivid picture of corporate fornication in their description of Israel as a harlot who went whoring after other gods.[63] The Old Testament shows Israel's first step towards spiritual infidelity took place when she allowed members of the community to commit immorality with no correction. This lax approach opened the door for the Israelites to indulge in forbidden behaviors with their neighbors, eventually leading them to spiritually fornicate with the gods of surrounding nations.

God's perspective of Israel's harlotry is poignantly recorded in the book of Hosea. As a visible demonstration of how he saw his relationship with Israel, his adulterous wife, Yahweh told the prophet Hosea to marry a prostitute and have children with her. In obedience, Hosea married the harlot, Gomer, whom he came to love and with whom he had three children. Tragically, just as Israel was unfaithful to Yahweh, Gomer broke her vows to Hosea and returned to prostitution.

Nevertheless, like Yahweh, Hosea continued to love Gomer and tried to win her back.

Through the failure of his own marriage, Hosea grasped the depth of Israel's sinfulness in rejecting God's love in a profound and personal way. As a result of Gomer's unfaithfulness, the prophet came to understand Yahweh's deep grief over Israel, his faithless spouse. In embracing other gods, Israel was not simply breaking rules or a moral code; she was rejecting God and his love. Distressed over his bride's adultery with other nations and their gods, Yahweh lamented that "*a spirit of prostitution* leads them astray . . . Israel is corrupt . . . they give birth to illegitimate children."[64] One scholar notes that as Hosea empathized with Yahweh through his own "bitter agony," the prophet "reached deeper than any other prophet into the secrets of religion." He observes it was no "accident that the most common metaphor for apostasy in this book is fornication."[65] In fact, this is a key metaphor in the rest of the Old Testament as well.[66] As a result of her repeated infidelity, God eventually judged Israel by sending her into exile in Babylon, the land of the very gods she pursued.

No wonder Paul was determined to raise the issue of the man sleeping with his father's wife with the Corinthians! In the apostle's view, tolerating the incestuous affair that created an unholy bond between the body of Christ and the body of Sin, as well other worldly mentalities, values, and behaviors, had the potential to corrupt the entire congregation and bring it under the most serious of judgments.

## Sinning Against the Body

Seeing *porneia* in this larger corporate context provides insight into why Paul told the community to "flee from sexual immorality," stating, "all other sins a person commits are *outside the body*, but whoever sins sexually, *sins against their own body*." While sins like drunkenness, gluttony, and other addictions may have a negative impact on the individual's body, they do not have the same type of impact on the body of Christ or even the person that illicit sex does. Scripture regards sexual immorality as a more serious sin because it violates relationships, corrupts the sacred purposes for which sex was designed, and mars the image of God that is to be portrayed to the world through right relationships in the new covenant community. It also sometimes produces unwanted offspring who bear the long-term consequences.

Sexual sin is even more serious when the improper relationship is between a member of the body of Christ and a member of the body of Sin. The incestuous relationship Paul is concerned about is not casual but is ongoing and has created a new "marital state" in which the unbeliever has been brought into the benefits of being married to a believer when there is no interest in following Christ. This is not comparable to the type of mixed marriages about which Paul advises in chapter 7:13-14. In this passage, he speaks to believers who had married a fellow unbeliever before being converted. He instructs the Christian to stay in the marriage if their partner is willing, explaining that the unbelieving spouse and children will be "sanctified" as a result of the union.

In the case of the man who is sleeping with his father's wife, however, the relationship is expressly forbidden so the woman is not afforded the same type of sanctification that God provides for an unbelieving spouse in a legitimate marriage. Not only is the so-called believer's body dishonored as a result of being in an unholy union, but also the illicit relationship uniquely compromises the believing community—a committed member of the body of Christ is introducing a non-repentant sinner into a level of involvement with Christ's holy bride through this illegal "matrimonial" union. This is creating a bridgehead for the kingdom of darkness. In this way, sexual immorality is a sin against the body of Christ as well as the individual's body. All other sins are "outside the body" in that no other form of sin creates this type of intimate link with the body of Sin or gives Satan such open inroads into the new covenant community.

As a corrective to Western individualism, this shows that in the New Testament's corporate framework, what one member of the body of Christ does has the potential to have an impact on the entire new covenant community in a very real and practical way. Contrary to popular thought, the reality for believers is that our bodies are not our own to do with whatever we like—they belong to Christ.

## The Harlot's Identity

Is there anything else we can discover about this Harlot's identity? Paul describes her as a corporate entity that parallels the church, so I say "yes," there are definitely some other clues. I propose she is that same *porné* (Greek for *whore*) the apostle John speaks of in Revelation 17:5:

> This name written on her forehead was a mystery:
> BABYLON THE GREAT
> THE MOTHER OF PROSTITUTES
> AND OF THE ABOMINATIONS OF THE EARTH.

John describes her activities in verses:1-2: "Come, I will show you the punishment of the great prostitute, who sits by many waters. With her the kings of the earth committed adultery [fornication, harlotry], and the inhabitants of the earth were intoxicated with the wine of her adulteries."

The fact that John, like Paul, has two communities in mind is evident by the fact that after describing the judgment of the Prostitute in Revelation 18, he presents a picture of the true Bride, adorned for her husband. In chapter 19, John writes,

> Then I heard what sounded like a great multitude, like the roar of
> rushing waters, and like loud peals of thunder, shouting:
> Hallelujah!
> For our Lord God Almighty reigns
> Let us rejoice and be glad
> And give him glory!
> For the wedding of the Lamb has come
> And his Bride has made herself ready.[67]

Will scholarship support the perspective that the Prostitute in 1 Corinthians 6 and the great Prostitute in Revelation 17 are one and the same? We do not have space to discuss the following theories in detail, but when it comes to identifying the Harlot described in Revelation, five distinct scholarly interpretations have gained traction over time:

- The historic interpretation equates Babylon, the great Mother of Prostitutes, with the entire Roman Empire.

- A second view maintains that Babylon is the city of Rome specifically, but also sees a wider application to godless society.

- The third interpretation, supported by the Reformers and many of their followers, sees Babylon as representing the papacy which links religious and secular authority, as it did in the Middle Ages.

- The fourth is an updated presentation of the Reformers' view. It sees Babylon as the Roman Catholic Church, and many of the images used in relation to the Harlot are seen as describing her influence in the emergence of a new Europe that will become a second Holy Roman Empire.

- The fifth view sees the Harlot as the entire mass of unredeemed human society that has lived throughout the ages.[68]

I want to share one scholar's perspective regarding this last view as it supports what I have been saying about the Prostitute mentioned in I Corinthians 6. In explaining why he believes the Harlot is unredeemed human society, George Eldon Ladd says,

The great harlot [in Revelation 17] is seated upon many waters. This is a very important statement and provides us with one of the clues in the identification of the harlot. This description does not fit historical Rome, for while the Tiber flows through the city, Rome was not built on many waters. The phrase does describe the historical Babylon because the city was built upon a network of canals. Jeremiah spoke of Babylon as the city which dwells upon many waters (Jer. 5:13). John himself interprets the meaning of this phrase, 'The waters you saw, where the harlot is seated, are peoples and multitudes and nations and tongues' (v. 15). *Babylon became the personification of wickedness,* and John has taken over the Old Testament symbolism and used Babylon to represent *the final manifestation of the total history of godless nations.* The city had a historical manifestation in first-century Rome, but the full significance of the wicked city is eschatological [pertaining to the end times]. Rome could be seated on many waters in the sense that she drew her strength and sovereignty from her conquest of many nations, but it will be even more true of eschatological Babylon *who will seduce all the world to worship that which is not God.*[69]

In this view, Babylon represents the city of man that is in opposition to God; it symbolizes "the world." While I agree with Ladd, I have gone beyond this to see the Harlot as having a deeper significance for the history of salvation. I suggest that Babylon is another name for the body of Sin, with all the covenantal implications that we have been discussing. Whether realized or not, to be a member of this unholy city, this collective body of unredeemed humanity, is to be in a covenant relationship with Satan, the god of this world.

I am not alone in identifying the Harlot of Revelation 17 with the Prostitute of 1 Corinthians 6. Speaking of the text in Revelation, one scholar points out,

> The whole passage is evidently grounded upon the comparison, which is instituted between Christ and His Church (Eph. 5:23ff), and it is not improbable that, when the apostle said that he that is joined to a harlot is one body with her, he had in view the great whore that sits upon many waters. (Rev. 17:1).[70]

T. F. Torrance's remarks about Babylon support the connection as well. Although he identifies John's immediate representation of Babylon with the Roman Empire, he sees a wider application. In his view,

> Babylon is, in fact, an imitation Kingdom of God; based on the demonic trinity. Ostensibly Babylon is a world-wide civilization and culture, magnificent in her science and arts and commerce, but it is drugged with pride and intoxicated with its enormous success—Babylon is the worship of this world, the deification of economic power and worldly security. There is no doubt but that our world is in the grip of this wicked Babylon today—*Babylon represents human collectivity.* [71]

The fact that Paul and the writer of the Apocalypse shared this theme implies it was a view known to the church at large.[72] Otherwise, the Corinthians would have missed the significance of what Paul was saying in 1 Corinthians 6 regarding the corporate nature of the Prostitute. In 2 Corinthians, Paul confirms that they did indeed understand the backdrop of his thinking. In this letter, we find the same grand themes as found in Revelation 17 – 21. Parallel passages include:

- The call to come out from among them (2 Cor. 6:17; Rev. 18:4).

- The promise that God would be their God (2 Cor. 6:18, Rev 21:7).

- God's promise to live with them (2 Cor. 6:16; Rev. 21:3).

This shows Paul's familiarity with and use of the same terms found in Revelation and which I have argued are the correct keys for understanding the identity of the Prostitute in 1 Corinthians 6.

As depicted in Revelation, the universal Prostitute represents the full extent of humankind's alienation from God throughout the ages and its relationship to Sin/Satan as his willing servant. What this reveals is that unredeemed humanity is not merely Satan's victim, but is also complicit in participating in the deeds of darkness. Through this Prostitute, also known as the body of Sin, Satan works to seduce, deceive, corrupt, and destroy the body of Christ by enticing members to betray their covenant relationship with Jesus. For this reason, Paul wants the Corinthians to understand how important it is to pursue holiness and protect the purity of their community not only spiritually, but also in what they do with their bodies.[73] I wish we had time and space to discuss these matters in more depth here, but my main purpose at the moment is to establish the connection between the Prostitute in 1 Corinthians 6 and the great Harlot in Revelation 17, and show how, in turn, this sheds further light on the body of Sin mentioned in Romans 6:6.

## A Clearer Picture

In conclusion, I can only say that the traditional individualistic inter-pretation of I Corinthians 6:12-20 is contrary to all contextual and grammatical considerations. The whole passage takes on a different meaning once the Hebraic setting with its corporate, New Exodus framework is properly identified. Seen in this context, Paul is addressing the church and speaking of her corporate experience.

This perspective not only resolves a number of problems created by individualistic, Greek-influenced interpretations, but it is also consistent with the larger end times context of 1 Corinthians 6. At the beginning of the chapter, Paul talks to the Corinthians about their future role as judges in the new era Christ will usher in with his return. In addressing sexual sin, as well as other forms of *porneia*, his greater concern is not with how such moral lapses affect the individual alone, but with the implications they have for the holy community destined to rule and reign with Christ.

This interpretation fits with Ben Witherington's suggestion that the focus of salvation is on the congregation, not the individual, and that the model Paul is drawing on in 1 Corinthians 5 and 6 is Israel's historic experience of judgment.[74] Indeed, Paul warns that if they do not deal with this situation and other forms of immorality in their midst themselves, he will be forced to come and deliver the whole congregation over to Satan. This is clearly in keeping with the discipline the entire nation of Israel came under in the Old Testament.

Putting together all that we have discussed in this chapter and paying close attention to grammatical concerns, when read through a corporate, Hebraic lens, 1 Corinthians 6:15-20 can be paraphrased like this:

> Our sexual appetites must not govern the ways that we use our bodies but the Lord himself and our relationship with him. Just as God raised his Son from the dead so he will raise you, his redeemed community, up also. Do you not know that, together, you are the body of Christ; you are its members? Do you want me to exercise my apostolic authority and deliver you all over to live in the unredeemed community, the Harlot, under its rules and serving Satan? That's what would happen because it is written that "The two will become one flesh." But it was never intended to be like this; your union was not to be with Sin but with the Lord.

> Because this is your relationship as God's redeemed people, flee from all sexual impurity. If you don't, it is not just your own body that is damaged, it is also the wider body of which you are members, the Lord's body, his church. Have you not appreciated how important all of this is? This greater body (the body of Christ, his virgin bride) that you are a member of is the temple of the Holy Spirit. God bought you, as he did the Jews out of Egypt, to be his spotless bride and to reside amongst you. So, realize that you are not your own but that you belong to God, and live as this fact demands.

This reading supports the view we have been considering that in Romans 5-8, Paul is comparing two communities—the body of Christ and the body of Sin—and which I have argued above is also the great Harlot described in Revelation 17. This link suggests, as I have claimed earlier, that the New Exodus theme with its emphasis on the divine marriage was fundamental to the entire church's understanding. Therefore, it is not appropriate to claim there is not a New Testament theology but many theologies. This does not deny the fact that each author might bring his own insights to the theme, but their viewpoints were under the control of the Old Testament model and not the result of flights of fantasy.

All we have explored so far shows that the first-century believing community made a very clear distinction between the church and the world, a distinction that was not merely one of belief, but involved living daily within the reality of a covenant relationship with God and one another. It also supports the contention the epistles are best read through a corporate lens, and that New Testament theology is nothing less than an extension of Old Testament paschal theology.

To round out our discussion of Romans 5–8, let's go back to chapter 6 now and look at Paul's understanding of corporate baptism, the great historic event in which God's people were freed from the body of Sin and formed into the new man (new humanity), the body of Christ.

CHAPTER 7

# Birthing the New Man

Foundational to the three major religions of Islam, Judaism, and Christianity, the iconic story of Moses and the Exodus is woven into our cultural consciousness. Born into a Hebrew slave family, but later adopted by the Pharaoh's daughter, Moses had once been a prince in Egypt. However, after he struck down a soldier who was beating a Hebrew slave, the Pharaoh tried to kill him, so he fled into exile. Forty years later, Yahweh came to him and speaking from the midst of a burning bush, told Moses to return to Egypt. He had heard the Hebrew people's cry for freedom and wanted to work through Moses to deliver them from slavery. Insecure and hesitant, nevertheless, he did what Yahweh said—Moses went back into hostile territory and challenged Pharaoh, the ruler of the world, to free the Hebrews so they could worship the one true God.

Ten times, Moses delivered Yahweh's message to Pharaoh to let his people go and ten times Pharaoh refused. The last time, Moses warned Pharaoh that unless he complied, Yahweh would strike down the firstborn of the land, both humans and animals. To protect Israel's firstborn, Moses did just as God said and told them to smear the blood of a lamb across their doorposts. This would be a sign to the angel of death to pass over their houses. On the night of the Passover, all happened as Yahweh said it would; the firstborn of the Egyptians died, but the firstborn of the Hebrews was spared. After this, Pharaoh relented and let Yahweh's people go. Moses, their divinely-appointed leader, led them out of the land of slavery and death, across the waters of the Red Sea to Mount Sinai where Yahweh pledged to be their God and they promised to be faithful to him. Through the obedience of this one man, Moses, the nation of Israel was born.

As I have wanted to show, the Exodus is key when it comes to understanding the New Testament. In fact, I propose this is the story Paul is drawing on when he describes our baptism into Christ's death in Romans 6:1-4. Just as a new nation was birthed when collectively all Hebrews—those present and those who would be born in the future—were united with Moses, their representative leader, and died to the rule of Pharaoh, through Christ, God birthed a new people who died to the rule of Sin/Satan. United with Jesus in his death and raised with him into resurrection life, this Spirit-birthed community emerged with a brand-new identity. At that time, all who looked to God in faith for salvation—past, present, and those who would do so in future—became what scripture refers to in singular terms as the new man, the body of Christ, God's holy nation.

Although Romans 6:1-4 is most commonly seen as referring to the experience of the individual believer, I suggest a corporate interpretation is far more consistent with the arguments Paul makes in chapters 5–8. As we have seen, chapter 5 describes two corporate entities—humanity in Adam and humanity in Christ. I have made the case that the body of Sin mentioned in 6:6 is also corporate; it is a description of the unredeemed community with Sin/Satan as its head. If this perspective is accepted, this passage about baptism is sandwiched between two corporate texts, Romans 5:12-21 and Romans 6:6. Reading Romans 6:1-4 in this context strongly suggests Paul's reference to baptism has a corporate dimension as well. The implication is the entire church was baptized together and at the same time into Christ's death. How can this be? How can all believers in all times be baptized into Christ at the same moment? Is there evidence to support what I am saying or am I just dreaming up a new theory? And if true, what difference does it make? This is what we want to consider next.

**ONE BAPTISM¶** Baptism has divided the church for centuries. To this day, opinions differ as to the significance of baptism and what texts speak of what reality. One of the main reasons is because there are different types of baptisms mentioned in scripture, most of which do not involve water. They are often mixed up with one another and read into other texts. These include:

- Baptism into, unto, or of repentance;[1]

- Baptism by, in, of, or with the Holy Spirit;[2]

- Baptism in fire;[3]

- Baptism into suffering;[4]

- Baptism into Christ's death;[5]

- Baptism into Moses;[6]

- Baptism in water.[7]

Clearly, we have to be careful when interpreting a passage not to assume we have chosen the right concept of baptism until all others have been considered to see if any make better sense of the passage.

There are some areas of general agreement about baptism. Most maintain its closely associated with the death of Christ and some agree certain texts emphasize the believer's inclusion into Christ's baptism of suffering (i.e. the cross) rather than water baptism. Many acknowledge that Paul used the Jews' Exodus from Egypt as a type when explaining the significance of baptism. It is also commonly believed Romans 6:1-4, the passage we are considering, is a key part of Paul's argument that not only reflects the theology of the rest of the letter, but actually pulls the various themes together.

Beyond this broad consensus, however, there is a smorgasbord of interpretations for Romans 6:1-4. Some see it as referring to baptismal rebirth, the point when the believer's spirit is made alive to God; others as the reception of the Holy Spirit in water baptism; and still others as the Spirit's baptism of the believer into the body of Christ at conversion. And then there are those who believe it has to do with water baptism either as a symbol of rebirth, or as a witness to having shared with Christ in his death.

Those who teach that it is associated with water baptism are divided into two groups. One sees water baptism as the time when the believer receives the Spirit and the benefits of Christ's work on the cross. The other group believes the Spirit is given *before* water baptism. In this view, water baptism is not when regeneration occurs; it is mainly a means of confession. The problem with these interpretations, however, is that they require *water* to be introduced into this text in Romans when there is no mention of it in the entire letter!

While interpretations of Romans 6:1-4 differ, what they all have in common is the belief that baptism has to do with to the experience of the *individual believer*. There is an alternative, however, that can help clarify the meaning of this classic text. It is a *corporate* view of baptism based on the type Paul uses in I Corinthians 10, where he says that all of Israel was "baptized into Moses in the cloud and in the sea"—an event in which the whole community shared at the same decisive moment.[8] It is already widely recognized that Romans 5:12-21, the passage on salvation that contrasts humankind in Adam and humankind Christ, has a corporate setting. I am merely advocating that we maintain this same perspective as we move into Romans 6.

When seen in context of Paul's corporate theology, I suggest the baptism Paul discusses in Romans 6:1-4 is not about water baptism, although that bears witness to the corporate baptism I believe he is describing. Nor is it about the individual being united with Christ at conversion. Rather, I propose it refers to a one-time major historic event that happened at the time of Christ's death, long before the work of regeneration in the individual takes place. As Paul sees it, this event is the ground upon which the Spirit does his work both in the church and in the individual believer.

I will explain more about this as we look at other texts. Let me say now these initial observations point again to the New Exodus narrative, which culminates in the divine marriage, as a framework for understanding Paul's view of baptism. There is no doubt the apostle sees Christ's death (into which all believers were baptized) in context of the Passover event with all of its connections to the original Exodus. In the Old Testament, the First Exodus was seen as the grand occasion when the glory and power of Yahweh were publicly displayed. Israel's baptism into Moses was key to this collective experience as it was through this event that God established Moses as the representative of his people. Following God's instructions, Moses led the Hebrews through the waters of the Red Sea and on to the other side where they entered into a covenant relationship with Yahweh and became a new people.

As we have seen, the Second Exodus from Babylon also plays a role in the New Exodus framework. The Second Exodus was the time God raised Israel, referred to in the Old Testament as the son of God, from the dead and brought the revived nation back from exile to himself to renew their covenant relationship. This too was a corporate event.[9] Together, these associations naturally link the two Exodus events to the death and resurrection of Jesus, the Son of God, a time when the power and glory of God would be supremely displayed in the midst of his people. This is also when God's promise to establish a new covenant relationship with his people would be fulfilled. Let's hold this idea of corporate baptism and resurrection in mind as we move on to explore key texts about baptism.

## Buried Alive

When I was studying Romans 5–8 as a young pastor, one of the problems I struggled with had to do with Romans 6:3-4, which says

> Or don't you know that all of us who were baptized into Christ Jesus were baptized into his death. We were therefore *buried with him through baptism into death* in order that, just as Christ was raised from the dead through the glory of the Father, we too may live a new life.

I discovered others were perplexed by these verses as well. If water baptism is a symbol of burial as some traditional interpretations teach and this text is about water baptism, then Paul is essentially saying that believers are buried with Christ *in order to produce death*. In other words, he is teaching that we are buried alive with Christ. This is an abhorrent picture! What I came to see, however, is that in Paul's view, believers were first united with Christ through baptism *while he was dying on the cross* and after we died with him, *then* we were then buried with him. In this way, the baptism into his death is quite distinct from his burial.

As you can see, there is no mention of water in this text; this reference to baptism is about sharing in Christ's death on the cross, which, historically, happened at one particular moment in time. This is when Jesus was established as the new covenant community's representative head. Just as Israel came before God on Mount Sinai through their representative Moses, so now Christians, who have been united with Christ in his death, resurrection, and ascension, appear in God's presence in and with Jesus.

I noticed something else about Paul's argument in 6:1-4 that is not usually identified. The language he uses is not about the individual—he is saying, "*we, together*, were baptized"—and his word choice in verse 4 implies that he was talking about a one-time past event that involved many. He also speaks of "*the* baptism into *the* death," which points to a singular moment. Maybe this grammatical evidence could be dismissed if it was presented on its own, but when seen in context of other passages on baptism, then Paul's choice of language carries serious weight.

## Parallel Baptisms

A crucial parallel text for understanding the concept of corporate baptism in Romans 6 is 1 Corinthians. There are several reasons for saying this. First, the two letters were written at approximately the same time. Second, the contexts of the letters are similar. Both have a section on the church as the pilgrim community; both refer to Jesus as the Passover offering; and both have a section dealing with baptism that is closely linked to becoming sons of God. Additionally, in the first part of 1 Corinthians 10, Paul writes about the church having been baptized into Christ.[10] In this passage, he warns his readers not to think they are safe because of their baptism. He points out the Jews also experienced baptism—in this case, a baptism into Moses—yet they came under judgment in the wilderness because of their unfaithfulness.

The phrase "baptized into Moses" is important for understanding at least one aspect of Paul's teaching on baptism. This baptism into Moses was nothing like the water baptism the early church practiced when individual converts confessed their faith in the name of the Father, Son, and Holy Spirit. As mentioned above, even though the Jews may not have been aware of it at the time, their baptism into Moses occurred when all of the children of Israel left Egypt and crossed the Red Sea with him. This was not a baptism into water; rather, it was the creation of a community with Moses as its divinely appointed representative. At that time, the Jewish people were brought into a covenant relationship with Moses—they were "baptized *into* or *unto* him"—and it was for the purpose of uniting Moses and Israel. From that point forward, all of God's dealings with Israel would be done through Moses as their mediator.

We can get some idea of the Jewish understanding of this momentous event when we read about how the Passover meal is celebrated. The eldest son asks the father: "What does this ceremony mean?"[11] Each generation of fathers then teaches the family, saying: "I do this because of what the Lord did *for me* when *I* came out of Egypt."[12] As the Jews see it, the entire nation was present as Israel came out of bondage, and not just those that had been enslaved in Egypt. Every succeeding generation, and each individual within those generations, saw themselves as actually involved in that act of salvation and could, therefore, speak of it as *their* personal baptism into Moses. Such is the power of solidarity the Jewish people had with Moses, their chief representative before God.

We have observed that in Paul's worldview there are two great solidarities governing humankind that are not based on class, nationality, or gender. Rather, they concern whether a person is in Adam or in Christ. Since all are in Adam (unredeemed humanity) at birth and under Satan's headship, how is solidarity with Christ, our representative head, established? Paul helps us understand this in 1 Corinthians 10 in his description of the solidarity that was established when the Jewish people were "baptized into Moses" as they left Egypt. The same type of corporate solidarity was created when the church was baptized into Christ's death.

This is where the New Exodus comes into play. In the passage about Jesus's transfiguration, Luke mentions Jesus's "coming departure."[13] A more accurate translation is "his coming *exodus*." Reflecting this same understanding, Paul says that when Jesus was leaving the realm of Sin and Death and setting out on his exodus from the world, just as the Israelites were "baptized into Moses," Jesus's people were united with him so that he became their representative head before God. From that time forward, God would deal with his people through Christ, our mediator. Just as the Jews could say, "this is what the Lord did for *me*" as a result of their corporate baptism into Moses during the Exodus, Christians can say, "this is what Christ did for *me*," because of our corporate baptism into his death. This is a clear picture of how the individual's experience is set within the larger context of the church's collective salvation.

When did this baptism into Christ take place? Paul explains—at the point of his death on the cross for "all of us who were baptized into Christ Jesus were baptized into his death."[14] Again, since Christ died at a particular moment in time and his death is not a reoccurring event, this suggests that collectively, all believers died with him at the same time. As we will see, the concept of a one-time corporate baptism is found throughout Paul's letters.

## Forming One Body

Those who propose an alternative interpretation to the one I'm suggesting often refer to I Corinthians 12:12-13, which says,

> Just as a body, though one, has many parts, but all its many parts form one body, so it is with Christ. For we were all *baptized by one Spirit so as to form one body*—whether Jews or Gentiles, slave or free—and we were all given the one Spirit to drink. Even so the body is not made up of one part but of many.

Based on these verses, some contend the baptism spoken of in Romans 6 is about the baptism of the Spirit, which as defined in their view, refers to the moment when the Spirit joins the individual believer to the body of Christ at conversion. For those who favor this individualistic perspective, the baptism Paul mentions in Romans has nothing to do with water; rather it is about the reality to which water baptism points—the individual's baptism by the Spirit into the body of Christ.[15]

While this understanding does not import water into the text, it is still making a choice from the range of meanings of baptism. How can we know if the right meaning has been chosen? To make sure, we need to look at the various options carefully and also to keep in mind that Old Testament theology is the foundation of all Paul is saying. Working within this framework will allow us to discover the hidden treasures that have been obscured by false methodologies.

In weighing how best to interpret these verses in 1 Corinthians 12, it is necessary to carefully consider Paul's use of language. I assure you this is not a matter of theological nitpicking, but his word choice has an important bearing on our discussion. Just as Paul made some unusual language choices in Romans 6:1-4 when he used the plural form of *you (we)* when speaking of our one-time baptism into Christ's death, another grammatical oddity occurs in 1 Corinthians 12:13 where he speaks of being baptized by one Spirit "to form one body." Although this is the most natural interpretation of the Greek, in most other versions besides the NIV it is translated as *"into* one body." This is understandable. If, as most believe, the phrase refers to incorporating individuals into a group one at a time, to speak of *forming* one body would mean the church would never exist or be complete until the last member had been joined to the body of Christ! However, the fact is that the church not only exists now but had already been formed in Paul's day.[16]

On the other hand, the meaning, "to form one body," makes perfect sense when seen in context of Paul's corporate Old Testament theology. The statement in 12:13 is the outcome of the running argument Paul began in chapter 10 in which he notes parallels between the Corinthian church and the old covenant community. Using Israel as an example, he warns the Corinthians about the dangers of unchecked sin and calls them as a congregation to live up to their high calling. In making this comparison, Paul starts by describing Israel's baptism into Moses when God formed the Hebrew nation and set it apart to serve him.

This corporate baptism, clearly at the forefront in I Corinthians 10, is about Israel, not as individuals, but as the designated covenant community. In that historic moment, the entire nation, including both present and future generations, received Moses as its representative head and was baptized into him all at the same time. God regarded Israel as a single entity. While this may be challenging for individualistic Westerners to understand, it is not at all difficult for people from collectivist cultures who strongly identify with their ancestors. As mentioned earlier, every succeeding generation of Jews and each individual within those generations saw themselves as being involved in the historic act of salvation when Moses led them out of Egypt.

In Paul's New Exodus framework, we can see how he views Israel and the church in terms of type and antitype. The corporate baptism of the Hebrews into Moses is the type, meaning a prophetic model that prefigures something fulfilled by a later reality. This foreshadows the antitype, or the parallel, which is the Spirit's baptism to form the one body in Christ as described in 12:13. When seen in the larger context of 1 Corinthians, I contend that in this verse Paul is not speaking of the individual being baptized by the Spirit into Christ's body at the moment of his or her conversion. Rather, he is referring to the historic, one-time corporate baptism that occurred when the Spirit took all the individuals who would look to God in faith throughout the ages, united them with Christ as he was dying, and through that union, formed the body of Christ.

Paul teaches that in the type, the Jews were baptized into Moses and drank water from the rock. Then he explains that in the antitype, the baptism is into Christ and the church partakes of the Spirit (represented by the water), who comes from Christ (represented by the smitten rock).[17] The difference between the type and the anti-type is that the baptism into Moses was limited to the Jewish community. The baptism into Christ, however, is part of Paul's great theme that everyone who believes in Jesus shares in the free grace of God on exactly the same grounds.

This helps us better understand the nature of Paul's arguments in 1 Corinthians 10–15—he is comparing the old order (type), with the new order (antitype) that has come into existence through Christ. In chapter 10, Paul describes the two patterns of salvation—one through Moses, one through Christ—and in chapters 11-14, he establishes what the Lord expects to see in the lives and the worship of his people. Clearly, the whole section is modeled closely on the Pentateuch, the first 5 books of the Bible. Just as the Exodus displayed God's power and established a community through whom the Gentiles could find God, so Paul tells the Corinthians that God's glory will shine through his church to the Gentiles as they continue to be led by the Spirit.[18]

## Baptized at the Same Moment

The idea of a one-time corporate baptism is further supported by Paul's arguments in Galatians 3:26-29, where he says:

> So, in Christ Jesus you are all children of God through faith, *for all of you who were baptized into Christ* have clothed yourselves with Christ. There is neither Jew nor Gentile, neither slave nor free, nor is there male and female, for you are all one in Christ Jesus. If you belong to Christ, then you are Abraham's seed, and heirs according to the promise.

Again, the grammar in 3:26 has a significance that is not generally recognized. The construction Paul uses suggests that he sees all of the Galatians being baptized at *exactly the same moment*. Scholars who maintain this text refers to water baptism of the individual have difficulty reconciling Paul's language. As one theologian stated,

> It would be possible to interpret the whole baptismal event as a unity in which the baptized are plunged . . . the imagery would attain its complete effect only under the presupposition that all were immersed unitedly into the baptismal water, but that is hardly possible.[19]

In other words, if this text were about water baptism, it would mean that all believing Galatians—even those who were converted *after* Paul left Galatia—were immersed into the baptismal water at precisely the same time. Obviously, this is impossible in human terms, which is why this scholar dismissed the idea of a corporate baptism. The problem with his view, however, is there is no mention of water here or anywhere else in the letter to the Galatians! This demonstrates how reading *water* into the text will prevent us from seeing Paul's intended meaning.

What we do find in this passage though is a reference to Christians being the children of Abraham—the true people of God. We also find echoes of the Exodus throughout the letter.[20] In other words, it seems this reference to the Galatians' baptism is similar to that found in other passages—it refers to the event when the Galatians were united with Christ in his death. Indeed, they were not the only ones who went through this baptism. They were in fellowship with the whole church of God in all generations, just as the baptism into Moses involved all generations of Israelites.

The significance of this passage in Galatians is that it clearly parallels Romans 6:1-4 and I Corinthians 12:13. In all three texts, the Spirit is the agent of baptism. The outcome of the union is the gift of the Holy Spirit and also sonship, which his presence establishes.[21] This corresponds to Israel's experience of becoming the Son of God, collectively, when the Hebrews were delivered from Egypt under Moses' leadership and the Spirit was given to guide them through their wanderings.[22] I will come back to the link between corporate baptism and sonship later, but for now, I want to explore another issue related to Paul's choice of language and the problem of reading individual-related baptism into key texts.

## When Was the Church Born?

Linguistic analysis has revealed that Paul deliberately used particular prepositions to convey the condition of the church at different stages of her development. When describing the historic experience of the church as she shares in Christ's death and resurrection, Paul uses the phrase "with (*syn*) Christ," but when he speaks of the life lived in fellowship with Christ he uses "in (*en*) Christ."[23]

To see why this distinction matters, if we look at the texts we've been discussing more closely, we can observe a pattern emerging. There is no mention of the community being united as one *before* the baptism into Christ's death occurred. Rather, the emphasis is on how the entire church was raised with Christ and seated in heavenly places with him *after* he died. The reason this is important is that if all believers were raised together, the corporate union we all now enjoy with Christ and one another must have happened sometime *before* the resurrection. This implies the death of Christ is the pivotal point when individual believers entered into a unified, corporate dimension of existence.

This leads to a critical question—at what point were we baptized into Christ's death and how exactly did this occur? What I mean by this is that if the individualistic views are correct, then believers are baptized into Christ's death and into his body *one at a time* and *all throughout church history* at the moment of their conversion, either by water or the Spirit or both depending on the view one holds. But if what I am saying is correct, then according to Paul, *all* believers of *all* ages were baptized into Christ's death in *a one-time historic experience* that took place when Christ died on the cross and *all* were raised with him *in the same moment*. Which view is true?

Looking at this more closely, scholars are aware of the need to emphasize that it is a historic fact that the entire church—past, present, and future—was raised and seated with Christ at the same time that he himself was raised and seated at the right hand of the Father. As portrayed by Paul, Christ and his church shared in that one-time exaltation.[24] The Greek makes it clear that there have not been countless millions of individual exaltations throughout the ages, but *only one* in which all have shared.

What is never asked, however, is how this exaltation of all believers could take place in one historic moment if individuals are only united with Christ *after* they are converted and baptized in whatever era they lived. To put it another way, in Paul's logic, Christ and his people were united long before the individual experiences conversion, water baptism, or receives the Spirit. Indeed, if all members of the church were raised with him at the same time, then the unity had to exist even before Christ left the tomb! But how could this be?

The problem is resolved once we realize the Old Testament type of the Israelites' baptism into Moses during the Exodus was the backdrop for Paul's teaching about baptism into Christ. According to Gamaliel the Second, the grandson of Paul's Jewish teacher, *all* Jews in *all* generations were present in "the coming out" of Egypt in the First Exodus and shared in the baptism that made Moses their representative leader.[25] As mentioned before, this is when Israel became the son of God, which is one way the nation is depicted in the Old Testament. Using another analogy, the nation was also betrothed as God's wife at Mount Sinai and given the Spirit to lead her through her wilderness journey, which shows a different side of Israel's relationship with Yahweh. We saw earlier that scripture itself teaches the Jews in all generations saw themselves as being part of this event.[26]

Now we can understand why Paul is so decisive in his use of the preposition *with (syn)* Christ when referring to our connection to Christ's death and resurrection. There is no unity of believers, either with each other or with Christ, without being united together *with* him through baptism. Paul has been careful to define this baptism in terms of its occasion—*it was the baptism into Christ's death*. Through the work of the Spirit and in this one historic moment, all believers of all times experienced this one baptism in which God's people were formed into the body of Christ. And then together, they died with him in order to be freed from the body of Sin headed by Satan.

Therefore, in answer to the question, "When did the church historically come into being?" I would say, "At the moment of Christ's death." It is acceptable to see the cross as the church's conception and the day of Pentecost as her birth, which is how most systematic theologians explain it. However, I would argue it is more accurate to say the church was formed when the Spirit baptized all members of the new covenant community into union with their Lord and Savior as he was dying. Once the union of all believers was established through this event, Paul was then free to use the preposition *en* (*in* or *into*) Christ as a term of ultimate reality. All believers were united *in* Christ so all experience a shared existence. This is the proper setting for the understanding our union with Christ. Even though our union with Christ is a familiar concept, when seen in this context it is far more glorious, far more significant than what most advocates of the doctrine have recognized.

**A BRIDE CLEAN AND READY.**¶Let's go on now to consider other key texts that further support the idea of a corporate baptism, one of which is Ephesians 5:25-27. In this text, Paul instructs husbands to love their wives,

> Just as Christ loved the church and gave himself up for her to make her holy, *cleansing her by the washing with water through the word,* and to present her to himself as a radiant church, without stain or wrinkle or any other blemish, but holy and blameless.

Clearly, Paul is not talking about individual water baptism here, but about the cleansing of the church as the bride of Christ. Cleansing is baptismal language and part of the vocabulary the Old Testament prophets used to describe the future New Exodus. The picture Paul paints in this text is based on a passage in Ezekiel 16:1-14 where the prophet recounts the history of Israel. Ezekiel reminds the nation that before God chose her for himself, she had no hope for future. She did not exist as a nation. She was like a baby who had been born without anyone to care for her—thrown by the side of the road and still covered in the blood of birth. Ezekiel said that Yahweh came by and, seeing her in her state of certain death, had mercy on her. He took her to himself and washed her as he spoke his Word of life to her.

This is the parallel that Paul draws in the letter to the Ephesians. The church is God's creation. She can boast in nothing other than the grace of God, for she was dead in trespasses and sins.[27] In the letter, Paul tells how this transformation has come about. Echoing the words Yahweh spoke to Israel: "I bathed you with water and washed the blood from you," Paul explains that Christ has cleansed his people from their defilement.[28] When the church died with Christ, she was made clean from sin's corruption and the stench of death and resurrected with him into new life. This may also reflect Ezekiel 37 where Israel in her exile is described as being a pile of dried bones.[29] Israel was brought to life when the word of the Lord was proclaimed to her. By implication, she was cleansed from the defilement of death to become the resurrected community. This is what the death of Jesus achieved for the people of God—we were freed from Sin/Satan, our former husband, and made clean and pure so that collectively, we could become his bride.

What ought to be clear is that Ezekiel and Paul are ultimately talking about the same thing. The prophet is describing Israel being taken as the bride of Yahweh and the apostle is describing the church being taken as the bride of Christ. The two washings are two baptisms, and both are corporate. Israel was baptized into Moses in the Exodus from Egypt and the church was baptized into Christ in his death and resurrection.

This helps shed light on the meaning of the one baptism mentioned in Ephesians 4:4-6. According to Paul,

> There is one body and one Spirit, just as you were called to one hope, when you were called; one Lord, one faith, *one baptism,* one God and Father of all, who is over all and through all and all.

It is obviously misplaced to import water baptism into such a statement that has to do with the great foundational realities of the church's existence. Water baptism of the individual simply does not have the same sort of significance as the eternal truths Paul lists in this passage. If, however, the "one baptism" is not a reference to water, but to the one great event in which the Spirit made the Lord one with his people through his vicarious atoning death, then it fits logically and naturally.

Not only is this in harmony with Ephesians 5:25 where the church is the bride and the cleansing clearly results from Christ's death, but it is also the same pattern we have observed in Romans 6:1 and 7:1. Both of these texts have to do with how the believing community died to the covenant relationship with Sin/Satan so that a new marriage could take place. Together, these passages in Ephesians and Romans, which are steeped in marital imagery, show the significance of Christ's death for his bride.

## Born Again

The concept of a corporate baptism also provides insight into another key passage—John 3:1-8, the much-quoted passage about being born again. In this text, Jesus explains to Nicodemus, a Pharisee and member of the Jewish ruling council, that "no one can see the kingdom of God unless he is born again . . . of water and the Spirit."[30] These verses are often seen as speaking primarily of the individual's need for spiritual regeneration and/or water baptism. I suggest, however, that before making individual application, this text first needs to be read in the same New Exodus framework that Paul drew on for his understanding of the church's corporate baptism in Romans 6, 1 Corinthians 10 and 12, Galatians 3, Ephesians, 5 and Colossians 2.

Looking at the surrounding context, the apostle John's reliance on New Exodus themes is evident. In chapter 1, he speaks of how Jesus tabernacled (dwelled, lived) among us, which is a reference to the First Exodus promise that God would dwell in the midst of his people.[31] Then he introduces Jesus as the Messiah, the king of the Jews, the nation's promised deliverer.[32] In chapter 2, a growing number of scholars appreciate that the wedding in Galilee points to Christ as the bridegroom, a theme which the Gospel writer develops in the second half of chapter 3.[33] Responding to concerns that Jesus was gaining a bigger following than him, John the Baptist identifies Jesus as the bridegroom, referring to himself as only a friend. Philip Long, in fact, makes a strong case that Jesus essentially sees his ministry as an on-going wedding celebration that signals the end of Israel's exile and the restoration of God's people to the position as the Lord's wife in the new covenant era.[34] Furthermore, others accept that this text in John 3 alludes to the vision of the valley of dried bones in Ezekiel 37, another New Exodus theme. Seen through this lens, in John 3:1-8 Jesus is speaking to a representative of Israel, Nicodemus, about the nation's need of a new exodus, a new birth, to bring her from death to life as Ezekiel prophesied.[35]

The mention of water in John 3:5 further strengthens the perspective that John is drawing on corporate, New Exodus themes. Some believe that like Ephesians 5, the reference to water is also linked to Ezekiel 16.[36] As we saw above, in this prophetic passage, God washed Israel with water and his Word when he rescued her from death and made the fledgling nation his beloved. What lends credibility to this view is that a few verses later in John 3:16, Jesus explains to Nicodemus that God sent his one and only Son to rescue his people from death and bring them into eternal life. This imagery ties into Passover, the event that led to the birth of Israel and the subsequent wedding between Yahweh and the nation. The connection between Passover and the divine marriage explains why, in the Jewish tradition, the Song of Solomon is always read out loud to the congregation during this time—it is a reminder of their status as Yahweh's wife and his love for them. The parallel, of course, is that Jesus died at Passover. This is when he took his people to himself, dying to free and cleanse the church from sin/Sin in order to make her the perfect bride.

Concerning the need to be born of the Spirit, Jesus's meaning becomes clearer when it is understood that John the Baptist's water baptism did not save nor was it associated with receiving the Spirit—it was simply for the purpose of calling the Jews to repent and be cleansed in preparation for the coming Messiah. While repentance is required, Jesus is saying to Nicodemus that Israel's birth into God's eternal kingdom will not happen through human effort. This is why water baptism is not enough. Rather, salvation will only come through a work of the Spirit like the one that occurred in the First Exodus when the Jews were freed from Pharaoh's rule and collectively baptized into Moses. In telling Nicodemus that anyone who wants to enter God's kingdom needs to be born again by water and the Spirit, Jesus is pointing ahead to the corporate baptism into his death and the birth of the new man that will be accomplished by the Spirit.

When reading this text, it is important to remember the Jews already had a corporate understanding of salvation. They were looking for a national, rather than a personal deliverer. Putting the pieces together, this evidence suggests Jesus's discussion with Nicodemus is about Israel's salvation. Viewed through this lens, John 3:1-8 is a parallel to 1 Corinthians 10:1-10 where Paul describes Israel's corporate baptism into Moses. Again, this is not to deny the importance of personal repentance and water baptism, but it must be emphasized that any understanding of these individual responses to God's offer for salvation needs to be set within this larger corporate framework.

## Sons of God

So far, we have seen that strong martial imagery is connected with corporate baptism. It is possible to argue, however, that while Paul's point of reference for the baptism described in Ephesians 5 is marriage, in other primary texts about baptism—Romans 6, 1 Corinthians 10 and Galatians 3—the focus is on sonship.[37] The reality is that all of three of these letters speak of marriage *and* sonship, the latter being another common concept relating to corporate baptism that runs through Paul's letters. This theme also ties these texts to the First Exodus, the event in which Israel became the son of God (singular). Let me briefly outline the connections:

- Romans 6, which I have argued has to do with corporate baptism and the birth of the Spirit-led community, is linked by the flow of Paul's arguments to 8:14, a text that highlights sonship. In this verse, Paul teaches, "those who are led by the Spirit of God are sons of God." This statement echoes the First Exodus in which Israel, the son of God, was led by the Spirit.[38]

- As previously discussed, in 1 Corinthians 10 Paul clearly uses the First Exodus when Israel became the son of God as the Old Testament antitype for the New Testament church. 1 Corinthians 6:1-11 supports this claim. In this passage, Paul urges the Corinthians to exercise their Messianic authority, meaning the authority they have presently received as sons of God and which they will also use when they judge the world at the end of the ages.

- In Galatians 3:26-27, Paul could not be any more explicit in drawing the connection between baptism and sonship. He says, "for you are all sons of God through faith in Christ Jesus. For all of you who were baptized into Christ have clothed yourselves with Christ."

- In addition, in each of these three letters, Paul claims the distinction between Jew and Gentile has ended.[39] Just as the baptism into Moses at the Exodus established a covenant community in which all Jews had equal standing, so the baptism into Christ creates a new community in which all distinctions are abolished and in which all believing Jews and Greeks, males and females, etc., are seen as sons of God who have an equal standing before God.

So how does sonship relate to the marriage imagery also associated with corporate baptism? As we have seen, in the Old Testament, Israel became the son of God when the Hebrews were baptized into Moses. At Mount Sinai, Israel also became the bride or wife of Yahweh, a description that points to the end times when the divine marriage will be fully realized. Following Paul's model of type/anti-type, it would seem that sonship applies to the church's existence in the present, and the role of wife is reserved for the time when the kingdom of God is finally consummated.

This is supported by Romans 8:23, which speaks of how "we ourselves, who have the first fruits of the Spirit, groan inwardly as we wait eagerly for our adoption to sonship." The adoption to sonship mentioned in this verse refers to the completion of the adoption process that ushers in the Kingdom of God. This is also when the betrothal period ends, and the church begins to fully relate to Christ as his wife. Corporate baptism connects the two themes. As with the nation of Israel, the church's status as son of God and Christ's betrothed were both established through the one-time event when together, the members of the new covenant community in all generations were baptized into Christ's death and assumed a new, corporate identity in him.

## Sons Now, Bride Later

If believers are already in union with Christ through corporate baptism, why then does scripture speak of the church as being betrothed to Christ in this age while describing the celebration of the divine marriage as an end times event? I can offer a couple of reasons.

First, if such a marital relationship were fully in place in this age, it would introduce concepts that could easily slide into the practices like the ones in the fertility religions in which sacred prostitution was seen as a means of worship. This type of practice is condemned in both the Old and New Testaments. While our bodies belong to the Lord, our relationship with him is not sexual—we are called to worship him in spirit and in truth and to maintain the purity of our bodies while we live on the earth, waiting for him to return for us.

The importance of seeing the celebration of our marriage to Christ as a future event was underscored to me recently when I heard Christian leaders teach and individuals testify about their personal experiences as the bride of Christ. Based on what they said, it was clear they had drifted into a form of Christian "mysticism" that is anything but Christian. This was evident by the fact that they saw themselves as being in a different sort of relationship with Christ than other "lesser Christians" who have not had these types of intimate experiences with Jesus. This view is simply heretical with a capital "H."

This is strong language, but I am using it deliberately because such a view runs completely counter to what Paul teaches in Colossians 2. In this text, Paul warns believers not to be deluded or "taken captive through hollow and deceptive philosophy" that depends on human tradition or the basic principles of the world rather than Christ. To help them discern the difference between true and false teachings, the apostle uses corporate terminology to remind the Colossians about who they are *together* as a result of being buried with Christ in baptism (into his death), forgiven, made alive to God, and raised with him. He explains that in Christ, "all the fullness of the Deity lives in bodily form" and that the *entire new covenant community* has been brought to fullness in him "who is the head over all power and authority." Joined to Christ, our head, from whom the *whole body* is nourished and "held together by its ligaments and sinews," the church grows "as God causes it to grow." While he acknowledges elsewhere that Christians may have different maturity levels, nevertheless, what Paul says in this text is true of all believers—*all* the members of the body of Christ have access to the Father through Christ and can enjoy his presence through the Holy Spirit.[40]

In light of these corporate realities, Paul tells the community at Colossae not to become excluded from this life by following any teacher who says we need to have additional experiences or jump through extra hoops in order to find favor with God. He warns about those who insist on practicing asceticism and worshipping angels, who go into detail about their visions, "puffed up with idle notions by their unspiritual mind." Observing that false teachers like this are *disconnected from the head*, he explains these are all elemental principles (spirits) of the world that believers have died to now that they are in Christ.

The entire new covenant community is betrothed to Christ, joined to him in corporate baptism but still waiting for the final wedding celebration. Therefore, any teaching that draws on marital imagery to claim that individuals should seek to experience a higher form of spiritual or physical intimacy with Jesus in this present age, especially one that makes them feel superior to other believers, is false teaching. And what is the root of this form of heresy? It comes from reading Paul's corporate arguments about the bride of Christ through an individualistic lens and treating the community's experience as though it applies to the lone individual.

The second reason I suggest that marital imagery is reserved for the future is because the concept of sonship in the church's present existence better serves the principle of obtaining an inheritance. Under Hebrew law, as it was later to be under Roman law, the son/husband was the one who received the inheritance from the father, not the daughter/wife. In the new covenant era, just as both men and women make up the bride of Christ, both are also referred to as the son(s) of God and seen as co-heirs with Christ. The concept that the corporate church is God's son in this age, and his wife in the next age not only avoids the danger of distorting biblical morality, but it also proves for a concept of salvation that already is, but at the same time is yet to be.

## Corporate Circumcision

The argument I have been making about corporate baptism based on Romans 6 is also fully supported by Colossians 2:11-13, the text we touched on above. In this passage Paul says,

> In him you were also circumcised with a circumcision not performed by human hands. Your whole self ruled by the flesh [body of flesh] was put off when you were circumcised by Christ, having been buried *(syntaphentes)* with him in baptism, in which you were also raised *(synēgerthetē)* with him through your faith in the working of God, who raised him from the dead. When you were dead in your sins and in the uncircumcision of your flesh, God made you alive with Christ. He forgave us all our sins.[41]

Here is confirmation of what we have already noted. Although the phrase, "your whole self" in the NIV creates the impression Paul is talking about the individual, the circumcision, burial and the raising mentioned in this text is a onetime corporate event. In using the preposition *syn* (with), and the plural forms of the Greek verbs *syntaphentes* (were buried with) and *synēgerthetē*, (were raised with), he is conveying the idea that collectively, *you all* were buried and raised together with Christ.

It is possible to see the phrase "having been buried with him in baptism" as a picture of a new convert emerging from the baptismal water. However, as we discussed earlier, Paul is not saying that we were individually buried alive with Christ in baptism to produce death, but that we have been buried with him *by* or *because of the* baptism into his death, which was a one-time corporate event. I say this because, although it is not reflected in most translations, in the original grammar Paul uses the definite article *tō* (the) with the singular *baptismō* (baptism).[42] Again, this indicates he is speaking of *the* baptism, a specific event that occurred at a specific point in time and has not been repeated.

I also want to point out that when Paul uses the preposition *en* in the phrase, "having been buried with him *in* the baptism" it can mean *by* as well as *in* or *into*. This helps us see that Paul is saying the same thing in Colossians as he says in Romans 6. Taking the grammar into consideration and paraphrasing, Paul is saying *by* the baptism, which the Spirit accomplished, we have been united *together* with Christ in the moment of his death. Because of this union, we died and have been buried *together* with Christ, and *together* with all the other members of the end times community from all generations, we have also been raised with him.

This interpretation also sheds light on the corporate circumcision that Paul describes. First, translating Paul's phrase, "Your *whole self* ruled by the flesh was put off when you were circumcised *by* Christ," as the NIV does, makes it sound like Christ did the circumcising and that it was performed on the individual. The language Paul uses shows this was not the case, however, as the removal of the flesh of both Christ and his people was a work of the Spirit that occurred in conjunction with his death and resurrection.

This is an important aspect of what was accomplished through Christ's death as circumcision plays a critical role in the relationship between God and his people. Going back to Abraham, all Hebrew males had to be circumcised in order to enter into the covenant with Yahweh that set Israel apart from the nations. Despite the insistence on physical circumcision, what really mattered, however, is what it represented—a circumcised heart, meaning one that was pure and passionately devoted to God.[43] Because Israel was stubborn and continued to reject Yahweh by following other gods, one of the new covenant promises God made to Israel as a people is that "I will remove from you your heart of stone and give you a heart of flesh."[44] In this context, a stony heart represents one that is hardened and rebellious, while a heart of flesh is soft and tender towards God.

In scripture, there is a strong link between circumcision and Passover. In the Old Testament era, circumcision was mandatory for partaking in the Passover, the event that led to and then commemorated the marriage of Yahweh and Israel at Mount Sinai.[45] In the New Testament, Christ's death is not only described as a Passover offering, but also the occasion of the church's corporate circumcision during which the body of flesh was removed and the new covenant community, the new man, was given a new heart and a new spirit. While physical circumcision is no longer required, this inward circumcision is necessary in order to be in a covenant relationship with God. For this reason, water baptism is not a guarantee of salvation; indeed, history shows that many have been water baptized without exhibiting any subsequent evidence of true repentance or love for Christ. Only those with circumcised hearts can keep the Christian Passover and experience the blessings promised to the new covenant community. This occurs when the individual, who responds to Jesus with genuine saving faith, enters into the believing community and shares experientially in the one-time corporate circumcision performed by the Spirit on Christ.

## Our Spiritual Circumcision

In Colossians, Paul explains that the Old Testament practice of circum-cision foreshadows our spiritual circumcision in Christ that took place through his death on the cross. At this time, he was freed from the body of flesh on behalf of his people and the covenant with Sin ended that Adam's disobedience had created. While the Spirit performed this circumcision—the removal of the flesh—on Christ, our representative head, it was applied to the corporate church and then to the individual members when they were made alive with Christ through repentance and faith.

This, again, follows the Old Testament type. Through physical circumcision, the individual Jew in each generation experientially entered into the reality *that already existed* as a result of the Hebrews' collective baptism unto Moses during the First Exodus. In the same way, under the new covenant, the believer's ability to come into the body of Christ and experience all the blessings promised to God's people is conditional on the spiritual circumcision of the heart. This was provided through Christ once and for all time for those who are his.

Let me say again that corporate baptism in no way alters the need for personal repentance and regeneration. What it does, however, is shift the goal of the individual's response to believing the good news of what God completed through Christ and by the Spirit, rather than performing external works like circumcision to become a member of Gods holy nation as was necessary under the old covenant. By faith, the believer gains entrance into the already-formed and Spirit-filled new covenant community that came into existence through its corporate baptism into Christ's death.

**BAPTISMAL BEWILDERMENT¶** The idea of a one-time corporate baptism leads to some inevitable questions. If what I am saying about our collective baptism into Christ's death is correct, then where does water baptism of the individual fit in and what significance does it have? Didn't Christ himself command the apostles to "make disciples of all nations, baptizing them in the name of the Father and of the Son and of the Holy Spirit?[46] And what about baptism *in* or *with* the Spirit that John the Baptist referred to in anticipation of the Messiah's coming? How or even does the Spirit baptism that initially occurred at Pentecost relate to the corporate baptism by the Spirit into Christ's death that took place at the cross? It is vital to clarify the difference between these two baptisms as similar language of being baptized *by, of, with,* or *in* the Spirit has been used in connection with both.

Further complicating the baptismal picture, a common teaching in some circles is that the baptism of (*with, in, into, by*) the Spirit is an individual experience. In this view, the baptism of the Spirit may occur at conversion or it may be a second, post-conversion experience that, depending on the tradition, the believer needs to seek in order to be empowered, gifted, or fully sanctified. Since not all have had this type of experience, the implication is that some Christians are "Spirit-filled" and others are not. Not only is this difficult to reconcile with Paul's statement in Romans 8:9 that "if anyone does not have the Spirit of Christ, they do not belong to Christ," but it has led to unfortunate divisions and hurts in the body of Christ.

My intention is not to get into a detailed discussion about these matters. However, in order to recover a clear view of the corporate baptism Paul describes in his letters, it is necessary to clarify some of the baptism-related language commonly used in the contemporary church. To this end, I want to briefly sum up the distinction between 1) the *corporate baptism into Christ's death* by the Spirit; 2) the *outpouring* of the Holy Spirit on the community that is referred to by John the Baptist as the baptism with the Spirit; and 3) the *infilling* of the Spirit that occurs on a corporate and individual level within context of the new covenant community. After this, we will talk about water baptism of the individual and see if or how it to relates to Spirit baptism.

*The baptism into Christ's death.* First, as we have seen, the baptism Paul refers to in Romans 6 and the other texts we have explored above is a *one-time* corporate event—all who looked to God in all generations were collectively, and at the same time, baptized into Christ's death by the Spirit. This took place when individual believers were united with Christ as he was dying on the cross, and then, having been made one with him were buried, raised, and seated in heavenly places in him. Notice, *the Spirit* is the one who is doing the baptizing, uniting, and raising.

*Baptism with or in the Spirit.* The one-time historic baptism into Christ's death as he was dying on the cross is not to be confused with the baptism or *outpouring* of the Spirit that initially occurred at Pentecost, and subsequently on the communities at Samaria, Cornelius's house, and the group of John's disciples at Ephesus. The baptism *with* (or *in*) the Spirit took place *after* Jesus died and ascended to the Father and was the fulfillment of God's promises to give the Spirit as a bridal gift to his people when the new covenant was established. Note that at Pentecost, God gave the Spirit to Jesus and *he* is the one doing the baptizing.[47]

By now, you probably won't be surprised that I believe the *outpouring* of the Spirit is also a corporate experience! Apart from Jesus's experience of the Spirit descending on him like a dove at his water baptism, the Spirit is never spoken of as being *poured out* on a lone individual in the New Testament.[48] The *outpouring* or the *baptism with the Spirit*, which were one and the same in the minds of the early church, always occurred within context of the believing community. Even when Paul encountered Jesus on the Road to Damascus, an event often used to teach that individual believers need to be "baptized in the Spirit," the Spirit was not *poured out* on the apostle in the same way that it happened collectively at Pentecost. Scripture says Paul was *filled* with the Spirit three days later, and then only when Ananias, a member of the new covenant community at Damascus, prayed with him per God's instructions.

The book of Acts shows that as the good news spread to other parts of the region after Pentecost, when people in a new location believed the gospel and bore witness to Christ, they were marked out by God as his own and the Spirit was poured out upon them as promised in the Old Testament.[49] Sometimes the corporate nature of this event is not explicitly stated, but it is most definitely implied. In several texts, the language clearly indicates *the community* received the outpoured Spirit.[50] We see this in the example of the Samaritans. After hearing they had accepted the message, the apostles sent representatives to see if, as a group, the new converts had received the Spirit. In another instance, when Cornelius welcomed the word of God, the Spirit came upon the newly formed believing community that was present in his home. Indeed, in reporting this back to the apostles, Peter told them that what happened to them on the day of Pentecost had also happened to this group of Gentile believers; as a household, they experienced the same baptism with or outpouring of the Spirit that Jesus had promised his disciples.[51]

Paul shared this understanding as well. When he met the group of disciples at Ephesus, he initially assumed they were Christians, but felt prompted to ask them, "Did you receive the Holy Spirit when you believed?" When they said they were only familiar with John's baptism and didn't know about the Holy Spirit, he told them about Jesus, they were baptized in his name, and all received the Spirit.[52]

All of these events are clearly corporate, which supports the Old Testament perspective that the outpouring or baptism of the Spirit is promised to the community. In other words, as Paul saw it, the Spirit was the vital gift from God for his people in the new covenant era. In the book of Acts, Christ poured out the Spirit whenever a believing community from a new national, ethnic, or tribal group came into existence. Through the Spirit, gifts such as preaching, teaching, administrations, prophecy, leadership, and others were bestowed on the group. These spiritual gifts were all essential for building up the community in faith, which explains why Paul told members to earnestly desire them.[53] From the first century forward, God has graciously poured out his Spirit on the new covenant community at various times to revive and strengthen the church when she has been threatened, in a weakened state, or preparing to face hardship. Nowhere in the apostolic letters are believers commanded to either seek the Spirit himself (the Spirit points to Christ) or a personal baptism of the Holy Spirit.

*The infilling of the Holy Spirit.* In Ephesians 5:18, however, Paul instructs the new covenant community to *keep on being filled* with the Spirit, which is a continual, repeated action. Right after he gives this command, the apostle goes on to show what this looks like. The Spirit, which indwells the community, enables members to walk in obedience, holiness, and love, inspires worship and prayer, and empowers the church to witness to the mystery of the gospel. There is no genuine infilling of the Spirit that does not express itself in corporate life, and the life of the sanctified community is meant to be pure and blameless.

As Paul's story shows, this infilling also occurs on an individual level. However, it should also be noted that each time scripture says a member of the body of Christ was filled with the Spirit, it happened in connection with the believing community and had to do with a mission-related event that advanced God's kingdom or edified the body of Christ.[54] In other words, it was not primarily for the individual's benefit, although there is no doubt the individual was certainly blessed as well.

I want to be clear that in no way do I question the Spirit's work in the lives of individual believers. But as a result of my understanding of the corporate nature of the faith, I believe this aspect of the Holy Spirit's ministry mainly happens in context of his work in the community to build up the body of Christ and accomplish God's mission. Or put another way, as the Spirit operates within the overall community, the life of the individual is also affected. Sadly, this order is usually reversed today, and the emphasis is often on the individual. This is not scriptural. As we can see from the Corinthians and the schism that occurred over tongues and prophecy, emphasis on individual giftedness does not unite a fellowship but often divides and damages. While I don't deny the reality of individual experiences, I question how they are often interpreted, labeled, and also the way their significance is explained.

## Water Baptism

Turning now to water baptism, from my earlier arguments you may have noticed that almost all the references to baptism in Paul's letters have a corporate dimension that relates to the birth of the new covenant community, not the water baptism of the individual. To be fair, the apostle does mention that he water baptized the household of Crispus and Gaius, and also of Stephanas; however, he also says he cannot recall baptizing any others.[55] Indeed, Paul was emphatic that Christ did not send him to baptize but to preach the gospel.[56] Without negating the importance of water baptism, this is hardly a ringing endorsement that it is the key means of salvation for God's people.

We do, however, find a slightly different emphasis in the Gospels. While a few references to baptism anticipate either the corporate baptism into Christ's death or the outpouring of the Spirit given at Pentecost, most clearly have to do with water baptism of the individual.[57] In the New Testament, John the Baptist was the first to practice water baptism and then Jesus's disciples did as well. Interestingly, Jesus himself did not baptize.[58] It is worth noting that water baptism was for the forgiveness of sin—nothing else was promised.[59] The purpose of the rite was for those who were baptized to prepare themselves for the coming of God's kingdom. When Jesus's disciples began to baptize in water, there was no suggestion it was any different from that which John practiced and the individual was never told he or she would receive the Holy Spirit as a result of water baptism. When John the Baptist said Jesus would baptize with the Spirit, he was looking forward to the corporate outpouring of the promised Spirit that initially occurred on Pentecost.[60]

There are two verses, however, that seem to challenge what I am saying about water baptism. One is Matthew 28:19, in which Jesus commands the apostles to "Go therefore and make disciples of all nations, baptizing them in the name of the Father and the Son and the Holy Spirit." Doesn't this imply that water baptism is essential to salvation? The other is in Acts 2. On the day of Pentecost, Peter preached such a convicting sermon to the crowds about their role in crucifying Jesus, they were prompted ask the apostles, "Brothers, what shall we do?" In response, Peter said, "*Repent* and *be baptized*, every one of you, in the name of Jesus Christ for the forgiveness of your sins. And you will receive the gift of the Holy Spirit. The promise is for you and your children and for all who are far off—for all whom the Lord our God will call." [61]

At first glance, this certainly sounds like Peter is saying the individual receives the Holy Spirit through water baptism. Since we have already ruled out any connection between the water baptism of the individual as practiced in the Gospels and the corporate baptism with the Spirit referred to by John the Baptist, we need to think through this carefully. Is Peter now saying that after Pentecost, water baptism of the individual is the key to receiving the Holy Spirit after all? If so, that's different than Paul's point of view.

In sorting through this, we first need to note that after Pentecost, some communities received the Spirit *before* individuals were water baptized. This happened in the case of Cornelius and his household. And some people like the Samaritans received the Spirit *after* water baptism. These examples clearly show the Spirit is not necessarily given through water baptism, although in some instances water baptism and the new community's baptism in the Spirit may happen close together as it did with the group of disciples at Ephesus.[62] In Acts 2, Peter is clearly talking about initiation into the body of Christ. Experientially, as individuals come to have saving faith in Christ they become members of the new covenant community where all of God's blessings are received. Because the body of Christ is the temple where the Spirit dwells, the new believer enters into the life of the Spirit and receives gifts from the Spirit to use for building up the community in love.

There is no evidence that water baptism is anything other than a public confession of repentance (as was the case when John and Jesus's disciples baptized) and turning to Jesus in faith. To arrive at a sacramental view, which teaches that the individual is saved and receives the Spirit through water baptism, it would be necessary to take the historical record of water baptism in the gospels, mix it up with the doctrine of the church's one corporate baptism into Christ's death by the Spirit, and ignore the distinction between the two.

Water baptism is a public declaration of faith in Christ which signals to the world that the believer has died with Christ and is now a member of his body. In this way, water baptism functions the same as it did in the Gospels—it is still the appointed way to confess faith. As Paul teaches in Romans 10,

> "The word is near you; it is in your mouth and in your heart," that is, the message concerning faith that we proclaim: If you declare with your mouth, "Jesus is Lord," and believe in your heart that God raised him from the dead, you will be saved. For it is with your heart that you believe and are justified, and it is with your mouth that you profess your faith and are saved.[63]

This shows that a person who genuinely believes and confesses Jesus as their Lord and Savior has born witness to Christ. Water baptism publicly testifies to this saving faith.

As mentioned above, it is important to remember that someone who is water baptized, but still has an uncircumcised heart cannot enter the kingdom of God. The circumcision of the heart is what fulfills Old Testament typology, not water baptism itself. The individual Jew had to be physically circumcised to be in a covenant relationship with Yahweh and enter into the community that was headed by Moses. In the New Testament era, this type is fulfilled in the spiritual circumcision of the heart that was accomplished by the Spirit when the body of flesh was removed through Christ's death and resurrection. Believers share in this corporate circumcision when they come to a saving faith in Christ and enter into the new covenant community.

Based on the reasoning I have presented here, I would argue that water baptism is mainly a symbolic act of forgiveness and cleansing that also re-enacts the church's corporate experience of dying to Sin/Satan and the world and being raised with Christ into a new spiritual reality. This does not lessen its importance as in this outward expression of faith, the believer publicly identifies with Christ and his people. The difference between John's water baptism and the water baptism Jesus commanded the apostles to perform is that the latter is done in the name of the Father, Son, and Holy Spirit, which makes it clear how this forgiveness has been achieved. John's baptism could not convey the certainty of acceptance that baptism in Christ's name denotes.

Because the corporate nature of the New Testament letters and their teachings has been overshadowed by individualistic readings, we have failed to see that most texts on baptism in the apostolic letters refer to something hugely different than the water baptisms recorded in the Gospels and Acts. This failure has led many church leaders to see all references to baptism as different facets of the individual's water baptism at conversion. In doing this, a sacramental theology has been constructed in which the Spirit's work is inextricably linked to, and even dependent upon, water baptism. This was not the case in the first-century church and it should not be the case today.

## One Baptism

To sum up, I have been arguing that most of the texts on baptism in the apostolic writings are not speaking about water baptism or even baptism into Christ's sufferings (even though these are important related themes). Rather, they are referring to a collective baptism that parallels Israel's corporate baptism into Moses, the time when the nation came into a covenant relationship with Yahweh through the representative he had appointed. In Romans 6, 1 Corinthians, Galatians, Ephesians, and Colossians, Paul demonstrated how the old order has been brought to an end and the new order has come into existence in the last days because all believers shared in the death of Christ. As a consequence of this historic, corporate baptism, together, they died to the covenantal demands of the old relationship that bound them to Sin and Death (Satan). The new covenant community that was formed at that time is now free to live unto God, who has made us his own through Christ and to walk by the Spirit, which has been poured out on God's people in fulfillment of the Old Testament promises. This one-time baptism, however, does not mean that individuals are automatically saved; each person must come to a saving faith in Christ in order to enter into the believing community where the Holy Spirit dwells.

In each of the letters mentioned above, sonship is part of the setting and marital imagery is also present. This reflects the Old Testament type in which Israel is both Yahweh's son in its earthly existence and is designated to be his bride when the marriage is celebrated at the end of the age. Moreover, Paul proclaims that the distinction between Jew and Gentile created by the Mosaic law has been ended. Just as the baptism into Moses at the Exodus established a covenant community in which all had equal standing, so baptism into Christ's death created a new community in which all distinctions are abolished. In Romans, Paul argues that all who trust in Christ for their salvation—whether Jew or Gentile—are children of Abraham.[64] This is stated even more explicitly in 1 Corinthians and Galatians when Paul says, "There is neither Jew nor Gentile, neither slave nor free, nor is there male and female, for you are all one in Christ Jesus."[65] He makes it clear in Ephesians that for those who are in Christ the division between Jew and Gentile has ended as far as God is concerned.[66]

This perspective is significant for a number of reasons. First, once again, we have seen that Paul stays within the corporate categories of the Old Testament while transposing them to reflect the new reality that came into existence through Christ's death and resurrection. In keeping with his Hebraic background, he framed the creation of the New Testament community using the same terms associated with Israel's birth as a nation. In going back to the original Exodus, Paul did not abandon the New Exodus motif as presented in the New Testament.

He drew on the paschal (Passover) sacrifice of the First Exodus from Egypt to interpret the death of Jesus and to depict the birth of the church, the new man. Since the Second Exodus from Babylonia was not based on a sacrificial rite, it was not sufficient to explain Christ's death. However, the promises associated with the new covenant were made in this period. So, in line with the New Exodus model initially given to the early church by Jesus, Paul combines the sacrificial element of the First Exodus with the promise of a new covenant made by the prophets in the Second Exodus era to shed light on Christ's person and work.

This merger is unique to the New Testament, for the Jewish writings did not look for a suffering Messiah whose death would bring about the birth and salvation of a new covenant community. Paul saw the death of Jesus to be the inauguration of the New Exodus and taught that the new covenant community's birth under its new representative occurred at the moment of the Messiah's death. Thus, all Christians have been baptized into his death. To be outside of that event is to be outside of Christ.

Understanding the corporate view of baptism into Christ's death also has implications for the unity of the church. For one thing, it makes the way for us to overcome old divisions that have been created by individualistic interpretations of key passages on baptism. It also brings into sharp relief the magnificent plan God has for us as a unified people and the part each of us has to play in building up the body of Christ in love. In turn, this can foster new appreciation for believers in various streams and camps within the universal church. While we must guard sound doctrine, our unity lies not in maintaining doctrinal conformity or correctness, but in the marvelous work of union accomplished through our baptism into Christ's death. This is the great foundational truth that unifies all who believe and follow Christ.

## Practical Effects

We have spent a good deal of time exploring the corporate framework of Romans 5-8. Since an individualistic, dualistic reading over the centuries has clouded this passage, it has been necessary to sort through a number of issues in order to get a clearer view of Paul's meaning.

Another step that can be immensely helpful in our efforts to recover scripture's corporate, Hebraic context is to go back to our family roots and see some of specific points where the biblical storyline first began to get muddled. To this end, I've included an additional chapter in the appendix entitled "Blurring the Lines" that looks at three pivotal developments in the early centuries of the church which had a long-term impact on the way we read scripture and practice spirituality. In this era, the Jewish context of scripture began to fade, and elements of Plato's journey of the individual soul to return to the spiritual realm were layered over the corporate narrative. This is when individualistic, dualistic assumptions inadvertently entered into the Christian thought stream and began to quietly blur the biblical picture. I encourage you to finish reading the main body of *Missing Lenses* before turning to it so that you have a deeper understanding of scripture's corporate framework first, as this will allow you to see the impact of the changes that began to occur in second century more clearly. But I do hope you won't skip over the appendix because I believe looking at these critical shifts together can help us identify the sources of some of our long-standing divisions in the body of Christ and frame issues that call for further discussion.

Going on, our next step is to unravel Romans 3:21-25, another foundational text in the West that encompasses the great salvation themes of righteousness, redemption, atonement, and justification. Often viewed within the framework of the Greco-Roman law court, it is exciting to see how these core biblical concepts take on a new, brighter hue when read against the corporate backdrop of the New Exodus storyline

PART THREE

# Recovering the Passover Lens

# CHAPTER 8

# Redemptive Threads

Weaving a tapestry is no small feat. The first step is to string a series of plain threads between two rollers on a large loom. The design is transferred onto this background and then many-colored threads—sometimes a dazzling array depending on the project—are woven back and forth through the strands to create the pattern or picture. In medieval times, tapestries could be quite costly depending on the quality of materials and the intricacy of the design. For instance, producing a set of six five-by-eight tapestries would have required the equivalent of thirty weavers working eight to sixteen months. And that's not counting the time it took to create and prepare the design and set up the loom![1] All the effort was considered well spent as tapestries often depicted stories that reflected or shaped the culture, plus they added beauty to otherwise austere surroundings.

In stating why she chose this ancient art form to express herself, contemporary artist Joanne Soroka noted her diverse ethnic background. "Through the medium of weaving," she explained, "I would be able to use the metaphor of interlacing to tell about who I am and eventually, although I did not know it at the time, to tell the stories of the unmarked lives of my ancestors."[2]

Given the nature of this art form, it makes sense why weaving is often used as analogy to portray the story of God's unfolding relationship with humanity over the ages. It is also an especially apt description of what Paul is doing in his letters. The apostle is gathering up various threads from the Old Testament, Jesus, and the twelve apostles—the entire storyline—and weaving them together to present a stunning tapestry of God's great work of salvation through Christ. These redemptive strands converge in a special way in Romans 3:21-26, a passage examined extensively in the West in attempts to find Paul's paradigm for redemption.

It may feel like I am skipping around in Paul's letters, but it has been important to lay the necessary groundwork for seeing his corporate mindset first before addressing this key text. This is crucial because several major salvation-related themes appear in this passage that are not only controversial in their own right, but also challenging for contemporary readers to relate to and understand. Weighty concepts like God's righteousness, sacrifice of atonement, redemption, and justification—key biblical terms not a part of our everyday vocabulary—are all in this one text. And all defy simplistic definitions as each of these strands ties into a subset of images and concepts drawn from scripture's ancient storyline. Essentially, each term is set within a mini-tapestry that, when laced together with the others, creates a fascinating, multi-faceted picture of God's remarkable efforts to save humankind from Sin/Satan's rule and address our own sin so that we could be reconciled to him through Christ.

The problem with our contemporary understanding of the bigger picture, however, is that, as we have been seeing, foreign ideas have been imported into scripture that have blurred the meaning of many salvation related terms. Our goal now is to pull apart three of the main conceptual strands in Romans 3:21-26 and see how each one becomes clearer, brighter, and more meaningful when read in context of Paul's Hebraic perspective rather than through an individualistic Greco-Roman tinted lens.

In the next two chapters, we will look at the phrases, *a righteousness from God* and *the sacrifice of atonement,* to see how reading against the corporate, New Exodus storyline, in which the Passover plays a central role, can shine a new light on these concepts. This will include an in-depth conversation about the controversial subject of God's wrath, so we can sort through how it relates—or doesn't relate—to the atonement when viewed within the New Exodus narrative. Then we will explore how this corporate framework provides fresh insight into Paul's view of *justification,* a foundational doctrine in the Western church.

## Why Did Jesus Have to Die?

In preparation for exploring the various threads let's look at the overall text so we can get a feel for what Paul is saying in this classic passage about salvation.

> But now apart from the law *the righteousness of God* has been made known, to which the Law and the Prophets testify. This righteousness is given through faith in Jesus Christ to all who believe. There is no difference between Jew and Gentile, for all have

sinned and fall short of the glory of God, and all are *justified freely* by his grace through the redemption that came by Christ Jesus.

God presented Christ as *a sacrifice of atonement*, through the shedding of his blood—to be received by faith. He did this to demonstrate his righteousness, because in his forbearance he had left the sins committed beforehand unpunished—he did it to demonstrate his righteousness at the present time, *so as to be just and the one who justifies* those who have faith in Jesus.[3]

This is a critical passage in that it definitively shows why Jesus is more than a wise man or good teacher. According to these verses, the Father presented his Son as a sacrifice of atonement (with Jesus's willing consent) so that those who believe in his saving work could receive God's righteousness, be redeemed, and rightfully reconciled to him. In other words, Jesus came not only to teach truth and impart wisdom but also to die, and in his death bring fulfillment to the great salvation story that has been unfolding ever since Adam and Eve first betrayed God in the garden. In our discussion of Romans 5–8, we delved into how Christ's death and resurrection freed the body of Christ from the law of sin and death that bound humanity to Satan. Now in this text, we will see additional aspects of Christ's work on the cross—how his sacrificial death remedied the breach with God created by humanity's sin and initiated the process in which God would restore all things to himself.

Jesus's sacrificial death taps into another reason why this is a challenging passage for many contemporary readers. The idea of requiring a blood sacrifice to atone for sin is not only foreign to most Westerners, it is also repugnant to many; it seems like something that belongs to a primitive culture from long ago, not an educated, civilized society. Taken at face value, it also appears to contradict the idea of a peaceful, loving God. The notion that God explicitly willed for his son to die on our behalf and that it was a violent, bloody death has caused some to wonder how the cross can possibly be seen as a demonstration of God's love, righteousness, or justice! What kind of loving Father would send his only son to suffer so horribly and be killed? Furthermore, it is asked, if God is all-powerful and can do anything he wants, why couldn't he just forgive us or find a less horrific way to deal with sin/Sin?

There is no doubt the sacrificial nature of Christ's death raises some tough questions. Nevertheless, the fact remains that in the New

Testament, Jesus is described as the Lamb of God, our Passover, who established the new and better covenant with his own blood.[4] And here in this passage from Romans, Paul plainly says, *"God presented Christ as a sacrifice of atonement, through the shedding of his blood,"* which portrays Jesus as a sin offering. So, if we are going to be true to the biblical text, there is no way to sidestep difficult, sometimes uncomfortable issues having to do with the blood of Jesus or the Father's role in his Son's death. Actually, it is good to talk about these matters, as coming to understand what God has done for us both corporately and individually is the foundation of becoming a new person in Christ. This is why, paradoxically, Christ's atoning death is such a life-giving subject!

As we'll see, one of the reasons Romans 3:21-26 is so challenging is that it's often interpreted individualistically and in context of the criminal law court. I contend, however, that strong, corporate New Exodus themes of deliverance, redemption, and covenant relationship are woven into this text that have not been fully appreciated. The atonement imagery drawn from the Old Testament sacrificial system is easily seen. However, what is often missed is that the Passover associated with the First Exodus, and imagery from the Second Exodus are part of the backdrop as well. This puts things in a different light as both of these were corporate events that involved saving the entire people of God, not a particular individual.

Before unraveling this text, I want to set the overall context of Romans 3 by briefly revisiting the dilemma created by sin/Sin. This will allow us to better see why Christ's sacrificial death was not only necessary, but also why scripture describes it as a supreme act of love on the part of the Father, Son, and Spirit.

## The Dilemma of sin/Sin

Earlier, we saw that humankind is in a terrible fix. As described by Paul, humanity and the rest of God's good creation came under Sin and Death's rule when Adam and Eve entered into a legally binding covenant relationship with Satan. Now subjected to his dark power, everyone who was born after them also wronged God and earned death for themselves. Compounding the problem, there is nothing humanity can do to break free from Sin or make things right. And as Paul makes clear, the Mosaic law that Yahweh gifted to the Jews is no help. While it is useful in raising awareness of sin and teaching God ways, the Law cannot free anyone from Sin/Satan, reverse the hold Death has on humanity, change our hearts, or give us life. Moreover, there is no way to cleanse ourselves, so we can come before God once again or restore his image in us that has been marred by sin. Consequently, all of humanity is stuck in sin/Sin, exiled from God's presence, and imprisoned in Satan's dark kingdom.

While God certainly has never been trapped in any way, it could be said that sin/Sin presented a dilemma for him as well (like Paul did upon occasion, I am speaking in human terms). In spite of humanity's betrayal and indifference, true to his nature, God never stopped loving the family he created in his image or longing for his relationship with humanity to be restored. Scripture clearly states that he wants all people "to be saved and to come to a knowledge of the truth" so they can return to him and live![5] The quandary, however, is that because God is holy, righteous and lives in unapproachable light, no one who is in solidarity with Sin/Satan and corrupted by sin can be in a relationship with him.[6] As Paul frames it, "what fellowship can light have with darkness? What harmony is there between Christ and Belial (the devil)?"[7]

To the question of why God didn't just forgive Adam and Eve and us as well, it is critical to understand that it is not because he is unwilling. The parables of the prodigal son and the master who forgives the servant's unpayable debt shows that God is ever ready to freely forgive those who come to him no matter how great their sin.[8] But here's the snag: even if God were to absolve everyone completely and unreservedly, Satan still has a binding claim on humanity because of the covenant alliance Adam formed with him. Furthermore, simply annulling the covenant would not be sufficient to maintain our freedom. Since sin leads to death, subsequent sins would put us right back in the same boat—condemned by the law and once again under Satan's thumb.

So, for humankind to be reconciled with God and once again become what it was created to be, it was necessary to overcome the devastating effects of the fall. To do so, humanity's covenant with Sin/Satan established through Adam had to be terminated legally, hostilities with God ended, and the Father had to make a way for his enemies to be able to return to him. This involved satisfying the law that says the consequence of sin is death and making a way for humankind to be cleansed and restored to its God-intended innocence. Furthermore, the covenant relationship between God and his people that Satan broke apart had to be re-established. Creation also had to be released from Satan's rule and renewed so that all would once again be subject to the Father. Clearly, no human being—no matter how powerful, brilliant, or gifted—could accomplish any of these things. Only God could rescue his people from Sin and Death, make permanent provision for our sin, and free creation.

As the apostle Peter observed, how God was going to work all of this out was a mystery even the angels longed to know![9] This is what Paul begins to unveil in Romans 3:21 when he describes the salvation God achieved for his people through the sacrificial death of his beloved Son, Jesus.

**GOD'S RIGHTEOUSNESS IN ACTION¶** In the passage we are considering, Paul begins with the matter of righteousness. This is a critical issue because without it, sinful humans cannot be reconciled to God, who is pure and holy. The question is, what exactly does Paul have in mind when he says, "but now *apart from the law the righteousness of God* has been made known?"[10] Notice the emphasis is on God's righteousness and that it comes from him. The fact that it is *apart from the law* indicates God's righteousness does not come through keeping the Mosaic law or any effort on our part. Some scholars have come to believe this concept is foundational to Paul's thinking about salvation, so understanding it can help unlock the meaning of the other terms he uses in Romans 3:21-26.[11]

A common understanding of "the righteousness of God" is that it refers to his *moral perfection and excellence.* Since the law was considered an expression of this, those who lived according to its precepts were seen as being righteous. In the Old Testament era, some Jews believed they were in right standing with Yahweh simply because they were in covenant with God. At the same time, the idea that righteousness requires self-effort was also prevalent in Jesus's time and, as we saw previously, is a mentality that persists today in the contemporary church.[12] Paul made it clear in Romans 3:23, however, that since all have sinned, no one is able to be right with God through law-keeping; rather it is a gift given through faith in Jesus Christ or, as framed by a number of scholars, through *his* faithfulness.[13]

Traditionally in the West, the righteousness that we freely receive from God through Christ has been viewed from an individualistic perspective. The questions that have continued to trouble the church is in what way does the individual believer become righteous when he or she places faith in Christ? Were we legally *declared* righteous or are we actually *made* righteous in some way? Since we sometimes sin after entering God's kingdom, does that mean we can each lose our right standing with God and so our salvation? Do we need to do good works to keep our individual righteousness before God? If we still have a permanent sin nature, as some contend, then what exactly does it mean to be righteous? How is it possible to be holy as God commanded if sin continues to live within us?[14] Momentarily setting aside these questions related to the individual, let's see how the viewing the concept of a righteousness that comes from God within the corporate, New Exodus storyline sheds a different light on the subject.

## God Moves to Save

In the Old Testament, the phrase "a righteousness from God" had a much greater significance than the individual's right standing with Yahweh or personal holiness, although that is certainly involved. In the larger picture of redemptive history, righteousness is set in a corporate, covenantal context; it is about *being faithful to the covenant relationship established between Yahweh and his people*. God is righteous because he faithfully keeps his covenant promises. Humankind, and Israel more specifically, are unrighteous because of their unfaithfulness to God. In this corporate setting, God's righteousness is defined by his fidelity to his word and also the mercy he extends to humankind even when it is undeserved.[15] It speaks of his saving activity in redeeming his people from exile and granting forgiveness for their wrongdoings.

Essential to understanding salvation history, this key Old Testament concept is illustrated in Israel's release from captivity in Babylon during the Second Exodus. To grasp the full meaning of the phrase, it is important to understand that God's righteousness involves judgment as well as blessing and deliverance. God is patient, longsuffering, compassionate, gracious, and slow to anger. But because he is also holy, righteous, just, and true, there are times when he will move to judge those who persist in doing evil and stubbornly reject his warnings to turn away from sin. We see these two sides of God's righteousness in Israel's story. When their covenant relationship was first established, Yahweh told Israel that if she remained faithful to him, he would shower her with blessings. At the same time, he clearly detailed the hardships or "curses" that would follow if the nation abandoned her covenant with him, pursued other gods, or went her own way.[16]

Time and again Israel was unfaithful, and time and again God graciously sent prophets to warn her, but Israel refused to listen. She continued to embrace other gods and, as a people, blatantly disobeyed him. After patiently trying to call her back to him, Yahweh kept his word about what would happen if she persisted in her flagrant infidelities—Israel finally experienced his righteous judgment. According to scripture, essentially, God divorced her.[17] Withdrawing his loving protection, enemies ruthlessly destroyed Jerusalem, Israel's capital city and swept the nation, along with its supporting network of communities, into exile. Cut off from the temple and deported to Babylon with her broken relationship with Yahweh displayed to all nations, captive Israel was unable deliver herself. Only God, in his mercy, could free her.

Yahweh's decree that Israel would be in exile for a certain period of time had to be fully carried out before he would act to save her. True to his word, once her hard service in Babylon was complete, he kept his promises to deliver his bride, so she could return to the Promised Land. Isaiah said that Israel was *made righteous* because God brought her back from exile.[18] By delivering Israel from her captors and publicly reconciling, God made it known to the nations that she was once again acceptable to him. Furthermore, in the prophet's view, being made righteous included not only forgiveness and reconciliation, but also the restoration of Israel's inheritance, meaning God would keep all the covenant promises he originally made to his people![19] Israel was released from exile not because the people kept the law or through any good works of their own—it happened *solely* as a result of Yahweh's gracious, covenant-keeping righteousness.

Paul's statement that *the Law and the Prophets testify to a righteousness from God* is evidence that his understanding of this key concept is set within this Old Testament context. Israel's inability to keep the Mosaic law proved that men and women could not make themselves righteous. This revealed the need for divine help, which God supplied through his Son, Jesus. The prophets pointed to Christ as well. Their predictions that Israel's inheritance would be restored and that she would enter into a new covenant relationship with God were not fully realized during the Second Exodus. Even though some of the Babylonian captives returned to their homeland and worked to rebuild the temple, other nations continued to oppress Israel, and she had not yet experienced the anticipated restoration of her national glory. As we saw earlier, this is why Israel was still waiting expectantly for a Messiah-King who would fulfill the prophetic promises at the time Jesus was born.

To sum up, this Old Testament backdrop shows that God is not only righteous because he is morally perfect; he is righteous because he keeps his covenant promises to deliver those who are suffering in captivity to Sin/Satan and who have no hope if he does not act to save them. Thus, when Isaiah speaks of God's righteousness being revealed, he means that God is about to act to rescue his people. This helps us comprehend what Paul means when he speaks of "a righteousness from God"—he is referring to God's faithfulness in redeeming and restoring his people to a covenant relationship with him through the death and resurrection of his beloved Son, Jesus.

## Righteousness and Redemption

In view of the way Paul draws on the Old Testament storyline, there is simply no need to turn to sources other than scripture, like the Roman criminal law court model, to determine how he understands God's righteousness and its relationship to redemption. Seeing God's righteousness against the backdrop of Yahweh's covenant with Israel allows us to recover a right view of both the relational and legal aspects of salvation. First and foremost, making a covenant is establishing a relationship—it involves making promises to another and then pledging to keep those vows. We saw that God is righteous because he was faithful to the covenant he made with his people, while Israel was unrighteous because she was unfaithful. This is the relational component that often gets downplayed or lost in the Roman law court model. As acknowledged previously, there *is* a legal aspect of salvation, but it looks different in the Old Testament covenantal setting. Since, in God's view, covenant relationships are binding, when vows made to him are broken he acts as judge, but more like one who presides over civil rather than criminal court.

What makes God's role as judge unique is that in a human court, typically the judge does not have a relationship with the offenders, so their actions do not affect him personally. This is not true in God's case. Sin involves *relational* violations that affect him in a very real and grievous way. All of humanity rejected God, our loving Creator, and went its own way, an offense far beyond any human comparison! In light of humankind's infidelity, God would have been completely justified in leaving us in Satan's dark domain, under the rule of Sin and Death. Instead, he demonstrated his own righteousness in that he faithfully kept the promises he made long ago, first to Adam after he fell, and then to Abraham to redeem his descendants from slavery and through his seed bless *all* the nations, not just Israel.[20]

Redemption is, therefore, indivisible from God's righteousness in the minds of the prophets, and consequently in Paul's. Indeed, redemption is the outworking of God's righteousness. This is why the righteousness of God cannot be understood properly outside of the Old Testament setting. Defining his righteousness predominantly as moral perfection and describing him as a criminal court judge presents God in detached, static terms that masks the full picture of his active, loving, saving involvement with humankind. It also overshadows the larger view that God's efforts are to redeem his bride, not just the individual.

When set within a corporate, New Exodus context it is easier to see that a righteousness from God has to do with his efforts to rescue his people from exile and bring them back into a position where he can accept and be happy with them once again. The entire new covenant community now enjoys this favorable status because of our union with Christ that took place at the time of his death. Redeemed from Sin, forgiven, cleansed, raised with Jesus into a new life and now betrothed to him, the church has become the righteousness of God in Christ![21] Together, we are living proof that God keeps his promises. We can once again enjoy fellowship with our Father as Adam and Eve did in the garden and it is all because of God's righteous faithfulness to his covenant!

The matter of the individual's righteousness, then, is set within this greater corporate context. Because the church, Christ's bride, is in union with him, all that belongs to him now belongs to us as a people—his righteousness and wisdom, his mind and Spirit, even his inheritance are now ours collectively! It is like the prosperous man who married a poverty-stricken woman. Even though she only brought debts to the marriage, her new husband willingly gave her everything he had—his wealth and status as well as his heart, all that she needed for life. In response to his generosity, she desired to serve him in return, not out of duty-bound obligation, but freely, out of love.

Likewise, the entire *church* (not the lone individual) is complete in Christ. Collectively, we have everything needed to live in a way that honors and pleases God.[22] As a wedding gift, God gave the Holy Spirit to the new covenant community and through the Spirit he continues to shower his people with spiritual blessings. When the individual comes into the body of Christ, he or she shares in all the benefits that belong to the community, receiving from others what is needed to live a fully faithful life and giving in return. In response to God's generosity, we are each to do our part so that all can grow in the grace and knowledge of Christ, and as an outgrowth of our union with him, "bearing fruit in every good work."[23] Together, we are also called to pursue holiness by putting off the old, sinful ways of relating that characterized our former lives in body of Sin and put on Christ instead.

We do all these things freely, joyfully, obeying out of deep gratitude, knowing that nothing we do can add to the righteousness of God, his great work of salvation that came to us through Christ's faithfulness. Unless we start with this understanding, it is all too easy to end up in some form of individualistic works-based religion in which we try to keep the law or make ourselves righteous to earn favor with God.

Without denying there is a forensic element to salvation, I contend the individualistic Roman law court metaphor obscures the rich layers of meaning that can only be seen when the concepts of God's righteousness and redemption are set within context of his historic, covenantal relationship with his people. Let's hold this in mind as we go on now to consider the atonement.

**THAT BLOODY SACRIFICE¶** We are moving into one of the most controversial parts of the redemption story—the atonement. Describing Paul's statement in Romans 3:25 that *"God presented Christ as a sacrifice of atonement, through the shedding of his blood"* as a 'mini-tapestry' doesn't quite do justice to the apostle's thinking. Christ's sacrificial death is the centerpiece of the salvation story.[24] This one phrase alone draws on several strands of thought from the Old Testament and weaves them into the New.

For some, the emotionally laden question of how a loving Father could consign his Son to die makes the atonement a challenging issue. But another reason Christ's sacrificial death is a difficult subject is because there is little agreement about how to explain the role it plays in saving God's people. While the *doctrine* of atonement—the teaching that our sins are forgiven as a result of Christ's death—has long been accepted as Christian orthodoxy, the church has never reached consensus regarding *how* or *why* his death effectively dealt with sin/Sin.

On the one hand, it could be said the how or why is not important because it doesn't alter the fact that we have a relationship with Jesus. But on the other, church history suggests that it does make a difference when it comes to how we relate to God. Over the centuries theologians have developed various theories that have not been completely satisfying scripturally. Nevertheless, they have had a powerful influence on our understanding of sin/Sin, salvation, God's nature, and how we view our identity both on a corporate and an individual level. While some models reflect aspects of a corporate understanding, they do not present the full picture of what Christ's death accomplished. Others place far more emphasis on the salvation of the individual, causing important features of the biblical story to be brushed out. Moreover, these theories have continued to be sources of conflict and division, with different groups in the body of Christ favoring one view over another.

In moving into this discussion, I want to first briefly outline several of the most influential atonement theories, so we can get the lay of the land and then see how they compare when the subject is set within the corporate, covenantal New Exodus framework. These include:

243

*The Ransom Theory.* God had to pay the devil a ransom to redeem believers from Sin and Death, so he sent Jesus to die in our place. Popular for the first thousand years of church history, this theory fell out of favor because the idea that God owed something to Satan, an outlaw, seemed unacceptable.

*Christus Victor.* In giving his life as an atoning sacrifice to free believers from Sin/Satan, Jesus defeated the powers of evil that held humankind in bondage. Many acknowledge this position has a degree of merit. While it presents a more corporate understanding of Sin/Satan's dominion over humanity, it is regarded as insufficient by some as it puts human beings in the role of being Sin's victim without also addressing the matter of our own participation in sin.

*Moral Exemplar or Moral Influence.* The purpose of Christ's death was to "influence mankind toward moral improvement."[25] In his death, Christ served as a perfect example of love, obedience, and humility. Individuals are changed for the good as we follow in his footsteps, live a moral life, and lay down our lives for others as he did. This view has a measure of truth as well, but it does not address the problem of humanity's captivity to Sin/Satan or the breach with God created by our personal sin.

*Recapitulation.* Christ is the new Adam who, by making atonement for sin so that we could be released from Satan, came to reverse the works of the evil one and sum up "the things in the heavens, and the things upon the earth" in him.[26] The Greek term for *sum up* means *to recapitulate* in Latin. According to Irenaeus, an early church father, Jesus's ultimate goal is for each of us to be conformed to his image, resulting in deification. By becoming one with us and defeating Sin and Death, he "became what we are, that He might bring us to be even what He is Himself."[27] The Eastern Orthodox branch of the global church favors this view.

*Satisfaction.* Developed by Anselm of Canterbury in the medieval ages, this position holds that God deserves all glory and honor. Sin is a failure to honor God, an offense that in his holiness he cannot overlook. Since God's honor demands satisfaction that no human can provide, God had to act on his own behalf. As both God and sinless man, Christ had abundant honor. Therefore, through his sacrificial atoning death he satisfied "God's offended character" by repaying the debt of honor each of us owed him.[28]

*Penal Substitution.* This is the doctrine that "Jesus suffered on behalf of sinners the death, punishment, and curse due to fallen humanity as the penalty for sin."[29] Although some form of penal substitution has been taught since the days of the early church, the theory is most often attributed to the Reformers of the sixteenth century.[30] Adapting elements of the satisfaction theory, it is set against the backdrop of the Roman criminal court and accounting metaphors. As described earlier, the traditional Reformed version holds that by sinning, all human beings have committed crimes against God and deserve the death penalty. God sent Christ to atone for our sins by taking the punishment we deserve so that his wrath towards sin could be satisfied and repentant individuals could be legally pardoned and declared (credited as) righteous.[31]

*The Governmental theory.* This view maintains that as Governor of the universe, it is God's task to maintain the moral foundation of his realm. To do this it was necessary for God to display his wrath towards sin, which he did when Jesus died as an atoning sacrifice on the cross. Since God himself upheld justice and appeased his own wrath, he could freely forgive those who repent without requiring punishment.[32] This view is objectionable to some for a number of reasons, one of which is that it denies Christ died in the sinner's place. Another is that it portrays God, the Father, as brutally punishing his own Son.

A number of other models have been proposed in more recent history as well.[33] In commenting on the various historic atonement theories influential in the West, theologian Robin Collins notes that

> Since the time of the Protestant Reformation, almost all Western theories of Atonement have been largely variations of Anselm's Satisfaction theory, the Penal theory, and the Moral Exemplar theory. All of these theories . . . share one thing in common: *they understand the basic relationship of God to the world primarily in terms of moral law, and the Satisfaction and Penal theories explicitly use judicial notions and the imagery of the courtroom.*[34]

Collins goes on to observe these "are fairly late interpretations of scripture, interpretations about which orthodox Christians have disagreed throughout the centuries, both in the East and West."[35]

Although it was criticized even in the Reformers' day, the penal substitution model has come under especially heavy fire since the eighteenth century, particularly the idea that God punished Jesus to satisfy his wrath.[36] Some, in fact, object to *any* kind of substitutionary model, maintaining that even before the fall God intended for Jesus to live among humanity at some point. In their opinion, this shows that God was not reacting to the events that took place in the garden when he determined to send his Son to us. So, in this view, any form of substitutionary atonement theory that says Jesus came to take our punishment for sin is in error.[37]

The controversial ideas that God punished Jesus in payment for our sin or to satisfy his wrath play a significant role in contemporary debates about the atonement. Therefore, it is important for us to address these notions if we are to get an accurate picture of why Jesus died. In doing this, I first want to show how viewing the atonement in context of the New Exodus narrative can help us come to a clearer, deeper understanding of God's heart and what was accomplished through Christ's death. My hope is that recovering this framework will allow us to move towards a more unified view of the atonement and develop a greater appreciation for the church's collective identity.

To this end, I will argue that the New Testament model of atonement is centered on two historic Jewish events: the Passover and the Day of Atonement, both of which had to do with the salvation of the entire people of God rather than the individual. Celebrated separately in the Old Testament after the first Passover, the prophet Ezekiel wove them together in a New Exodus, end times setting. I contend the New Testament authors looked to this combined corporate model, along with writings of the other prophets, when explaining the purpose of Christ's death. In addition to clarifying the how's and why's of the atonement, identifying this framework will put us in a better position to sort through the difficult subject of God's wrath, which we will do in the next chapter.

## Life is in the Blood

Broadly defined, the concept of *atonement* has to do with covering a wrongdoing so that a relationship can be restored.[38] Simply put, it means "at-one-ment, i.e., the state of being at one or being reconciled"[39] Atonement is necessary because as God said through the prophet Ezekiel, "All souls are mine, but the soul who sins will die."[40] At the same time, he stated elsewhere that he takes no pleasure in this and wants all to live.[41] So, in the old covenant era, Yahweh made a way to avert death by instituting the sacrificial system to make atonement for Israel's wrongdoings. By allowing for animals to take the place of humans, it was meant to be a temporary but just solution to the breach with God created by sin. Sacrifices were to be made once a year on the

Day of Atonement to redress the nation's collective sin and on occasion for certain types of sins committed by individuals. Central to each sacrifice was the pouring out of the animal's blood on the base of the altar. [42] In explaining why this was effective, God told Israel: "The life of a creature is in the blood; and I have given it to you to make atonement for yourselves on the altar; it is the blood that makes atonement for one's life."[43]

By providing for an animal to die in place of those who sinned, God protected the Israelites in that the sacrifices temporarily satisfied the law which says the consequence of sin is death.[44] On Israel's part, offering the animals were concrete acts of repentance given to make peace with God. They also cleansed the community from sin, thereby re-establishing and maintaining the purity of the people.[45] In this way, the atoning sacrifices made it possible for Israel to continue to have a relationship with Yahweh. It is important to note that the ritual sacrifices alone were not enough to please him. Yahweh's desire was for the one presenting the sacrifice—be it the nation or an individual—to have a humble, contrite heart, recognizing the gravity of being unfaithful to him, and seeking forgiveness and restoration [46]

The sacrificial system was merciful because it spared the nation or person from death, yet it was also just because it did not overlook the seriousness of wronging God. The sacrificial rites "taught the necessity of dealing with sin and, at the same time, demonstrated that God himself had provided a way for dealing with sin."[47] This is the imagery Paul is drawing on when he says in Romans 3:25, "God presented Christ as *a sacrifice of atonement, through the shedding of his blood*—to be received by faith." Christ became the ultimate sacrifice whose blood was "poured out for many" and covered (atoned for) the sins of all who trust in him, once for all time.[48] No animal sacrifices were necessary after Jesus died on the cross as a sin offering!

## An Elusive Model

One of the challenges in achieving a unified theory of atonement today is that it is not exactly clear what occasion Paul had in mind when he described Christ's death as an atoning sacrifice. The two great annual Jewish religious celebrations that incorporated animal sacrifices were the Passover and the Day of Atonement. Traditionally, Romans

3:21-26 has been seen to compare Jesus's death to the sacrifice on the Day of Atonement. This is understandable because Paul uses the word *hilasterion*, which the NIV translates as a *sacrifice of atonement.*

This term can also be interpreted as *propitiation, expiation, conciliation, placation* or as the *mercy seat* or *place of atonement*. The latter two phrases specifically reflect the way *hilasterion* is used in Hebrew 9:5, a passage that describes Christ's role as our high priest. Each year on the Day of Atonement, the high priest would stand in front of the ark of the covenant where the mercy seat was and offer a sacrifice to God to atone for Israel's sin.

In recent history, the term *hilasterion* has been controversial in the West, as scholars have debated whether it is best rendered as *expiation* (covering or cleansing) or as *propitiation* (making atonement or appeasing).[49] The difference between the two is the object of the act— expiation is focused on a problem (removing sin) and propitiation is centered on making amends with an offended party (making peace with God). While cleansing or removing sin was an important element of the Day of Atonement, most Western evangelical scholars have recognized *propitiation* as the primary meaning of *hilasterion.*[50]

However, since the middle of the twentieth century, scholars have been uncertain whether the Day of Atonement was the main setting Paul had in mind after all. This is because, while the term *hilasterion* has clear links to the Day of Atonement, the rest of the imagery in the text points away from it. The phrase translated "God *presented* Christ as a sacrifice of atonement" in the NIV is more accurately translated as "God made a *public display* of Jesus as the sacrifice of atonement."[51] This stands in stark contrast to the complete solitude of the Most Holy Place, the inner chamber of the temple where only the high priest presented the annual sacrifice to Yahweh on the Day of Atonement.[52]

Scholars unhappy with the Day of Atonement model have suggested the reference to the *hilasterion* links Jesus's death with the sacrificial death of the Maccabean martyrs, who gave their lives to defend the true God.[53] When a martyr prepared to die, he prayed that his death would be a *hilasterion* (propitiation) for the nation's sins. The Jewish martyrs were inspired by the story of Abraham's son, Isaac, and his determination to be faithful to God unto death. As a result, Isaac became the prototype of all martyrs and his willingness to die links into an extensive Rabbinic theological structure of atonement.

We have already seen some of the problems with relying on martyrdom theology in chapter one—it simply does not do justice to the full biblical picture of what Christ's sacrifice accomplished or the uniqueness of his death. The fact that Paul repeatedly claims the Law and the Prophets bear witness to the redemption Christ achieved suggests it is far more natural to look to these Old Testament writings to understand the apostle's perspective rather than to problematic extra-biblical texts like Maccabees 1–4.[54]

## What about the Passover?

Even if the Day of Atonement is ruled out as the primary setting, this leaves the Passover, the other national event involving a blood sacrifice, as a potential model for the atonement. Considering Passover as a setting for atonement in Romans 3:21-26 has been resisted primarily because the sacrificial offering in this text is described as a *hilasterion* (a means of propitiation) and most interpreters see no propitiatory value in the Passover. In their view, the lamb's blood smeared over the doorpost during the Exodus event averted the Angel of Death, but it did not atone for Israel's sin.

However, the idea that Paul relied on this motif actually makes good sense for a number of reasons. The Passover is the only religious rite in which redemption is celebrated and the only one that could be practiced away from the temple. Also, because it was observed in homes throughout the entire Roman Empire, it is the one God-ordained, Old Testament festival about which both Jews and Gentile God-fearers had detailed knowledge.

Also, since the First Exodus is when the nation was formed, the Passover event controlled both Israel's self-consciousness and her existence. She could not define herself apart from the reality that Yahweh had rescued her from captivity in Egypt. Even Israel's ethical system was founded on the fact that God displayed mercy by redeeming her from slavery.[55] If the Passover was at the heart of Israel's self-identification and understanding, then given that most of the New Testament writers were Jews, it should not be surprising to find this same imagery at the center of the end times salvation to which Israel had been looking forward. But most important of all, this is the only feast Jesus used to interpret his death![56]

Furthermore, some experts make the case that the Passover actually does have an atoning content in that the lamb's blood was a substitute for Israel's firstborn who were spared. The problem is that even those who see propitiatory value in the Passover offering, either originally in the Mosaic era or in the New Testament period, have not seen a connection between the Passover and references to the atonement in Romans 3:21-26. However, I contend evidence exists that links these two great sacrificial events together but has not been considered before now. Found in the prophet Ezekiel's writings, this evidence is vitally important to our discussion as it can help identify how the authors of New Testament understood the atonement and the purpose of Christ's death in redeeming God's people.

## Ezekiel's Combined Model

We have already established that if Paul were following the New Exodus model as I am arguing, his main source material would have been the Torah, which includes the Mosaic law given during with the First Exodus. And he would have also looked to the prophets' predictions of a Second Exodus that was to follow Israel's period of exile in Babylon and culminate in the restoration of her covenant relationship with God.

A crucial contributor to the expectation of another exodus was Ezekiel, who, like Isaiah, envisioned a coming Prince who would sit on David's throne. In Ezekiel's writings, this priestly Prince's main task was to build the end times temple and provide abundant sacrifices to atone for the sins of God's people.[57] What is significant about Ezekiel's version of events is that these offerings are *not* made on the Day of Atonement, which is the usual time set aside to address the nation's sin. In fact, Ezekiel never mentions the Day of Atonement in context of the end times temple. What he says is that these abundant atoning sacrifices will be offered *during the Passover.*

This has great significance! If Ezekiel, a priest who had preached against the sins of tampering with the laws of Yahweh, alters the sacrificial system so dramatically in his writings by identifying Passover as a time of atonement, he can only be doing one thing: he is emphasizing the importance of the Passover for addressing the sins of the people. [58] To make this point, he does the unthinkable and changes the Mosaic law in his prophetic writings by merging the two events.

Indeed, Ezekiel anticipates what the Son of David, the Messiah himself, will do by bringing atonement right into the center of the Passover celebration.[59] In this way, *Ezekiel combines concepts from the Passover and the Day of Atonement into one model!* Jesus is the Lamb of God, whose blood ensures that death will pass over God's people, and also the sin offering that makes atonement with God. The next question is whether Ezekiel's model was an obscure, little known concept or was it a major influence on Paul and the other New Testament writers?

## The New Testament and Ezekiel's Model

Substantial evidence suggests the entire first-century church, including Paul, understood and drew on Ezekiel's combined Passover/Day of Atonement model. James Dunn claims the introduction of atonement in Ezekiel 45 is grounds for seeing an atoning significance for the Passover in New Testament thought.[60]

Another contends the connection between the two events was widely understood before Jesus came. In his view, those who heard John the Baptist would have had no difficulty in understanding his declaration when he saw Jesus—"Behold, the Lamb of God who takes away the sins of the world."[61] This imagery draws on both the Passover (the Lamb of God) and the Day of Atonement (removes sins).[62] If these scholars are right in believing the link between Passover and atonement in Ezekiel 45 was well known in New Testament days, then those who read both the Gospels and Paul's writings could be expected to understand the connection.

Others have previously noted the link between Passover in Ezekiel 45 and the Day of Atonement, but the implications of this for understanding Paul's view of the sacrificial nature of Jesus's death have not been fully appreciated. For one thing, the apostle draws extensively on Ezekiel's prophecy in his writings; Ezekiel has long been recognized as the source of Paul's ideas that the church is the temple of the living God that was brought into existence by the Messiah's death. To see the Davidic leader offering sacrifices in the temple for the people would naturally lead Paul's thinking in the direction of the cross. This is supported by the fact that in Romans, Paul introduces Jesus as David's descendant. He couples this with language that indicates it is Jesus, the Son of David, the Son of God, who atones for sin and, as our Passover, achieves redemption for his people through his own death.

The idea that Paul, along with other New Testament writers, relied on Ezekiel's model is further supported by texts from the letter to the Hebrews. The tabernacle imagery in Hebrews is also based on the end times temple that Ezekiel describes.[63] This explains how the writer who penned Hebrews could speak of Christ as having obtained eternal *redemption* through his sacrificial death. This is strange for virtually all scholars recognize how heavily Hebrews 9 depends on the Day of Atonement imagery, a feast in which there was no concept of redemption. Again, redemption is associated with Passover.[64] A comparison of the themes in both Hebrews 9:1-10 and Romans 3:24-26 has shown them to be the same. Some have specifically linked *hilasterion* from Romans 3:25 with its use in Hebrews 9:5, which describes the altar where propitiation was made. In turn, this same language is used in Ezekiel.[65] If scholars are correct in seeing these associations, then it further connects Ezekiel with Paul's letter to the Romans.

In addition to the significant fact that Ezekiel linked atonement and redemption together, the prophet also used the preposition *huper* (in place of) throughout his writings in the LXX, a usage that is particularly unique to him. *Huper* is repeatedly used in the sacrificial imagery in the book of Hebrews and also throughout the Pauline passages about Christ's sacrifice. It became the standard expression in the New Testament church for describing the substitutionary death of Christ, the Lamb of God.[66] We will discuss substitution in more detail in chapter 12 when we look at Jesus's familial role as the firstborn of all creation, but for now, let me say the New Exodus framework provides fresh insight into this concept.

Other texts show Ezekiel's influence on Paul as well.[67] The reliance on this prophet would make it quite natural for Paul's readers to also hear the connection between Ezekiel's promises of atonement offered on Passover and the explanation that Paul gives regarding the death and resurrection of Jesus. Such clear dependence on Ezekiel's writings, either directly or indirectly, underlines the importance of the prophet's modification to the sacrificial system that combined the Passover with atonement, and the use made of it by the early church.

## Passover and God's Justice

The view that Paul looks to the Passover for understanding Christ's death is further supported by his reference in Romans 3:25 to the *paresin* (the passing over) of sins previously committed. This clearly echoes the passing over of the Angel of Death on the night of the Passover. The Egyptians' firstborn were not the only ones who were in danger that night. Because Israel had been unfaithful and worshipped the Egyptian gods, she was in danger of being judged by Yahweh as well.[68] Mercifully, he provided the blood of the lambs to serve as a substitute for Israel's firstborn, thereby, sparing them from judgment and death.

With the advent of the new covenant era, God no longer passes over sin; he has fully and permanently addressed it through the death of Jesus, the firstborn of all creation.[69] Paul explains that in this way, Christ's death is a demonstration of God's justice. The cross answers the dilemma as to how God, who is holy, just, and does not lie could apparently deal so "lightly" with sin in the past, especially when he said himself that sin leads to death. Over the course of human history, there have been many times when it seemed like God was ignoring sin and therefore, not keeping his own word. Paul is saying this was never the case! The apostle explains that in God's patience and forbearance, he passed over the sins committed beforehand because he had a plan to rescue his people from exile and death. Through the cross, God proved that he took sin seriously—so seriously in fact, that he presented his own beloved Son (with the Son's consent) to be both the Passover Lamb and a sin offering. This made the way for all who believed in Jesus to be released from Sin and Death, forgiven, and reconciled with God.

Another Passover theme is found in the use of *proetheto* in verse 25, which speaks of *the public display* of Christ's death. This is the statement that caused some to reject the Day of Atonement as the sacrificial setting of this text because on that day, the sacrifice was offered privately to God in the Holy of Holies. In all of the Old Testament, the only sacrifice that was publicly displayed was the Passover lamb, whose blood was daubed on the lintel and doorposts of the homes it protected. The blood of this sacrifice was foundational in redeeming the Israelites both from Pharaoh and God's judgment and it is, I would suggest, the only sacrifice that fits this description given by Paul.

The language Paul uses in Romans about Christ being the last Adam also dovetails with the emerging picture. The redemption Paul describes in Romans 3:21-26 is intended to undo the catastrophic effects of the fall. This points to the unity of the sacrificial language Paul uses throughout Romans, which presupposes Adam's role in bringing man into a covenant relationship with Sin.[70] The death of Jesus, who is described as the last Adam, reverses this tragedy. The redemption that comes through Christ's atoning death brings humankind out of the spiritual bondage in which it has been imprisoned since Adam broke covenant with Yahweh and formed a binding alliance with Sin/Satan. This salvation comes through the righteousness of God and the faithfulness of Jesus, not the law. To underscore this, Paul makes it clear the requirement of the law was met in the redemption and atonement that was accomplished through Christ's sacrificial death.

## A Consistent Theme

There is yet another source that likely influenced Paul in interpreting Christ's sacrificial death in the setting of Passover—Jesus himself. It is clear that Jesus regarded his death as an act of atonement, and equally clear that the timing of his death on Passover was deeply significant both for himself and for the early church.[71] Furthermore, he deliberately took the symbols of the First Exodus and reinterpreted them so that they spoke of the deliverance he was about to accomplish for his people in the New Exodus.[72]

The fact that Paul followed this same pattern is evident not only in Romans, but in his other letters. In 1 Corinthians 5:7, Paul speaks of Christ, our Passover having been sacrificed for us, and he connects the atonement with Passover in 1 Corinthians 15. In verses 3-4, Paul says Christ *died for our sins* according to the scriptures and was *raised on the third day* according to the scriptures. Then in verse 20, he says, "Christ has indeed been *raised from the dead*, the *firstfruits* of those who have fallen asleep." In these texts, Paul states that the one who died to atone for our sins was also raised from the dead as the firstfruits of those who have fallen asleep (died). What ties it all together is that in the Old Testament the firstfruits offering was associated with Passover.

In Jewish law, the firstfruits was a grain offering of the harvest's first produce to be presented to Yahweh in gratitude for what he had given Israel. As proscribed in Leviticus 23, the offering was to take place *on the third day after Passover began* during the Feast of Unleavened Bread, the seven-day festival when Israel commemorated this important historic national event.[73] Deuteronomy 26 clearly explains the link between firstfruits and the First Exodus.[74] When the priest set the offering on the altar, the Israelites were instructed to declare how the Lord delivered them from slavery in Egypt with a mighty hand, and brought them to a land flowing with milk and honey where he richly provided for all their needs.

Naturally making the connections in light of this Old Testament background, first century believers saw Jesus as our Passover who died to atone for sin, and on the third day rose from the dead as the firstfruits. Just as the firstfruits offering was a token to remind Israel that the harvest came from Yahweh, Jesus, who was raised as the firstfruits of the dead, is a token of the great harvest of those who believe in God's resurrection power and will be raised with him.[75] This imagery has been overlooked in 1 Corinthians 15. This is because the atonement, Passover, and firstfruits have not been linked together and seen as the backdrop for Paul's statements that Christ died for our sins and was raised on the third day as the firstfruits offering.[76]

If we are to allow any basic consistency in the apostle's thought, we should also look at 2 Corinthians to discern how he understood Christ's death. In 2 Corinthians 5:21, Paul says "God made him who had no sin to be sin for us, so that in him we might become the righteousness of God." At the very least, Paul describes Jesus's death in a way that suggests it is a sin offering.[77] Since it flows from the New Exodus theme that immediately precedes it, this statement should not be isolated from the previous verses and treated as a distinctively different strand of thought. Going back to 2 Corinthians 5:17, the phrase, "if anyone is in Christ, the new creation has come" is a clear echo of Isaiah's prediction of a new creation.[78] This was an integral part of the New Exodus promises made by the prophets. Indeed, going even further back to the beginning of the chapter, Paul describes the temporal nature of our life on earth as we journey home to our Heavenly Father, a theme that depicts the church as the pilgrim New Exodus community.

This is all part of the Paschal-New Exodus typology that guided the theology of Paul and the early church. Additional evidence that Paul saw a link between Passover, atonement, and the New Exodus narrative can be found in Galatians, Ephesians, and Colossians as well.[79] I also talk at length about other related themes and theological motifs that support the Paschal-New Exodus model for interpreting Christ's death in my earlier work, *Contours of Pauline Theology*.[80]

## The Two Goats

We have been speaking of the Passover and Jesus in his role as the Lamb of God, but there is another perplexing matter that needs to be taken into account—where do the two goats presented as a sin offering on the Day of Atonement fit into the picture? I want to touch on this briefly as it sheds light on how Yahweh could rightfully take Israel as his bride if she was in a covenant relationship with Sin/Satan along with the rest of humanity. This is important because, as we saw earlier, if God took Israel to be his own without satisfying the law of sin and death that gave Satan claim to her then he could not only be accused of adultery, but also of violating his own word.

You can read the details in Leviticus 16, but during this annual rite two goats were presented before Yahweh. One goat was sacrificed as an atonement to remove Israel's sin and uncleanness, so the nation could be at peace with Yahweh. The high priest presented the offering to Yahweh in total solitude within the Holy of Holies. Using his fingers, he sprinkled the blood on and in front of the mercy seat seven times. Next, he laid both hands on the second animal known as the scapegoat and confessed Israel's sins, transferring them onto the animal. Since he was not instructed to wash his hands until later in the ceremony, it would have been almost impossible for the blood of the slain goat on his hands not to be smeared on the live one. The second goat was then driven out into the wilderness to an entity called Azazel, who was understood in those days to be an evil spirit that personified wickedness.[81] Some believe this figure represented Satan.[82]

If this is correct, then a very powerful image is being played out. The atoning sacrifice not only delivered Israel from judgment and death, but it also showed that the nation was not under Azazel's (Satan's) control. A common understanding is that the scapegoat was a symbolic representation of Israel's sin being sent into the wilderness where the people would never encounter it again.[83] But some scholars suggest the blood-stained scapegoat also served as evidence to Azazel (Satan) that an acceptable offering for Israel's sins had been made to Yahweh; it demonstrated that the requirement of the law had been satisfied, and therefore, Satan's rule over the nation had been curtailed.[84] Although Israel had given herself to Satan through her pagan worship of false gods in Egypt, he no longer had claim on her because she now legitimately belonged to Yahweh.

Seen in context of the New Exodus framework, this annual sacrifice temporarily addressed Israel's sin so that she could be spared from death, and also reminded Azazel (Satan) that as God's bride, the nation was under his protection. The evil one could only exercise control over her if she played the harlot once again. Of course, this narrative is not likely to have been understood early in Israel's history with the clarity I am suggesting. But with all of the pieces in place, later on Israel's prophets could clearly see the storyline of the divine marriage and write about it in powerful ways.

By relying on the prophets and Ezekiel's combined model of the Passover/Day of Atonement, the New Testament writers interpreted the meaning of Christ's death within context of the Old Testament scriptures that Jesus himself explained to them. It is important to note that this tradition emerged before a thinker of Paul's caliber came along. The way he uses traditional material suggests this model was evidently well in place before he encountered Christ on the Damascus road. Again, this shows there is no division between Jesus, the early church's understanding, and the explanation of Christ's death found in Paul's letters.

## A Corporate Act of Salvation

Identifying the Passover as a central motif for understanding the atonement provides a window into the mindset of Paul and the other NT authors when they write about salvation. First, everything about the Passover is corporate. The Jews celebrated the Passover meal together as families and remembered God's saving power as he spared them on the night of judgment. As a nation, they were led out of Egypt and were baptized into Moses when they passed through the Red Sea.[85] God entered into a covenant with them as a nation when they appeared before him at Sinai, and it was as a nation that he swore himself to them to be their husband and took them as his bride. Unless we understand the significance of this corporate perspective and embed it into our thinking we will miss vital truths regarding our own salvation.

As mentioned above, a critical but often overlooked part of Israel's national salvation story is that she needed to be saved not only from Pharaoh and her Egyptian taskmasters, but also from the consequences of her own sin. We tend to focus on the suffering Israel experienced as an oppressed slave people. This is an important part of the story, but what is not often emphasized is that Israel was no innocent "damsel in distress" when she lived in Egypt; she was also suffering the consequences of embracing Egypt's gods and abandoning Yahweh who, through their ancestor Abraham, had elected her as his own people.

In looking at the situation more closely, it was understandable why the Hebrews initially went to Egypt to be under Joseph's protection—there was a famine in the land and they needed food. However, it was not understandable why they remained in Egypt once Joseph died. In fact, Joseph himself had anticipated their return to the Promised Land, giving them instructions to take his remains with them so that he could be buried with the nation's fathers. But like the Babylonian captives hundreds of years later who were freed to return to Zion yet chose to stay, the Israelites did not go back to Canaan even though they were free to do so at the time. Instead, Israel opted to remain in Egypt, which meant putting herself under Pharaoh's patronage and accepting his gods along with their demands. Ironically, one of Egypt's primary deities was Isis, the god of death.

Thus, instead of being the holy nation Yahweh called them to be, Israel chose to align herself with Pharaoh's gods and become the willing servants of sin and death. In rejecting the loving relationship with God, her Creator, she had done the same thing as Adam and entered into a covenant relationship with other gods. Even though Yahweh's intention was to make Israel his bride, she had broken the vows Abraham made on behalf of his family and their descendants. By getting into bed with Egyptian deities, she also broke the heart of Abraham's God. The Hebrews led comfortable lives under Egypt's patronage. Sadly, they only cried out to Yahweh for deliverance when a new Pharaoh took over and began to oppress them.

Because of the choices she made, in God's eyes Israel was as vile as Egypt. When the Lord concluded that he must judge the most powerful nation on earth, justice required him to judge Israel as well since she had become one with its gods. Although individual Jews who remained faithful to Yahweh may have been unhappy with the actions of their fellow countrymen, nevertheless, in keeping with the dynamics of corporate solidarity they were all members of that sinful, adulterous generation. Which is why the entire nation of Israel was in mortal danger of experiencing God's wrath and judgment when the angel of death passed through Egypt.

Appreciating these realities shows that God had to work on several levels to accomplish salvation for Israel. First, Yahweh had to overcome Egypt so that Pharaoh would let her go. Furthermore, since Israel now belonged to other gods he had to make a way to free her from these deadly alliances. He also had to work in Israel's heart so that she would want to be with her God. And then he had to protect her from the act of judgment that was coming on Egypt, the nation with whom she had chosen to align herself. This is why some form of atonement was necessary in order to deliver Israel—unless her sins were addressed, she too was in danger of judgment. As we have seen, Yahweh's merciful provision of smearing the blood of a lamb on the doorpost of each home on Passover night is what saved her firstborn from death and averted his wrath from Israel.

Serving as a type and shadow, Israel's national story enables us to understand why it was necessary for Christ, our Passover, to make atonement for humanity. As we saw earlier, without addressing our sin, there would be no way for anyone to be freed from Sin/Satan as the evil one would still have a claim on humankind in the same way that Pharaoh and his gods had a claim on Israel. It also allows us to see that just as blood of the lambs saved Israel from Yahweh's judgment on the night of Passover, the blood of Jesus, the Lamb of God, will protect his people from God's wrath when he exercises final judgment on Satan and his followers at the end of the age.

This brings us to the difficult subject of God's wrath. Since it is such a controversial matter, our discussion of the Paschal-New Exodus model for the atonement would not be complete without considering how it may—or may not—be related to Christ's work on the cross. This is what we will consider in the next chapter.

CHAPTER 9

# Loving Wrath

In Greek mythology, the gods were immortal but had qualities similar to humans. Known for their jealousy and irrational, often immoral behavior, they frequently quarreled among themselves and were quick to punish any mortal who upset them. The people saw adversities like disease, natural disasters, and other misfortunes as divine retribution for some perceived wrong.

For instance, Zeus, the god of the sky who also was king of the gods at Mount Olympus, was sometimes depicted as throwing a thunderbolt, a symbol of punishment. The ancient Greeks believed lightning and thunder during rainstorms were signs that he was angry with them. And Zeus's wife, Hera, had a reputation not only for feuding with her husband, but also for being vindictive, especially towards her husband's lovers and the children that came from those illicit unions. In the famous legend of Hercules, Zeus's illegitimate son, Hera sent two enormous snakes to kill him in his crib, and when that didn't work she found numerous ways to make his life miserable. Given the nature of their deities, it is no wonder the ancient Greeks lived in fear of the gods' anger and made offerings to appease their wrath.

Integral to the Western culture, these myths and legends explain, in part, why God's wrath is not an easy topic to discuss—for many, the subject conjures up images that are more in keeping with the false gods of antiquity than the God of the Bible. A common idea is that the God of the Old Testament is an old, white-bearded, easily angered deity who sits up in the sky and capriciously smites people or smashes cities whenever he is displeased. Another is of a stern, disapproving father figure who harshly punishes anyone who fails to live up to his exacting standards. The concept of "Sinners in the Hands of An Angry God," a famous sermon delivered by Jonathan Edwards during the First Great Awakening, is an enduring part of America's religious heritage that brings up frightful pictures of God for many.

Apart from these images, how God's wrath relates to Christ's atoning death is a touchy subject among Christians for other reasons. Some adamantly contend the idea that Jesus appeased God's wrath towards sin on the cross is an essential doctrine of the Christian faith. But for others, no matter how it's explained or defended, the idea that God would take out his anger on his Son—especially given that Jesus died such bloody, violent death—simply does not line up with other truths about his character. Since, in our human experience, anger rarely has a positive effect it is understandably difficult for many to reconcile how a loving God can also express wrath. For this reason, some would prefer to jettison the concept altogether in favor of a kinder, gentler God who never gets angry.

The problem with doing so is that references to God's wrath run throughout scripture from beginning to end. We can acknowledge that the concept has often been misunderstood or misused, and also that is an uncomfortable and sensitive subject for some. But there is no way to throw it overboard without excising major portions of scripture, which is something we are not at liberty to do. While it may not be a popular topic, since it is a significant biblical theme we can assume that it is to our benefit to consider why God, who by very nature is love, sometimes becomes angry and what, if anything, his wrath has to do with the atonement Jesus made for humanity's sin. I suggest that looking at God's wrath in context of the corporate Paschal-New Exodus setting will help us better understand the relationship between God's love and anger, bring greater clarity to what did and didn't happen on the cross, and also provide even more insights into what Christ's death accomplished.

**FROM GOD'S PERSPECTIVE¶** What clouds the picture when talking about God's wrath is that we have a tendency to view God through a human lens. However, as the prophet Isaiah explains, God thinks, sees, and does things differently than we do.[1] When approaching this subject, it is important to understand that God's anger is not like ours. As humans, it is not always wrong for us to be angry. In fact, there are times when it can spur us to take action in the face of injustice. But in his letter to the saints, James instructs his readers to be slow to anger because "human anger does not produce the righteousness that God desires."[2] Since our motives may be mixed with self-interest or self-righteousness and we cannot see into the hearts of others, we do not always have the wisdom to express anger in a productive manner.

On the other hand, scripture depicts God's wrath as stemming from his love, so it is pure and aimed towards that which corrupts and destroys. Because he knows the hearts of all, the judgments he makes are right and true. When expressed, God's anger is completely justified, and unlike us, he knows exactly how to direct it to accomplish his good purposes.

We can get a better understanding of God's anger by looking at the two main Greek words New Testament writers used when referring to God's wrath—*orgé* and *thumos*—both of which are characterized by passionate opposition. *Orgé*, the word that is used most frequently, is a steadfast, "controlled, passionate feeling against sin;" it is "a strong and settled opposition to all that is evil arising out of God's very nature."[3] *Thumos*, on the other hand, is "an outburst of passion" that may erupt suddenly and then subside.

For the most part, the apostles used *orgé* to speak of God's anger and *thumos* in reference to human wrath or anger. In Revelation, however, the word *thumos* is used multiple times to describe the full measure of wrath that God pours out on Satan and all who side with him at the end of the ages.[4] Here, God's anger towards sin/Sin blazes into a deliberate, passionate outburst of wrath as he executes final judgment on the kingdom of darkness through Christ, the Word of God, who "treads the winepress of the fury *(thumos)* of the wrath *(orgé)* of God Almighty."[5] It is important to note that this type of wrath is only unleashed after numerous God-given opportunities to repent and turn from evil are rejected. [6]

Another complicating factor is that some tend to talk about God's wrath as though it is one of his defining attributes and it is not. [7] Rather, when God expresses anger in the scriptures, it is in response to the sinfulness of man and even then, it is often tempered by compassion so he does not act on it hastily or thoughtlessly. [8] To see from God's viewpoint, it will be helpful to consider two passages that provide the most significant self-disclosure of his nature in the entire Old Testament. When Moses asked to see God in the book of Exodus, he was only allowed to glimpse Yahweh's back as he passed by. At this time, God described himself saying,

> The LORD, the LORD, a God merciful and gracious, *slow to anger*, and abounding in steadfast love and faithfulness, keeping steadfast love for thousands, forgiving iniquity and transgression and sin, but who will by no means clear the guilty, visiting the iniquity of the fathers on the children and the children's children, to the third and fourth generation. [9]

The prophet Jeremiah echoes these same themes when he writes:

> Thus says the Lord: 'Let not the wise man boast in his wisdom, let not the mighty man boast in his might, let not the rich man boast in his riches, but let him who boasts boast in this, that he understands and knows me, that *I am the Lord who practices steadfast love, justice, and righteousness in the earth*. For in these things I delight, declares the Lord. [10]

Notice that wrath is not listed as one of God's primary attributes. To the contrary, God describes himself as *slow* to anger, a characteristic that is repeated throughout the Old Testament. [11] Reflecting what we saw above, judgment only enters the picture when people repeatedly refuse to repent, and his forgiveness is spurned. When God says, "he will by no means clear the guilty, visiting the iniquity of the fathers on the children and the children's children," he is not making the children responsible for the father's sins. Rather he is saying that if the fathers do not address their sin and come to him for forgiveness, which he is willing to freely give, then subsequent generations will experience the negative effects of their wrongdoings. In his lovingkindness, this is something he wants to prevent. In addition to God's self-disclosure, the Old Testament also depicts him as a loving husband to the widow and a father to the orphan who cares deeply about the poor and sets the lonely in families. This picture of God has absolutely *nothing* in common with the stereotypes of ancient deities or abusive fathers who vindictively punish anyone who displeases them.

The commonly held view that God, in his anger, punishes people at will can be traced, in part, to an excessive emphasis on the forensic model. In this framework, sin is taken out of its covenantal context and primarily defined in terms of disobeying God's laws. Sins are seen as crimes that deserve punishment, with death as the ultimate penalty. We saw that in this view, God sent Jesus to take the punishment we deserve and die in our place so that he could legally pardon sinners. Some versions of this model maintain that when Jesus was crucified, God poured out his wrath towards our sin on his Son, who, it is said, absorbed it within himself in order to appease or satisfy (propitiate) the Father's anger. In this way, it is said, Christ's sacrificial death saved all who believe in him from God's fierce wrath.

One of the problems with this version of the penal substitution model of atonement is that it is in danger of glorifying God's wrath and treating it as though it is a primary attribute by which he wants to be known. If this view is allowed to dominate our understanding it will not bring us to the God who disclosed himself so powerfully and tenderly to Moses, and even less to the God who is so lovingly revealed in the person of his own Son, Jesus.

## The Relational Context of God's Wrath

In contrast to the forensic view, the New Exodus model can help us come to a much clearer understanding of how God's wrath and judgment fit into the picture that God himself has given us of his character and being. In this corporate framework, God's wrath towards sin is set within context of the divine marriage, his desire to have a people who know and love him wholeheartedly, and his steadfast opposition to all that violates or destroys that love. Since this subject is so often misunderstood, it will be helpful to explore a few other key texts about God's wrath in the biblical narrative. Once we get a clearer picture of what angers God, we will apply this to our conversation about the atonement.

To see how God's wrath relates to his love in the corporate New Exodus setting, let's go back to the blessings and cursings in

Deuteronomy 28–32 that we touched on earlier. As the children of
Israel were preparing to enter the Promised Land after their time in the
wilderness, Moses and the elders conducted what could be described as
a vow renewal ceremony. Israel's representative leader reminded the
people of the covenant they entered into with Yahweh at Mount Sinai,
and also of several sins that would violate that covenant and bring
judgment.[12] Number one on the list was worshipping idols and false
gods. Others included such things as dishonoring parents; withholding
justice from foreigners, the fatherless, and widows; and certain forms
of sexual perversion and murder—all things that harmed others and
were, therefore, offensive to God. Moses reaffirmed that if they would
be faithful to Yahweh and do as he said, he would treasure Israel as his
holy people and set her high above the other nations he made, just as
he promised.

On this occasion, Moses described the multiple ways God would
bless Israel if she remained true to the covenant.[13] This was the path of
life and prosperity. He also warned that terrible curses would come
upon the nation if they broke the covenant and turned away from
Yahweh to worship other gods.[14] Moses explained that if the people
took this wayward path and stubbornly resisted correction, eventually
Yahweh would become angry because of their ongoing betrayal and
allow Israel's enemies to carry her off into exile.[15] Separated from his
presence and subject to foreign kings and false gods, she would
experience the terrible desolation, despair and adversity that comes
from being separated from God.

We know from Israel's history that eventually this happened. As we
saw earlier, because of her serial infidelity and refusal to respond to his
patient, repeated warnings God finally brought judgment on Israel
(Judah), which led to her exile in Babylon. In Old Testament language,
this is when Yahweh, Israel's husband, turned away and "hid his face"
from her.[16] Israel's story shows that what rouses God's wrath is not
simply breaking his rules and disobeying his commands, although this
is part of it. Yahweh was angry because, as a nation, Israel had
abandoned her covenantal relationship with him and shamelessly
persisted in worshipping dumb idols and false gods. Furthermore, she
failed to care not only for the poor and needy, but also for the land he
had entrusted to her.[17] In context of the narrative, God is likened to a
loving husband who is rightfully upset by his wife's repeated affairs and

neglect. Inevitably, he is pushed into divorcing even though that is not what he really wants. In short, God finally kept his word and sent Israel into exile because of her ongoing unfaithfulness.

To have a right understanding of God's wrath, it is important to realize that when Yahweh turned Israel over to her enemies, his primary purpose was not to take revenge, nor did he take pleasure in it. In fact, the prophet Hosea shows it grieved God to take this step.[18] Rather, he did it to discipline (chastise) Israel and bring correction so that his relationship with her could be restored. The intended outcome of exile was to turn the hearts of his people back to him by allowing them to experience the bitter hardships of life when separated from his love and protection.

In this setting, God's wrath was *redemptive*. His right and just anger was directed at the sin that was destroying his relationship with Israel and her willing participation in it. Because their hearts were hard, and they would not listen to correction, in his severe but gracious mercy, God let Israel experience the consequences of her choices so that she could realize the utter futility of sin. Exiling Israel was an act of love on God's part that was intended to produce a change of heart. If she did not repent, she would finally be given over to the deities she had chosen to serve and be cut off from Yahweh forever.[19] In this state, Israel would eventually discover the full extent of all she had rejected as she came to see how utterly different her new lovers were from the One who had called her into existence and set his affection on her.

God's steadfast love for his people was apparent in that, even before they were sent into exile for repeatedly betraying him, he always held out the promise of restoration. Moses told Israel at the renewal ceremony that when she was scattered among the nations for her unfaithfulness (as he already knew she would be), if the people would turn back to God and obey him wholeheartedly, he would have compassion and bring them back to their home, the Promised Land. Not only would he restore Israel, but also, he would make her more prosperous than ever before. God also promised to circumcise their hearts and the hearts of their children, so they would love him with their entire being and live.[20]

Seen in this context, the most powerful model that reveals the true nature of God's wrath is not the criminal law court metaphor but the divine marriage, which is central to the New Exodus narrative. Not only was God heartbroken because of Israel's unfaithfulness, she knowingly aroused his anger by continuing to reject his love and give herself to deities who used and abused her. He was also angry with Satan who, in the guise of false gods, had captivated her heart. Would anyone claim that it is unreasonable for a faithful husband to be angry if his wife became so enthralled with another that she willingly abandoned the marriage? Or argue that his anger toward the one who seduced his wife was somehow unjustified?

In addition to shedding light on God's anger, this model also helps us better understand the corporate nature of his judgments. Far from being a vindictive, mean-spirited deity who punishes people on a whim, the reality is that Yahweh, as the psalmist says, is "compassionate and gracious, *slow to anger*, abounding in love" and does not "harbor his anger forever."[21] In his patience and unwavering love, God not only offered mercy to Israel after she betrayed him, but he graciously gave other wayward cities and nations, including Egypt, the opportunity to turn to him as well. As seen in the story of Jonah, the reluctant prophet whom Yahweh sent to the city of Nineveh, some people groups did repent and received mercy.[22] Others, however, that rebelled and persisted in perpetrating deep evil eventually brought judgment on themselves or sometimes, in exceptional cases, suffered God's direct judgment.

## The Purposes of God's Loving Wrath

This backdrop can help us better grasp the purposes of God's wrath in scripture, where we see two types of judgment—*redemptive* and *punitive*. God's wrath is also spoken of in two tenses—*present* and *future*. The first type and tense can be seen in Romans 1, where Paul says God's wrath is *currently* being revealed in the lives of the unredeemed who have overtly rejected him. Rather than taking direct action against them, God, in his righteous anger, steps back and gives them what they want. Since they prefer to worship created things rather than the Creator, God turns them over to the "sinful desires of their hearts," leading to practices that degrade the body.[23] And because they have no interest in knowing him, he gives "them over to a depraved mind, so that they do what ought not to be done," resulting in an evil, faithless, heartless lifestyle.[24] In describing the lives of unredeemed humanity, Paul provides a disturbing picture of what it looks like to be separated from God and living in Satan's domain.

However, as we have seen, God's desire is for "all people to be saved and to come to a knowledge of the truth."[25] When people choose to reject God, just as with Israel, he allows them to experience the painful consequences of their choices with the aim of producing repentance. But also, just as he did with Israel, he continues to offer the promise of reconciliation and restoration in this age to all who want to come back to him. In this way, God's anger can have a *redemptive* purpose.

The church is a clear example of the positive effects of God's redemptive wrath. Paul reminds the saints in Ephesus that before they became members of the body of Christ, they were in the same boat as the rest of humankind. They used to be followers of the "prince of the power of the air," he says, "sons of disobedience who were dead to God" in their trespasses and sins.[26] In their former lives as members of the body of Sin, they too lived in the passions of the flesh (unredeemed humanity), "carrying out the desires of the body and the mind" and were by nature "children of wrath" like the rest of humanity.[27] Exiled from God's presence and experiencing the darkness of life apart from him, they had no hope until, in his great love and mercy, he rescued them from Sin and Death and made them alive with Christ.[28] The same can be said of all believers.

The New Testament also reflects Israel's experience by showing that God, in his forbearance and mercy, delays judgment as long as possible. The apostle Peter explained to anxious believers who longed for Christ's return that God is not slow in keeping his promises to make all things new and establish his visible kingdom. Rather, in this present age he is patiently giving all of humanity an opportunity to repent and return to him because he does not want anyone to perish when he exercises final judgment on Satan and the kingdom of darkness![29]

This points to the second type and tense of God's wrath in scripture—what numerous texts refer to as God's *punitive* wrath.[30] Examples of this type of wrath are found in the Old Testament when people refused to repent, and Yahweh finally moved to put a stop to evil. This was demonstrated in the stories of the Great Flood, God's response to Sodom, and the death of Egypt's firstborn.[31] In keeping with his long-suffering nature, in each instance, God's punitive wrath was only expressed after providing repeated warnings and ample time for the evildoers to turn back to him.

Echoing the Old Testament prophets, the New Testament writers refer to God's *punitive* wrath as a *future* event to take place at the end of the age.[32] Jesus himself warned that the cities of Chorazin and Bethsaida would suffer greater consequences than other unrepentant cities in the final judgment because they still rejected him even after witnessing the miracles he performed.[33] Paul alerted some of his readers that because of their stubbornness and unrepentant heart, they were *"storing up wrath"* against themselves for *"the day of God's wrath, when his righteous judgment will be revealed."*[34] And in his second letter to the saints, Peter describes *a coming judgment day* in which ungodly men will be destroyed and unrighteousness purged from the earth.[35] This future event, in which God will exercise his punitive wrath against evil, will be like nothing that has ever been seen in the history of humankind!

More details about this time are found in Revelations 16, where the apostle John writes about the seven bowls of God's wrath that will be poured out on those who have cooperated with Sin/Satan. The hardships associated with the first five bowls are redemptive efforts meant to turn the hearts of evildoers back to God, but they will refuse to do so. The sixth is when God's enemies gather to fight against him. When the last bowl is poured out, John says, "God remembered Babylon the Great and gave her the cup filled with the wine of the fury of his wrath."[36]

This is when God finally says "enough" to evil and, in his *punitive* wrath, moves to bring destruction on the great Prostitute who "corrupted the earth by her adulteries."[37] As we have seen, the Prostitute is unredeemed humanity who reject God and chose the favors that Satan offers instead. At this time, God avenges the prophets, saints, and the blood of all others she is responsible for shedding.[38] Jesus also "treads the winepress of the fury of the wrath of God Almighty" by pronouncing judgment on those who have warred against God and his people in the last days.[39] Eventually, God executes final judgment on his great adversary, Satan, along with his minions and all who prefer darkness to light.[40] The old order passes away, the new comes, and the long-anticipated celebration of the marriage between God and his people finally takes place!

Looking at the final judgment in Revelation alongside the celebration of the divine marriage, we see the big picture of humanity's sin, rebellion, and God's redemptive plan. Right at the heart of the biblical story is humankind's rejection of God's love and the choice to be with another god, reflecting Sin/Satan's identity and character rather than the benevolent nature of our Creator. God's wrath is directed towards everything represented in this act of rebellion. His judgment towards humankind's unrepentant sin comes into sharp focus in this context. Seen in this light, God's judgment is part of the spiritual warfare that began on earth when Satan enticed Adam to rebel against God and form a covenant alliance with him. Anyone who continues to reject God and side with Satan will experience the judgment God is reserving for the evil one and his kingdom on that final day.

The idea that the unredeemed are "children of wrath" and under judgment is in line with Jesus's teaching that anyone who does not believe in "the name of God's one and only Son" and loves the darkness rather than the light is already judged.[41] This sheds light on why God did not send his Son to judge or condemn the world but rather to save it.[42] Jesus came to announce the day of salvation, inviting all to return to God and escape this judgment by believing in him. A similar understanding is reflected in Paul's first letter to the Thessalonians. Noting that their faith had become an example to believers in other cities, the apostle wrote, "For they themselves report ... how you turned to God from idols to serve the living and true God, and to wait for his Son from heaven, whom he raised from the dead, *Jesus, who rescues us from the coming wrath.*"[43]

Ultimately then, how we are judged on that day depends on the community to which we belong—those who are unrepentant members of the body of Sin headed by Satan will experience God's wrath and judgment; those who belong to the body of Christ headed by Jesus, our Passover, will be safe.

As we continue our discussion, it is important to remember the two different forms of God's wrath. The first is his *redemptive* wrath in which he allows people to make their own choices and then experience the consequences of sin with the aim of producing repentance. The other is his *punitive* wrath that eventually comes on those who refuse to turn away from evil and come to the light. In this type of righteous wrath, God exercises judgment upon determined perpetrators of evil and vindicates those who have suffered unjustly for his name's sake.[44]

It should be emphasized that *only God* is to dispense justice in this manner; Christ instructs his disciples to follow him in loving and doing good to their enemies, trusting God to avenge evil in his time and according to his divine wisdom.[45] In both cases, God's wrath is an expression of his truth, love, justice, and holiness.

**ADJUSTING LENSES—ISAIAH 53¶** Coming back now to the matter of how God's wrath may or may not relate to the atonement, we have another task—we need to carefully sort through Isaiah 53. This is a key text for evangelical theology; in fact, some consider it to be the controlling Old Testament passage for interpreting Jesus's death as a vicarious atonement. It is also often used to support the idea that God punished Jesus on the cross to satisfy his wrath towards our sin. For instance, in commenting on this text, one respected theologian acknowledges that Jesus experienced pain and disgrace "at the hands of lawless men" and then states, "but we dare not miss what was going on 'behind the scenes.' While human agents were killing an innocent man, God was *pouring out His wrath* on this same man—His incarnate Son. He was crushing Jesus 'for our iniquities.'"[46]

Given the language of this passage, it is possible to understand why Isaiah 53 is seen in this light. In the text, the prophet Isaiah describes someone he refers to only as the servant, who most Christians believe is Jesus. Quoting from the NIV with terms used in other translations in parentheses, the prophet says,

> "we considered him *punished (stricken, plagued)* by God and afflicted. But he was *pierced* for our transgressions, he was *crushed (bruised)* for our iniquities; the *punishment (chastisement)* that brought us peace was on him, and by his *wounds (scourging, stripes)* we are healed."[47] The text also explicitly states that it was "the Lord's will to *crush (bruise)* him and *cause him to suffer (put him to grief)*" as "an *offering for sin (guilt offering, reparation)* . . . for he *bore the sin* of many."[48]

However, in spite of what seems to be obvious atonement and wrath-related language, I believe there is good reason to question the traditional interpretation of Isaiah 53. First, let me say I agree that it is a crucial text for Christian understanding. I do not deny that it informs us about the death of Jesus or that the early church looked to it, along with other materials, when developing their theology of what Christ achieved on the cross.[49] But my position is that certain elements of New Testament doctrine have been imported back into this passage that inadvertently altered how we understand the meaning. I suggest that when read in its original Old Testament setting and in context of the Paschal Exodus framework, we will discover that Passover and redemption, not atonement, is the proper setting for Isaiah 53 and that it does not say what it is typically thought to say about God pouring out his wrath on the servant.

Getting to the bottom of this will require us to patiently sift through a number of issues that have a bearing on how the text is read. Once this groundwork is in place, we will put the pieces together to get a clearer picture of what exactly is—and is not—going on in this important Old Testament passage.

## First Things First

When engaging with Isaiah 53 it is necessary to begin by reflecting on methodology; that is, how should the evidence be interpreted when determining the meaning of the passage? The initial step is to consider how Isaiah's original readers would have understood Isaiah 53. Then we need to need to ask if it is right to read back into the text what the first-century church came to make of it seven hundred years later.

In other words, is it reasonable or correct to believe that when Isaiah penned these words, it was initially understood by its original readers to be speaking about Christ's death, the event to which it was eventually linked by the church? Taking the time to see the author's perspective in key Old Testament texts that are later appealed to by the New Testament writers can help us understand what was in their arguments and what was not. This, in turn, will enable us to discern if we, as contemporary believers, are reading a particular text through the correct historical lens.

Looking at the original context, the first question, as mentioned, is to consider who the servant was in the eyes of the original readers? This issue has occupied a central position in Old Testament studies for hundreds of years. Theories range from the prophet Isaiah himself to Israel who, it is reasoned, suffered for the sins of the world. All of the suggestions have elements of truth and are possible. However, some key clues have been overlooked that could help solve this quandary, one of which is found in the immediate introduction to this song about the servant. I want to take the time to explain who I see the servant to be and why I believe considering this will help our thinking,

The introduction to the passage we know as Isaiah 53 actually starts in 52:

> See, my servant will act wisely;
> he will be raised and lifted up and highly exalted.
> Just as there were many who were appalled at him—
> his appearance was so disfigured beyond that of any human being
> and his form marred beyond human likeness—
> so he will sprinkle many nations,
> and kings will shut their mouths because of him.
> For what they were not told, they will see,
> and what they have not heard, they will understand.[50]

This text clearly speaks about one who suffers innocently (as does the rest of Isaiah 53), but it is the statement "and kings will shut their mouths because of him" that is significant. The ancient kings see the suffering of this important figure; he is a victim of brutal violence and they are rendered speechless. Now, the reality is that few kings in the ancient world would be silenced if a nondescript person suffered, as this happened every day in their world. Rather they are speechless because the servant they have heard about is one of their own; he too is a king! They are struck by the realization that if this could happen to the sovereign of a neighboring nation, it could also happen to them. Their families could also be dispossessed of their thrones and treated as criminals. An analogy is when the Bolsheviks killed the royal family of Russia. The news must have stunned the royal families of Europe as they realized this horrific event could herald their own downfall. These kings are also awestruck because this is not just any ruler—it is Israel's king, the one who served his God and is innocent, yet has suffered greatly. He is also the one who, after having been treated so cruelly, will be highly exalted and "sprinkle many nations." (We will look at the meaning of this phrase in a moment.)

A second clue to the servant's identity is found in Isaiah 55:3-5. After describing the attributes and outcomes of the servant's death in chapter 53, Isaiah goes on to let his readers know that the servant is David's descendant, who in Old Testament terms was the son of God, a title that was applied to the king of the Jews in Samuel and the Psalms.[51] In this passage, Isaiah speaks of a covenant Yahweh establishes with the servant, one that upholds the promises made to David.

So, in the introduction to Isaiah 53 we learn that the servant is identified as Israel's king, and from Isaiah 55 we are told that he is

David's descendant, appointed by Yahweh to be Israel's representative leader. In both texts, we also see that he has a role to play that involves other nations. Having clarified these aspects of the servant's identity, we can now begin to consider Isaiah 53 itself.

## Questions About the Traditional Lens

The next step is to ask what the servant's death accomplished? Based on traditional understanding, the natural response would be to say that he died to atone for our sins. It's true that Isaiah says the servant was "crushed for our iniquities" but we need to be careful here. I suggest seeing this as an atonement-related statement is an example of using statements by New Testament writers as a lens to read back into Isaiah 53. What we need to ask first is what did Isaiah and his ancient audiences understand regarding the purpose of the servant's death. Then we can look to see how Jesus and the apostles used it when constructing the Christian doctrine of the atonement.

This is a critical issue because the Jewish community has a very different take on the meaning of Isaiah 53; they believe the servant is the nation of Israel. Given this, how then do we get from the Jewish understanding to the Christian view, and is the Christian adaptation a legitimate use of this key passage? It is important not to automatically assume that we know the answer to the question of what the servant's death accomplished or we will skip over critical evidence that can shed light on the meaning of this text.

It was in asking this myself that I began to question the traditional understanding. In the larger context of Isaiah 40-66, Israel is exiled in Babylon. Most see the servant in chapter 53 as paying the price (atoning) for Israel's sins so that she could be released from exile. Christian theologians then expand on this understanding to say Jesus is the servant and he died to atone for humanity's sins.

The first problem I have with this traditional reading stems from Isaiah 40:1-5, which says:

> Comfort, comfort my people, says your God.
> Speak tenderly to Jerusalem,
> and cry to her
> that her warfare is ended,
> that her iniquity is pardoned,
> that she has received from the Lord's hand

double for all her sins.

If we are to take this text seriously, it shows that Israel had already paid for her sins. In fact, she paid double, indicating that God was fully satisfied that the covenant curse Israel brought on herself as a result of her unfaithfulness had been addressed. Having spent the allotted time in exile for her sins, Yahweh was no longer angry with her and Israel could return to the land from which she had been removed. So here is the question: If Israel's sins had already been paid for, why would there be a need for the servant, a national leader, to make atonement for her?

The second problem not normally discussed is that many translations of Isaiah 53 says the servant was "crushed" as a sin offering. This totally contradicts the Old Testament sacrificial system, which states that no blemished animal could be offered to Yahweh for sin. Atoning sacrifices had to be perfect, yet in Isaiah 52, the servant is described as horribly disfigured; his appearance was marred beyond human likeness. Furthermore, in the Old Testament, sacrificial animals were not crushed, beaten, or tortured as the servant was, nor did God take out his wrath on them to satisfy his anger towards sin. In fact, care was taken to use humane means when they were sacrificed. Furthermore, in serving as a substitute for humans, the animals *averted* the judgment due to sinners; there is no indication they *absorbed* God's anger.

So here we have two major contradictions: first, Israel had already paid for her sins by completing her allotted time in exile, yet the traditional understanding is that someone else—the servant—was dying to atone for her sins. And second, it's commonly believed that the servant was crushed as a sin offering which is contrary to Old Testament sacrificial law. These facts should provoke us to ask what exactly is going on in Isaiah 53? If Israel had already atoned for her sin, why did the servant-king need to die?

## Clues in the Context

As is normally the case, the immediate context provides the answer. The flow of Isaiah 40-66 is about how Yahweh will redeem Israel from Babylon similar to the way he redeemed her from Egypt during the First Exodus. References to redemption, Passover, and the divine marriage are laced throughout the context. In fact, there is a clear echo of the Passover event in Isaiah 52, just before the section on the death of the servant-king is introduced in verse 13.

I suggest stopping here to read Isaiah 52 in your own Bible. The chapter has to do with God's call to Israel to leave Babylon and return to Zion. Verses 1-12 are clearly about Israel's immediate exodus from Babylon (also referred to as Assyria, the nation that conquered Babylon). Israel is to be made clean and put on new garments, having no uncircumcised in her midst. She will be redeemed without money and will once again know God's name. Yahweh will keep his promises to save and restore her just as he foretold, and all the nations of the world will see it. Unlike the First Exodus, however, Israel will not go out in haste or flight because the Lord will lead her and be her rearguard.[52] In other words, here we see exodus language being applied to Israel's immanent deliverance from Babylon.

As we have seen, the divine marriage was at the heart of the Egyptian Passover and the First Exodus; Yahweh had redeemed Israel to be his bride. This theme also plays a central role in the Second Exodus from Babylon; the restoration of the divine marriage was promised to Israel as the final triumph of her return from exile. In Isaiah 52, Israel is described as coming back with great joy and excitement to the relationship she had forfeited as the bride of Yahweh. This is the significance of knowing Yahweh's name once again; restored as his wife, she will have all of the privileges that come from being united to him. The greater context surrounding Isaiah 53 is studded with imagery of the divine marriage:

> Lift up your eyes and look around; all your children gather and come to you. As surely as I live, declares the Lord, "you will wear them all as ornaments; you will put them on, like a bride." (Isa. 49:18)

> For your Maker is your husband—the LORD Almighty is his name—the Holy One of Israel is your Redeemer; he is called the God of all the earth. The LORD will call you back as if you were a wife deserted and distressed in spirit—a wife who married young, only to be rejected," says your God. "For a brief moment I abandoned you, but with deep compassion I will bring you back." (Isa. 54:5-7)

> I delight greatly in the Lord; my soul rejoices in my God. For he has clothed me with garments of salvation and arrayed me in a robe of

righteousness, as a bridegroom adorns his head like a priest. (Isa. 61:10)

As a young man marries a young woman, so will your Builder marry you; as a bridegroom rejoices over his bride, so will your God rejoice over you. (Isa. 62:5)

The restoration of the divine marriage is clearly intended to be the climax of a new creation. Returning will be like going back to Eden, the time when humankind was in a sacred, covenantal relationship with God. The prophet speaks of this homeward journey as being the manifestation of God's glory to the earth. This is conveyed in Isaiah 51, which says, "The LORD will surely comfort Zion and will look with compassion on all her ruins; he will make her deserts like Eden, her wastelands like the garden of the LORD. Joy and gladness will be found in her, thanksgiving and the sound of singing."[53]

The suffering of the servant-king in Isaiah 52 and 53 also carries powerful Paschal Exodus imagery for the end result of his anguish is that he shall "sprinkle many nations."[54] Given the redemptive context, there is reason to believe this sprinkling echoes the first Passover. It may refer to the blood of the lambs that dripped from the doorposts and covered Israel when the angel of death passed over. Or it could refer to the blood that was sprinkled to consecrate Israel when she entered into a covenant relationship with Yahweh at Mt. Sinai. In either case, the sprinkling of many nations points to the eventual cleansing and reception of the Gentiles that will also be made possible by the servant's suffering and death.

Furthermore, the servant is described in 53:7 as being led like a lamb to the slaughter, and silent as a sheep before her shearers. The paschal imagery of lambs in the text provides an important clue to the meaning of the servant's death. Remember, without the Passover in the First Exodus, the divine marriage would not have been possible as it was through this event that Israel was released from the covenant relationship she had entered into with foreign kings/gods. No Passover meant no divine marriage.

While noting the connection between the Egyptian and Babylonian Exodus events, there is also a critical difference that needs to be taken into account when interpreting Isaiah 53. As I pointed out earlier, in the first Passover, atonement and redemption occurred together. Following Mount Sinai, however, these events were separated. The annual Day of

Atonement became the regular time for dealing with Israel's sins, while the yearly Passover celebration, which occurred on a different day, was simply an important commemoration of the redemption Yahweh had achieved for Israel. Having addressed the matter of Israel's sin and God's forgiveness earlier in the narrative, Isaiah's focus in chapters 52 and 53 is on the need for *redemption*, release from bondage to her masters in Babylon—both kings and foreign gods—rather than atonement for sin. This is a critical factor to keep in mind as we continue our discussion.

## A Different Lens

So how does this inform the way we should interpret Isaiah 53? The Paschal Exodus imagery embedded in both the larger and immediate context suggests that the royal servant did not die to make atonement, as the traditional understanding goes; rather he died as a Passover sacrifice. If this is so, it is a very important part of Israel's redemptive story—the restoration of the divine marriage and the inauguration of the new creation are not through the death of a lamb as in the Egyptian Exodus, but the death of her king!

In the immediate context, this representative servant-king, the promised descendant of David, dies to redeem Israel from captivity. Redemption was necessary because Israel had been unfaithful to Yahweh even before the Babylonians took her captive. Embracing foreign deities as lovers and swearing allegiance to them, she had become the bride of another god(s). In doing this, the prophet Isaiah writes that Israel had entered into a covenant with death.[55] Even though she had paid for her sin in exile, Israel was still bound by law to another god in an unbreakable covenant that could only be annulled through the death of one of the parties.

In our discussion of Romans 5–8, we touched on the idea that covenants are terminated through death. A number of other examples indicate this principle was commonly understood in the Old Testament era. For instance, when Israel worshipped other gods at the time Moses was on Mount Sinai receiving the law, Yahweh told Moses that he was going to cut Israel off, a term normally associated with being put to death, thereby ending his covenant relationship with her.[56] Moses, as Israel's representative leader, pleaded with God to spare the lives of the people and take his life instead.[57] Likewise, Israel's exile in Babylon is also described as a form of death in that she was separated from Yahweh, the source of life. In Ezekiel's vision of the valley of the dry bones, the nation is pictured as being dead, and the renewal of the covenant relationship with Yahweh when she receives the Holy Spirit is seen as being brought back to life.[58]

This dynamic runs throughout the Old Testament. People who deliberately violated the law were given the opportunity to make things right through repentance and sacrifice. However, if they did not repent and follow God's instructions for addressing their sin they were to be cut off, that is, put to death or exiled, thereby ending their covenant relationship with Yahweh and his people.[59] This may sound severe, but what is not normally noted is that death was intended to be more of a solution than a punishment. Violators were cut off from the covenant community to prevent others from being corrupted by their influence and defiled. (As we saw earlier, this is why Paul was so concerned about unchecked sin in the Corinthian church.)

We will come back to the relationship between punishment, death, and exile later, but for now, the point I want to reinforce is that death is the prescribed way of terminating covenants, including those Israel entered into with other gods. If Israel could die, her covenant with foreign deities could be ended, and if she could be raised from the dead she would be a new person, a new creation; she would have left everything behind that had separated her from Yahweh. But how could an entire nation die? All of this could be accomplished if the servant-king, Israel's representative leader, stood in for her and died in her stead. Admittedly, this is sounding very much like Pauline theology, but there again, where did he get his understanding? Since, according to the apostle himself, it was based on the law and the prophets, the similarities should not be surprising.

This, then, sheds light on the *purpose* of the servant's death in Isaiah 53. Although Israel had already atoned for her sins, the servant-king died as a Passover sacrifice on her behalf in order to annul the covenant she had entered into with foreign gods. In this way, he made it possible for Yahweh to bring Israel back to himself. This perspective also helps to clarify the *nature* of the servant's pain and death; in identifying with his people, he was suffering *because* of Israel's sins, not to make atonement *for* them, for as we have seen the nation's sins had already been addressed. We'll talk more about this distinction in a moment, as it is an important factor in understanding Isaiah 53.

**REDEMPTIVE LANGUAGE¶** One of the difficulties with accepting the view I am presenting is that atonement-related language seems to run throughout Isaiah 53. The text says the servant was pierced *for* our transgressions, crushed *for* our iniquities, and the Lord has *laid on him* the iniquity of us all, a phrase that seems to echo the Day of Atonement offering of the two goats. Verse 8 is rendered as *"for the transgression of my people* he was punished"* and 53:10-11 explicitly says, "The Lord makes his [the servant's] life an *offering for sin"* and that "he will *bear their iniquities."* In light of this language, there seems to be no question that the servant in Isaiah 53 died to atone *for* his people's sins.

Given the context, however, I want to gently suggest this is one of those places in which some translators have read New Testament theology back into the Old Testament. I say this because if we read Isaiah 53 through the Paschal Exodus framework embedded in the context, the possibility of an alternative picture emerges—one that is centered on redemption rather than atonement. Since many are so used to reading this passage as though it is set against the backdrop of the atonement, it can be quite challenging to see it differently. For this reason, it will be necessary to address a number of specific language-related issues and questions in order to comprehend the meaning of the text in its redemptive, Paschal setting. Once this process is complete, I believe it will become clear that Isaiah 53 is not about atonement, nor does it support the idea that God poured out his wrath on the servant.

The first language-related issue I want to draw attention to has to do with the difference between suffering to *pay for* someone's sin (atonement), which is the language used in a number of translations, and suffering *because of* someone's sin, which is how it is often rendered in ancient Hebrew. For instance, looking at verse 5 in the NIV, the text reads, "but he was pierced *for* our transgressions, he was crushed *for* our iniquities."[60] In contrast, verse 5 in the Holman Bible says, "He was pierced *because of* our transgressions, crushed *because of* our iniquities." The NET Bible, which also uses *because of*, notes that this preposition has a causal sense.[61] In other words, even though the servant was innocent, he suffered *because* he identified with his people who had sinned. This rendering is more consistent with the passage's redemptive context—the servant enters into the suffering of his people to actually free them from captivity, not simply to pay for their wrongdoings.

Since the distinction between *for* and *because* is so critical to the argument I am making I want to share a fictitious story to illustrate the difference between the two. Imagine that a man named Steve visited a warm, welcoming community in South America on a trip through the area and decided to stay a while. To his dismay, he discovered that all of the villagers were hooked on cocaine and that it was slowly destroying the community. Addicted from birth, even the children were dependent on the drug! Steve observed that a man drove into the village two days a week and sold packets of cocaine to the villagers. He also discovered the dealer worked for a local government official who used his power to protect the regional drug cartel and intimidate anyone who tried to interfere.

As Steve came to understand the plight of the community, he longed to see them break free of the drug. Becoming deeply concerned for the people's welfare, he found numerous ways to help them. Suspicious of his motives at first, his steady acts of kindness began to win some of the villagers' trust. Steve also told them stories of what their lives could be like if they were willing to get away from the official's corrupt influence and stop using cocaine.

Over time, the dealer began to notice that his sales were dropping due to Steve's influence. Concerned that his livelihood was being threatened, the dealer reported this turn of events to his boss, the government official, who was furious at Steve's attempt to disrupt the operation. Determined to eliminate the threat, he instructed a couple of local thugs to incite a crowd to turn against Steve and do "whatever was necessary" to silence him.

News of the plot got back to members of the village. Fearing for his life, those who had come to trust Steve urged him to escape while he could. Though he certainly didn't want to face an angry mob, he was not willing to leave until he knew that those who wanted a new life had safely left the village. Only ten people agreed to go, but that was enough for Steve to act. He quickly arranged with his friends to bring a bus and transfer the small band of villagers to a different jurisdiction where the corrupt official had no power. Unfortunately, just after the bus pulled away, the dealer and his thugs arrived. Praying he had not been seen, Steve headed towards his car to escape, but before he could get to it, he was tackled from behind and brutally kicked and beaten. Dragged to his feet, the mob surrounded him, shouting and demanding to know why he stayed in the village and tried to interfere with their lives. Before he could explain, one of the men pushed through the crowd and thrust a knife deep into his heart, killing him.

The point I want to make is that in this story, Steve functioned as a *redeemer*. The primary goal of his rescue effort was to make it possible for the villagers to escape from the corrupt government official's control and move to a safe environment where they could become drug free. In this situation, Steve was not making atonement for the wrong the community had done—in fact, that did not even enter his mind— and that is not why he was beaten and killed; he did not suffer *for* them. Rather, he suffered *because he had identified with the villagers and sought to rescue them.*

Of course, all analogies fall short, so there is a major difference between this story and Isaiah 53. In Steve's case, he did not need to die to redeem the villagers since they were not legally bound to the official; his suffering and death was the unfortunate result of mob violence. However, the servant-king's death *was* necessary to redeem Israel because she had entered into a binding covenant with the Babylonian gods, one that could only be terminated through death. When the servant, her representative leader, died on her behalf, Yahweh reckoned that Israel died as well. Dying to the covenant that bound her to foreign gods, she was then free to be restored to Yahweh as his bride. This is the same dynamic we saw when looking at Paul's understanding of what Christ's death achieved in Romans 7:1-6. By dying with Jesus to her old husband, Sin/Satan, the new covenant community was free to become Christ's bride.

As a reminder, let me say that we must be careful when referencing the New Testament in relation to Isaiah 53 so that we don't jump ahead in our thinking and impose the apostles teaching upon the passage. If we do, we will never learn what the writer of Isaiah 53 was saying. In considering the meaning of the servant's death in the immediate context of Isaiah 53, it is critical to remember that redemption and atonement are not the same thing, and that at this stage of Israel's history, they were separate events. Later, when we discuss how the early church applied Isaiah 53 to Christ's death, we will see how the New Testament writers came to understand that redemption and atonement were joined together at the cross to present the one glorious truth that "Jesus died for our sins according to the scriptures."[62] But for now, we need to continue exploring what Isaiah 53 means in its precise Old Testament setting.

## Was the Servant a Sin Offering?

Another obstacle to accepting the view I am proposing has to do with the language in verse 10 that specifically says, "The Lord makes his life an *offering for sin* (*asham*)."[63] Some versions of the Bible use the phrase *guilt offering* or *offering for guilt.*[64] One of the reasons some translators have favored these atonement-related concepts is because the Hebrew word *asham* is found most often in Leviticus 5 and 6. In this context, it refers to a specific type of offering given to make atonement for an unintentional trespass against the Lord. Since the rest of Isaiah 53 has normally been seen as having to do with atonement, at first glance, interpreting *asham* as a sin or guilt offering seems to make good sense.

There are a number of problems with this, however. For one thing, as we have seen, Israel had already paid for her sin so there was no need for the servant to make atonement. Furthermore, in this passage there is no mention of the Temple or the altar that are associated with the sacrificial system in the Old Testament. However, redemptive themes related to the Passover-Exodus framework run throughout the context, and at this point in Israel's history, Passover and atonement were two separate events. When seen in this light, the reasons for interpreting *asham* in Isaiah 53:10 as a sin or guilt offering are not quite as obvious as they first appear to be.

This raises an issue that has been problematic for biblical studies and has a direct bearing on how best to translate *asham* in Isaiah 53:10. As James Barr has shown, a common mistake is to take a word used in various contexts and then combine the meanings to create a one-size-fits-all definition.[65] Take the word *trunk* for instance. In some settings, it can mean the base of a tree, a storage box, the back-end of a car, the center part of a person's body, or an elephant's nose. If we try to say that *trunk* usually means the base of a tree because that is the first definition given in some dictionaries we are sure to misinterpret the word when it's used in other settings. The meaning of *trunk* can only be determined by paying close attention to the context. In the same way, to interpret *asham* as a sin or guilt offering because that is how it is most often used in Leviticus is no guarantee that it has this same meaning in Isaiah 53. We must look at the immediate context.

Given the redemptive setting of Isaiah 53, I suggest that among its range of meanings, a more appropriate interpretation for *asham* is *reparation* or *restitution*. Verse 10 would then read, "The Lord makes his life *a reparation.*" Or, as the Jewish Bible states, "to see if his [the servant's] soul would offer itself in *restitution.*" A number of other scholarly works support this rendering.[66] Used in this sense, *asham* has to do with repairing the damage that was done by sin. We need to be careful, however, as some works that interpret *asham* as *reparation* also go on to translate the term in context of atonement. For instance, the New American Bible (Revised Edition) uses the phrase *reparation offering,* which suggests it is a sin offering. However, as we have seen, while Leviticus mainly centers on atonement, the context of Isaiah 53 has to do with redemption, so this is a case where the importance of the context has been forgotten as warned by Barr. For these reasons, we cannot look to Leviticus to define the meaning of *reparation (asham)* in Isaiah 53.

John Goldingay lends support to the view I'm presenting. He too favors *reparation* as an interpretation of *asham,* saying that in context of Isaiah 53 the term does not necessarily carry the idea of guilt. He also points out that *bearing the sins of many* is not a reference to the sin offering; rather it is about how the servant identifies with the suffering that Israel has brought upon herself because of her unfaithfulness. Furthermore, although he misses vital clues related to the paschal-divine marriage theme in the surrounding context, Goldingay also sees the parallels to the First Exodus in the text, a framework which I propose Isaiah references. As he observes, "The servant goes through Israel's experience in Egypt which is also what the people [are] once more going through."[67] In light of these considerations, the question we must ask now is what does *reparation (restitution)* mean in the redemptive context of Isaiah 53?

Generally speaking, reparation has to do with putting things right. For instance, Germany had to pay reparations to the allies after the First World War. The money was not given to make atonement; rather it was a contribution to repairing the damage caused by the war. We have seen that in the Paschal Exodus context of Isaiah 53 Yahweh was reclaiming his bride. Israel had completed her "hard service" in exile and now, having pardoned her, God was moving to keep his promise to bring her home to Zion and restore their covenant relationship.[68] Unfortunately, part of the damage caused by Israel's sin was that she was legally bound to another god; she was not free to be reunited with Yahweh until the covenant was rightfully dissolved. Identifying with his people and stepping into their suffering, the servant-king made reparation in that through his death he satisfied the requirement of law, thereby annulling her covenant with death. By freeing Israel from foreign powers, which allowed her to return to Yahweh, the servant-king made it possible to repair the breach in the covenant relationship caused by Israel's sin.

## Did God Pour Out His Wrath on the Servant?

We are coming now to language that as some see it, seems to clearly support the idea that God punished the servant to satisfy his wrath toward sin. In the NIV, Isaiah 53:4 says "we considered him *punished by God, stricken by him*, and *afflicted*." Verse 5 says the servant "was *crushed* for our iniquities; the *punishment* that brought us peace was on him." Verse 8 states "for the transgression of my people he was *punished*," and in verse 10, Isaiah writes, "it was the *Lord's will to crush him* and *cause* him to suffer." Given these combined statements, it is not surprising why some believe that God, in his wrath, was punishing the servant. I suggest these texts, however, take on a different hue when set within the redemptive context of the Paschal Exodus framework.

One of the reasons this is such a challenging passage is that *punishment* can have various connotations, some of which can be emotionally charged for contemporary readers. As mentioned earlier, it may conjure up images of severe treatment by violent, abusive, or vengeful authority figures. Or within a law-court setting, it may be understood in a punitive sense as a "penalty inflicted on an offender."[69] *Punishment*, however, can also be defined as *chastisement*, in which case it has the connotation of correction and instruction. In reading through Isaiah 53, it is not always easy to decipher in what sense *punishment* is being used. What we don't want to do is to make the mistake described earlier and assume it has the same meaning across the board in Isaiah 53.

Before considering the first use of *punishment* in verse 4 (NIV), it will help to review what is happening in the story. Earlier in Isaiah 40, we saw that Israel had paid for her sins by suffering the covenant curses referred to in Deuteronomy 29-32. Now, in chapter 52, God intends to redeem his people from captivity and he calls them to prepare to return to Zion. He plans to accomplish this glorious redemption through the servant figure. Isaiah states the servant will act wisely and be exalted among the nations, but then the story takes an unexpected twist. Rather than delivering Israel with strength and might as expected, the servant experiences brutal treatment at the hands of his enemies, causing many to be horrified. In addition to the humiliation, his appearance was so disfigured that it was "marred beyond human likeness." However, as Isaiah points out, even in his youth, the servant was not a charismatic figure—no one was attracted to him; in fact, he was despised, and people avoided him, much like a leper.

Judging by appearances, his people draw a faulty conclusion. As Isaiah writes in 53:4, they thought God was punishing the servant for something *he* had done. This was wrong on two counts. First, the servant was suffering because of *the people's* sin, not his, and second, they misunderstood God's role in it. The Hebrew word the NIV translates as *punishment* in this verse is *naga*, "to touch or lay a hand on."[70] It has a range of meanings that include *to strike violently, to beat, bring down,* or *plague,* and is rendered in many translations as *stricken.* This language certainly creates the impression that the servant was being beaten or afflicted in anger.

However, it is important to note that in this verse, Isaiah does not say Yahweh was the one who was "laying a hand" on him; rather observers *assumed* this based on a common cultural belief that anyone who was afflicted in such a manner had done something to incur divine punishment. We see this notion in the Gospel of John. Referring to a man who was born blind, the disciples asked, "Rabbi, who sinned, this man or his parents, that he was born blind?" Jesus answered, "Neither . . . but this happened that the works of God might be displayed in him."[71] There is absolutely nothing in verse 4 that indicates Yahweh was angry or that he was the one who was striking the servant in a violent manner.

We get more insight into Yahweh's role in verse 5, which uses a different word for punishment. As the text goes on to explain, the servant's suffering actually has a redemptive purpose—he endures the suffering his people deserve so they can find peace with God, return to him, and be healed. The Hebrew word Isaiah uses here is *musar*, which is translated as *punishment* in some versions of the Bible and *chastisement* in others. *Musar* is not about punishment in an angry, vengeful, or penal sense; rather it has to do with the type of *chastening, discipline, correction or instruction* intended to teach or tutor, such as that given by a caring teacher to a student or a loving father to his child.

As used in 53:5, *musar* has the same connotation as the Greek *paideuo* and its derivative, *paideia* used in the New Testament by the author of Hebrews to speak of God's *loving discipline*. In Hebrews 12, the reader is reminded to "not make light of the Lord's *discipline*," for "the Lord *disciplines* the one he loves."[72] Jesus, too, uses the term at the end of days when he tells the angel of the church in Laodicea, "Those whom I love I rebuke and *discipline*. So be earnest and repent."[73] Discipline in this context is related to a child's training and is used for enabling someone to reach maturity.

The author of Hebrews observes that while some form of pain or hardship may be involved in the chastening process, our heavenly Father "disciplines us for our good, so that we may share His holiness."[74] Acknowledging that God's loving correction may produce momentary sorrow, the writer says that in the end, it leads to peace, righteousness, and healing.[75] As we saw, when God judged Israel because of her unfaithfulness and chastised her by allowing the nation to be carried into exile, it was for redemptive purposes—the goal was to bring correction so that Israel's relationship with him could be restored. Furthermore, he was not eager to take this step; he wanted to spare Israel, but she would not listen and continued to engage in destructive behaviors. For this reason, he finally gave her over to enemies who exercised violence against her.

This is a crucial distinction—Israel's enemies, *not God*, were the ones who cruelly mistreated her after she turned to foreign gods instead of Yahweh. There is no suggestion whatsoever in Isaiah 53, Hebrews, or anywhere else in scripture that God metes out harsh forms of punishment for sin in order to pacify his own anger or that he chastens his people, including the servant, in a vengeful, abusive manner. God's judgments are always a righteous expression of his justice. In the case of the nation's exile to Babylon, he stepped back and let Israel have what she wanted, even though, as she soon discovered, it would lead to pain and hardship. Now the servant, whom Yahweh sent, was suffering on her behalf so that she could be redeemed.

Going on to verse 8 Isaiah says, "for the transgression of my people he was *punished*." The Hebrew word for punished here is *nega*. It means essentially the same thing as *naga* used in verse 4—it carries the idea of being stricken physically in some sense, whether by blows or afflicted by a plague. In addition to having the connotation of physical violence, the terms *naga* and *nega* can also mean, "afflicted with leprosy." While there is no indication the servant actually had the disease, this language could imply he was suffering as a consequence of Israel's uncleanness, which, because of his identification with the people, was attributed to him. Also, if the flow of Isaiah 53 is about how the servant is treated by Israel's enemies—*and not about how he is treated by God*—then like the village that was under the control of corrupt government officials in the illustration above, it's possible the nation's oppressors, or even rebellious members of Israel herself, saw the servant's message as having an unwelcome influence on the people and sought to put him to death.

But what about the phrase in verse 10, "It was the *Lord's will to crush him and cause him to suffer?*" As stated in another translation, "But *the LORD was pleased to crush Him, putting Him to grief.*"[76] Doesn't this show that God himself was directly responsible for the servant's tortuous sufferings? Here, we gain additional insight into Yahweh's involvement in these events. We have already established that Israel's enemies were the ones who were doing the beating, piercing, and tormenting, not the LORD. However, going back to verses 5 and 6, we see that Yahweh had a role in the servant's suffering. As one commentator observes, the LORD "*let* the wrongdoing of all of us fall on him" or, put another way, he "*causes* or *allows*" the people's wrongdoing and the punishment (chastisement) they deserved to fall on the servant instead of them.[77] This shows that Yahweh was indeed at work behind the scenes, so to speak, but as the passage goes on to make clear, it was not for cruel or abusive purposes or with the intent to do harm; rather it was so that all the faithful Israelites who wanted to be in a restored relationship could return to him.[78]

Moving to verse 10, to say the LORD was *pleased* to crush the servant and *cause* him to suffer does not mean that Yahweh took some kind of perverse delight in inflicting pain on the servant. First, in this setting, *pleased* or *to take pleasure in* is a "term used of sovereigns."[79] When speaking of kings and queens, "Their pleasure is equivalent to their will in a matter" as expressed, for example, in the statement that "It was the King's good pleasure to send an edict throughout the land."[80] In the same way, it was Yahweh's good pleasure (sovereign will) to work through the servant's suffering to accomplish his good purposes. This is evident when looking at the entire verse. While the beginning of 53:10 says it was Yahweh's will for the servant to be crushed, the end of the verse also says it was his will for the servant to see his offspring and prolong his days, and also that "the will of the LORD will prosper in his hand." This shows that the servant's sufferings were temporary and God's intentions toward him were benevolent.

Second, in Hebrew, active verbs like *cause* do not necessarily refer to direct action taken by an agent but can speak of the permission granted to do it. This dynamic was reflected in the language used by the commentator above when he noted that Yahweh *let, allowed,* or *caused* the people's sins to fall on the servant. While it can be said on one level that Yahweh caused the servant's suffering by directing or permitting the people's sins to fall on him, this does not mean that Yahweh himself exercised violence against the servant. Furthermore, the language in verse 10 does not suggest that Yahweh caused or allowed the servant to suffer against his will. To the contrary, as we see in the following verses, the servant voluntarily gave up his life for his people, resulting in the justification of many. This shows that Yahweh and the servant were in agreement.

Seen in the broader context, the servant was beaten, stricken, and punished by enemies, but it was Yahweh's will (good pleasure) to use the servant's suffering for redemptive purposes. His intent was not only to restore those in Israel who had remained faithful to him in the midst of their captivity, but also, as Isaiah 55 reveals, to bless many other nations. And after his sufferings, Yahweh richly rewarded the servant. There is simply no evidence in this passage to support the idea that Yahweh punished the servant to satisfy his wrath.

## Isaiah 53 Reframed

Looking at the full picture now in context of the Paschal Exodus framework allows us to discern what is happening in Isaiah 53. As we saw earlier, Yahweh told Israel that if she continued to betray him, in his redemptive wrath he would discipline or chastise her by allowing the nation's enemies to overtake her. After refusing to listen to his many warnings, Yahweh finally turned his face away and let Israel have what she wanted—he gave her over to the foreign kings and gods with whom she had been unfaithful. No longer under Yahweh's protection, the Babylonians took Israel captive and carried her into exile.

Having paid for her sins by serving her full sentence in exile, in Isaiah 52 and 53 Yahweh is calling for Israel to leave Babylon and return to him as his bride. However, before this could happen, the covenant alliance Israel had foolishly entered into when she rejected Yahweh for other gods had to be legitimately annulled.[81] As we have seen, a covenant can only be ended through the death of one of the parties. So, in order to redeem her, the servant-king identified with his people and, enduring the chastening Israel had brought on herself, he died on her behalf to free her from the covenant that bound her to another. Because the servant died representing Israel, his death cancelled the control the Babylonian gods had over her and she was released. By his wounds the nation found peace and healing, as through his representative suffering and death, the servant-king made it possible for those who were willing to return to Yahweh, the source of life.

In summary, then, Isaiah 53 is not about atonement and forgiveness; it is about redemption. And God was not pouring out his wrath on the servant; rather the text shows the servant-king voluntarily endured the sufferings inflicted by Yahweh's enemies in order to redeem his people. Thus, he died as an innocent Passover sacrifice, knowing that Israel's exile could only come to an end through his death. It was not about a political victory, but a spiritual one. Reflecting Yahweh's benevolent will, through the servant's suffering many were justified.

Although aspects of the Paschal Exodus storyline in this passage have not been widely recognized, it is important for those who may not be familiar with reading Isaiah 53 against this backdrop to know that I am not introducing a novel approach. Influenced by trends that became popular starting in the eighteenth century, Isaiah has often been treated as a collection of prophecies or oracles. Since it was not regarded as a literary unit, there was no expectation of finding continuity in Isaiah's writings. More recently, however, scholarship has recognized that common themes run throughout the book. Consequently, Isaiah is now being approached as a unified whole. My reading of Isaiah 53 is simply a result of applying this recognized continuity. By interpreting this difficult passage in context of the unfolding biblical narrative, we are able to see it in a new light.

## Christ, the Servant

Now that we've seen what Isaiah 53 means when read in its Old Testament context, we are in a better position to understand how it was used—and not used—by the first-century church. As stated earlier, there is no doubt the early church looked to Isaiah 53 when developing their theology of Christ's death. Certainly, in line with this text, they understood Jesus to be the Servant-King, the Passover sacrifice who died to redeem his people from captivity. It is important to note, however, that what we learned about the death of the servant in Isaiah is not identical with what we find in the New Testament regarding Christ's sacrifice. The New Testament writers wove together two strands of truth to describe what Jesus's death accomplished. As Ezekiel 45 shows, in the end times the Passover lamb was to become a sacrifice of atonement once again. In other words, as Paul teaches in Romans, Corinthians, and Ephesians, in the Passover of Christ, Jesus redeemed his people, his bride, from captivity to Sin/Satan *and* atoned for their sins.[82]

This demonstrates why Isaiah 53 is a crucial text for the Christian understanding of what Jesus accomplished through his death. While in its original setting this passage does not speak of atonement or God's wrath, its expanded use by the New Testament writers does not violate biblical truth. By understanding Ezekiel's prediction of how sacrifices of atonement were to be offered by the Davidic prince during the end times Passover, we can see how the first-century church correctly understood that redemption and atonement were both achieved in Jesus's paschal death. What the apostles did not do, however, was use Isaiah 53 itself to support the idea that Christ made atonement on the cross or that God punished Jesus to satisfy his wrath towards sin in humankind.

Let's wrap up this part of our discussion now by looking closely at what New Testament writers say in regard to God's wrath and Christ's death.

**CLEARING AWAY MISCONCEPTIONS¶** We have been taking time to explore the subject of God's wrath as it relates to atonement as it is a significant factor in the contemporary controversy about the purpose of Christ's death. One of the unsettling claims we have wanted to weigh is the belief that the New Testament doctrine of the atonement is abhorrent because it presents God as a cosmic child abuser, who, in his anger, cruelly punished his Son for sins that he did not commit. Thankfully, seeing Christ's death in context of the Paschal-New Exodus framework can lead us out of such a scandal and help us get a clearer understanding of how God's wrath fits into the biblical picture of a loving God.

Applying what we have learned so far, what scripture clearly states is that Jesus will save all who are in him from God's *coming wrath.* This takes place in the future when God exercises final judgment on Satan and his allies. Like the Passover lamb and subsequent atoning sacrifices in the Old Testament, the blood of Christ will protect the believing community by averting God's wrath from his people. But—and here is where we need to think things through carefully—*nowhere* does the Bible say that Jesus *satisfied God's wrath while he was on the cross.* According to the apostle Paul, what Jesus satisfied or fulfilled was the *righteous requirement of the law*, which says the consequence of sin is death.[83] This is a critical distinction.

In the New Testament, Jesus is described as "the atoning sacrifice (propitiation) for our sins" and "also for the sins of the whole world."[84] In the Old Testament, the death of the sacrificial animal was evidence that the conditions of the law had been met. Blood had been shed; a life had been given up so that the covenant curses Moses outlined to Israel did not have to be applied to the offender. Because of this merciful provision, the one who sinned did not need to be cut off from God by death or exile, but fellowship with him could be restored and continue.

In the same way, by offering himself as an atoning sacrifice in place of his people, Jesus satisfied the law's requirement so that all who believe in him could be restored to God and enjoy fellowship with him. God presented Jesus as an atoning sacrifice for this reason, not so that he could satisfy his anger by punishing his Son. We can say this with confidence because the full fury of God's righteous, punitive wrath on all that is evil will not be poured out until the end of the ages, and it will be directed *at Satan and the kingdom of darkness*, not his Son or those who are in union with him.

This leads to another misconception of God's wrath and the atonement that needs to be addressed. A common teaching is that God severely punished Jesus in payment for our sins. In this view, since sin is an infinite offense against God's glory and honor, it deserves an infinite judgment. Consequently, God poured out his wrath on Jesus with a degree of intensity that corresponds to the magnitude of humanity's sin. Because Jesus absorbed the punishment we deserved, it is said, believers will be spared from the eternal torment that God will inflict on those who reject him.

The problem with this picture is that it is not taught in scripture. The Bible is clear that the wages of sin is *death*, not death to which God deliberately adds infinite torture and sufferings. As we have seen in the Old Testament narrative, the consequence of sin was either physical death, or spiritual death that comes from being separated from God's presence. Our first parents experienced both when they were excluded from the Garden of Eden after betraying Yahweh. Some of the Israelites who died physically during the First Exodus did so as a consequence of the nation's sin. And Israel experienced a spiritual death when she was cut off from Yahweh and sent into exile in Babylon because of idolatry. The subsequent sufferings experienced in each case were the outcome of being alienated from Yahweh and not because he purposely devised additional ways to torment them.

I realize a number of texts can be used to support the idea that God imposes post mortem punishment on those who reject him.[85] What the biblical narrative shows, however, is that judgment is eternal exile from his presence. Period. The language of eternal suffering and of the lake of fire found in some of these texts is drawn from the Old Testament exile narrative where Israel's separation from God is described as being in the midst of destruction and fiery flames. Virtually all the references to fire are associated with wars that occurred when Israel's enemies overran her and carried her into exile.[86] As noted by one theologian, wrath in Jewish thought "refers to hostile military action."[87] As a result of her own choices, the nation had been sentenced to death, which they experienced when they were cut off from God's presence and subject to their enemies. Clearly, this was not a literal termination of the entire nation, for the people continued their physical existence in the land to which they were taken as captives. In this context, being sentenced to death meant that in their new home they were dead to God.

This is the destiny of those who refuse God's forgiveness and reject him—they will experience eternal exile from his presence. Scripture describes this as the second death. Exactly what this will entail we cannot say other than if interpreted consistently with Old Testament imagery, references in Revelation to burning in a lake of fire mean neither extinction nor unbearable physical sufferings.[88] In her exile, Israel was not completely eradicated, nor did she suffer never-ending physical agony. Initially, the nation did go through great physical distress. However, this did not continue after Israel's enemies took her captive for, as time went on, those who allied themselves with their captors and refused to return to Zion clearly preferred their exiled state! What these Israelites lost that was never to be restored was their relationship with God. Having chosen to stay under the protection of Israel's conquerors and their gods, they became God's enemies, a condition that had long-term consequences.

So, let us be clear, the punishment for sin is death, exile from God's presence and nothing more. Whatever suffering may be experienced in eternal exile is the consequence of being cut off from God and not because he intentionally and cruelly torments humans forever in a lake of fire.

Clearing away these misconceptions helps us see that the atonement is not about God's need to appease his own anger by punishing his Son instead of us. Nor is it about the need for Christ to suffer intense pain on a grand cosmic scale so that he could pay for humanity's sin. Scripture does not speak of Christ enduring eternal suffering in the hours he was crucified; it simply says that he died for us, in our place. Admittedly it was a shocking and excruciating death, but the pain that he suffered was not the essence of the atonement; rather, the cross was a public display that the death sentence required by the law had been fulfilled.

So, what do we make of the claim that the New Testament teaching about the atonement portrays God as a cruel, unloving father? Here again it is important to see things from God's perspective. As presented in scripture, sending Jesus to die in order to free us from Sin/Satan was an act of love towards humankind on the part of the Father and the Son, who were in agreement. A helpful analogy is D-Day, which was the turning point in World War II. On June 4, 1944, 160,000 Allied troops landed on the beaches of Normandy, France to begin a push that would ultimately end the war. When the plan was conceived, General Dwight Eisenhower, leader of the Allied troops who was charged with executing it, knew the cost would be high. The Germans held a fortified position on the cliffs above the beaches, which meant the soldiers who stormed the beach would be sitting ducks. However, it was understood not only by the military commanders, but also by the men who were being sent into battle that even though many of them would suffer and be killed, unless the Allies gained a foothold in Europe and defeated Hitler, millions more could die.

Both the Allied commanders who made the gut-wrenching decision to send men into the battle and the soldiers who followed their directive accepted that the sacrifice was necessary so that others could live. In a similar way, even before the foundations of the earth were laid, God foresaw what would happen in the garden and made the costly decision to send his beloved Son, his Servant, to defeat Satan and free his people, knowing that he would suffer. And the Son willingly gave himself so that through his sacrificial death many could return to God and live. As Paul said, in this way "God demonstrates his own love toward us, in that while we were yet sinners, Christ died for us. Much more then, having now been *justified by his blood* (present), *we shall be saved from the wrath of God* (future) through Him."[89]

## Clarifying the Picture

To sum up, when Jesus assumed humanity's sin and died in our place, as depicted in Isaiah's description of Israel's Servant-King, he was handed over to God's enemies and endured the chastisement that we deserved. Having sifted through Isaiah 53 and other relevant passages, we can confidently say the accusation that the Son suffered at the hands of the Father is a gross distortion as scripture clearly states that he died at the hands of sinful men.[90] The wider biblical picture also shows us the cost to God in sending him to rescue humankind from sin/Sin.[91]

However, in the mystery of his divine wisdom, God used this devastating event for good in that Christ's death was essential if the Father was to "be just and the one who justifies those who have faith in Jesus."[92] On the cross, Christ suffered because of and for our sin, having been made a curse for us so that we could be restored to the Father and spared from eternal exile.[93] The biblically focused view that judgment is exile from God's presence explains the nature of Jesus's suffering; it was proportional and it was adequate. As the Servant-King, he represented his people in the same way that Adam had represented humanity and the servant represented Israel in Isaiah 53. In allowing Jesus to die, God momentarily turned his face away from his Son as he suffered exile on our behalf. However, because Jesus himself was sinless, Death had no right to hold him and he came back from the dead, bringing the new covenant community with him. Through his death and resurrection, he has ended the exile of his people and inaugurated the New Exodus!

Of course, the Bible does speak of a future judgment in which God's punitive wrath, so long withheld from humanity, will finally be meted out. On the day of God's wrath there will be no further offering of mercy. Those who have sided with Sin/Satan will be excluded from the kingdom and the separation will be final and irrevocable.[94] All who prefer the kingdom of darkness will never again have the chance to hear the loving voice of God or be invited into his presence. They will have chosen the god they want to serve, and in time, they will know the full horror of his perverted, abusive "love."

Scripture teaches that when that day arrives there will be no display of God's wrath toward his people, as he does not have an ounce or gram of anger toward those who have called upon Christ! The believing community does not need to fear punishment because God's infinite love has already been revealed to us in Christ, our Passover representative.[95] Just as the blood of the lambs protected the Israelites from Yahweh's judgment when the angel of death passed over Egypt, the blood of Christ will protect the believing community from God's punitive wrath when he exercises judgment on the kingdom of darkness. All who are in Christ will be safe, and Jesus will deliver the new covenant community to his Father as his adoring bride with great joy.

Contrary to the idea that God is angry with us most of the time and quick to punish wrongdoings, the biblical picture reveals just the opposite. In his dealings with humanity, God is shown to be a loving, patient, longsuffering husband/father who agonizes over the breach with his wayward bride/son. He hates the sin that has destroyed the relationship and takes it upon himself to do everything that is needed to put things right again. In this present age, his redemptive wrath is aimed towards humankind's ongoing participation in the sin of Adam and is intended to bring those whom he so lovingly created back to the path of life and light. If this course of correction is refused, then for all who stubbornly persist in pursuing evil, God's redemptive wrath will become his punitive wrath when he moves against Satan and his kingdom at the end of the age.

To the question of whether it was cruel and unloving for God to allow Jesus to experience such a brutal death, from the Father, Son, and Spirit's perspective the answer is no. If anyone had a right to object or complain it was Jesus himself, but he had an eternal view of the momentary suffering he experienced. The writer of Hebrews says that it was *for the joy set before him* that our Savior "endured the cross, scorning its shame, and sat down at the right hand of the throne of God."[96] And to the question of whether God could have found a different, less horrendous way of dealing with sin/Sin, as we learn from Paul's reflections on the mysteries of salvation, this is not something we can answer. Observing that God's judgments and ways are ultimately incomprehensible, in humility the apostle exclaimed, "Who has known the mind of the Lord? Or who has been his counselor . . . To him be the glory forever! Amen."[97]

## A Unified Model

In these last two chapters, we have examined two key redemptive threads that Paul writes about in Romans 3:21-26. First, we looked at the phrase, "a righteousness from God." We discovered this is not just about God's moral excellence and perfection. Based on its Old Testament setting, it also describes his saving activity and faithfulness to his covenant promises. God's righteousness is revealed in that even "if we are faithless, he remains faithful, for he cannot disown himself."[98] United with Jesus at the time of his death and delivered from exile in the kingdom of darkness, together the church displays the righteousness of God in Christ. Knowing this perspective can not only help us appreciate God's saving actions more fully, but it can also free us from the burden of a false perfectionism. Even if we stumble or fall short at times, we are still accepted in the beloved based on God's works, not our own.

We also explored Paul's sacrificial language related to the atonement and concluded there is only one sacrifice that holds all these strands together, and that is the Passover. However, this does not deny the importance of the Day of Atonement for dealing with sin. As we saw, the prophet Ezekiel re-established the link between these two events by looking forward to a final Passover offered by the Son of David that would be similar in achievement to the first Passover made by Moses. As Ezekiel saw it, the end times Passover would have propitiatory value in that the Paschal sacrifice would also atone for sins. The New Testament writers inherited and developed this understanding.

Far from being an abusive act, we also saw that by sending his Son to enter our suffering, Christ's death was actually a great expression of our triune God's love and mercy. As Jesus taught his followers, "greater love has no man than this, that he lay down his life for his friends."[99] Christ's death was unique, and the cross was no ordinary instance of one person dying for another. In Paul's view, it is not only that "Christ dies in the place of others so that they can escape death."[100] What is even greater than this vitally important truth is that the entire church was united with Jesus as he was dying through the Spirit's corporate baptism. Consequently, she shared in his death. This is a key distinction as it was in dying together with him that the body of Christ was freed from Satan's dark covenantal domain and transferred into the kingdom of light. Only the death of Jesus, which brought an end to Adam's covenant control over fallen humankind, could achieve this. Safe under the blood of Jesus, our Passover, the body of Christ has not only been saved from Satan's hold, but she will also be protected from God's just, righteous wrath that will be poured out on the kingdom of darkness at the appointed time.

Once again, we have found that Paul did not depart from what Jesus and the twelve apostles taught. He shared the same view Jesus had regarding what his death achieved. One of the benefits of recovering this perspective and seeing Christ's atoning sacrifice in context of Passover is that it puts it right in the heart of the corporate, New Exodus narrative. This allows us to better appreciate the grand story of redemption that unfolds all throughout scripture. Identifying this model also opens the door to understanding other aspects of Paul's theology that have been obscured by the individualistic Roman law court metaphor and other atonement theories. Being familiar with Paul's combined Passover/Atonement model and the corporate nature of our salvation will be particularly helpful as we explore the other great redemptive strand in Romans 3:21-26—justification by faith.

# CHAPTER 10

# Making Things Right

The painful saga of the faithful lover betrayed by a wayward partner is one of the universal themes found in everything from soap operas and classic literary works to he-done-me-wrong songs and movies. Perhaps one of the most heart wrenching accounts of love and betrayal is no work of fiction—it is the real-life story of Yahweh's relationship with the nation of Israel that led him to send her away because of adultery.[1]

The prophet Ezekiel recounts the story in gripping and sometimes graphic detail.[2] In the beginning, Israel had nothing to commend her. The prophet describes her as being like a newborn child who was tossed into a field, naked, unwashed, unwanted and despised. Passing by, Yahweh noticed her and chose to set his affection on the infant nation. Speaking words of life to her, he caused Israel to grow strong and healthy. Yahweh washed her, clothed her with fine linens and silks, and invited her to enter into a covenant relationship in which he would be her God and she would be his people. In a dazzling display of his love, Yahweh adorned Israel with gold, silver, and jewels, and gave her a magnificent crown that identified her as royalty. In return, he asked her to love him wholeheartedly and to be faithful. Israel flourished in the relationship; her beauty and splendor became renowned among all the other nations.

Unfortunately, this is where the story takes a tragic turn. Becoming arrogant and enamored with her own beauty, Israel began to play the harlot. Forgetting what Yahweh had done for her in her youth, she took the good gifts Yahweh lavished upon her and fashioned them into idols that she worshipped instead of him. If that were not enough, Israel began committing serial adultery by taking the gods of other nations as her own in the place of Yahweh, one after another. To his horror, she even sacrificed her children to other deities. In Yahweh's eyes, Israel acted far worse than a common prostitute; rather than taking money in exchange for her favors, she actually paid others to be her lover!

Yahweh sent numerous prophets to warn her about the consequences of her shameless behavior, but she would not listen.

Reluctantly, Yahweh finally turned away from her, just as he said he would; as the prophet Jeremiah describes it, Yahweh gave her "a certificate of divorce" and sent her away into exile because of her adulteries. Yet in his faithfulness, he did not forget the original covenant he made with her. After the designated period of captivity was complete, Yahweh made good on his promises to rescue Israel and bring her into a new relationship with him, one that would be sealed by a new and better covenant.[3] Through his gracious, saving actions, Yahweh *justified* Israel, meaning he made it possible for their broken relationship to be made right.

We have touched on this poignant story in previous chapters. However, I am going into more detail now as it, along with other Old Testament accounts like Adam and Eve's betrayal in the garden and God's covenant with Abraham, is essential for appreciating the next conceptual strand we want to explore in Romans 3:21-26—the great theme of justification by faith. Often referred to as the heart of the gospel, very simply, justification has to do with how humanity can once again have a right relationship with God. In exploring the redemptive threads in Romans 3:21-26, we have considered what the corporate perspective of the phrases "a righteousness from God" and "sacrifice of atonement" mean when seen in the context of the ancient storyline. Now we want to see what Paul has in mind when he says that we are "justified freely by his grace."[4]

## A High Stakes Subject

Justification by faith is a subject of great importance in the Western church. The Catholic Catechism contends that the justification of the wicked is even greater than the creation of the world because "heaven and earth will pass away but the salvation and justification of the elect . . .will not pass away."[5] As stated by one Catholic theologian and writer "everything is at stake here. The question is nothing less than how to get to heaven."[6] Representing the position of many of the sixteenth century Reformers, Martin Luther maintained the Protestant version—justification by faith *alone*—is the "chief article of the whole Christian doctrine."[7] In his view, if this article stands, the church stands; if it falls, "everything falls."[8]

Justification is also a tough subject. Not only is it one of the main issues that sparked the Reformation, leading to the divide between Catholics and Protestants, but also has been an ongoing source of tension. For centuries, Catholics and Protestants have been debating whether believers are justified by a combination of faith and good works (Catholic) or by faith alone (Protestant). More recently, a number of Protestant scholars associated with the New Perspectives on Paul created a stir by raising questions about the historic Reformed understanding of the doctrine.[9] Justification by faith is also a point of difference between the Eastern and Western Church, as Orthodox Christians do not emphasize it in the same way.

In an attempt to overcome historic differences, Lutherans and Catholics issued a joint declaration in 1999 stating several areas of common understanding.[10] A subsequent document published in 2015 outlined additional areas of agreement.[11] Protestant Evangelicals, Catholics and Orthodox Christians have been in dialogue as well.[12] However, despite these positive steps, participants acknowledge there is still a way to go before the global church reaches agreement.

As I mentioned previously, I am convinced there is an often hidden, but significant factor in the West, particularly in Protestant circles, that has complicated the matter—we have been reading key passages about justification against the backdrop of the individualistic criminal law court and accounting metaphors rather than the corporate setting of God's covenant relationship with his people. In my opinion, this has confused terms and obscured the proper context necessary for seeing the full meaning of justification. What I want to do next is consider how looking at justification by faith through the corporate lens of the New Exodus paradigm can help us move past some of the historical sticking points and see the amazing tapestry of God's great salvation story with new eyes.

## Different Views

To be clear, I do not plan to tackle all the issues involved in the historic dispute. Nevertheless, it will be helpful to briefly review the traditional Catholic and Protestant positions as this will allow us to see why the debate has been challenging to resolve and why the backdrop against which we read scripture is so critical. Notice that in both of the views that follow, the focus is on the individual believer.

*The Catholic View.* According to the Catholic Catechism, "justification includes the remission of sins, sanctification, and the renewal of the inner man."[13] As Catholics see it, justification (coming into a right relationship with God) and sanctification (being made holy) are inextricably linked together. Therefore, justification is not just a one-time event, but rather a process that takes place throughout the believer's lifetime.[14]

According to Catholics, the initial stage of justification occurs when the individual believer is regenerated through water baptism and adopted as God's son or daughter. At this time and completely by God's grace, the guilt and corruption of original sin is removed, and the person is infused with the principle or habit of grace, which becomes a permanent part of his or her being. As a result of this infusion, one is not only *declared* righteous (justified), but is *actually made* righteous (sanctified).

However, Catholics also believe that while justification is fully rooted in faith, final justification occurs through a combination of faith *and* good works or, as they frame it, faith working through love.[15] For this reason, they reject the Protestant formulation that justification is by faith *alone*, and in fact, point out the word *alone* is not found in Romans 3:28, a classic text about justification. Catholics also maintain that if a mortal (as in grave or serious) sin is committed after baptism, the believer can be separated from grace and lose his or her justification. If this happens, one must begin the process again through confession, repentance, and acts of penance.[16]

Because there is no way to know if one's good works are adequate to offset the guilt of whatever sins are committed after baptism, there is no way to be certain one has made enough progress in holiness to be justified in the end. Therefore, Catholics do not believe it is possible to have assurance of final justification and teach that after death, the believer goes to purgatory to be refined before going on to heaven.

Catholics often quote James 2:14-26, Galatians 5:19-21, and Matthew 19:17 to support their view that final justification depends on a combination of faith, visible works and one's success in avoiding certain sins.

*The Protestant View.* Protestants, on the other hand, make a distinction between justification and sanctification. They maintain that justification is *not* a process but a one-time event in which the individual believer is legally acquitted of his or her sins and *declared* righteous without being *made* righteous internally. Once justified, or legally pardoned, sanctification, which is the lifetime process of actually being made holy, follows. In explaining the Reformed Protestant position, theologian Michael Horton states,

> Although all of Christ's gifts are given in our union with him through faith, justification is a verdict that declares sinners to be righteous even while they are inherently unrighteous, simply on the basis of Christ's righteousness imputed to them. Whereas Rome teaches that one is finally justified by being sanctified, the evangelical conviction is that one is being sanctified because one has already been justified. Rather than working toward the verdict of divine vindication, the believer leaves the court justified in the joy that bears the fruit of faith: namely good works. [17]

As some Protestants see it, justification does not actually change one's corrupt condition. In this view, although believers are forgiven, legally pardoned, and *positionally* transferred from the kingdom of darkness into the kingdom of light when they are justified, *conditionally*, they remain sinful. In other words, "Sin's dominion has been toppled, but still indwells believers."[18] Since, in the Reformed view, indwelling sin taints even the believer's best efforts, this means no work will ever be sufficient to meet the standard of holiness God's law requires.

In this view, the believer's right standing before God, then, is not—in fact, cannot be—dependent on good works or law-keeping; it is based solely on the fact that Christ's righteousness that is none of our own has been imputed or credited to our individual account. As Horton states, "the understanding of justification as an *exclusively forensic [legal] declaration*, based on the imputation of Christ's righteousness through faith alone, was the chief insight of the Reformation."[19]

Because they believe it is a gracious, divine legal verdict that in no way depends on human effort, Reformed Protestants teach that genuine Christians cannot lose their justification and, therefore, can count on being justified in the end. While confession of sin and forgiveness are important for maintaining a close relationship with God, unlike Catholics, Protestants do not believe it is necessary for the Christian to recover their right standing with God when they sin by doing acts of penance or spend time in purgatory in order to be refined.

Reformed Protestants rely on Ephesians 2:8, Acts 16:14, and Philippians 1:29 to prove that Christians are justified by faith *alone*, not faith plus works. In their view, if faith is genuine, good works will naturally follow. In this view, while the believer will never be free of the presence of indwelling sin in this lifetime, with the Spirit's help one will grow in holiness (sanctification) as he or she continues to put away sin.

*The Historic Impasse.* Both sides agree faith is necessary for salvation, grace plays a central role, and believers are commanded by God to do good works. However, as Protestants see it, by teaching that final justification depends in part on works, the historic Catholic view leads people to falsely believe they can merit or must earn salvation in part through their own efforts. In the Protestant view, this is a grave error that can lead believers to trust in themselves instead of in Christ alone. In turn, Catholics see the historic Protestant view as opening the door to a false view of salvation and lawlessness by teaching that once justified, our actions have no effect on our status before God. Since in their opinion one can lose his or her justification as a result of mortal sin or failure to do good works, this is a dangerous position that can result in eternal damnation.

Commenting on progress made toward resolving this impasse, one Catholic theologian notes, "It is becoming clear to both sides that we are saved only by Christ, by grace; that faith is our acceptance of that grace, so we are saved by faith; and that good works, the works of love, necessarily follow that faith if it is real and saving faith, so we cannot be saved by a faith that is without good works."[20] Yet, there is also recognition that a number of outstanding differences related to this crucial doctrine have yet to be resolved, and that "more theological work is needed."[21]

*New Perspectives on Paul.* In recent years, new tensions surfaced among Protestants when several scholars claimed that the Reformers read their own dispute with Rome regarding faith alone into Paul's debate with Judaism. This, it is said, skewed the Reformer's understanding of biblical justification, causing them to misread Paul. In N.T. Wright's view, because the New Testament concept is rooted in the Old in which Jews were already in a covenant relationship with God, justification is not about being acquitted from sin or made righteous. That is, it is not about how one becomes a Christian so much as "how you can tell who is a member of the covenant family."[22] In this framework, justification has to do with the declaration that one is *in* the covenant and already acceptable to God rather than the process by which someone comes into a relationship with him.

Originally, this new line of thinking was of interest mostly to scholars, but it has steadily seeped into the mainstream. I have already discussed the ins and outs of the New Pauline Perspective in *Contours of Pauline Theology*, my previous work, so I will simply say here that I believe some of the ideas presented by this group of scholars have merit.[23] Their viewpoints have provoked others to reconsider some of their inherited presuppositions, a process which, although uncomfortable at times, can be beneficial. However, as I explain in *Contours*, I also believe some of the methodology used by New Perspective theologians is flawed, leading to what, in my opinion, are less than satisfactory conclusions.

## Relational versus Legal Language

There is one more bit of background information I want to cover before we go on as it highlights one of the problems that exist in modern day debates. I want to point out that the language used to describe the Reformed position regarding justification by faith differs among Protestants, which has muddied the waters by creating confusing impressions of the doctrine. For instance, historian Patrick Collinson observes that Protestants have historically viewed justification in relational terms with an emphasis on the marriage covenant with Christ. In describing their view of the gospel, he states that Protestants have understood

> That man enjoys that acceptance with God called 'justification', the beginning and end of salvation, not through his own moral effort even in the smallest and slightest degree but entirely and only through the loving mercy of God made available in the merits of Christ and of his saving death on the Cross. This was not a process of gradual ethical improvement but an instantaneous transaction, *something like a marriage, in which Christ the bridegroom takes to himself an impoverished and wretched harlot and confers upon her all the riches which are his.* The key to this transaction was faith, defined as a total and trustful commitment of the self to God, and it is itself not a human achievement but the pure gift of God.[24]

In contrast, the Westminster Confession, an influential historic Reformed document, presents justification in a more legal, business-like fashion. There is not room to include the entire section on justification here, but the following paragraph will give you a taste of the language:

> Those whom God effectually calls, he also freely justifies; not by infusing righteousness into them, but by *pardoning* their sins, and by *accounting* and accepting their persons as righteous, not for anything wrought in them, or done by them, but for Christ's sake alone; not by *imputing* faith itself, the act of believing, or any other evangelical obedience to them, as their righteousness; but *by imputing* the obedience and satisfaction of Christ unto them, they receiving and resting on him and his righteousness by faith; which faith they have not of themselves, it is the gift of God.[25]

Using a combination of legal and accounting metaphors, the Westminster Confession goes on to speak of how "Christ, by his obedience and death, did fully *discharge the debt* of all those thus justified, and did make a proper, real, and *full satisfaction to his Father's justice* in their behalf." And how "God did, from all eternity, *decree to justify* the elect."[26]

As you can see, while some Protestants describe justification in terms of marriage, trust, and relationship, the Westminster Confession presents it as more of a legal, business transaction. According to Baker's Evangelical Dictionary, the latter's law-oriented approach "makes it unpalatable to many in our day."[27] However, after noting the downside, Baker's goes on to defend it by saying that, nevertheless, "justification is *a legal term* with a meaning like 'acquittal'; in religion it points to the process whereby a person is declared to be right before God."[28]

One of the things I want to show as we discuss this critical doctrine in context of the New Exodus paradigm is that justification in the New Testament does indeed have a forensic element as understood by the Reformers. But at the same time, it has a much wider context that has to do with how God brings people into a covenant relationship with himself. Seeing the legal verdict in context of this broader relational dimension will allow us to recover a richer, more expansive picture of justification. Let me say at the outset that *to justify* or *justification* has more than one meaning in scripture, but in this part of our conversation, the focus is on the concept associated with the traditional, historic debate.

**JUSTIFICATION: BACK TO THE ANCIENT STORYLINE¶** To understand Paul's framework for justification, we need to go back to the Old Testament predictions that Israel would be restored after being sent into exile as a consequence of betraying Yahweh. The prophets spoke about the exile as God "putting away" or "cutting off" his people.[29] In this context, justification had to do with redeeming *an entire community* from exile so that as a people, they can enter into new relationship with God. Declaring that he would not completely forsake her, God promised to deliver Israel from her enemies, pardon her sins, bring her back to her homeland, betroth her in righteousness, create a new covenant with her, and gift her with the Holy Spirit.[30] At some point in the future, the Gentiles would be incorporated into this new relationship.[31] As the prophets saw it, justification or being made right with Yahweh was a blanket description that included redemption from captivity, atonement for sin, forgiveness, reconciliation, and all the blessings Israel would receive when she returned to claim her inheritance. While this is the language that Isaiah especially uses, it is not restricted to him; it is a common theme that links the Psalms and the classic prophets together.[32]

Viewed within context of the Old Testament storyline, Israel's justification will be complete only when *all* of the promises Yahweh has made to her are finally fulfilled. Justification, therefore, covers the whole scope of salvation history from Israel's election as the nation through whom Yahweh would bring salvation to the rest of the world to being perfected as God's bride.

Drawing on their Jewish heritage, the primitive church used this same concept to describe the activity of God in electing, redeeming, making atonement for sin, and entering into a covenant relationship with the redeemed community. In other words, *justification is the technical description of the whole of the salvation experience from beginning to end.* While there is definitely an individual application, which is crucial, again, the primary focus in the biblical narrative is on the justification of the new covenant community. It should also be noted in light of the current debate within Protestantism that while the New Testament speaks of justification as a past achievement and centers on what God has done through the death of Jesus, it also has a future sense. Because it has to do with the salvation of God's people from beginning to end, the justification of the saints will only be complete when they finally receive their full inheritance at the end-times resurrection.

In trying to grasp how the biblical writers viewed justification, it helps to know that in Hebrew, the words, *justified* and *righteous* are essentially saying the same thing. In the Old Testament, the verbal form of the noun *tsedeq*, meaning *righteousness*, expresses the idea of how God's people are made right with him.[33] So when Yahweh says he will make Israel righteous, it means that he will justify her. In the New Testament, the noun for *righteousness* is *diakaiosune*, which also means *upright* as well as *justness,* and the related verb is *dikaioo* is translated as *justify.* [34] The verb is used to describe God's divine initiative in saving the elect community, and in so doing, bringing them into a right relationship with himself.[35] Everywhere Paul uses this term it denotes God's active outworking of his covenant-keeping grace.

Isaiah provides key insights regarding the scope of righteous actions Yahweh performed in order to justify Israel. First, Isaiah said Yahweh would *forgive* and *deliver* Israel; second, the prophet said God would *protect her on pilgrimage* as she returned to the Promised Land; and third, Yahweh would *safely establish Israel in her inheritance* once she got back to Zion.[36] Paul clearly echoes these themes when he speaks to the saints and says, "He has delivered us from such deadly peril, and he will deliver us. On him we have set our hope that he will continue to deliver us."[37] And as we have seen, in Romans 3:26, Paul writes that God took saving action "so as to be just and the one who justifies those who have faith in Jesus."[38] Paul's statement echoes Isaiah's understanding that salvation had to do with Israel's return from exile in which both Yahweh and Israel were justified.[39]

How did exiling and then rescuing Israel justify both God and Israel? Yahweh was shown to be just when he demonstrated to all that he did not ignore Israel's sins. Although he extended grace for a lengthy period of time, eventually he kept his word that he would address Israel's sins by sending her away from his presence if she did not repent. Yahweh also proved to be just in that he kept his promise to bring Israel back from exile even though she had been unfaithful. In turn, Israel was justified when God forgave her betrayal, rescued her from exile, and restored the relationship. In taking this action, he was declaring to the watching nations that Israel's claim to be his chosen people was justified.

Building on this framework, Paul shows how God was just by redeeming humanity from captivity to Sin/Satan, lawfully addressing our sins through Christ's atoning sacrifice, and making a way for the nations to return from exile and be reconciled with him—Gentiles as well as Jews. In his faithfulness, God kept the covenant promises he made to Abraham long ago that through his seed all the nations of the earth would be blessed.

## The Justified Community

As the New Exodus model is increasingly appreciated, we can begin to see how justification fits into Paul's doctrine of corporate baptism. Previously, we discovered the major texts in Paul's writing about baptism are not about water baptism or baptismal regeneration of the individual; they describe a one-time corporate baptism in which the Spirit took all who would look to God in faith—past, present, and future—and united them with Christ as he was dying so that together, they shared in his death and resurrection.[40] Furthermore, all the passages we considered had a New Exodus context. Paul's framework for this is clearly seen 1 Corinthians 10:1-4. These verses refer to Israel's corporate baptism into Moses that occurred during the First Exodus and are used by Paul as a parallel to the church's corporate baptism into Christ in the New Exodus.

In 1 Corinthians 6:11, Paul makes a definitive connection between justification and corporate baptism. Referring to the wicked, he says, "And that is what some of you were. But you were *washed*, you were *sanctified*, you were *justified* in the name of the Lord Jesus Christ and by the Spirit of our God."[41] Here, cleansing, sanctification and justification are linked together, there is no recognizable *ordo salutis* (order of salvation), and Paul is not referring to a series of separate events. Rather, he is describing various aspects of *one corporate experience*.

This may sound startling at first as this verse is usually applied to the individual. However, what must govern the interpretation of this statement is the introduction of the section that begins in 1 Corinthians 5:7. It leads with "Christ our Passover has been sacrificed." This is a New Exodus theme that applies to God's people collectively. Plus, as we have seen previously, jumping ahead to the last part of I Corinthians 6,

Paul talks about the body of Christ, so it too has a corporate emphasis. This squarely places 1 Corinthians 6:11, which is sandwiched between these two passages, within a larger corporate context. Furthermore, the washing referred to in 6:11 is not the rite of individual water baptism, but the historic event of Christ's death. This is evident because the setting of this text is the same as in Ephesians 5, which speaks of the corporate washing of Christ's bride.[42] We also found this corporate baptism in 1 Corinthians 10 and 12.[43] It was clearly Paul's default model when explaining what was achieved through corporate baptism into Christ's death.

The significance of these parallel passages in 1 Corinthians and Ephesians 5 is that the justification of the Christian community took place in this New Exodus washing or cleansing. We can see this by comparing Israel's story with the church's experience. Israel was freed from her oppressors, baptized into Moses, and brought into a covenant relationship with Yahweh during the First Exodus. Similarly, the church was freed from Sin and Death, baptized into Jesus's death, and brought into a covenant relationship with God in the New Exodus. The nation of Israel was sanctified (cleansed, washed, set apart as holy) during the Second Exodus when she was removed from the defilement that came from living in Babylon; in like fashion the church was sanctified in the New Exodus when she was removed from the defilement that came from living in the kingdom of darkness, the body of Sin.[44]

The mention of justification in I Corinthians 6:11 is important because there is no evidence the church in Corinth was confronting Judaism. This shows that justification was not just a concept Paul came up with for the sake of argument while debating the Jews, as some New Perspective scholars claim; rather, it was an integral part of how he understood the whole process of redemptive history. To sum up, in Paul's view, *justification was a historical act having to do with the corporate salvation of the new covenant community that was accomplished through Christ's death and resurrection.*

Because some of the passages mentioned so far have traditionally been read through an individualistic lens, I realize seeing justification as a corporate experience is a paradigm shift that may be challenging to make. If you have reservations at the moment, I encourage you to just hold the idea in your mind while we consider additional evidence.

## RECOVERING THE CORPORATE, COVENANTAL BACKDROP⸶

A key text in understanding Paul's view of justification is Romans 4:3, which speaks of the time when Abraham was *justified* or *declared righteous* by Yahweh. After noting that Abraham was not justified by works, Paul writes: "what does the Scripture say? 'Abraham believed God, and it was credited to him as righteousness.'" Traditionally, this text is seen as having to do with the justification of the individual and the forgiveness of sins. I want to argue, however, that it is speaking primarily about the justification of people groups—specifically the Jews and Gentiles—and how they come into a covenant relationship with God. In saying this, I am not downplaying the fact that Christ's redemptive work made it possible for our personal sins to be forgiven; I am only saying that it is not the main point of this particular passage for reasons I will explain.

The traditional, Protestant understanding of Romans 4:3 is an example of why the backdrop against which we read scripture is so important. In addition to reading this passage with the criminal law court in mind, the idea that God credited Abraham with righteousness is often seen as referring to the type of credit ledger used by accountants that lists debts in one column and assets in another. Since, in this view, all of our best efforts are tainted by sin, there is nothing we can do to make ourselves righteous or justify ourselves in God's eyes. Therefore, none of our works can ever be recorded in the plus column. Those who favor this reading say that when we trust in Jesus we are legally pardoned (declared innocent) and even though sin remains in us, Christ's merits are *imputed* or *credited* to our asset column. We are justified not through any effort of our own, but only because Christ's righteousness is credited to our ledger sheet. In other words, when God looks at our personal account, he sees Christ's righteous acts of obedience on our list of assets and therefore, counts us as being righteous even though, in reality, we are still sinners.

However, when we look at Paul's statement in the context of the Old Testament storyline, a different picture emerges as to what it means that Abraham's faith was "credited to him as righteousness." Paul took this quote directly from Genesis 15:6, which has a covenantal rather than a legal, accounting setting. (I encourage you to stop and read Genesis 15 at this point, as it will make it easier to follow what I'm about to say.) The backdrop of the text is that God promised Abraham that he would give him a son and that his descendants would become a great nation. Abraham believed that God would keep his word. As a result, God counted Abraham as being righteous and entered into a covenant relationship with him. There was no ledger sheet involved, no asset or debit column to be calculated, and Abraham's sin is not central to the story. In this context, being counted righteous simply means *being accepted by Yahweh.*

To impose an accounting or legal meaning on the phrase *credited with righteousness* in Genesis 15 rather than allowing it to be understood in its own context is not likely to help us uncover the original meaning. The main point of the chapter is that God established a covenant relationship with Abraham (then called Abram). In addition to the promise of a son, Yahweh told Abraham that his seed will be as numerous as the stars in the sky and also vowed that he would give him the land in which he was living sometime in the future. Abraham asked God how he could know for certain that all of this would happen. Yahweh's response was to formally establish the covenant that had been implicitly in existence from the time Abraham first responded to God's call to leave his original homeland and follow him.[45]

Based on the covenant-making ceremony described in Genesis 15, the initiative in establishing this relationship is clearly all God's, as Abraham had nothing to bring to the table. Yahweh was the one who sought out Abraham, laid out the terms, and gave specific instructions for formalizing the covenant. In explaining what the covenant guarantees, Yahweh specifically told Abraham that his descendants would be enslaved at some point in the future and that, as their God, he would act to deliver them from oppression. God kept that promise. When the Hebrews were enslaved in Egypt and then later exiled in Babylon, in both instances Yahweh rescued his people and brought them back to himself.

This promise to rescue and restore the relationship with his people is the key to understanding the biblical framework of justification. Based on what Yahweh said, it is clear that an important part of the covenant has to do with his commitment to deliver Abraham's offspring from bondage and exile. This is at the heart of how being credited with righteousness should be understood—justification *cannot be separated from the Exodus events in which God moved to deliver his people from slavery.* The purpose of the First and Second Exodus was to release Israel from her tyrannical oppressors so that she could enter or re-enter into a covenant relationship with Yahweh. God justified Israel or, put another way, regarded her as being righteous, when he freed her from captivity and brought her back to himself.

## A Corporate Covenant

What must not be missed is that the corporate, covenantal setting of Genesis 15 is *the backdrop of Paul's arguments in both Romans 3 and chapter 4.* In Romans 3:21-26, the text we have been exploring, Paul is speaking of redemption and justification. We have seen that right at the heart of these verses is the statement that "apart from the law the righteousness of God has been made known, to which the Law and the Prophets testify." The use of *righteousness* here is the same as in Romans 4:3 where Paul writes, "What does the Scripture say? 'Abraham believed God, and it was credited to him as *righteousness.*'" There would have to be very good reasons for severing the statement in 3:21 from the context that controls the meaning of righteousness in 4:3. And as we have seen, the context of Paul's arguments in Romans 4 is linked to Genesis 15, which is *saturated with covenant imagery.*

This shows the corporate nature of Paul's arguments in both chapters. Even though Paul is discussing how our father Abraham was justified, Paul's primary focus *is on the justification of God's people, not the individual.* This can be said with confidence because at the end of chapter 3, Paul is talking about the Jews and Gentiles. He reasons that since all are justified by faith, ultimately the Mosaic covenant did not give the Jews any greater privilege over the Gentiles. This reveals that the whole section leading into Paul's use of the story of God's acceptance of Abraham has to do primarily with the covenant status of *people groups.*

In chapter 4, Paul goes on to explain that the Gentiles and the Jews are justified in the same way—by faith (believing God's promises) and not the law. To prove this, Paul points out that Abraham was effectively a Gentile when God promised him a son and made a covenant with him. Clearly, Abraham had not been circumcised and the Mosaic law had not yet been given when God counted him righteous and entered into a covenant. relationship with him. This meant Abraham's right standing with God had nothing to do with works like circumcision or law keeping. God's declaration was based *solely* on the fact that he chose Abraham to be the one through whom he would accomplish his mission to bring salvation to the nations and Abraham responded in faith, meaning he trusted God to keep his promises. Paul argues these facts must be front and center when considering how the new covenant community, which now consists of both Jews and Gentiles, is justified or made righteous before God.

If Paul's view of justification comes from the Law and the Prophets and not the Greco Roman law court or accounting models, then it must affect how we understand Romans 4:3. As I have explained, the Old Testament provides a distinctly covenantal and corporate framework for Paul's argument. What Paul is saying is that Abraham believed God's promise to give him an heir and that he would be the first of millions of offspring. Yahweh was, in fact, so committed to fulfilling his covenant promises that he *already attributed* to Abraham the status of what he was to become in the future—the head of a redeemed new covenant community through which all the nations of the world would be blessed. In other words, this covenant promise was *not just for Abraham as an individual*; it also applied *to the extensive community* that would be birthed through his seed!

Based on this understanding, then both Genesis and Paul are showing that the primary issue in Genesis 15 is Yahweh's acceptance of Abraham and his descendants. God committed himself to Abraham, saying that he would act righteously toward him and always keep his covenant promises. Abraham's faith was his response to the promises Yahweh made to him; it was his "Amen, I want to be in a covenant relationship with you."

Surely the matter of Abraham's sin and his forgiveness was important—no covenant could be established with Yahweh without properly dealing with sin—but at the risk of shocking some, it was secondary. To make sin the *primary* focus of justification in Romans 4 is to miss the significance of what was happening when "Abraham believed God and it was credited to him as righteousness." Clearly, the point of the story is that God entered into a covenant relationship with Abraham and his descendants. This helps us see that being *counted as righteous* or *justified* has to do with being accepted and brought into a covenant relationship with God that is entirely his doing. This is the basis of what occurred in all three of the exodus events—the First and

Second Exodus in the Old Testament, and the New Exodus through Christ.

## The Gentiles Made Right

Is there any further evidence to support this interpretation? That in Romans 4 being credited with righteousness refers to Yahweh bringing Abraham into a covenant relationship with himself? Yes, there is. The only other Pauline text that refers to Genesis 15 is Galatians 3. In verses 6-8 Paul says,

> So also Abraham "believed God, and it was credited to him as righteousness." Understand, then, that those who have faith are children of Abraham. Scripture foresaw that God would *justify the Gentiles by faith*, and announced the gospel in advance to Abraham: "All nations will be blessed through you."

In this letter, Paul is admonishing the Galatians that any attempt to go back to the Mosaic law would mean they were leaving the true gospel. The argument he uses is a condensed version of what he says in Romans 6 and 7. Death has already fully satisfied the requirement of the law, so no one will be justified by observing it. When Paul speaks of death in this context, he is referring to the death of Christ in which all believers have shared. For him, this is not a mere theoretical concept. The reality is that Christ's death has brought Paul, a faithful Jew, into a totally new relationship with God. He argues that the new covenant, which is grounded on the death of Jesus, has brought *all* believers into a relationship with God that the law was unable to secure, mainly because it was never intended to.

To drive this point home, Paul asks the Galatian believers in 3:2 how they came into the covenant—was it by works of the law or by faith? This question sets the stage for his statement that Abraham was credited with righteousness and his discussion of the justification of the Gentiles. So, in this passage, we again see the link between entering into a covenant with God and justification.

What is significant here is that Paul is not asking if their sins were forgiven. This shows that he did not see the forgiveness of sins as the primary purpose of justification. Surprisingly, he asked if they *received the Spirit* by keeping the law or by faith.[46] Receiving the Spirit was one of the main promises associated with entering into the new covenant. The gift of the Spirit and not circumcision or law-keeping was the main evidence that the Gentiles had been justified or accepted by God into the new covenant community. Peter makes exactly this same point at the Council of Jerusalem in Acts 15:7-11:

> Brothers, you know that some time ago God made a choice among you that the Gentiles might hear from my lips the message of the gospel and believe. God, who knows the heart, showed that he accepted them by giving the Holy Spirit to them, just as he did to us. He did not discriminate between us and them, for he purified their hearts by faith. Now then, why do you try to test God by putting on the necks of the Gentiles a yoke that neither we nor our ancestors have been able to bear? No! We believe it is through the grace of our Lord Jesus that we are saved, just as they are.

Peter and Paul are on the same page. As they see it, the Spirit is the evidence that proves God has accepted the Gentiles into a covenant relationship with him. It's also abundantly clear that the debate in the Council of Jerusalem was not concerning the acceptability of an individual Gentile, but the believing Gentiles as a group. We are seeing the same sort of corporate argument that we have found to be running throughout Paul's letters.

Psalm 106 provides one of the strongest arguments that the phrase *credited with righteousness* has to do with entering into a covenant relationship with God. This passage describes the story of Phineas, the Old Testament priest, who took action against his fellow countrymen after they engaged in sexual immorality with those outside the covenant, something Yahweh had forbidden. As a result, God counted him as righteous and entered into a "covenant of peace" with him and his descendants that endured for endless generations.[47] If you want to explore additional evidence to support the idea that being counted righteous has to do with entering into a covenant relationship with God, I refer you to my earlier work, *Contours of Pauline Theology*.[48]

## The Paschal-New Exodus Connection

Corporate, covenantal justification is also plainly seen in the link Paul makes between Passover and the New Exodus in Romans 5:9. In this text he says, "Since we have been justified by his blood, how much more shall we be saved from God's wrath through him!" One scholar notes, "The fact that in Romans 5:9 the blood protects us from the future wrath of God again suggests a reference to the Passover."[49] We saw the connection between justification, redemption, and Passover earlier in our discussion of Romans 3:24-25. Looking at it once again, Paul explains that we "are *justified freely* by his grace, *through the redemption* that came by Christ Jesus whom God put forward as a propitiation by his blood, to be received by faith."[50]

Here we can see that justification is the *outcome* of the redemption that was accomplished through the Passover sacrifice. Just as it was in the Old Testament, redemption has to do with being delivered both from a tyrannical oppressor and God's wrath. This has distinct echoes of Israel's deliverance from Egypt when she was not only brought out from under her enemy's control, but also protected from Yahweh's judgment by the blood of the lamb on the night of the Passover. To use Isaiah's language, she was justified; the object of Yahweh's righteous, saving activity. In Romans 5, Paul also describes the role of the last Adam in ending humanity's exile from God. Merging language from Passover and justification in this critical passage is clear proof that the New Exodus is a dominant metaphor in Paul's doctrine of salvation.

Often overlooked, Romans 5 is vitally important when it comes to understanding justification. Expanding on the theme of justification that Paul has been discussing in chapters 3 and 4, Romans 5:12-21 is about Christ, the last Adam, who delivered his people from the consequences of the fall. Few would dispute the backdrop of Paul's thinking here is that the fall brought humankind under the domain of Sin/Satan. In fact, justification—the redeemed community's deliverance from bondage and exile through Christ—is the essence of the argument Paul is making in Romans 5. As one prominent theologian observed, the "Adam-Christ parallel is based on justification."[51]

This evidence lends further weight to the argument I am presenting that while justification involves a legal pardon from sin, it has a much broader scope—it covers the full range of God's merciful, saving activity in rescuing a captive people who had betrayed him. This deliverance is achieved through the death of Jesus. This is why I believe it can be said that the heart of Paul's doctrine of justification is in Romans 5:16-18:

> Nor can the gift of God be compared with the result of one man's [Adam's] sin: The judgment followed one sin and brought condemnation, but the gift followed many trespasses and *brought justification.* For if, by the trespass of the one man, death reigned through that one man, how much more will those who receive

God's abundant provision of grace and of the gift of righteousness reign in life through the one man, Jesus Christ! Consequently, just as one trespass resulted in condemnation for all people, so also one righteous act *resulted in justification* and life for all people.

This passage is unmistakably about deliverance and renewal. It is about being brought from Satan's control into the realm where Christ rules, for he is the new community's representative head. It is not about declaring or identifying who is in the new covenant community as some New Perspective theologians contend; it is about Christ's death and resurrection, the means by which the transfer into God's kingdom was made possible.

I also want to point out this passage is not about the justification of the individual believer, but of the many who have been made righteous. In other words, the argument being put forward in this critical chapter is essentially corporate. Some might say it could be talking about all the individuals who are justified, which happen to be many. However, as we saw earlier, Romans 5 is focused on two *communities* and their representative heads—unredeemed humanity in Adam and redeemed humanity in Christ. This is consistent with Paul's arguments in chapters 3 and 4 that have to do with the justification of people groups rather than individuals.

Yet another important dimension of corporate justification can be seen in Romans 5 when Paul describes the imputation of sin and righteousness. Imputation is another one of those weighty theological words that is not part of our everyday vocabulary. It means to credit someone with the debt, curse, blame, blessing, or status of another. The argument Paul makes is that even though Adam's descendants did not necessarily sin in the same way he did, all people were made sinners and condemned because of his disobedience. As we saw, this happened because Adam, humanity's representative head, entered into a covenant alliance with Sin and Death that was binding on subsequent generations. Consequently, all of his offspring were born into the unredeemed community, the body of Sin that is at enmity with God. In this way, Adam's sin was imputed to all of humankind.

Conversely, Paul explains that through the death of Christ many will be made righteous and receive life. As the last Adam whose work is to undo this unholy alliance with Sin and Death, Jesus not only delivers all who call on his name from captivity, but also imputes his own righteousness to the new covenant community, the body of Christ. This is surely a critical part of the argument. The setting for this imputation, however, is not the criminal law court or an accounting transaction; rather it is within a covenantal context and based on our union with and betrothal to Christ, the church's representative head. A legal element is still involved in that marriage covenants are binding unless rightfully dissolved. In the New Exodus framework, the righteousness of the husband becomes that of his bride as she shares in all that belongs to him.[52] His standing before the law becomes her standing before the law so, in this sense, Christ's righteousness is imputed to the collective church.

For this reason, while there are texts that should not be used to speak of such an imputation—for example Genesis 15:6 or Romans 4:3 which we considered above—the important doctrine of the Reformation regarding the imputation of Christ's righteousness cannot be so easily jettisoned as some New Perspective scholars have done. The correction I would introduce to the Reformers understanding is that the imputation of Christ's righteousness is corporate; it applies to the community that is in Christ, and individuals enter into this glorious state as they believe and avail themselves of the blessing of the gospel. In other words, while not individually given, the individual receives it, along with all other spiritual blessings that are in Christ upon entering the community as a member of the body of Christ.[53]

## Finding a Proper Home

The question we must ask now is why has this corporate, covenantal dimension of justification so often been overlooked? As I mentioned earlier, I believe it is because the emphasis on the criminal legal setting and accounting metaphors that have dominated the traditional understanding have overshadowed the original covenantal context of Romans 3, 4 and 5.

This has created a number of problems. Terms like sacrifice, redemption, and the gift of the Spirit are not naturally at home in a business model. Also, the individualistic law court metaphor has elevated the personal, forensic aspect of justification over the greater context of the corporate, covenant relationship between God and his people. This has caused us to lose sight of the New Exodus narrative that sheds a more relational light on what it means to be counted righteous.

On one level, it is understandable why this happened. In certain contexts, *logizomai*, the Greek word for *count, reckon,* or *credit* is an accounting metaphor. There is also a legal component to justification.[54] However, as we have seen before, words have different meanings depending on the context. Thus, when interpreting Romans 4:3, since Paul directly quotes Genesis 15:6, the first step is to consider what being credited with righteousness means in this setting. And then we must consider what Paul intends to convey each time he speaks of justification in Romans 3–5. What does the particular context dictate when Paul is explaining what it means to be credited with righteousness or justified? Whatever it means, what is not permissible is to trawl the range of meanings from all across biblical literature and fuse them together into a new model or metaphor that becomes the key to all uses of the word regardless of the context. In regard to Romans 4:3, it is what Genesis 15 says about being credited with righteousness that matters.

What has happened in the linguistic confusion surrounding this term is exactly what expert linguist/theologian, James Barr, warned against—various meanings have been imported from other passages and used to construct an illegitimate hybrid definition. This collective meaning is then applied to a particular verse—in this instance to Genesis 15:6—without considering the surrounding context. As discussed earlier, in the setting of Genesis 15, *logizomai* is not an accounting term; rather, in this context being counted righteous has to do with entering into a covenant relationship with God.

Mounting evidence shows that Paul stayed within the relational framework of Old Testament covenant theology and the New Exodus storyline, developing it in light of the Christ event that brought the covenant promises to completion. I suggest this is the correct paradigm for understanding his thinking on justification. While there is a legal aspect to justification in that Christ's bride was pardoned and is no longer condemned for her sin, the setting is covenantal law, which has to do with the relationship between God and his people, not the impersonal criminal law of the Roman court system or a business accounting model. Making this adjustment and interpreting justification in a New Exodus, covenantal context does not remove the necessity of receiving God's free and gracious acquittal from the guilt of sin that has been at the heart of Protestant theology. Rather, it places justification in its true biblical home, the relational setting of the corporate covenant God made with his people.

## What About the Individual?

The idea that Paul is speaking primarily of the justification of the new covenant community in Romans 4 naturally leads to a crucial question—where, then, does the individual fit in? What about personal repentance and salvation? Romans 4 and related texts can serve as a test case to see how a corporate reading can help us recover a more biblically balanced view of the relationship between the justified community and the individual.

The idea that Paul is primarily concerned with imputation of righteousness to the individual in Romans 4 has been understandably based on his statement in verse 5. He says, "the one who does not work but trusts God who justifies the ungodly, their faith is credited as righteousness." The use of the singular *one* coupled with his references to two men in the passage, Abraham and David, can create the impression that individual justification is indeed the main subject. Such a reading, however, loses the greater plot of the discussion.

First, the work mentioned in Romans 4:5 clearly refers to the old covenant requirement for being accepted into a covenant relationship with God, which was circumcision. Once the issue Paul is discussing— the status of the Gentiles as a people group—has been identified, there is no suggestion in this text that he is talking about the individual working to gain acceptance through self-effort involving religious observations, moral achievement, or the like. And, as important as it may be, nor is he addressing the acquittal of the individual sinner from guilt as is traditionally taught.

Second, the individualistic accounting metaphor often used to interpret this verse violates the corporate and covenantal context of the passage. As I have shown, Romans 3 and 4, and also Galatians 3 are loaded with New Exodus concepts, specifically with Passover. This is important because as we have seen, the Passover, which is steeped with propitiation imagery, was at the heart of the Old Testament's understanding of covenant making and justification. Although the individual Jew benefitted from Passover, as we have seen, this was a corporate event involving the entire people of God.

Thus, it is essential to first understand that justification of the individual is simply not the focus of the Paul's discussion in Romans 4. As noted above, Paul is addressing God's acceptance of the Gentiles into the covenant. Based on this acceptance, all of the blessings of election that were once exclusive to Israel, which include deliverance, pardon and forgiveness, justification, the Holy Spirit and the covenant community's future inheritance, are now flowing out to the nations. And these are the blessings that individuals enter into experientially when the same Spirit works in their hearts to produce faith in the God who justifies the ungodly. Just as the individual Jew had to be circumcised to belong to the covenant community, so in the New Testament the individual must be circumcised in heart in order to become a member of the body of Christ. In the biblical model, this happens when the individual believer repents, believes in the name of Christ, and enters into the justified community.

The problem is that when we read Romans 4 and other key New Testament texts as being primarily about the individual, the vital role of corporate justification and the corporate community gets pushed to the background. The result is that key elements of the salvation story having to do with God's people as a whole are diminished and the individual assumes more importance than is warranted by scripture. This, in turn, can prevent the individual believer from seeing and walking in the fact that their personal justification flows from the community of which they are a part.

## When Paul Speaks to the Individual

All this may sound foreign to Western ears, but as I have been trying to show, the corporate community is central to the biblical narrative. In stressing the importance of reading through a communal lens first, let me also say that Paul does, in fact, address the individual at times, but always in context of the individual's identity and role within the corporate body of Christ. For instance, while I have argued that, like Romans 4, Galatians 3 is also based on a corporate argument, this is not the sole dimension of Paul's thought in this passage.

The appeals in the letter to the Galatians are to those individual members who are seceding to Judaism. [55] In Galatians, the argument about justification is certainly corporate, but the warnings to the individuals emphasize that justification has to be appropriated or applied personally by faith. If the individual Gentile believers accept physical circumcision as the means of being justified, they are embracing the Mosaic law as their way of salvation. In basing their salvation on a ritual that requires self-effort, they are putting themselves outside the covenant of grace, which is to say, outside of the body of Christ.

In the same letter, Paul describes how this corporate salvation applied to him personally when he says, "I have been crucified with Christ and I no longer live, but Christ lives in me. The life I now live in the body, I live by faith in the Son of God, who loved me and gave himself for me."[56] Also, in Paul's testimony in Philippians 3, he speaks of not desiring to have his own righteousness based on old covenant privileges, but on Christ's.[57] Both of these clearly show the idea that faith must be personally appropriated, a familiar concept, was part of Paul's understanding, but also that his acceptance was set within context of a larger corporate reality.

The illustrations Paul uses must be viewed through a similar lens. Even though he discusses Abraham and David in terms of their role as representatives of God's people, their personal faith and consequential acceptance into a covenant relationship with Yahweh are obviously also cases of individuals being justified. But again, they were not justified as stand-alone individuals, as they too were part of the justified community. Even Abraham's justification was integrally related to that of his descendants.

For individualistic Westerners, the challenge in shifting to a corporate mentality is to understand that what is true of the community is not necessarily true of the individual alone. In Paul's framework, terms such as the body of Christ, the temple of the Spirit, the bride of Christ, the new man, the royal priesthood, and the holy nation describe the entire new covenant community, not the solitary believer. While personal repentance and obedience is vital, the individual believer can only experience the full benefits of God's covenant when he or she responds by faith in Christ, takes their place in community, and lives with the other members of the body of Christ in mutual submission.

**FREED OR JUSTIFIED?** ¶ Before leaving this subject, I want to show how the corporate, covenant-making dimension of justification can resolve some other longstanding interpretive problems that many have recognized. Let's circle back now to the conundrum I described when we first began discussing Romans 5–8. I stated that I was uneasy with the commonly accepted interpretation of Romans 6:6-7, which reads:

> For we know that our old self was crucified with him so that the body of sin might be done away with, that we should no longer be slaves to sin—because anyone who has died has been *freed* from sin. [58]

If you recall, I was concerned that interpreters almost always translated the Greek word *dedikaiōtai* in this text as *freed* or *set free* when, in all of the other sixteen times it appears in Paul's letters, it is translated as *justified*. This led me to suspect something was amiss with the common interpretation of this passage.

Paul's use of *dedikaiōtai* (justified) in verse 7 has caused considerable difficulty for those who favor the individualistic, forensic model. If Paul truly meant to use *justified* (declared innocent), according to the Reformed understanding he would have reversed his theology. Instead of teaching that justification is a free gift of grace, as is commonly accepted, he would be saying, "because a believer has died with Christ, he or she is justified." In other words, the experience of dying with Christ would come first and be the *source* of justification. Put another way, justification would be the *outcome* of dying to sin/Sin. As many see it, this is contrary to Paul's insistence that justification is not dependent on any prior event, effort, or experience, a line of thinking which supposedly he developed previously in Romans 4.

Because of this conundrum, the overwhelming consensus of translators and commentators is that in this one instance, Paul must have intended *dedikaiōtai* to mean *freed* and not *justified*. Those who support this interpretation contend Paul is arguing that the person who died has been freed from any charge the law could have had against him or her. According to this rationale, Paul's statement that "anyone who has died has been freed from sin" is based on the legal precept that it is useless taking a dead man to court—once dead, he is effectively freed from the punishment of sin.

This popular forensic explanation, however, not only imposes a meaning upon Paul's vocabulary not ascribed to *dedikaiōtai* (justified) anywhere else in his letters, it also ignores the meaning of *hamartias* (sin) in 6:7 as it equates sin with crime (*aitia*). That is undisciplined thinking. *Hamartias* (sin) is a theological term—an offense against God—while *aitia* (crime) is an offense against fellow humans. People are taken to criminal court for crimes, not sins against God. If Paul had wanted to be understood in the way suggested, he would have used the term *aition* (criminal charge).

The forensic meaning of sin as a crime also does not work when we talk of death freeing a person from sin/Sin. Scripture clearly states, "Man is destined to die once, and after that to face judgment."[59] Death may free a person from paying for a crime committed against a fellow human being. However, it does not remove the responsibility for sin (*hamartias*) against God and Paul clearly anticipated some kind of judgment at the end of the age that will address how we responded to God during our lifetime.[60] Furthermore, by reverting to the little "s" definition of sin as transgression, the traditional forensic view has abandoned the big "S" concept of Sin generally agreed to be found in Romans 6, namely, the personification of Satan.[61] This is important because if a person is still a member of the body of Sin when he or she dies, death does not release that individual from Sin/Satan. If Paul had said, "He that is dead is freed from crime," or even better, "he is freed from the law regarding crime," then the traditional forensic understanding would be plainly true, for *human* law cannot pursue a person beyond death.

A simple way to test an interpretation is to try and put it back in the original setting. If it doesn't fit, then there is good reason to question its validity. To have any possibility of retaining the suggested forensic meaning, we not only have to change the text as far as the term *justified* is concerned, we also have to alter the definition of *sin* (*hamartias*). The increasing number of required adjustments makes the suggested traditional interpretation seem ever more unlikely.

How can these interpretive problems be resolved? Only, I maintain, by placing these verses into a corporate, covenantal New Exodus context. As discussed previously, Sin is the personification of evil; it is Satan, the body of Sin's husband. Because of this covenant relationship, humanity belongs to Sin and cannot enter into a relationship with Christ, as he would then be involved in an act of spiritual adultery. However, if death were to annul the relationship, then all who died with Christ to the law of sin and death would be justified in remarrying. In other words, if it were truly possible for the believing community to share in the death of Christ to Sin, the covenant with the old husband would be cancelled. The church would be *justified* from Sin before both the civil law and God's law. Consequently, she would then be free to become betrothed to Christ. This, I suggest, is exactly what Paul was conveying in his letter to the Romans.

In this scenario, Paul was right to use the term *justified* and anyone who changes this meaning is departing from what he intended to say. The traditional preference for translating *dedikaiōtai* as *freed* results from the failure to appreciate the theological and corporate framework of the argument. To be justified from Sin as referenced in Romans 6:6-7 fits naturally into the corporate model for which I have been arguing; it describes the release from the covenant that bound humankind to Sin and Death since the garden. The validity of this reading is confirmed in that Paul goes on to make the same argument in Romans 7:1-6.

## Reframing the Debate

The corporate, covenantal view of justification we have been exploring has the potential to shift the contours of the historic debate about this critical doctrine. Regarding the current conversation among Protestants, there is support for the Reformers' interpretation that justification has to do with the believer's acquittal from sin and judgment. But at the same time, there has been confusion about the way the Reformers used various terms related to justification.

As discussed, it is a violation of linguistic principles to collect a range of texts that contain the same term, mash the meanings together to create a hybrid definition, and then apply it to every use of the word. The same linguistic rules apply to theology as to other areas of literary study—the context must determine the meaning. This has been the weakness of the Reformed method. Focusing primarily on the forensic aspects of justification prevented some of the Reformers from seeing the wider theological meaning of the term. In context of the biblical narrative, justification is about far more than legal pardon and acquittal from guilt for the individual; it is about the entire process of restoring God's people to a covenantal relationship with him.

I have pointed out that Passover is at the very heart of the New Exodus framework and is the crucial event around which Paul builds his doctrine of justification. We have also seen that an important strand of the Old Testament doctrine of justification has to do with Israel's release from exile and subsequent restoration of her relationship with Yahweh during the Second Exodus. Paul picks up these threads of Old Testament thought by maintaining a corporate, covenantal view of justification. However, in keeping with God's promises to Abraham, he widens it to include those from any nation who renounce their alliance with Sin/Satan and turn to Christ in faith. All who believe in Jesus as Messiah, no matter what nation, ethnic group, gender, or class can now belong to the justified community.

In considering alternative ways to read Paul's letters, New Perspective advocates unwittingly highlighted the linguistic confusion of the Reformer's method, which has been a helpful contribution to the conversation. However, as our discussion has shown, justification is not about how to define the people of God or how you can tell who a member of the new covenant community is, as some New Perspective advocates claim. Rather, it refers to the *creation* of a covenant between Yahweh and his people and how they enter into that sacred relationship collectively. One of the methodological problems associated with the New Perspective is that key arguments were framed in reaction to the Westminster Confession. By isolating the more systematic, business-like language of the Westminster Confession from the wider theology of the Reformers, including the writers of the Confession itself, they produced a caricature of the Reformed view.

Despite the widespread problem with the Reformers methodology and individualistic approach, in my view, they still had the heart of the biblical understanding of justification. Earlier, I noted the historical Protestant understanding of justification. I want to reflect on it again, but this time in light of the entire argument I have now presented. I have been making the case that justification is about God's salvation in which he freed his people from Sin/Satan, forgave their sins, and established an indissoluble covenant with them that scripture describes as a marriage.

Although admittedly explained in terms of the individual, the Reformers, along with other Protestants, understood

> That man enjoys that acceptance with God called "justification," the beginning and end of salvation, not through his own moral effort even in the smallest and slightest degree but entirely and only through the loving mercy of God made available in the merits of Christ and of his saving death on the Cross. This was not a process of gradual ethical improvement but an instantaneous transaction, something like a marriage, in which Christ the bridegroom takes to himself an impoverished and wretched harlot and confers upon her all the riches that are his. The key to this transaction was faith, defined as a total and trustful commitment of the self to God, and is itself not a human achievement but the pure gift of God. [62]

Shifting to a corporate view of justification and understanding the full scope of what it entails may be challenging, but I hope you can see how it opens up new dimensions in scripture that have been blurred over time by individualistic readings. In light of this more expansive view of justification we would do well to reframe the debate in the West, both among Protestants, and between Catholics and Protestants. Until the whole matter of justification is set within its proper corporate, covenantal framework, it will be difficult, if not impossible, to accurately pinpoint the exact causes of the conflicts about this doctrine. This correction is essential if we are to resolve the long-standing differences that have divided the Western Church and erected walls between Eastern and Western believers. I know that I am leaving many questions unanswered at this point, but as there is much more to be discussed than what is covered here, rethinking the contours of the historic debate is something that will need to be done in subsequent conversations over time.

### An Amazing Picture!

In the last three chapters, we have pulled apart several conceptual strands in Romans 3:21-26 to see how they looked when set within their Old Testament corporate, covenantal context. This enabled us to gain insight into Paul's understanding of key terms and how he wove them together in context of the New Exodus framework to show the panoramic story of the salvation that God accomplished for his people through Christ's death.

This critical passage reveals how, together, the Father and Son through the agency of the Spirit resolved the dilemma created by sin/Sin in order to begin making things right. We saw that in his covenant-keeping righteousness, the Father moved to rescue his people from Sin and Death by presenting his Son as a Passover sacrifice that also made atonement for sin. On humanity's behalf, Jesus satisfied the requirement of the law spoken in the Garden that says the consequence of sin is death. This made the way for God to rightfully redeem his people from exile in the kingdom of darkness, pardon their sins, and bring them back into a covenant relationship with him. In this way, God justified the new covenant community. Any individual who calls on the name of Christ for salvation and whose heart is circumcised can enter into the justified community and enjoy the never-ending blessings that God has bestowed on his people collectively.

If what I have been saying up to this point is correct, then it opens the door to a much fuller understanding of what Christ's death accomplished. As we have seen, a traditional view of salvation is that Christ paid for the sins that we, as individuals, committed so that we could have eternal life. This is definitely part of Christ's saving work, but I want to argue that it is secondary to something far more amazing. I contend the justification of the new covenant community that we read of in Romans 1-8 is even more glorious than the idea that Jesus died so that our personal sins could be forgiven. Indeed, I suggest the bigger picture the New Testament presents regarding the significance of Christ's death is that Jesus freed his people from Sin/Satan's control once for all time!

I would further argue this is the basis of the message preached by the early church—that all who are outside of Christ are in exile from God and captives of Sin and Death. But through Christ's death, God made the way for all who trust in his Son to be delivered from the realm of darkness and transferred into the kingdom of light. In the first-century church, matters related personal sin and forgiveness were set within the larger context of the redeemed community. As we discussed previously, and scripture so clearly reveals, sin is not just a problem for the individual, but it threatens the community's fellowship with God and with one another.

Although he fails to appreciate the corporate and covenantal dimension of Paul's thought, E.P. Sanders supports the argument I am making by identifying the larger picture of Sin and the purpose of Christ's death. He states:

> Paul has a more radical conception of sin than that it is transgression. Humans are not just sinners; they are enslaved by a power: Sin. Repentance and acquittal of individual transgressions do not fully meet the human problem. People are not just guilty, they are enslaved, and they need to escape. Paul thought that the power of Sin was so great that one must die to be set free of it... People who become one person with Christ share his death and thus escape bondage, and they then share his life, being free from the power of Sin. Herein lies Paul's distinctive contribution to thought about the death of Christ.[63]

This statement is even more meaningful when it is understood that the enemy who enslaved humanity is no less than Sin/Satan, the former husband mentioned in Romans 7, and that the power he once had over God's people was the covenantal authority the law gave to husbands. The abuse of this law and the way it became an instrument of Sin/Satan is what led Paul to debate the question, "Is the law sin?" in Romans 7. The incredibly good news is that the representative death of Christ has broken Satan's authority over the believing community by ending the covenant relationship with Sin and Death, and with it, Sin's power. Now, through Christ, God is making everything right!

Recovering this larger framework allows us to see how the New Exodus storyline brings together various elements of the different atonement theories to form a more cohesive picture of Christ's sacrificial death. In giving his life for us, Jesus, our Passover, paid the ultimate price to deal with humanity's sin so that he could ransom (rescue, redeem) his bride from Sin and Death. As humanity's representative, Jesus atoned for our sins by dying in our stead so that we would not have to suffer the ultimate consequence of sin—eternal exile from God. He was chastened on our behalf so that all who are willing could return to the Father without fear of punishment. Also, as the Lamb of God, his blood will protect those who are at home in him from God's future wrath that will be poured out on Satan and the kingdom of darkness at the end of the ages.

On the cross, Jesus also defeated the powers of evil that held humankind in bondage in the kingdom of darkness. Even when suffering brutal violence at the hands of his enemies, Jesus continued to love them and offer forgiveness. In this way, he overcame evil with good so that in both his life and death he served as an example for all to follow. Having redeemed his people from Sin/Satan, he initiated the New Exodus in which he began leading the pilgrim community home to Zion, the city of God.

Through his saving work, God proved to be just in that by presenting Jesus as a sacrifice of atonement (with the Son's consent), he in no way ignored our sin or violated his own word. And he showed himself to be the one who justifies by bringing those who have faith in Jesus back to himself and establishing the promised new covenant. Together, the justified new covenant community is a public display of God's righteousness that came to us through the faithfulness of his Son.

Furthermore, as the last Adam who came to reverse the work of the evil one, Jesus inaugurated the new creation and began the process of recapitulation through his work on the cross. The new man, the church that was birthed at the time of his death, is being conformed to Christ's image so that his glory can be reflected in his people, who together, are his body. In defeating Satan, Jesus, in his role as King of kings and Lord of lords, also redeemed creation through his death and, by means of the Spirit, is in the process of summing up (subjecting, regathering) all things in himself to present to the Father so that God may once again be all in all.[64]

This is why we are to remember Jesus's death by taking communion together until his coming. Just as celebrating the Passover event was central to Israel's national identity, every time we eat the bread and drink from the cup we celebrate all that Christ, our Passover, accomplished on our behalf and who we are as a result of our collective union with him—the new man, the body of Christ, his beloved bride, the living Temple in whom the Spirit now dwells! Together, we are renewed by the Spirit as we come to the table and recall what he achieved through his love and sacrifice in the New Exodus event.

We are nearing the end of our journey now to recover the corporate, New Exodus framework for God's salvation story. To finish this part of our discussion, I want to explore one more concept related to Christ's work as the last Adam, as in my opinion, it puts the crowning touch on this breathtaking picture—and that is Paul's understanding of Christ as *prototokos*, the firstborn of all creation.

CHAPTER 11

# First of All

When faulty assumptions are made, it is easy to overlook the obvious. This is the premise of *The Purloined Letter*, a classic tale by Edgar Allen Poe. The story tells of how detective, C. Auguste Dupin, ingeniously solves a mystery involving a stolen letter. Seeking help, the Prefect of the Police tells Dupin that a devious public official known as Minister D had taken a letter that contained compromising information from a prominent lady's home. He was now using it to blackmail her.

Every day for three months, the frustrated Prefect and the detectives on his team had searched Minister D's hotel room while he was out, but to no avail. They had looked behind the wallpaper, under the carpets, behind pictures, in and under drawers, probed cushions, and even examined the tables and chairs using their most advanced methods but turned up nothing. Intrigued, Dupin asked him to share a detailed description of the letter, which he memorized. A month later, Dupin calmly turned the letter over to the baffled Prefect.

How did Dupin solve the mystery? He first reasoned that Minister D was smart enough to know the Prefect would assume that he put the letter in a cleverly devised hiding place. Dupin further deduced that D would hide the letter somewhere the police would never think to look. Where would this be?

With an idea in mind, Dupin visited Minister D in his hotel room. Surveying the room, he noticed a half-torn letter openly displayed in an organizer rack on the fireplace. Based on the Prefect's description, he recognized it as the purloined letter, noticing the envelope had been changed slightly so it would not be immediately spotted. When the visit ended, Dupin left a personal item behind as an excuse to return the next day. When he did, he discretely replaced the real letter with a facsimile he had created. As Dupin explained, ultimately, the solution to the mystery was simple—the letter had been there all along, hidden in plain sight.

In the effort to recover a clearer view of the biblical picture, we have been considering how the New Exodus storyline unifies scripture and gives definition to the Messiah's death and mission, which is to be carried forward by the new covenant community. Our aim now is see how this paradigm shines a light on straightforward clues about other aspects of Jesus's person and work that have been previously overlooked due to faulty assumptions. In our earlier study of Romans 3:21-26, I made the case that the Passover is the central theme Paul used to describe the sacrificial nature of Christ's death. If so, there is a strong possibility it also shaped his views on Jesus's life and work. This brings me to a major Passover-related clue about Jesus's identity that, as we shall see, has been in plain sight all along but not fully appreciated—the phrase *the firstborn of all creation (prototokos)*.[1]

It is not that scholars have ignored this concept; in fact, for centuries, there has been ongoing debate about what it means that Christ is the *prototokos*. Observing that commentators still disagree, one scholar notes it is "one of the unsolved problems of the New Testament."[2] In my opinion, one reason is because the paschal setting of the term has been overlooked. Also, it has sometimes been interpreted against a Greek or Jewish-Hellenistic backdrop, which has masked key elements of its meaning.

Let's first see why the term has been controversial and challenging to define. After this, we will look at *the firstborn of all creation (prototokos)* in context of the Old Testament and then see how this provides exciting insights about what the phrase means in relation to Christ, his practical role as the firstborn son of God's family, and the new covenant community's corporate identity.

**THE MYSTERY OF THE FIRSTBORN¶** The term *firstborn* is used in several places in the New Testament, but the text that has received the most attention by far is Colossians 1:15-20, which describes Jesus and what he accomplished through his death in the highest of terms.

> The Son is the image of the invisible God, *the firstborn over all creation*. For in him all things were created: things in heaven and on earth, visible and invisible, whether thrones or powers or rulers or authorities; all things have been created through him and for him. He is before all things, and in him all things hold together. And he is the head of the body, the church; he is the beginning and the *firstborn from among the dead*, so that in everything he might have the supremacy. For God was pleased to have all his fullness dwell in him, and through him to reconcile to himself all things, whether things on earth or things in heaven, by making peace *through his blood, shed on the cross.*[3]

This passage is generally seen as speaking about ontological matters related to Christ's pre-existence, status, supremacy, or nature. Ontology, another word we do not use in our everyday vocabulary, is a philosophical term that has to do with abstract theories about being and existence. For instance, ontological discussions about Jesus address subjects like, does being the firstborn mean he had a beginning or that he has a higher rank than other creatures? What is the essence of his being? Is he the firstborn in the sense that he is the first to have a divine/human nature? Is he the first to come back from the dead? Or does the term refer to his sovereign status over all?

Because verse 16 describes Jesus's role as creating all things, there is no question that it relates to Christ's pre-existence. As such, the passage certainly has an ontological dimension, but I would say not in the way that it has been traditionally understood. What has been missing in most of the discussions about this text is that in scripture, "the firstborn of all creation" is not an abstract term that primarily describes Christ's nature, essence, or his status—rather it is defined by his *concrete actions*, namely, his saving work in redeeming creation. As we will see, in the Old Testament the firstborn son had specific responsibilities he was to carry out on behalf of the family, which pointed ahead to the specific work that Christ, the firstborn of all creation, was sent by God the Father to do for his family. This Old Testament background is crucial for understanding how the primitive church understood the person and work of Christ, and why they believed that Jesus was God very early on. Before going on to explore this in more detail, it will help to first look at some of the various ways this passage has been read and interpreted.

## Firstborn Controversies

Historically, controversy erupted over the phrase, "the firstborn of all creation," in the fourth century, when Arius, an influential presbyter in the Christian community, used it to support his claim that Jesus was a created being and, therefore, not fully God. This generated a fierce debate about the deity of Christ and the Holy Spirit that had a long-lasting impact on the church. Even though it was eventually declared heretical, to this day some groups like the Jehovah's Witnesses adhere to the Arian position.

In more recent history, controversy has centered on the authorship and source of Colossians 1:15-20. Some claim Paul wrote Colossians, some say not, and still others say he was the author of the letter, but not this passage. One line of thinking is that the text is a hymn sung by the first-century church Paul adapted and incorporated into his letter as a confessional statement. In this way, he could start the letter from a place of common agreement. Those who embrace the evolutionary model for how New Testament theology developed, however, contend the text was invented and inserted later in an effort to prove that Jesus was superior to pagan gods. In this view, there is no way the early church could have come up with a sophisticated theology of the cosmic Christ so soon after Jesus's death.

A number of scholars and theologians suggest the hymn, along with the particular reference to "the firstborn of all creation," is best understood when viewed through the lens of Wisdom Christology. In this framework, Jesus is seen as a form of personified wisdom, be it the divine pre-existent Son of God who came to earth, a wise but human-only son of God, a prophet or a son of the goddess Sophia (wisdom).

Some who favor Wisdom Christology contend the New Testament writers adapted, alluded to, or incorporated Greek wisdom motifs into their theologies. Another influential view is that Paul and other New Testament writers relied on a combination of Old Testament texts and extra-biblical Jewish-Hellenistic works shaped by Greek thought such as the *Wisdom of Solomon*, *Sirach*, and the *Books of the Maccabees* when drafting their works. Others theorize that Paul's views of Christ's work and person was shaped primarily by the Jewish Wisdom tradition such as that found in Proverbs 8, where wisdom is personified as a female.

In looking at these theories, I can only say that as a lens for understanding his person and work, the Wisdom Christology that draws on Greek philosophy is problematic for several reasons. For one thing, the Greeks could never accept that the Logos (another name given to Wisdom in their belief system) would ever become a bodily being because for them, physicality itself is an inferior state. Since Plato's followers saw the human body as a prison house for the soul, there is no way that wisdom could become flesh in their framework. Also, the connection between *firstborn* and *wisdom* is not as clear as has been claimed by some who embrace Wisdom Christology. The text in Colossians links the firstborn with redemption and reconciliation, themes that have nothing to do with Greek wisdom in any shape or form.[4] The Greek concept of wisdom also does not have anything in common with sacrifice, a theme central to Paul's teaching, and specifically to the text in Colossians.

This raises the question—why import the meaning of *prototokos* from Hellenism, when Paul's theology is so heavily impregnated with Old Testament sacrificial language? As with other statements made by the apostle, I contend there is no need to go outside of scripture itself to understand what Paul meant when he described Jesus as "the firstborn of all creation." This is supported by the fact that although Jesus is indeed described as the wisdom of God in John's gospel, it is now widely agreed he did not get this understanding from Greek sources as previously thought. Rather, he drew it from the Old Testament account of creation in Proverbs 8 where God's word (Wisdom) created all things. However, as encouraging as it may be that some scholars look to Old Testament scripture for the framework for understanding Jesus, as we'll see, even the Jewish Wisdom tradition based primarily on Proverbs 8 is simply not sufficient when it comes to determining the meaning of *prototokos*.

## Retrieving the Paschal Setting

One of the main reasons it makes sense to interpret *prototokos* within a paschal, New Exodus setting is because the firstborn's death was at the very heart of the Passover. In the First Exodus narrative, the firstborn son was designated by Yahweh to represent the family, and this role was bound up with each family's deliverance from the angel of death.[5] It is vital to note that it was the firstborn son and not the entire family who faced the threat of death as the angel of death moved through Egypt to kill the firstborn of man and animals. The reason the firstborn son's life was threatened is because he represented the family. Thus, the lamb that was slain for each Hebrew household was not to spare the family as a whole, but only the firstborn son.

This representative role is what links the New Testament declarations that Christ is the Lamb of God and our Passover with the statement that he is the firstborn. To be more precise, Christ is the firstborn, the one who represents his family and protects his people from death. Because no one else could fulfill his representative role and face the angel of death on humanity's behalf, Jesus died as the paschal lamb had done in the First Exodus. In this way, he was both the firstborn and the Passover offering, for in the Christian Passover, they are one.

This double designation of firstborn and Lamb of God is not a problem when it comes to the argument I am making as, in Christ, many offices and titles converge. Prophet and priest converge with king; priest converges with victim; and savior converges with judge. The New Testament writers would have little difficulty applying this same principle to yet another realm of Christ's offices and work, so the firstborn and paschal lamb converge to become one and the same entity. Since the First Exodus foreshadowed the redemptive work of Christ, it is somewhat astonishing that so many scholars have failed to look into the significance of the firstborn's role in that initial Old Testament act of redemption when seeking to interpret how the title applies to Christ.

I want to be clear— by placing it firmly in the context of redemptive history, the position I am presenting rejects Wisdom Christology or any Greek-influenced ontologically-based framework for interpreting *prototokos*. I contend the main point of the title is not that Christ *is* the firstborn—it is not primarily about his nature, essence, or status—but that he *acts* as the firstborn. In other words, *the title describes the actual work he has done in his death.*

The significance of this for comprehending what it means that Christ is the firstborn of creation becomes apparent when looking at the biblical storyline. For Paul, redemption, like the fall, has a cosmic dimension. Romans 8 shows that having come under Sin/Satan's rule, the whole creation is waiting to be restored to God, the Creator. This will happen at the climax of Christ's redemptive work when the sons and daughters of God are finally revealed and glorified. In the First Exodus, the firstborn's significance was only for his nuclear family. However, the impact of Christ's death, the Christian Passover in the New Exodus, goes beyond his own family to the entire creation. This links the title *firstborn* to the creation that was caught up in the tragedy of the fall. Thus, Jesus is the firstborn of creation—the one through whom God created the world—is also tasked with redeeming and restoring it to his Father. And reflecting his familial role as the redeemer of his brethren, Paul also describes Jesus as the "firstborn of many brothers" in Romans 8. This places Jesus squarely in the center of our corporate identity as God's new covenant community. He is God's only begotten firstborn Son, who carries all of the responsibilities for his family.

When seen in context of the Paschal-New Exodus paradigm, the title, "the firstborn over all creation" describes Jesus's specific *function as redeemer.*[6] This understanding is the first and most important meaning of *protokos.* If we do not see this as Paul's primary meaning, then we will not only miss what he is saying, but the rest of the Bible as well. The reason is because the apostle draws important implications based on this understanding, many of which, in turn, explain Jesus's status and great work of being the creator before he became creation's redeemer. In other words, Christ's practical role as the firstborn who redeems God's family is what sheds light on ontological matters related to his nature, being, and pre-existence. This is why it is critical to first realize that the meaning of the term *firstborn* is based on his actual *work* rather than on philosophical abstractions. We will see the importance of this more clearly after looking at the firstborn's role and responsibilities to the family that are spelled out in the Old Testament. Later, we will also see that the introduction and conclusion of the Colossians hymn support the view I am presenting.

## Responsibilities of the Firstborn

In the ancient Hebrew culture, the firstborn is synonymous with *the redeemer*, the designated person who acts on behalf of the family. They are one and the same. This is never explicitly stated in scripture, probably because the equation was obvious to any Jew, but the connection is clearly present. As mentioned previously, the firstborn-redeemer had three main responsibilities.

*Securing justice.* Based on the law of retribution, when a member of the family was murdered, the redeemer's duty was to seek justice by avenging their death.[7] In the later part of Isaiah, where Yahweh is often called the redeemer, he promises to act as the avenger of his people.[8] In the New Testament, Christ is presented as fulfilling this same role.[9]

*Securing lost property.* Another function of the firstborn-redeemer in the Old Testament was to secure property that had been lost to the family through debt. As outlined in Leviticus, the redeemer also had responsibilities in connection with the year of Jubilee.[10] Every 50 years, all debts were to be forgiven. Whenever possible, it fell to the nearest relative to act as the redeemer by recovering the family's property. Once again, we find Yahweh promising to act as Israel's redeemer in securing what had been lost by making sure her land would be returned to her possession.[11] And again, we find this role attributed to Christ as he recovers the kingdom of heaven for those who were deprived of it by sin/Sin.[12]

*Securing protection for family widows.* The third role of the redeemer was to fulfill the law that required the redeemer to act as protector for any widows in the family. If a woman was widowed and childless, it was the redeemer's responsibility to take her as his wife and raise a family on behalf of the deceased brother.[13] This aspect of the redeemer's role is also used to illustrate the salvation Yahweh promises his people. The prophet Isaiah says, "He will save Jerusalem from her widowhood and raise up children for her."[14] This same role is applied to Christ, who takes the church to himself as her husband.[15]

The argument I'm making about Jesus *acting* as firstborn assumes two important points: that the firstborn's role in the Exodus event was vicarious—he represented his family; and the Old Testament title *redeemer* was dropped by the New Testament writers in favor of *firstborn* when describing Christ. To test these assumptions, we will need to look into the significance of the firstborn's role, and then see if we can discover why Jesus was referred to as firstborn and not redeemer even though he fulfilled that function.

## Chosen to Represent

To this end, our first task is to delve more deeply into the firstborn's role in the Passover. Why were the firstborn sons central to the event? Why was it necessary for a lamb to serve as a substitute? Did the firstborn have anything to do with making atonement for the people? Although scholars differ about these matters, I would say evidence suggests the original Passover, in which a lamb was substituted for Israel's firstborn, was regarded as an atoning sacrifice for the entire nation.[16] However, subsequent Passover celebrations were memorials of the original act of redemption but had no atoning value. If so, this indicates that Israel's sin, which involved her covenant unfaithfulness in worshipping the Egyptian gods, was originally dealt with in the first Passover. The annual Day of Atonement is when the subsequent sin of the nation was addressed.

A major clue regarding the firstborn's role in the initial Passover is found in Exodus 4:22. At this point in the storyline, Pharaoh is threatening Israel, the nation who Yahweh elected to be his special people. God has decided it is time to deliver his people from the Egyptian ruler's control and chose Moses to be his spokesman. In this verse, Yahweh is giving Moses instructions about what he is to say when it is time to issue the final warning to Pharaoh. He tells Moses:

> Then say to Pharaoh, "This is what the LORD says, 'Israel is my firstborn son, and I told you, let my people go, so that they may worship me.' But you refused to let him go, so I will kill your firstborn son."

Commenting on the correlation between Israel and the Egyptians, Alan Cole observes,

> Israel, considered collectively, is God's firstborn, presumably as being His chosen people and as "first-fruits" of all the peoples (Jer. 31:9). If Pharaoh will not give God's firstborn up to God, to whom all firstborn belong in any case, then Pharaoh's own firstborn must die instead. Since "Israel" is a collective here, it is reasonable to suppose that "Pharaoh" is also a collective term; thus, "your firstborn" includes all the firstborn in the land. Otherwise we

should have to assume that the original reference was to Pharaoh's son alone and no other.[17]

The comparison is between Israel *collectively* and all of the firstborn sons of Egypt. Pharaoh had sought not only to control Yahweh's firstborn son—the nation of Israel—but his command to kill the male Hebrew babies at one point was a deliberate action that endangered Israel's very existence.[18] This, plus the grinding enslavement of the Hebrews, bore witness to the fact that Pharaoh regarded Yahweh's firstborn as being dispensable. Now, Yahweh will demonstrate his own might in his dealings with Egypt.

Yahweh's intention to strike the firstborn is repeated in Exodus 11. In this passage, he impresses upon the Israelites that they will be safe in the coming judgment, but how Israel's firstborn will be protected is not fully explained until chapter 12. This is when Yahweh tells them the blood of a lamb, an innocent victim, is to be substituted for the life of their firstborn as a protection to them, and also as a safeguard for every family. While the blood only spares the firstborn, the whole family is instructed to eat the lamb. Eating the lamb together is described as sharing in the Passover. This is a clear sign the entire Jewish community will share in the deliverance that will come about because the firstborn sons who represented the family were spared by the blood of the lamb.

Additional clues regarding the significance of the firstborn are found in Exodus 13. In the midst of giving instructions about the Passover event, Yahweh tells Moses to "Consecrate to me every firstborn male. The first offspring of every womb among the Israelites belongs to me, whether human or animal."[19] The firstborn males were to be set apart for Yahweh to act as his priestly people.

Together, these chapters show that the firstborn sons had a representative role—during the First Exodus they stood between the angel of death and their families. In turn, it was necessary to make provision for the firstborn in order for their lives to be spared, which Yahweh himself supplied by providing for a lamb to die in their stead.

## Constant Reminders

The significance of the firstborn son's role is further revealed when it is realized that celebrating Passover was not just an afterthought to the Exodus event; it was meant to be a perpetual memorial for the entire nation of Israel through all generations.[20] In fact, in Yahweh's design, the Passover was not only to be celebrated annually by every succeeding generation of Jews, but reminders of it were woven into their daily lives. And one of those reminders had to do with the birth and redemption of the firstborn males.

The birth of a firstborn son, a treasured moment in the lives of any Jewish couple, was accompanied by the reminder that he did not belong to his parents; he was to be presented as a sacrifice to the Lord. To be very clear, Israel was not to practice child sacrifice as other nations did. Although the firstborn son was presented to Yahweh, he also instructed the Hebrews to "redeem every firstborn among your sons."[21] The father could do this by paying five shekels to the priest on the thirtieth day after his son's birth.[22] This was a gracious reminder of how God spared the firstborn, as the ceremonial sacrifice of the firstborn and their redemption harkened back to the first Passover.

Yahweh also made provision for redeeming the firstborn animals as well. Although instructions were for the firstborn donkey, an unclean animal, to be destroyed, it had such a practical value to the Israelites that Yahweh allowed for it to be redeemed by the death of a lamb. At lambing time, the air must have carried the stench of burning flesh throughout the land, which was yet another reminder of Passover and the role of the firstborn.

Through the practice of consecrating and then redeeming the firstborn males, the vicarious nature of the firstborn's role was clearly to be taught to succeeding generations. As Moses explained,

> In the days to come when your son asks you, "What does this mean?" say to him, "with a mighty hand the LORD brought us out of Egypt, out of the land of slavery. When Pharaoh stubbornly refused to let us go, the LORD killed every firstborn in Egypt, both man and animal. This is why I sacrifice to the LORD the first male offspring of every womb and redeem each of my firstborn sons." And it will be like a sign on your hand and a symbol on your forehead that the LORD brought us out of Egypt with his mighty hand.[23]

Yahweh intended for the Passover and its significance to be at the forefront in other areas of Hebrew thought and theology as well. Their experience of being strangers who were oppressed in a foreign land and then redeemed determined their treatment of aliens.[24] Indeed, it molded their whole ethical framework, as they were to relate to others out of the wellspring of gratitude that came from being redeemed. Truly, the implications of the Passover surrounded the Jews daily.

## The Levites and the Firstborn

The vicarious nature of the firstborn son's role also seems to be reflected in God's selection of the Levites to assist the priests. As explained in Numbers 8, Yahweh allowed the firstborn who belonged to him to be redeemed, and then gave the Levites to Aaron, the priest, and his sons to serve in the tabernacle instead. In other words, the Levites became substitutes for the firstborn. Yahweh gives an unusual explanation for their role:

> From among all the Israelites, I have given the Levites as gifts to Aaron and his sons to do the work at the tent of meeting on behalf of the Israelites and to make atonement for them so that no plague will strike the Israelites when they go near the sanctuary.[25]

This verse again reveals the representational solidarity we have been discussing with the Levites serving as representatives for the firstborn and, in turn, for Israel. But it also contains the unexpected statement, "to make atonement." This cannot be a reference to offering animal sacrifices because the Levites were excluded from this service. Only Aaron and his sons were allowed to offer sacrifices. The passage, therefore, suggests the very presence of the Levites, as substitutes for the firstborn, performed a propitiatory function by averting the wrath of Yahweh from the people.

This protective role is described earlier in the book of Numbers when instructions were given as to where the different tribes were to camp in relation to the tabernacle. In Numbers 1, it says, "The Levites, however, are to set up their tents around the tabernacle of the covenant law so that my wrath will not fall on the Israelite community."[26] Just as the lambs served as substitutes and saved the firstborn from God's judgment on the night of the Passover, so the Levites later performed the same function of protecting the congregation from Yahweh's wrath. The atoning value of the Levites' role is supported by a rabbinical interpretation, which says, "This prerogative was then conferred upon the tribe of Levi who, moreover, dedicating themselves, man for man, to the service of the Lord, served as an atonement for the firstborn, that they might not be destroyed as they deserved."[27]

This further underscores the propitiatory function that the death of the lamb and the presence of the Levites played. They are not separate roles but linked in that they both represent the firstborn. It also supports the idea that the firstborn sons were under the threat of death on the night of Passover because they fulfilled a representative role for the family; if no provision for atonement was made for them, they would also die bearing the wrath of God. This dovetails with the case made earlier about how the prophet Ezekiel merged Passover with the Day of Atonement, thereby, establishing the propitiatory value of the Passover. For more evidence regarding the link between the firstborn, Passover and atonement please see *Contours of Pauline Theology*.[28] I have also included a discussion about why the firstborn and not the father represented the family.[29]

## Working Titles

Another question to explore regarding the significance of the firstborn's role and work has to do with the two titles, *firstborn* and *redeemer*. If they refer to one and the same person in the Old Testament, then why not have just one title? This may seem like a minor question, but actually, it opens the door to an exhilarating exploration of Jesus's work, and how the various Messianic titles connect and complement one another in the paschal setting.

The reason for the two titles is that they describe separate functions. The firstborn was the sacrificial representative for the family, and this function could not be abdicated or handed on. The only way the firstborn could avoid this role was if a God-ordained substitute took his place. While the firstborn son was also intended to be the family's redeemer, he was not always so in practice. This role could be, and often was, handed on to the next of kin, either because of death or abdication. Also, there was no vicarious sacrificial role in the work of the redeemer. It was essentially concerned with the social welfare of the nearest kinsmen.

The two titles are never explicitly brought together in the Old Testament. However, this does not undermine the argument that the two are interrelated. To the Hebrews, the identity of one with the other was so obvious it would be like saying rain is water. In Jewish society, because the firstborn son was also meant to be the redeemer, by law he received twice the inheritance of any other family member so that he had the means to fulfill this function. If the eldest was dead or refused to act, his responsibilities went to the next brother in line. If there were no brothers or if they all refused to act, the role of the redeemer fell upon the nearest relative who would accept the duty. No one could assume the role of redeemer without honoring this relational chain, which started with the eldest son.[30]

The other sphere, in which the roles of the firstborn and redeemer are seen to be interrelated if not synonymous, is in Jewish expectations of the Messiah. Although the title, Messiah, was not applied until later, based on Hebrew scriptures the Jews were looking for a king or priest who would redeem the people of Israel from political oppression and give Israel favored status among the nations. In the Old Testament, Israel's king in Psalm 89:27 was called the Lord's firstborn. This originally referred to the Jewish king's promised superiority over the kings of the earth. A fact especially relevant to our discussion is that the king of Israel, the Lord's firstborn, played a central role in celebrating the Passover.[31] If you recall, in Ezekiel, it was the princely descendant of David who made sacrifices during the end times Passover. The first-century church would have recognized that this anticipated the ultimate sacrifice that Jesus, as firstborn king, provides and makes.

The Messianic titles used by Jesus and the New Testament writers provide even more insights into the significance of the term *firstborn*. The description of Jesus as the last Adam points to the representative role the firstborn fulfilled. As the Lord's firstborn, Jesus is the federal head and redeemer of his brethren.[32] One theologian observes that by comparing the first Adam to Christ, who is the last Adam, Paul expresses the reality that Jesus is the firstborn of God's new creation. As the new Adam, he stands at the head of all as the initiator of the perfect redeemed creation.[33]

This view is supported by another claim that the firstborn of every creature is not only linked to the idea of Christ as the last Adam, but it is the very cornerstone of Paul's Christology, which, he contends, was implicit in the resurrection of Christ. He states, "In other words, from Christ's significance as the second Adam all the categories are derived which further defined his significance as the firstborn of every creature."[34] To sum up, we can add all Paul that said about the last Adam to the other material we have considered about the firstborn.

Both titles are inseparably linked with the concept of the *firstborn-redeemer* figure.

As I explain in more detail in the original *Contours of Pauline Theology*, when looking at this, along with the other titles of Jesus in scripture, we can see that like facets of a diamond, each illuminates the significance of the others. Jesus's role as the firstborn of creation is colored by all the redemptive concepts inherent in the work of the priestly king, the descendant of David, the Royal Servant who is also the suffering Servant. Who is also the Son of Man, who fulfills a priestly function and serves as Judge. Who is the paschal victim, the firstborn of the dead, and the last Adam. And who is also the firstborn-redeemer at the heart of the Passover and the New Exodus. For all of these reasons I suggest that the proposed paradigm is called the Paschal New Exodus.

**THE FIRSTBORN AND GOD'S FAMILY**¶We have covered a lot of ground, but it was important to do so as we are now in a position to make several observations about Christ's work and how it relates to our identity as the people of God. First, far from the Passover event having little influence on the New Testament writers, we can see that it actually formed the very substructure upon which they built their concepts. As one scholar observed, "Palestinian Christianity arrived at its Christology via a Passover setting."[35]

While I mostly agree with this statement, I want to make a note about the timing of the first-century church's understanding of the person and work of Christ. Once it is realized that much of the New Testament's perspective of Christ is rooted in the Old, there are compelling reasons to believe it came together very early on. The primitive community arrived at their insights as the Spirit enabled them to reflect on the significance of Christ, who, through his death as the paschal sacrifice, inaugurated the New Exodus for his people. This shows the first-century church's view of Christ did not originate with Paul; it was given to him in a highly developed form, which served as the basis of his theology.

But we can go even further than this. The doctrine of Christ's person is illustrated and clarified by the doctrine of his work. Therefore, rather than the phrase, "the firstborn of creation" creating difficulties when it comes to the doctrine of Christ's divinity, it turns out to be the very opposite; it actually becomes a key statement in proving it! No creature, no matter how exalted, could redeem creation. Only God himself could be the firstborn-redeemer of the whole creation. Thus, as the early believers reflected on the Old Testament scriptures about how Yahweh promised to redeem creation and saw this to have been achieved in the death of Jesus, they could come to no other conclusion than Jesus was God.

And this brings us to the title's ontological versus practical function. Although the inevitable ontological conclusion was that Jesus is God, it is important to realize the early church's Christology was *functionally* based for a couple of reasons. First, rather than grappling with lofty, intangible definitions of Christ's pre-existent being, the first-century Christians were glorying in how God's promises were actually being fulfilled in redemptive history. This is in keeping with the predominately Jewish character of the church at this time. On the whole, the Jews were far more interested in the practical side of life and discovering what God wants humans to do, than in "describing God's essence."[36] As we have seen, when the focus is primarily on the ontological definition of firstborn, the concrete, practical aspects of what this term means in context of redemptive history are often overlooked or minimized. Consequently, critical layers of meaning that help define the person of Christ can easily be missed.

Throughout the New Testament, Jesus is shown to be actively fulfilling the very promises Yahweh gave to save his people, which culminate in his death and resurrection. This work is intimately tied to his practical role as the firstborn-redeemer. This helps us see that the description of Jesus as the wisdom of God in the New Testament is not about the incarnation of pre-existent wisdom, as Wisdom Christology would have it. The problem with this view is that it removes wisdom material from its New Exodus context. Rather it is about the display of God's wisdom in redeeming his people through his firstborn Son.

A functionally-based understanding of the person and work of Christ also helps to safeguard against attempts to reduce Jesus to a human-only figure. While some may argue that Jesus is no more than Yahweh's appointed agent, wisdom personified in flesh and blood, this view fails to take into account all of the New Testament evidence. Not only was Jesus seen to be fulfilling the Messianic promises, but also, in connection with these concrete activities many of Yahweh's titles and unique claims were attributed to Jesus. For instance, Jesus was referred to as "the resurrection and the life" as well as the "first and the last," titles that are clearly linked to the description of the firstborn.[37] These statements can mean nothing other than Jesus is uniquely and ontologically identified with God.

Finally, a functional view of "the firstborn of all creation" helps the body of Christ to more completely understand Jesus's role not only as Lord and the head of the body, but also as the firstborn of many brothers and sisters. All of the functional acts described above continue to flow from the work he performed as the firstborn son on behalf of his covenant family. To embrace this is to deepen our identity as a people and empower our everyday life in carrying out God's purposes.

I hope you can see that I am not saying there is no room for ontological reflections about Christ's being and nature; however, I am saying that following the first-century church's lead, they need to be grounded on a *functional* Christology. With this background in mind, let's return now to the Colossians hymn and see how viewing it within context of the Paschal-New Exodus paradigm affects the interpretation.

## The New Exodus Setting

Despite the varying opinions about the context of the Colossian's hymn, it is widely accepted that the introduction (1:12-14) is based on the promise of a New Exodus. In 1:12-14, Paul writes,

> And giving joyful thanks to the Father, who has qualified you to share in the inheritance of his holy people in the kingdom of light. For he has rescued us from the dominion of darkness and brought us into the kingdom of the Son he loves, in whom we have redemption, the forgiveness of sins.

In fact, the New Exodus theme is so emphatic that it is one of the few uncontested aspects of the letter. As noted by several commentators, the statement about how we have been rescued from the kingdom of darkness and brought into the kingdom of light reflects the description of the exodus events, return from exile, and Jewish themes of redemption.[38]

One observation is that this passage is about the people of God corporately as it echoes Israel's national experience. In evoking the imagery of the exodus events, the introduction brings to mind the time when Israel's God showed himself to be God of the whole world by defeating both the Egyptians and the mighty waters of the sea. The New Exodus was regarded as the beginning of the new creation, in which the new humanity would be birthed out of chaos and slavery.[39] The verses that follow the Colossians poem give the same impression and reflect a corporate perspective. The God of all the earth has become responsible for reconciling the Colossians to himself and grafting them into his true people. So, the hymn is sandwiched between two corporate passages.

Normally, the introduction of a work is seen to set the context for the interpretation of the material that follows, and as we have seen, context determines meaning. This being the case, Paul's introduction points to the paschal setting for interpreting the hymn, as the Passover sacrifice was the means of redemption in the First Exodus. Consequently, *the hymn must be read in a paschal, New Exodus context.* Some scholars recognize this to varying degrees. One view is the entire hymn is speaking of redemption, while another is that verse 18 alone relates to this theme. Surprisingly, however, few see this is what the introduction itself determined. This oversight has left the door open for considering other sources and settings as a possible backdrop for establishing the meaning of "the firstborn of all creation."

It is not only the introduction, however, that fixes the interpretive framework of a main text, but the conclusion also helps to tell us what should be understood when reading or hearing a text as well. In fact, the importance of the introduction and conclusion for establishing the context is so obvious that it does not need to be argued. Yet scholarship has repeatedly failed to take note of the Paschal-New Exodus setting for the conclusion of the Colossian hymn in 1:19-20, which also has a redemptive theme. Here, Paul writes that God was working through Jesus to "reconcile to himself all things, whether things on earth or things in heaven, *by making peace through his blood, shed on the cross.*"[40] The end of the poem clearly speaks of an act of cosmic reconciliation achieved through the shedding of Christ's blood.

Whatever the passage is about, surely to force it into a discussion of philosophical abstractions of any sort, as some have done, is to miss the mark by miles. The Colossians hymn is a reflection on the act of redemption that has been achieved through Christ's blood. Therefore, it must be interpreted within a sacrificial context. This limits the choices for identifying the hymn's background. In reviewing the options given by scholars, it is either one, or a combination of the following.

a. Greek hymn in praise of wisdom;
b. Jewish hymn in praise of wisdom;
c. Hymn celebrating the Day of Atonement;
d. Hymn celebrating the Passover;
e. Confessional statement of the creativity of Israel's God.

By now, you already know what I think. In my opinion, the strong emphasis on redemption in the introduction and conclusion of the hymn supports "d," a celebration of the Passover. This brings the term *prototokos* into the realm of salvation related themes rather than ontology, which is normally understood to be its setting. In turn, this supports the idea that a paschal theology exists in the New Testament writings, the scope of which has been previously unidentified. While the Passover context is central, I suggest "c" is also present because, as we discovered, propitiation was involved in the original Passover sacrifice. And "e" also applies because the New Exodus is about Yahweh's new creation.

## In Praise of Christ, the Firstborn

Within this context, let's look at the hymn verse by verse. We have already touched on some of the major themes, but the goal is to bring it all together now, so we can get a clearer picture of Christ's role as the firstborn of all creation and how this sheds light on our collective identity, mission, and inheritance. Referring to Jesus, the hymn in Colossians 1 states that,

> 15 - He is the image of the invisible God, the firstborn over [of] all creation.

Summing up our discussion, the reference to Christ as the image of the invisible God refers to Jesus's practical role as the last Adam, who represents Yahweh in the work of rescuing creation. This does not weaken Trinitarian orthodoxy; it strengthens it. No created being can redeem creation; the Old and New Testament alike make it clear that only the Creator, the Lord, can do this. The work is accomplished through the power of the Holy Spirit who baptized believing individuals into Jesus's death to form the new man, the body of Christ that was raised with him into a new life. This was the beginning of the new creation.

Regarding the second part of the verse, in calling Christ the *prototokos* of all creation, Paul is attributing to Christ's death something that no other firstborn's death ever achieved—the redemption of God's creation. One of the great themes of Isaiah's prophecy was that the redeemer would not only rescue Israel from her distress, but also bring all of creation out from under the curse it came under because of Adam's sin. In the section of Isaiah's writings where these prophecies appear, the dominant theme is that Yahweh is Israel's redeemer who will restore the nation to her inheritance, the land. He redeems creation from the curse of the fall for her sake.[41] In Romans, Paul predicts that creation will finally be renewed when it is set free from slavery to corruption and brought into freedom and glory at the time God's children, who have been redeemed by the firstborn son, are revealed.[42]

Looking at the next verses,

16 - For in him all things were created: things in heaven and on earth, visible and invisible, whether thrones or powers or rulers or authorities; all things have been created through him and for him.

17 - He is before all things, and in him all things hold together.

The language used to exalt Christ further strengthens the hymn's connection to the Passover. These exalted titles are being ascribed to Jesus, not to compete with the pagan deities to which the Colossians were in danger of turning as suggested by most scholars, but to underline that fact that as Yahweh's firstborn, he was the only one who could act as redeemer. This section states Jesus's credentials to be the redeemer of creation, the primary qualification being that he is the Creator of all things.

18 - And he is the head of the body, the church; he is the beginning and the firstborn from among the dead, so that in everything he might have the supremacy.

An important observation made by Stephen Bedale is that in this context, *head* (*kephale*) does not mean the head of the community as it does in classical Greek. Rather, following the LXX, it has the same connotation as *prototokos*, which is husband and leader-king.[43] This is significant for these are the very titles that were explicitly associated with the Passover. As Israel's king, Yahweh spared the firstborn and led the people out of Egypt, so the nation could become his bride. In other words, the connection between the Old and New Testament noted earlier, that only the Creator can redeem, is being followed here with precision.

Furthermore, Passover language lurks at the back of this verse. While the statement primarily refers to the Adam figure, the Davidic king who is the firstborn of the rulers of the earth, here it is applied to Christ's lordship over the ultimate enemy, death itself. By using the title, "firstborn from the dead," Paul is drawing these redemptive themes together. As redeemer, Christ conquered death and delivered his people from the realm of darkness in which they once lived in fear. If Paul had wanted to say Christ was the first to rise from the dead, as is so often suggested, he could have—and I contend would have—used the term "firstfruits." The significance of the term "firstborn from the dead" is that it speaks to the fact that Christ is the promised Messiah-King. Through his death and resurrection, he has brought everything, including death itself, under his lordship. This parallels the original

Passover at which time Pharaoh, Israel's oppressor was humbled and made to recognize the supreme lordship of Yahweh.

19 - For God was pleased to have all his fullness dwell in him,

This Old Testament setting is further supported when it is appreciated the claim that in Christ all God's fullness dwells is not an ontological statement about Jesus's divine nature and being; it is based on an Old Testament prophetic expectation in which *fullness* refers to the completion of Yahweh's purposes. His covenantal promises are brought to their climax in the person of Christ, the promised Redeemer, as is seen in the next verse,

20 - and through him to reconcile to himself all things, whether things on earth or things in heaven, by making peace through his blood, shed on the cross.

The redemption of creation by the firstborn is upheld here as the hymn expands the significance of the firstborn son's death in that it achieves the reconciliation of *all things*. This is the high point of the hymn, which culminates in the redemption of creation. The entire hymn is in praise of the Creator-Redeemer, the last Adam who is the Servant, the king of creation, the only begotten Son of God, the firstborn of the new creation. It is only through the atoning death of Christ, our Passover, that all things have been reconciled to the Creator!

## The Firstborn and the Family

So, what does all of this have to do with the church's collective identity and mission as God's people? In the two chapters that follow the hymn, Paul describes the implications of these truths for the new covenant community. After noting the riches and wisdom that belong to God's people in Christ, he explains that the cross is at the center of the victory that Jesus, the firstborn of all creation, achieved over all his opponents.[44]

Their power was shown to be impotent in the face of his self-sacrifice. Here again are echoes of the First Exodus when the power of Pharaoh was broken on the night of the Passover. The central message of the Colossians letter is that there is no other Lord. As the firstborn son, Christ is the head over all of creation. All other claims to this position are false. This is the plumb line the Colossians can use when weighing other teachings, claims, human traditions, and philosophies.

Paul also addresses the issue of circumcision.[45] In the Old Testament, this rite was required in order to participate in the Passover and through that experience share in the exodus event. Paul asserts this requirement has now been perfectly fulfilled in the death of Christ. It is no longer an act done *to* them, but it has been done *for* them through the death of Christ himself. There is no danger that circumcision will ever be seen as a required work of faith now because it was done to Christ, once and forever, on the believing community's behalf. This underscores that salvation is an act of grace from beginning to end.

The New Exodus theme continues as Paul addresses the forgiveness of sin and freedom from all forms of bondage. Every opponent—the law, which excluded the Gentiles from the covenant, as well as all powers and authorities—has been overcome in order to secure the new covenant community's freedom.[46] Just as Yahweh's triumph over Pharaoh took place on the night of the Passover when the firstborn of Egypt were slain, so Christ has triumphed through his work on the cross when, as God's firstborn, he died to redeem all of creation.[47]

Because of this once-for-all-time victory, the Colossians are free from the ceremonial regulations that governed the Jews in the previous age as these were merely shadows that point to what has now come in Christ.[48] The church's death with Christ also means that Jewish believers have died to the Mosaic law as a way of achieving righteousness. They, along with the Gentiles believers, are now the righteousness of God in Christ. Because the Colossians died with Christ, they have also been raised with him and share in his final victory![49] They are to live in light of this fact. Just as the Jews were called to live a new lifestyle after their deliverance from Egypt, so the Colossians are urged to live in a way that is worthy of the Lord, their Redeemer.[50]

Overall, this appeal is not to individual believers per se, although each person must personally respond to the responsibilities of being part of the new covenant community, but to the Colossian church collectively. The corporate basis of Paul's appeal is supported by his exhortation to live in light of our identity as the new man.[51] As we have seen, the new man is not an individual, but is the Christian community that was birthed at the time of Christ's death. Together, the community is to live in God's presence and put aside any practices that do not reflect the character of Christ.

## Missing Lenses

After reading the Colossians hymn in a New Exodus setting, I hope you can see for yourself why there is no need to turn to extra-biblical sources—whether Greek or Jewish—to understand its meaning. Nor is there a reason to treat Colossians as anything other than a letter written by Paul. The same Paschal-New Exodus motif fundamental to his other writings runs through Colossians as well. As we have seen, understanding the concrete role of the firstborn in context of the Old Testament shows how reading scripture through a Greek-tinted lens can actually cause us to miss valuable clues regarding the person of Christ and the scope of the work he accomplished on the new covenant community's behalf. In the phrase, "the firstborn of all creation," a treasure has been sitting before us for centuries, hidden in plain sight. In light of the growing acceptance of the New Exodus theme, this shows why there is good reason to recover the central role of the Passover for understanding the person and work of Christ.

# CHAPTER 12

# In Bold Relief

Commissioned in the later part of the eleventh century, the Bayeux Tapestry is an incredible example of medieval craftsmanship that depicts the Norman invasion of England in 1066, a significant turning point in the history of Great Britain. The size and scope of the piece is quite astonishing. It is close to 20 inches tall, nearly 230 feet long, and displays over 50 scenes, each portraying a particular event in the two years leading up to the final battle when William, Duke of Normandy, defeated Harold, Earl of Essex, and won the throne. In addition to featuring 11 battles, the tapestry also provides invaluable insights into the period's historical context by incorporating numerous scenes of every day medieval life that contain hundreds of images.

Since no one piece of fabric could accommodate a design of this magnitude, the tapestry was created as eight separate panels that were pieced together later. This finishing step was a pivotal part of the process. Although each panel showed an important part of the bigger picture, the full scope of the storyline was not visible until the panels were assembled in proper order. Only when viewed in its entirety was it possible to see the critical sequence of events that forever altered the course of a nation. Once connected, it was also possible see that in the midst of all the people and events portrayed in the intricate tapestry, one person stood out in bold relief—the victor, William the Conqueror.

## Putting the Pieces Together

In many ways, we have been in a similar process. We have focused on various aspects of the biblical picture to see how reading scripture through the corporate, Hebraic lens of the first-century New Testament writers changes our understanding of key texts that have to do with Christ's saving work and the identity of his body, the church. This involved exploring the Jewish backdrop of the Old and New Testaments and the narrative that binds the two together. Seeing this helped us appreciate that Jesus and the Hebrew writers of the New Testament, Paul included, had a collectivist rather than individualistic mindset, but one in which the individual is still highly valued. We discovered they shared the same corporate, covenantal Paschal-New Exodus framework for understanding Christ's person, work, and mission. Also, the marriage between God and his people, which is the culmination of each exodus event, is a theme that runs all throughout scripture.

Identifying this cohesive storyline allowed us to see that Paul viewed Israel's national experience during the First and Second Exodus as a *type* or *picture* that foreshadowed the formation and salvation of the corporate body of Christ; it was a preview of the New Exodus led by Christ. Imagine a complex jigsaw puzzle with many pieces. Without a picture on the lid of the box that shows how the completed puzzle should look it would be almost impossible to put it together. The doctrines of the New Testament are just like those jigsaw pieces, and the typology Paul uses from the pages of the Old Testament is the picture that guides us to arrange the pieces in their correct order.

Viewed from a corporate, Hebraic perspective, we found some of the key terms Paul uses such as *the old* and *new man*, *the body of Sin*, and also the *Wretched Man* in Romans 5–8 described communities, rather than individuals. A closer look at 1 Corinthians 6 revealed that the mention of the Prostitute and the phrase, "your body is a temple of the Holy Spirit" have corporate dimensions as well.

We also found that the Hebraic concept of corporate solidarity and the holistic view of the human person that undergirds New Testament thought may challenge some of the traditional Western views of sin based on Augustine's doctrine of original sin and the criminal law court metaphor. After seeing sin in a covenantal context and recovering the understanding that scripture speaks of sin in two distinct senses—as either transgressions, (acts of sin or sins), or as Satan personified (Sin as a power)—we saw that sin/Sin is even more serious than is sometimes understood. When our ancestor and representative leader, Adam, entered into a covenant relationship with the evil one, all of humanity came under Sin's power and was exiled from God.

Next, we circled back to the church's collective baptism into Christ's death as described in Romans 6:1-4, the time when the new man (the church) was birthed and freed from captivity to Sin. During this great historic event, the Spirit formed the body of Christ by taking all the individuals from all generations who looked to God in faith— past, present, and those who would do so in the future—and joined them to Jesus when he was on the cross. Baptized into his death and dying with him to the law that bound us to Sin/Satan, collectively, the believing community was raised into a new life, betrothed to Christ, and seated with him in heavenly places. At Pentecost, the newly formed church was filled with the indwelling Holy Spirit just as God promised. As a result of our union with Christ, we now have constant access to the Father through the Spirit, and all who are his share a bond that transcends external differences to make up the church, the body of Christ.

To be clear, this corporate baptism does not mean people are automatically saved; individuals must still come to a saving faith in Christ—whether it occurs in a definable moment or through a process—in order to become members of the new covenant community experimentally. Placed in the body just as God desires and joined together as living stones to form God's temple, together, we are called to live in a way that is worthy of our high calling as saints, holy ones who are set apart for God's glory, for that is who scripture says we are.

We then examined separate conceptual strands related to the redemption of the new covenant community in Romans 3–5. Seeing this passage in the corporate context of the New Exodus narrative provided fresh insights about God's righteousness, Christ's atoning sacrifice, and the justification of the body of Christ. Our investigation showed that Jesus and the New Testament writers all relied on the prophet Ezekiel's model for the atonement that combined imagery from the Passover and the Day of Atonement to explain the nature and purpose of Christ's sacrificial death. We saw that the Paschal-New Exodus theme, which is a central motif in scripture for explaining Christ's sacrificial death and resurrection, has either been overlooked or not fully appreciated. This framework helped us understand God's wrath as it related to Christ's death in a different light as well. We also learned that in Paul's view, justification is a corporate event in which the entire church of every generation shares. On pilgrimage in the present age, the church's justification will be complete when Christ returns for his bride and she receives her promised inheritance in full.

Looking at the flow of Paul's arguments in Romans 1–8 revealed how the apostle skillfully wove these redemptive threads together to portray the God of Israel's astounding plan to save his people from Sin/Satan, make the way for our sins to be forgiven, and bring all who are willing back from exile to himself. The central figure in the entire storyline is Jesus, our Passover, who, as the firstborn of all creation, conquered Sin and Death so he could redeem his bride and begin restoring all things to the Father. Just as Yahweh promised, all the nations of the earth were blessed through Abraham's offspring, Jesus, who freely transfers all who call on him—Jews and Gentiles alike—from the kingdom of darkness into the kingdom of light. Together, Paul's writings reinforce that the New Testament is a collection of Jewish documents showing that Jesus is the fulfillment of everything to which the Old Testament pointed.

Along the way, we sorted through several faulty assumptions and methodologies that have complicated and obscured the biblical picture. We disproved the notion that Paul Hellenized the Christian message and transformed it into something different from what Jesus and the twelve apostles proclaimed. Furthermore, we countered the idea that Christian theology is inherently dependent on Greek philosophy, and that Jewish intertestamental literature is the key to understanding the mindset of the first-century church. Ample evidence repeatedly showed it is not necessary to go outside of scripture to discover the meaning of key biblical concepts.

## The Benefits of New Eyeglasses

Identifying the New Exodus narrative and recovering the holistic, Hebraic view of the human person has numerous benefits and practical implications. First, this unified storyline allows the body of Christ to reclaim the simplicity of the biblical message. It is something all can grasp from the least to the greatest, yet it also honors the complexity and diversity of scripture, the profound mystery of the Trinity, and the wonder of God's eternal purposes for all he has created. By presenting a cohesive view of scripture, this framework can help *all* believers become more confident in understanding our sacred texts and assessing the various teachings to which they are exposed. Knowing the background of key passages makes it easier to see when someone is twisting scripture, preaching a different gospel, or teaching a false view of Jesus. As the narrative shows, he was, and is, a specific person—uniquely divine and human—whom the God of Israel sent at a specific point in time within a specific historical context to accomplish the specific mission of defeating Sin/Satan and inaugurating the new creation.

Second, the story has two dimensions that have a significant bearing on Christian spirituality. On one level, it is historic in that it shows how the God of Israel operates in concrete ways within time and space to rescue humanity from Sin so all who are willing can be reconciled to him. Through Jesus, God defeated Satan, the ruler of this world, and established his kingdom here on earth.[1] But the story also has a cosmic dimension in that heaven and earth are now connected in Christ and his body, the church. Having been united with him in his death and resurrection, and seated with him in heavenly places, the new covenant community has entered into an eternal existence even in the present age.

Wrenching Jesus or the church from either of these realities will lead to a faulty picture of his person and work and an imbalanced understanding of the Christian life. As citizens of heaven and members of Christ's body, the church is called to set her mind on things above, but at the same time, to function as God's servant on the earth. It is the Spirit dwelling within us, collectively and individually, who makes this two-way communication between heaven and earth possible, and who comforts, guides, and protects the pilgrim church as she journeys home to Zion.

Reading scripture through a corporate, Hebraic lens also provides a clearer vision of the church's identity as a living, unified entity in which each person has a crucial role. We saw that the new covenant community is central to God's plan for humanity, and that recovering the proper relationship between it and the individual can foster a deeper appreciation of our bond in the Spirit and shared purpose as the people of God. Not only is the centrality of the corporate body an effective antidote to unbiblical brands of individualism, but also, paradoxically, within this larger context individuals can better realize their own identity, meaning, and purpose as they use their unique abilities and spiritual gifts for the common good.

Further contributing to a healthy sense of self, we discovered that in keeping with their Hebraic background, Jesus and the New Testament writers had a holistic view of the human person. The Hellenistic dualism that portrays the individual's body and spirit, or higher and lower parts of the soul as being opposed to one another was not part of their thinking. Nor did they conceive of a split between the head and the heart. Additionally, we learned that from a biblical perspective, whether or not an individual is a sinner depends on the community to which he or she belongs—all who are members of the body of Sin, headed by Satan are sinners, while members of the body of Christ are holy ones. This does not mean Christians never sin; only that it does not define our identity.

Thinking through the implications of Paul's holistic view of the human person also helped us realize our battle with sin/Sin has a corporate dimension. Without minimizing the individual's responsibility to deal with personal sin, in the apostle's corporate framework the battle with sin/Sin is set within the larger body of Christ, which stands in opposition to Satan and all he represents and controls.[2] We are to address personal sin not just for our own sake, but also for the health and well-being of the local congregation. This shifts the focus from a primarily inward-facing introspective of personal failings to God's outward-facing purposes. As his holy people, a city set on a hill, we are called to be ambassadors, shining as light in the darkness, appealing to others to come out of the world and be reconciled to God through Christ; to tear down strongholds, free the captives, and love one another as he has loved us.[3]

Given this corporate mission, holiness is something we are called to grow in together so that through our purity and love, the body of Christ can reflect God's holy character.[4] On a practical level, we do this by becoming part of the local church, where we find grace and help to turn from the old, sinful, self-centered ways in which we used to live in the kingdom of darkness and learn the self-sacrificing, other-oriented ways of Christ. The local church is where God's word is taught and where the Spirit of God meets with his worshipping people. In this community, we build one another up in love so that we may be equipped to do his work.

Reading scripture through a corporate, Hebraic lens has other ramifications for the unity of the church. It can help us re-establish common ground and a common language. For instance, we saw earlier that Protestants sometimes use different terminology when describing justification—the relational language of marriage is favored in some cases, while in others, more business-like frameworks are used. A similar dynamic occurs between Catholics and Lutherans. Merold Westphal notes that, according to commentators, the two sides operate in different languages: "the Catholics in a scholastic, metaphysical language, the Lutherans in an experiential, relational language."[5]

I believe some of these "language barriers" can be traced to differing underlying philosophical assumptions that have influenced biblical interpretation in each tradition. It is also being recognized that interpretive differences between the Eastern and Western church stem, in part, from this as well.[6] Recovering a common biblical "baseline" can help us see when divisions in the church may be rooted in cultural differences or competing philosophical frameworks rather than in scripture itself.

## Our Challenge

Summing up, we have seen that two major lenses have been missing from most interpretations of the Bible, and this continues to have a detrimental effect on properly reading the New Testament, particularly Paul's writings, and fully appreciating its relationship to the Old. They are not separate books, but when read in the ancient way of the first-century apostolic church, form one grand narrative tied together by the corporate, Paschal-New Exodus storyline. Although not completely lost, critical elements of the apostolic understanding were obscured when hidden assumptions inherited from our Greco-Roman background seeped into Christian thought while, at the same time, aspects of our Hebraic heritage were minimized. Together, these factors have clouded the biblical picture.

I started the book with the bold claim that we have been reading scripture through distorted lenses for centuries. I would like to end with another strong statement. Many so-called problems of scripture interpretation used to undermine the Bible's authority have been rooted in an interpretive paradigm that is both individualistic and dualistic. As we have discussed, when considering what scripture means, it is critical to stay focused on the context that influenced, and often determined, the understanding of those who wrote the texts. To this end, we should avoid interpreting them through frameworks not shared by their authors. I believe that holding to this basic principle would not only restore confidence in scripture, but also bring a reformation to our understanding of a whole range of biblical truth that we can then seek to apply to our present circumstances.[7]

In my opinion, the seriousness of this major hermeneutical flaw, which is found in today's prevailing theological methodology, demands a review of all theological literature so that we can detect and appreciate the extent of this problem. For the sake of the church's unity and well-being, I am pleading that we begin the vital task of reform. The news from those I am acquainted with who are in pastoral charges and have begun this process is encouraging: they tell me it has helped to transform their ministries.

However, the need for this reformation extends not just to churches in Western nations, but also to Christian communities throughout the world. Because the Western church has exported its theological methodology through various missionary endeavors, it has given spiritual birth to children who have followed this same road. Tragically, by introducing our Western, Hellenized, individualistic mindset into other international communities, we have sometimes adversely affected cultures where a corporate mentality naturally existed, one that would have given the new believers in those settings valuable insights into the New Testament.

If there is any concern about committing ourselves to this monumental task for fear of where it will lead, I want to assure you that if we follow this path, we will come out with a biblical orthodoxy that does not reject the core Christian beliefs expressed in many of our historic confessions. Rather, we will see that God, in his mercy, kept the church despite her many confusions. I am not naïve about the challenge this process represents. However, I am hopeful that as we consider our common apostolic roots, the church's fundamental unity, which already exists in Christ, will become increasingly visible and attractive in a chaotic world that continues to experience such massive, unsettling change.

# Paul's Quotes from Isaiah in Romans

Here are the texts from Isaiah that Paul cited in Romans in the order he used them. An explanation of how they exemplify salvation history follows.

- "As it is written, 'God's name is blasphemed among the Gentiles because of you.'" (Rom. 2:24; Isa. 52:5, LXX)

- "Their feet are swift to shed blood: ruin and misery marked their paths and the way of peace they have not known." (Rom. 3:15-17; Isa. 59:7-8)

- "Isaiah cries out concerning Israel: 'Though the number of the Israelites should be like the sand by the sea, only the remnant will be saved. For the Lord will carry out his sentence on earth with speed and finality.' It is just as Isaiah had said previously." (Rom. 9:27-28; Isa. 10:22-23, LXX)

- "Just as Isaiah said previously, 'Unless the Lord Almighty had left us descendants, we would have become like Sodom, and we would have been like Gomorrah.'" (Rom. 9:29; Isa. 1:9, LXX)

- "As it is written, 'See, I lay in Zion a stone that causes men to stumble and a rock that makes them fall.'" (Rom. 9:33a; Isa. 8:14)

- "And 'the one who trusts in him will never be put to shame." (Rom. 9:33; Isa. 28:16, LXX)

- "As the Scripture says, 'He who believes in him will not be disappointed.'" (Rom. 10:11; Isa. 52:7, LXX)

- "As it is written, 'How beautiful are the feet of those who bring good news!'" (Rom. 10:15; Isa. 52:7)

- "For Isaiah says, 'Lord, who has believed our message?'" (Rom. 10:16; Isa. 53:1, LXX)

- "And Isaiah boldly says, 'I was found by those who did not seek me, I revealed myself to those who did not ask for me.'" (Rom. 10:20; Isa. 29:10, LXX)

- "What then? What Israel sought so earnestly it did not attain, but the elect did. The others were hardened as it is written: 'God gave them a spirit of stupor, eyes so that they could not see and hearts so that they could not hear, to this very day.'" (Rom. 11:7-8; Isa. 29:10, LXX)

- "And so all Israel shall be saved: as it is written, 'there shall come out of Zion the Deliverer, and he shall turn away ungodliness from Jacob; for this is my covenant until them, when I shall take away their sins.'" (Rom. 11:26-27; Isa. 59:20-21, LXX)

- "Who has known the mind of the Lord? Or who has been his counselor?" (Rom. 11:34; Isa. 40:13, LXX)

- "For it is written, 'As I live, sayeth the Lord." (Rom. 14:11a; Isa. 49:18)

- "Every knee shall bow to me, and every tongue shall confess to God." (Rom. 14:11b; Isa. 45:23, LXX)

- "And again, Isaiah says, 'The root of Jesse will spring up, one who will arise to rule over the nations; the Gentiles will hope in him.'" (Rom. 15:12; Isa. 11:10, LXX)

- "Rather, as it is written, 'Those who were not told about him will see, and those who have not heard will understand.'" (Rom. 15:21; Isa. 52:15, LXX)

These passages show the perspective that Paul had in regard to salvation history. He had the mindset of an evangelical prophet. The quotations work systematically through the various stages of development of God's purposes in the salvation of humankind.

- Israel had not responded to her calling to be set apart for God, she acted like the other nations. (Rom. 2:24; Isa. 52:5 and Rom. 3:15-17; Isa. 59:7-8)

- God's purpose is to show his faithfulness to his promises to Israel by saving a remnant. (Rom. 9:27-29; Isa. 10:22-23)

- God will appoint a savior for both Jews and Gentiles (Rom. 9:33; Isaiah 8:14, 28:16 and Rom. 10:11; Isa. 8:16) Notice how Paul stressed the universality of Christ's salvation as he follows up the quote from Isaiah 28:16 with: "For there is no difference between Jew and Gentile—the same Lord is Lord of all and richly blesses all who call on him, for 'Everyone who calls on the name of the Lord will be saved'."

- Paul then goes on to speak of the church's responsibility to declare the salvation of God, as it had been fulfilled by the remnant in the previous age. (Rom. 10:15; Isa. 52:7)

- But there would be the same response of unbelief to the gospel message. (Rom. 10:16; Isa. 53:1)

- Even so, the electing purposes of God would not be overturned by the sinfulness of humankind. What God purposes he will achieve. (Rom. 10:22; Isa. 65:1 and Rom. 10:21; Isa. 65:2. Also, Rom. 11:8; Isa. 29:10)

- God's purposes will be fulfilled, and all Israel, as Paul has already defined her in Rom. 4:11-12, will be saved. (Rom. 11:26-27; Isa. 59:20-21)

- All of this is beyond humankind's design; it is of God alone. (Rom. 11:33-34; Isa. 40:13)

- The salvation promised to Abraham, in which the nations are to share in the covenant blessings, will finally be fulfilled. Those who were never part of the people of God have come into the end times community. (Rom. 15:21; Isa. 52:15)

# Blurring the Lines

Researchers are affirming what conventional wisdom has long known —storytelling has a vital impact on how our identities are formed. As one author points out, "Everyone lives out of some narrative identity, whether it is thought out and reflected upon or not."[1] These stories "give meaning to our lives, sketch our character in outline, and tell us what is important in life."[2] They also provide a connection between the past, present, and future. We know from personal experience that family histories—whether positive or negative—often ground our identities as individuals. Stories also shape the characteristics of nations, tribes or other types of groups with whom we may identify. For instance, a narrative about Norway may involve "winter and skiing," "the importance of being in nature," and "upholding peace and democracy."[3] On the other hand, American identity has been shaped by stories about "rugged individualism," "the new promised land," or being "a cultural melting pot."

One of the most powerful examples of a life-shaping master narrative is the story of the Hebrews' Exodus from Egypt, which, as we have seen, was a defining event in forming Israel's national identity. Each year when the Jews celebrated the Passover, God instructed them to tell the story of how he rescued them from slavery, the nation's identification with Moses as their leader, and who they are "as God's chosen, as God's beloved." It was also to remind the Israelites of their unique calling among the nations.

In *Missing Lenses*, we have followed this ancient storyline into the New Testament to see how the narrative of a New Exodus led by Jesus, our Passover, can help us recover the meaning of key terms and our identity, both as a people and as individuals. The case I have been making is that in the West, we are going through a paradigm shift when it comes to the way we read scripture. For centuries, we have been viewing key texts that are rooted in the Jewish culture through Greco-Roman eyeglasses. Looking at various passages within context of the corporate, New Exodus storyline has given us a taste of what it's like to shift to a predominantly Hebraic lens.

## Missing Lenses

What we want to do now is go back into our early family history to look more closely at specific ways the corporate, Hebraic context of scripture was eclipsed after the twelve apostles died. To do this, we'll explore three pivotal places where new developments began to skew the biblical storyline. The first has to do with how the biblical narrative changed when the Jewish backdrop of scripture began to recede as Judaism and Christianity parted ways. The second involves what happened when elements of Plato's account of the individual soul's journey to return to the divine realm were layered over the corporate biblical storyline. This was the point where individualistic and dualistic presuppositions began to cloud the picture. And finally, we'll see how these Platonist concepts affected some of the influential views of Christian spirituality and sin that we inherited from Augustine, one of the most revered and influential church fathers in the West.

Identifying the long-term effect of these changes on Christian thought and practice will not only help us clarify the picture, but also see the importance of recovering scripture's original context. In addition to providing an opportunity to adjust our eyeglasses if need be, this will also offer reassurance that we are not on some lofty intellectual quest with little practical relevance. To the contrary, rediscovering scripture's corporate, New Exodus framework has the potential to change the way we live out our faith, together and individually.

What I am presenting here is not intended to be a complete discussion of these matters, partly because it would take an entire book to do justice to the complexities involved. Rather, the goal is to frame several critical issues for further exploration that I believe will help the church live into her true identity as the unified people of God.

**PARTING WAYS¶** To appreciate how the biblical narrative began to change and impact the way the church understood scripture we need to go back to the end of the first century. Before 70 AD, the young church was mainly focused on internal matters such as how Jewish believers and new Gentile converts should relate to one another and the Mosaic law, and to address other cultural issues. In this era, the leaders of the church mainly came from a Jewish background and spirituality was decidedly corporate—its primary focus was on the body of believers as a whole. The individual's walk with God was set within this larger context.[4] As we've seen, the idea that the people of God comprised a single, unified entity was already well established in the Hebraic culture.

As the story unfolds, after the original apostles died and the gospel spread into regions beyond Palestine towards the end of the first century and into the second, the fledgling community began to face a new set of challenges from within and without. At this time, the complexion of the church shifted—many of the church's members, including the new leaders, came from a Greek background so the Jewish backdrop of the faith was not as well known. The church was also compelled to engage more directly with pagan critics and philosophers. Also, a number of diverse groups claiming to be Christian promoted teachings that sparked controversy. Additionally, the determination had to be made as to what texts among those circulating at the time should be considered as authoritative or valid. As some of have observed, this was a messy but critical time in the life of the church.[5] In fact, scholars are now recognizing that during the second century, *"more important decisions were made for the whole of Christianity than were made from the end of the second century to the present day."*[6]

Three things should be noted as we begin to look at this period. First, it is necessary to approach our discussion with humility and charity. In addition to sorting through many difficult issues for the first time, the early fathers were in vastly different social contexts than we are today. Without excusing or defending any of the ways they may have erred—and it's acknowledged that some did—the fact is the fathers inherited a set of assumptions that were at play in the cultural context of their day, some of which they saw and overcame, and some of which they didn't.[7] The same can be said of Christian theologies since then, including ones being written today. Those who follow us may look back one day and see the shortcomings of our work as well. For this reason, we are in no position to sit in critical judgment of the fathers, even if some of their views are disturbing to us or it is determined that correction is warranted in certain areas. Humility is also required because not all Christian groups share the same view of the early church fathers or their authority, and not all agree on what constitutes error.

Second, we will be looking at select issues, not the full theology of the fathers we will be discussing. This may seem obvious, but it is important to say because no matter how careful we may be to honor their overall thought, there is still a risk of creating a misimpression of their work by only looking at only a part of it. I am bringing this up because I do not want to inadvertently mispresent any of the fathers nor do I want anything I say to be used against them in an unjust manner.

And finally, while a good deal of theological diversity existed in the early Christian community, it is important to remember there was also "a core set of beliefs that unified most Christians" going back to the apostles.[8] And there was something more. As theologian Thomas Oden observed, "if we listen carefully to the tradition speak of itself," the central thread that unifies the historical varieties of Christianity is *life in Christ*.[9] Oden points out that no matter how different the language and theological formulations used by various fathers and later church leaders may be, "Christianity owes its existence then and now to the continued presence of the person" of the resurrected Christ in the church, even in the midst of severe historical setbacks.[10] It is important to hold fast to what we have in common as we explore sensitive issues that have also contributed to some of our differences.

## The Jewish Backdrop Recedes

In looking at how the narrative began to change in this era, as the church transitioned into the second century, the number of Gentile converts eventually outnumbered the original Jewish members. Due to changes in both groups, an antagonism began to emerge between the increasingly Gentile church and the Jewish community that served to further distance the young church from her Jewish roots. In the early years, Christianity was regarded as a sect within Judaism—in fact, a number of Christians continued to attend the synagogue—but over time, Jews and Christians became more deeply divided about theological issues.[11]

On the one hand, the Jews, who were scattered in various places after the Temple was destroyed in 70 AD, had to figure out how to retain their identity since it was no longer possible to offer sacrifices in Jerusalem. To protect the integrity of their religion from outside influences, Jewish leaders devised methods to identify and expel those in their midst, including Christians, who did not adhere to the core teachings of Judaism as the Pharisees now defined it.[12]

On the other hand, Christians were claiming that God's promises to Israel now applied to them, which was offensive to the Jews. To make their case, Christians tried to show from the Hebrew Bible how and why Jesus was the Messiah. Despite their best efforts, Jewish leaders were not convinced. Frustrated by what they regarded as a stubborn refusal to accept the truth, "a new spirit of arrogance" emerged towards the Jews within the increasingly Gentile church.[13] Rather than seeing the church as being grafted into the Jewish root as Paul taught in Romans 11, some Christian leaders began to claim the church had *replaced* Israel—a belief referred to today as *supersessionism*—and was now the new spiritual Israel.[14] In this view, the Jews were seen as no longer being part of God's plan. Noting the apostle Paul would not have supported such a position, Marvin Wilson observes,

> This displacement resulted in many institutions and concepts of Israel being de-Judaized or Hellenized by the gentile church . . .The tearing away from Jewish roots resulted in the Church defining itself largely in non-Jewish terminology.[15]

For these and other reasons, by the middle of the second century Judaism and Christianity had not only become separate entities, but an open hostility had developed between the Jewish "elder brother" and the increasingly Gentile "younger brother" with both sides committing offenses against the other.[16] Unfortunately, the contempt for Judaism expressed in the writings of the early fathers and later in other Christian texts was sometimes used to justify terrible persecutions against the Jews from the second century to the present day.[17]

## Relating to the Old Testament

This new reality brought challenges to the young church's relationship with the Hebrew Bible. On one side, Jewish leaders wanted to know how Christians could justify using Israel's sacred texts while not keeping the Mosaic law as they required. On the other, some early Christians believed the Old Testament was obsolete now that Christ had come. Others wanted to reject it because, in their view, the harsh, war-like God of the Hebrew Bible seemed incompatible with the loving Father described in the New Testament.[18] Consequently, Robert Wilken notes, "during the first three centuries Christians were forced to develop a systematic and thoroughgoing interpretation of the Old Testament."[19]

To prove the new covenant community could lay claim to the ancient Jewish texts, Christian leaders needed to demonstrate both continuity and discontinuity with Israel, to show "what was *old* and what was *new* about the Christian revelation and interpretation of the Bible."[20] To do this, the case was made that the Hebrew Bible belonged to the church because it is all about Christ. As it was reasoned, the Old Testament prophecies pointed forward to Jesus, who fulfilled them in concrete ways through his virgin birth, genealogy in the flesh, life, death, and resurrection. This meant that without realizing it, the faithful in Israel were actually following Christ. Looking at it this way, natural Israel could be seen as a natural, earthly "type or shadow" (typology) that pointed ahead to the church, which was a spiritual entity.[21]

Where the early church fathers believed the Jews got it wrong is that they were reading their sacred texts too literally and had become spiritually blind as a result. They were expecting the Messiah to come and free them from an earthly tyrant. Instead, Jesus came to liberate all of humanity, including the Jews, from a spiritual oppressor (Sin/Satan). Therefore, it was reasoned, the Old Testament could be interpreted *spiritually*. Furthermore, it was argued, since the Jewish nation as a whole had rejected Jesus, this meant that as the new spiritual Israel, the church, now inherited all of God's promises to the Jews recorded in the Hebrew Bible. As one early father framed it when dialoguing with the Jews, the Hebrew Bible is "not yours, but ours."[22]

Unfortunately, although the church successfully defended its claim to the Hebrew Bible, many of the Gentile fathers did not know Hebrew or understand the Hebraic mindset.[23] They accepted the Old Testament as God's authoritative word, but apart from a few exceptions, because most had no direct access to the original texts their knowledge of it was "often limited to selected passages and proof texts."[24] And there was little incentive to learn more as in the eyes of many, the Old Testament "was and remained a book, describing a history that was past and finished."[25] Consequently, Jaroslav Pelikan notes that apart from a few exceptions, in the patristic era Christian theologians

> no longer gave serious consideration to the Jewish interpretation of the Old Testament or to the Jewish background of the New. Therefore, the urgency and the poignancy about the mystery of Israel that are so vivid in the New Testament have appeared only occasionally in Christian thought, as in some passages in Augustine; but these are outweighed, even in Augustine, by the many others that speak of Judaism and paganism almost as though they were equally alien to "the people of God"—the church of Gentile Christians.[26]

Commenting on these developments, Augustinian scholar Philip Cary states, "What is important and beyond question (and the depth of which has not yet been fully appreciated by many patristic scholars) is that the Jewish context of scripture was not well known by the Gentile church after about the second century."[27]

Again, it should be noted that it was not completely lost. Although Jewish-Christians were in the minority by this time, their perspective still had influence, which is reflected in the writings of some of the fathers.[28] This served to counter-balance the growing Gentile presence and gave the church a lasting collection of texts more informed by a Hebraic mindset than it would have had otherwise. Nevertheless, Pelikan states that "most of Christian doctrine developed in a church uninformed by any knowledge of the original text of the Hebrew Bible."[29] This general lack of knowledge about the Jewish background of scripture caused some of the fathers to flounder when it came to unpacking the meaning of key New Testament passages. And, as might be expected given their Greco-Roman upbringing, secular patterns of thought also affected the way some texts were understood. Not surprisingly, the fathers adopted different, sometimes conflicting ideas about how best to interpret scripture.[30]

## Changes to the Narrative

In particular, the claim to be the new spiritual Israel had a far-reaching impact on the church's understanding of the larger biblical narrative. Adopting this view of the church when knowledge of scripture's Hebraic background was fading caused the Christian community to lose sight of the essential role Israel plays in the ongoing story. This is important because, as R. Kendall Soulen points out, the biblical narrative provides a critical interpretive framework for scripture by showing how the whole Bible forms a unified witness to the ways "the God of Israel has acted in Jesus Christ for the sake of all."[31]

We have seen how Israel's First Exodus from Egypt and her Second Exodus from exile in Babylon pointed forward to the New Exodus led by Jesus, the Christ. This cohesive storyline reveals how God is moving to restore creation and bless all the nations through Jesus, Abraham's promised seed and Israel's Servant-King. In the biblical narrative, there are five main plot points:

1. Creation and God's eternal plan for humankind;
2. Adam and Eve's betrayal and humanity's fall (exile);
3. God's choice of Israel as the nation through whom he will bring salvation;
4. Redemption and reconciliation in Christ;
5. Restoration and the final consummation of God's plan.

But in the way the narrative developed, Israel's vital role was pushed into the background. Commenting on this loss, N.T. Wright states that in order to be true to scripture,

> It simply will not do to tell the story of salvation as simply creation, fall, Jesus, salvation. If we ask the question of how this particular human being [Jesus] is the instrument of salvation and do not say as our first answer, "because in him God's Israel-shaped plan to save the world came to fulfillment," then we leave a huge vacuum in our thinking (and in our reading of scripture). I believe it is because of this vacuum that people have elevated minor themes, such as the sinlessness of Jesus, to a prominence which, though not insignificant, they do not possess in the NT itself.[32]

Soulen observes that by shaping the way Christians have read "great expanses of the biblical story," supersessionism had a decided impact on the "doctrinal structure of classical Christian theology in fundamental and systematic ways."[33] In noting how it affected the doctrine of God, he points out that by minimizing Israel's role in salvation history, the traditional four-point storyline also masked the fundamental understanding of God's identity as the God of Israel.[34] Clarifying it is not that God's interaction with Israel doesn't receive *any* attention, Soulen adds that in the way it's been construed

> Israel's story contributes little or nothing to understanding how God's consummation and redemptive purposes engage human creation in universal and enduring ways. Indeed, the background can be completely omitted from an account of Christian faith without thereby disturbing the overarching logic of salvation history. This omission is reflected in virtually every historic confession of Christian faith from the Creeds of Nicaea and Constantinople to the Augsburg confession and beyond.[35]

For this reason, in Soulen's opinion, to correct matters by rejecting the idea that the church replaced Israel would also entail reevaluating "the whole body of classical Christian divinity."[36] Not all may agree with this statement, but it serves to highlight the problem with minimizing Israel's role in the narrative.

This is where caution is warranted. These observations certainly call for thoughtful consideration, but it is important not to overreact and write off either the early church fathers or all of Christian doctrine. As noted earlier, the patristics were writing within the social context of their day, and they got many, many things right, which is why we must be careful when weighing their work. Open, charitable dialogue is vital as we continue to learn more about events in the second century and recover the Jewish context of scripture.

What we want to see next is how adopting a christianized version of Plato's story of the individual soul's journey to return to the divine realm further skewed the biblical picture.

379

**ENGAGING THE PHILOSOPHERS¶** In a second major development, just as the increasingly Gentile church was in the process of disengaging from Judaism, by necessity it began to engage more directly with the pagan culture. In addition to addressing issues within the Christian community, the additional task now was to defend the gospel from pagan critics. It was also necessary to help the influx of new Gentile converts, some of whom were educated Greeks, assimilate into the community. Furthermore, because several of the new Christian leaders had been trained in philosophy and the Greek classics, the Gentile fathers had to sort through how best to relate to their own cultural heritage as well.

A dispute about philosophy sprang up very quickly, revealing mixed and sometimes contradictory opinions about its value and role. All of the early church fathers were agreed on condemning pagan religion, and all actively refuted philosophical views that overtly contradicted the gospel. [37] However, they were divided as to whether or not select concepts derived from Greek philosophy could or should be used in Christian theologies.

While acknowledging philosophy's weaknesses, some of the fathers saw what they believed were notable parallels between it and Christianity, with several suggesting that Plato had read Moses and drew ideas from the prophet. Believing that all truth—whether found in scripture or the secular culture—comes from God, a number of the fathers proposed that some of the wisdom, insights, and methods discovered by the philosophers could be useful to Christians. Based on this line of reasoning, some have felt "there need be no contradiction between Greek and biblical thought."[38]

Others, however, strongly opposed this view, agreeing with Tertullian (155-240 AD) who posed the famous question: "What does Jerusalem have to do with Athens, the Church with the Academy, the Christian with the heretic?"[39] In this analogy, Athens was home to Plato's academy and regarded as the center of secular learning while Jerusalem represented the divine revelation upon which the church was founded. In Tertullian's opinion, most of the heresies that troubled the church and drew believers away from the simplicity of the faith stemmed from philosophy. He acknowledged there were fragments here and there in Plato's work that might be compatible with Christianity, but that what stood out when looking at the two systems side-by-side, was *difference*. Believing the various philosophers had contours of thought that were not just "*sub*-christian but *anti*-christian," he was deeply concerned that if the two systems were mixed, alien or evil ideas could compromise Christian truth.[40]

These two views, which were framed in the second century, have shaped the parameters of the debate about Greek philosophy and Christian theology that is unresolved to this day. Unraveling this historic tangle is certainly not something to take on here. However, this background helps set the stage for seeing how hidden philosophical assumptions began to affect the way the church read scripture and practiced spirituality.

## Enter Plato

In this part of our discussion, we will be looking at two leaders in the early church—Clement of Alexandria (150-215 AD) and Origen (185-254 AD)—who lived in the Greco-Roman city of Alexandria. Along with Irenaeus, another father in the second century, these men are sometimes referred to as the founders of Christian theology. Origen was so widely read, in fact, that speaking of theologians universally, one respected father called him "the whetstone of us all."[41] As Orthodox theologian Validmir Lossky explains, they play a critical role in our family history because "the Hellenistic world enters the Church with Clement and Origen, bringing with it elements alien to the Christian tradition—elements of religious speculation and intellectualistic spirituality belonging to a world altogether different from that of the Gospel."[42]

Clement and Origen are of particular interest because they were the first to christianize Plato's story of the individual soul's journey to return to the spiritual realm and weave it into the biblical narrative. In fusing elements of the two frameworks, they introduced a novel, personalized form of mysticism into the faith that clouded scripture's central focus on corporate spirituality. It also opened a conduit for individualistic and dualistic presuppositions to begin seeping into the Christian thought stream. Not only did this affect the way certain texts were read over time, but as we'll see, it also shifted the biblical narrative by further obscuring Israel's role in God's plan. Speaking of the enduring effect of Clement and Origen's innovative ideas, Lossky observes that it has taken "centuries of struggle and superhuman effort" in the Eastern tradition to fully christianize the Hellenistic ideas they introduced.[43]

Others would argue, however, that a number of the philosophical concepts they and other fathers introduced have not yet been fully transformed. As a result, they have become "a burden in the history of Christian thought."[44] As Robert Casey notes "the doctrine of God did not lose the Platonic stamp first deeply impressed upon it by Clement of Alexandria" in the East or the West.[45] And classicist Werner Jaeger stated that Origen "built into Christian doctrine the whole cosmic drama of the soul, which he took from Plato."[46] He commented that although Christian fathers later decided he took over too much, "that which they kept was still the essence of Plato's philosophy of the soul." Rowan Greer also observes "the themes Origen used in giving definition to the Christian life persist to this day in the classical expositions of Christian spirituality."[47] In light of these and other developments, Marvin Wilson concludes "The widespread influence of Plato upon the history of Christian thought can hardly be overestimated."[48]

Let me say at the outset that any discussion of Clement and Origen's legacy is a sensitive subject.[49] Because of the perception that their theologies were tainted by Hellenism or in error in one way or another, the work of both men has been suspect at various times in history.[50] However, in recent decades, a number of patristic scholars have come to see aspects of Clement and Origen's involvement with philosophy in a more favorable light.

In defending the Alexandrians, it's been pointed out that scripture was of primary importance for both men and the careful use of philosophy is what enabled them to refute paganism, preserve the faith, and help it spread.[51] One contention is that Clement's approach in using the best of philosophy to join together educated Greek pagans and Christians who were sometimes hostile to one another "under one rational and acceptable Christian religion" is what enabled Christianity to grow in Egypt. [52] And one Orthodox theologian observes that key elements of Clement's theology are foundational to the entire Eastern tradition.[53]

I do not wish to argue that Clement and Origen were Platonists or make a case that they "Hellenized" Christianity, nor do I want to detract from their positive accomplishments. Nevertheless, evidence suggests that a number of philosophical concepts entered Christian thought through the Alexandrians that muddled the biblical picture and have had far-reaching effects that, in my opinion, have yet to be fully appreciated.

## The Alexandria Connection

Given how social context affects theologies, it's to our benefit to know a little about Clement and Origen's world, including their philosophical influences. To the question of what Jerusalem has to do with Athens, as David Runia observes, the two converged in Alexandria.[54] Known as the "queen city of the eastern Mediterranean," Alexandria was the center of a powerful confluence of intellectual and religious trends at the time Clement and Origen lived there. In fact, from the second century on this wealthy city went on to eclipse Antioch and Jerusalem as one of the centers of the Christian faith, eventually coming to rival Rome.[55]

Reflecting its diverse population, a syncretic mix of Egyptian, Greek, and Roman religions was widespread in Alexandria, which gave rise to a number of multi-service temples. Gnosticism was an influence as well and Alexandria was also home to the great Library and Museum that attracted intellectuals from throughout Greece.[56] Philosophy was a subject of great interest in the city.[57] *Timaeus*, Plato's account of the origin of the universe and humankind was especially popular in Alexandria. Regarded as the "Platonists' Bible" because it gave the philosophical student "a clear vision of the divine," up to the third century, *Timaeus* "was the only Greek prose work that . . . every educated man could be assumed to have read."[58]

A thriving Jewish community also existed in Alexandria, although its prominence later diminished when the Jews were quashed after the Jewish-Roman war in 115-117.[59] Alexandria is where the *Septuagint* translation, the Greek version of the Hebrew Bible was produced. A number of Jewish writings that incorporated Hellenistic thought such as the *Book of Wisdom* were generated there as well.

Additionally, Alexandria was home to Philo (25 BC- 50 AD), the Jewish-Hellenistic philosopher who was dedicated to Moses while embracing aspects of Platonism.[60] According to David Runia, Philo's writings "were ignored or neglected by Jews and pagans alike."[61] Nevertheless, Philo is an important figure in our story because he is one of the first to use philosophy to expound Old Testament truths, an approach which had a decided impact on Christian thought.[62] It's not so much that Philo tried to read philosophy into scripture; rather he was convinced that Plato and other famous Greek lawgivers and philosophers had read Moses and based their doctrines on his writings. Therefore, as Runia notes, Philo believed "Plato was already contained *in* the law of Moses."[63]

To show how, in his opinion, they were connected, Philo used a Greek-inspired allegorical method of interpretation to assert that

> Abraham's wife, Sarah, symbolizes philosophy; her handmaiden, Hagar, the general studies that prepare for philosophy; and Abraham, the soul that learns by instruction. Sarah gives Abraham Hagar because philosophy cannot bear fruit until the soul is prepared for it. [64]

The Greeks had adopted this allegorical approach to preserve their beloved classic literature. As they grew more sophisticated, many of the educated Greeks, including Socrates and Plato, were disturbed by the gods' immoral, all-too-human antics depicted in the ancient myths. To downplay their embarrassing behavior, the gods were said to be symbols that represent hidden meanings in the text. For instance, Zeus signified the mind; Athena symbolized art; the various gods depicted powers of nature.[65] In applying this allegorical approach to scripture, Philo set a precedent that Clement, Origen, and other fathers followed. This had long-term effect on the interpretation of key biblical texts.

We'll talk about this more later, but to avoid confusion let me quickly point out here that biblical writers also sometimes used a form of allegory, commonly referred to as *typology*, in which the natural points to spiritual. For instance, Paul taught that Hagar and Sarah in the Old Testament represented the old and new covenants. The difference between this and the Greek allegorical method is that in biblical typology, the spiritual meaning is not arbitrary—it is tied to specific objects, persons, or events that are visible to all in scripture. In the Greek method, however, the interpreter has a greater personal role in determining meaning. Looking at Philo's perspective above, there is *nothing* in scripture that says or even remotely suggests that Sarah symbolizes philosophy or that Hagar represents general studies—those are Philo's own ideas that differ with scripture, which says they represent two covenants. This is a clear example of the difference between using the Greek allegorical method and biblical typology.

## Plato's Framework

With this backdrop in mind, we've come to the place now where it is necessary to briefly review elements of Plato's work, so we can understand the context for his teaching about the individual soul's journey to the spiritual realm. We'll also need to touch on a few of the ways Platonism evolved as it had assumed different forms by the time Clement and Origen came on the scene.

For those who don't like philosophy, even a small amount may seem like too much. However, it will be difficult to appreciate the enduring influence Platonism had on Christian thought and practice without patiently laying this groundwork first. My goal is to describe the overall framework of his individualistic narrative, so we can see the differences when it is set next to scripture's corporate storyline with its emphasis on communal spirituality. Even though the fathers were united in rejecting Plato's views about the Greek gods, I want to include this so that we can get an accurate picture of his general system of thought. As you will see for yourself, the Greek gods play a critical role in the creation of the human body and soul so if they are set aside, it leaves a significant gap in Plato's explanation of how the universe works. Let's look now at some of the fundamentals of his scheme.

Building on the philosophers who went before him, Plato set out to offer a more cohesive understanding of the universe and its divine source than his predecessors. When looking at how the universe functioned harmoniously as a unified whole, Plato reasoned it must be the product of an Intelligent Mind (*nous*). He also presumed there was a hierarchy to the universe that brought order to each descending level.

- *The Forms.* In Plato's system, the highest place in the universe belongs to the inanimate *Forms.* These are the Ideas or Principles after which all created things are patterned. For instance, in a well-known example, a table that can be detected by the senses is patterned after an *idea* or *form* of a table that originates in the mind. Plato reasoned that if every created thing first exists in the realm of Ideas, then these Forms must be the *First Principle* or *First Cause* of all else. Observing that goodness permeates the universe, Plato placed the Form of the Absolute Good, also referred to as the One and the Beautiful, at the top of his reality structure.[66]

In Plato's dualistic worldview, the *intelligible realm* of the Forms, which can only be accessed by the intellect, is permanent, stable, trustworthy, and therefore superior to all else. In comparison, the *sensible realm*, the material world that can be perceived by the senses, is in constant flux. This makes it unstable, unreliable, and therefore, inferior.[67]

- *The Divine Craftsman.* Since the Forms do not have the ability to create, in Plato's system this work is accomplished by the Demiurge, a benevolent but mysterious figure with unknown origins, who serves as a bridge between the intelligible realm of Ideas and sensible material world. Referred to at times as Intellect (Mind, Reason), God, Architect, and "maker and father" of the universe, this Divine Craftsman used pre-existing material to model the universe after the Forms.[68]

- *The World Soul.* The Demiurge also created a living soul for the world. In Plato's framework, souls have intellect so in this way the Demiurge endowed the world with intelligent life, making it a living god like the other celestial bodies (sun, moon, stars). The World Soul functions as "the ordering principle in the visible universe."[69]

- *The gods.* The Craftsman also made the other Greek gods, which are described as "living immortals whose bodies and souls are united for all time."[70] To elevate the deities, Plato gave them a makeover, transforming them into morally excellent, benevolent caretakers of the sensible world, with Zeus retaining his role as chief god who "the Father of gods and of mortal beings."[71] The Demiurge tasked the gods with creating human bodies and the lower parts of the soul. Along with caring for humanity, the gods were "involved in contemplating the Ideas, nourishing themselves through intellect and pure knowledge."[72] Plato encouraged citizens to worship the gods and to please them by pursuing the virtues in order to become like them.[73]

- *The individual soul.* In one of his classic descriptions, Plato says the Demiurge fashions individual souls from the "residue" or "soul stuff" that was left over from creating the World Soul.[74] Though the material is inferior, nevertheless, all individual souls share in the same "soul stuff of the universe," *which makes them divine and immortal.*[75]

  In *The Republic* and *Timaeus*, Plato depicts the soul as having three parts: 1) reason or intellect (*nous*) is the highest, immortal part; 2) the mortal mid-soul is the spirited, active part concerned with honor or social status; and 3) the lower part has to do with the sensual appetites. While the Demiurge creates the highest part of the soul, the Greek gods form the two lower, mortal parts of the individual soul when it falls into a body.

- *Individual bodies.* Since the human body is patterned after the Forms, on the one hand, Plato saw it in a positive light. However, he also described "the body as a prison house of the soul" because it confines the divine soul to the inferior, sensible world where it forgets its innate divinity.[76]

## Plato's Narrative: The Journey of the Individual Soul

This brings us to Plato's narrative of the soul's fall to earth and its journey back to the divine realm, a theme that as one scholar points out, "loosely ties together much of his thought."[77] First, in his influential allegory of the charioteer, Plato portrays the tension between the three parts of the soul and how it *descends* or *falls* from the spiritual realm into the material world. He likens the soul to a chariot pulled by two winged horses. The driver is reason, which is the divine part of the soul (higher soul); the white horse (mid-soul) represents honorable desires and appetites; and the dark horse (lower soul) symbolizes dishonorable ones.

While still in the divine realm, the chariot (soul) joins a procession of the gods led by Zeus into the heavens to view the Forms. The white horse wants to go higher and see more, but the dark horse, which is enticed by sensual pleasures, tries to pull the chariot back towards the earth. If the charioteer (reason) fails to successfully guide the two horses to gaze on Goodness, Beauty and Knowledge and other higher

Forms, their wings either wither from lack of nourishment or break off when other unruly horses or chariots collide. The soul then falls to the earth, where it becomes imprisoned in a human body.

Unfortunately, once it's trapped in the sensible world, the soul becomes disoriented and forgets its divine origin until it is unexpectedly awakened by beauty and love (*eros*).[78] This fills the highest part of soul with longing for the "blessed perfection of the Good," which rightly belongs to it. [79] In Plato's system, *conversion* takes place when the soul turns away from the sensible world and goes inward to seek its true self, which is divine, and return home to the spiritual realm.[80]

In the famous allegory of the cave and other writings, Plato describes the soul's path of *salvation,* which involves contemplating the higher truths that can only be known to the intellect.[81] After awakening and realizing it is imprisoned in a deep cave in which it only sees dim, shadowy reflections of truth, the soul begins to *ascend* upward towards the light of reality.[82] First, the wisdom-seeking soul goes through an arduous, sometimes painful process of *purification* in an effort to acquire virtue. This is followed by *illumination*, which takes place through rigorous general studies that prepare the soul to understand higher truths. Eventually moving beyond concepts and words, the ascent culminates in a participatory *union* with the First Principle—the Absolute Good or the One, which, like the sun, radiates upon all else.[83]

## An Experiential Encounter with Plato's One

This last step is where things become more mysterious and abstract. Taking a closer look, Plato taught that the First Principle or Ultimate Reality cannot be described in words; rather, the philosopher can only say what it is not.[84] This is the concept that inspired a method for approaching God known as the *via negativa* or *apophatic way* that had great influence on the Christian mystic traditions in both the East and West. We'll look at this in more detail later, but those who practice the apophatic way believe that because God is incomprehensible, ultimately nothing can be said about him; he can only be experienced by going beyond all words, concepts, and symbols.

In Plato's scheme, after the soul is enlightened through instruction, it must engage in a series of negations in which all mental ideas of the

Absolute One are laid aside. For example, Plato reasoned "if the One exists it cannot be many; if it has no parts, it can have no beginning, middle, or end; the one has no name, there is no description, knowledge, or perception of it."[85] Moving past the negations, the philosopher then enters into the silence of higher contemplation. At this time, an intuitive knowledge of the Absolute may suddenly flash directly upon the *intellect* (nous) "as a light that is kindled by a leaping spark."[86] This creates an affinity or union with the Absolute that awakens the innate divinity of the soul.

According to Bernard McGinn "this is the height of Platonic contemplation—not merely a seeing, but an awareness of identity with the present Ultimate Principle."[87] He goes on to say that, "*Divinization then is the goal of Plato's philosophy*: the philosopher gains immortality by being assimilated to God," an experience that Platonists sometimes described as being accompanied by a type of ecstasy.[88] In Plato's system, this divinization is not for all. In fact, only an elite few can attain knowledge of the Absolute Good, as it requires an advanced education for which, according to Plato, most people are not suited.[89] However, it is meant to benefit all. Ideally, once deified, the enlightened few will become benevolent philosopher-kings who govern the city-state with wisdom, justice, and truth, and also serve as examples of virtuous living for others to follow.[90]

## Plato Evolves

What makes Plato's theology so challenging is that it contains a number of puzzles, contradictions and vague ideas that were open to various interpretations. For instance, as one expert on Plato points out, "Plato's views on God and the divine are notoriously difficult to unravel."[91] Sometimes he refers to God in the singular, sometimes in the plural. Since there are many gods in his scheme, then who or what is referred to as God, singular?

At first glance, it may seem like it may be the Form of the Good, but the problem is the One does not create, nor does it interact with human beings like the biblical God. So, is Plato's God the Demiurge, the Intellect that creates the world, the other gods, and the divine part of soul? Is it Zeus, who Plato also refers to as "father" and the god of gods? The other gods who created the human body and the mortal parts of the individual soul, and who are charged with actually caring for humans? Or is Plato's God all of the gods combined? As stated by the authors of *Philosophy for Theology*, the philosopher's views on the soul are also difficult to reconcile.[92]

In attempting to resolve these and other conundrums, Plato's followers amended his thought system in various ways. First, claiming to have knowledge of his unwritten doctrines, Plato's student, Aristotle, offered views that differed significantly from his master's written work.[93] Rejecting Plato's theory of the Forms, Aristotle looked to the sensible world as a valid source of knowledge. He also did not believe the soul was immortal or that it could be separated from the body. Therefore, according to Aristotle, the human soul is not "on a journey seeking release from the body in order to return to its place of origin," as Plato taught.[94] He also reframed the First Cause as the "Unmoved Mover," a divine Intellect that is the source of all movement but is not moved itself.[95] As the highest God, Aristotle's Unmoved Mover "must think necessarily that which is most divine and of the greatest worth," which means it can only think about itself. Consequently, unlike the biblical God, it cannot care about anything outside of itself.[96]

Not only did Aristotle's views spark intense debate among the Platonists, but Plato's Old Academy went through significant changes as well. As a result, by Clement's day different versions of Platonism had emerged that relied heavily on Plato but also combined various ideas from Aristotle, and other philosophies like Stoicism as well.[97] There was no unified view of metaphysics or the divine in this era. However, reflecting Aristotle's influence, the supreme God was often seen as a transcendent *Mind* and Plato's Forms were placed *inside* this Intellect rather than *above* it.[98] Many of the Platonists at this time did not necessarily regard "the supreme God as *unknowable, but simply difficult to know.*"[99] Some of these ideas influenced Clement.

## Neoplatonism

Further complicating the mix, a new adaptation, later called Neoplatonism, began to surface around the time Origen taught at the religious school in Alexandria, which had a significant impact on Christianity. Plotinus, the primary founder of Neoplatonism, retrieved Plato's idea that the highest level of Reality is the One or the Good.[100] In an effort to resolve some of the conundrums in Plato's thought, he firmly positioned the One as *beyond being* and *beyond knowing*, which set it above all other levels of reality.[101] As a result, he taught that nothing could be said about the One; it could only be apprehended in "the silence of the mind, rising above thought altogether."[102] Like Plato, he also stressed the importance of the individual soul turning within to find her true self and realize *"her inner identity with the whole Intelligible world"* before finally ascending to the One.[103]

Modifying Plato's thoughts, Plotinus is also known for conceiving the influential idea of *procession* and *return*. He supposed that all things flow out from the One and eventually return to it based on the principle that like is attracted to like. Although we won't be discussing it here, later, this concept had a far-reaching impact on Christianity through the works of Pseudo-Dionysius, a writer from the fifth or sixth century.[104] Also influencing Christian thought, the conflicting ideas about whether God is knowable or unknowable to the intellect spawned different forms of mysticism and are one of the underlying causes of division between the Eastern and Western church.

On one level, it's possible to see why some of the fathers saw certain parallels between Platonism and Christianity—initially, they appear to have a number of things in common like seeing goodness as a foundational quality of the universe, envisioning a just society, and the emphasis on pursuing virtue. However, as philosopher Etienne Gilson notes, in reality *the two worlds are incomparable* "for the fundamental reason that their metaphysical structure is essentially different."[105]

This taps into one of the overall reasons why it is problematic to make direct comparisons between the Platonic and biblical concept of God or to integrate the two systems. As you can see for yourself, there is no one version of God in Platonism (or other forms of philosophy); it can mean different things depending on who is using the term. And for another, as Jewish theologian Michael Wyschogrod points out, the philosophical One—no matter which version—is simply *not the same* as the living God of Israel who interacts with his people and will someday be worshipped as the only one God by all the nations.[106] What I also want to point out here is that if Plato had read Moses as some of the fathers believed, the philosopher would have clearly known that the first of the ten commandments given by God is that "You shall have no other gods before me." Yet the Platonists not only continued to worship other gods, they also steadfastly opposed Christianity. [107]

Keeping this basic background in mind, let's see what happened when Clement of Alexandria and Origen introduced modified version of Plato's individualistic narrative about the soul's ascent and other philosophical concepts into Christian thought.

## Fusing Frameworks

Believing that Plato had read Moses, Clement saw the philosopher and prophet as being "mutually complementary, each one explaining the other one."[108] Consequently, like Philo, he assumed that *Plato's ascent of the soul* was a parallel to *Moses's ascent to meet with God on Mount Sinai.* This is a critical premise because it served as Clement's underlying rationale for blending the two storylines, and like Philo, he relied on the Greek allegorical method to arrive at this conclusion.

While Philo believed meditating on the law of Moses was the means of ascent, Clement offered a christianized version of Plato's account of the soul's journey. Based on the assumption that Plato's "region of Ideas" was the same as the "region of God" on Mount Sinai, Clement presumed that when Plato read the account of Moses ascent, he realized the prophet had reached "the summit of things known to the intellect" by way of contemplation.[109] Having arrived at this peak through intellectual analysis, Moses then grasped those things that exceeded what could be known by the mind and entered the "darkness" where he "confronted the invisible and unspeakable."[110] Clement maintained that like Moses, individual believers should also seek to go beyond thought and concepts to enter into "the abyss of the Father" where they could achieve union with him.[111]

As Clement taught, in order to be initiated into these divine mysteries and attain perfection, the individual Christian needed to follow a threefold contemplative path similar to the one Plato outlined. Here we see what is known as the *mystic way* or the *mystic ladder* beginning to emerge that is foundational to many forms of contemplative Christianity to this day.[112]

- *Purification* or *purgation.* Christianizing a concept from the Stoics that he mixed in with Plato's storyline, Clement taught that in order to become perfect like God, it was necessary for one's soul to reach a state of impassibility or *apatheia* by learning to suppress the passions (negative emotions) and also to subdue the body. Seeing beyond our physical existence brings us into an open space in which we can perceive a certain underlying spiritual unity that connects all of humankind, a view only accessible to the intellect.

- *Illumination.* The second step involves learning more about these elementary spiritual mysteries through doctrine and instruction. This knowledge eventually ushers the individual into the majesty of Christ where the soul is sanctified.

- *Deification/Union.* In the third stage, individual believers begin contemplating the more advanced mysteries. To do so, Clement taught that it is necessary to move past what can be known and discover the truth of God that is beyond comprehension. Reflecting Plato's perspective in part, Clement believed that by means of intellectual analysis, the seeking believer comes to understand God not for what he is, but *for what he is not.* Here we see Clement embracing the *apophatic way* for approaching God. This method leads the contemplative into the depths or *abyss* of the incomprehensible Father, who contains all things. The few who reach this place are united with the One and experience *deification*, meaning that once assimilated, they "become a divine image, resembling God."[113]

One theologian observed that for Clement, contemplation seemed to "involve man's intellectual faculty almost exclusively."[114] To be fair, it should be noted that Clement was not a pure intellectual in that he did not advocate relying on reason alone; he clearly believed that faith in Christ, which is founded on divine revelation, is the doorway into the Christian life.[115] Clement also emphasized the central role love played in pursuing God. However, in teaching that perpetual contemplation was the pathway to deification, he implied that union with God is attained through knowledge *higher* than faith. Furthermore, like Plato, he believed only the "pure in heart," meaning the advanced, perfected few, can experience the deifying vision of God.

Commenting on Clement's approach, Eastern Orthodox theologian Vladimir Lossky states this elitist version of spirituality is "literary fiction." He observes "Clement is providing a Christian disguise for the intellectualistic contemplative whom he had found outside the experience of the church's life."[116]

Nevertheless, the assumption Clement shared with Philo, that Moses and Plato were both describing the soul's ascent to God, became widely accepted, as was his view that Moses is a pattern for the individual believer's journey to achieve union with God.[117] An enduring theme in mystic literature is based on the image of Moses entering into the "darkness of ignorance" on Mt. Sinai, referred to by later writers as the "cloud of unknowing."[118]

Furthermore, modified versions of the apophatic way that Clement introduced became foundational not only to some forms of Christian mysticism, but also to the entire Eastern Orthodox tradition.[119] In reference to Moses entering into the cloud, one Orthodox theologian explains this is "a favourite symbol for the incomprehensibility of the divine nature. The divine darkness signifies that God is essentially inaccessible and unknown to man. It also signifies the impossibility of describing God or predicating anything of him."[120] Before discussing these developments further, let's first look at some of the ways Origen added an individualistic, dualistic overlay to the biblical storyline.

## Origen's Innovations

Influenced by Plato and Clement, but also an independent thinker, Origen adopted Clement's christianized version of Plato's account of the soul's ascent and the threefold contemplative pathway, but with some changes. He went much further than his predecessor in using the allegorical method to apply key typologies to individuals that, in scripture, have to do primarily with the covenant community as a whole, not individuals in particular.

Known as "an authentic master of the spiritual life" who practiced a strict ascetic lifestyle, Origen tended to read scripture "in light of his own spiritual experience."[121] Reflecting this, one of the innovative interpretive principles Origen introduced is that "God acts towards each soul in just the same kind of way as he operates on the larger scale of Israel, Christ, the Church, and the eschaton."[122] Consequently although he never lost sight of the central role of the church, he interpreted many corporate passages as also being about the interior life of the individual Christian.[123]

This shows up in Origen's influential interpretation of the Song of Solomon. Whereas most of the fathers, Origen included, saw this as applying to the marriage between Christ and the church, Origen believed it also described Christ's love for the individual soul and the soul's response. The problem, however, is that as we saw earlier, marriage imagery is *never* used to describe the relationship between the individual and Yahweh or Christ in scripture—it is *only* used corporately, in reference to God and his people.

Along with individualizing this text, Origen also added an intellectual twist that differed from Clement's by teaching that this intimacy, which only the spiritually advanced can achieve, leads to the illumination of the mind. Origen did not embrace the apophatic way, as Clement did. While he agreed that language is insufficient when communicating about God, at the same time, he also believed God is accessible to the intellect and is the object of knowledge. In fact, in Origen's framework, intellectual illumination is the "truer, closer, holier kiss, which is said to be given by the lover, the Word of God, to his beloved, the pure and perfect soul."[124]

The idea of the solitary celibate believer seeking the kisses of God's mouth, along with several other intimate images arising from the individual application of the Songs, became central themes in mystic thought.[125] Harvey Egan notes, "The impact this book [the Songs] has had on the Christian mystical tradition cannot be overemphasized."[126] In a statement to which some might take exception, Egan goes on to say, "in fact, the power of Western mysticism comes from its deliberate eroticizing of the relation between the human virgin and the divine Bridegroom."[127]

## A Solitary Exodus

In another classic and highly influential example of individualized typology, Origen took the story of the Exodus of God's people traveling from Egypt through the desert to the Promised Land and applied it to the individual soul. Using Plato's framework of the soul's ascent and the allegorical method, Origen taught that each stage of Israel's journey describes the steps the soul goes through on its pilgrimage to have a vision of God and become perfect. This fusion of the Platonic and Christian storylines is clearly evident in his statement that, "the Savior descended so that He might accompany and assist *the soul in its journey of ascent* to the promised land."[128] In describing the individual soul's flight from Egypt, Origen says, "It is better to die in the desert than to be a slave in Egypt. It is better to die on the journey, on *the quest for the perfect life*, than never to undertake that quest."[129]

In his use of this personalized typology, Origen unwittingly individualized the church's understanding of perfection, holiness, and union with Christ. First, as John Zizioulas observes, Origen attached "the notion of holiness to perfection and, therefore, to a certain group of Christians, a spiritual elite."[130] When he did this, Zizioulas points out, *"the idea of holiness was dissociated from the community of the church as a whole."* [131] As a result, practicing holiness was often seen as more an individual pursuit rather than something the entire holy covenant community, which is already purified and united to Christ, walks in together as members relate to God and others.

Although it is true that Christ commands his followers "to be perfect, as your heavenly Father is perfect," this is not a personal, moral perfection that comes by disdaining the physical body and acquiring virtue through the contemplative process.[132] Rather, in context, it has to do with loving others as God loves and is lived out within the entire corporate and embodied church. As the apostle Paul said, "goal of *our* instruction is love," a love that is perfected as members of Christ's body serve God and others, including our enemies.[133] Likewise, the command to "mortify the deeds of the body" in Romans 8:13 (NASB) is not a call to individual perfection. Rather, it's a *communal* practice in which we put away the old habits and patterns of relating to one another that characterized our former lives in the flesh, the body of Sin.

Moral excellence certainly plays a role in this, but scripture portrays it as a stepping-stone towards the community's greater goal of loving others as Christ has loved us. In contrast to Plato's account of the solitary soul's upward climb to reconnect with the divine and achieve personal perfection, the apostle Peter paints a much different picture. He first describes the entire community's escape from the world's corruption and its present, ongoing participation in the new divine order, i.e. God's kingdom.[134] He then shows the pathway by which its members attain true knowledge of Jesus. Speaking to the corporate body, he instructs them all to:

> Make every effort to add to your faith goodness;
> To goodness, knowledge;

And to knowledge, self-control;
And to self-control, perseverance;
And to perseverance, godliness;
And to godliness, mutual affection;
And to mutual affection, love.

He goes on to say,

For *if you possess these qualities in increasing measure*, they will keep you from being ineffective and unproductive in *your knowledge of our Lord Jesus Christ*. But whoever does not have them is nearsighted and blind, forgetting that they have been cleansed from their past sins.

Peter concludes by assuring the community that if they confirm their calling by doing these things, they will never stumble and "will receive a rich welcome into the eternal kingdom of our Lord and Savior Jesus Christ."[135] The point I want to emphasize here is that while each individual member has a part to play in the process, this is no individualized journey and it does not involve the way of negation or being personally divinized. Participating in the divine order is already possible because of the community's corporate union with Christ and gaining greater knowledge of Jesus is something the community does together as members mature in their love for one another.

Furthermore, by embracing a modified version of Plato's journey of the soul, both Clement and Origen individualized and privatized the concept of union with Christ. In Plato's scheme, union comes at *the end* of the journey; it is the culmination of the individual soul's arduous ascent that can only be experienced by the elite few. As described in the New Testament, however, it is just the opposite. Union comes *at the beginning* of the salvation process; it is a privilege that *all believers from the least to the greatest*, enjoy from the moment they trust in Christ and are brought into the present life of the church.

We saw previously that our union with Christ was a corporate event accomplished by the Spirit at the time of Christ's death. Raised together with him, the entire covenant community is presently seated with Christ in heavenly places while waiting for the final consummation of this union at the end of the ages. Some may have a greater experiential knowledge of this union than others depending on their level of maturity and other factors. Nevertheless, as a result of the Spirit's work at the cross, *all believers are united with Christ* and can experience his love and care. Presenting union with God as something to be achieved by the individual at the end of a lengthy contemplative journey is contrary to scripture.

In looking at the fusion of these two frameworks, the question we need to ask is if there is any biblical evidence to support Origen's idea that Israel's Exodus is a metaphor for the stages of the individual soul's journey of ascent? As popular as this motif may be, what I would say is that, in scripture, Israel's experiences are meant to be an *historic example for the entire new covenant community*. In 1 Corinthians 10, Paul begins with a description of Israel's corporate solidarity with Moses through baptism. He shows that even though Yahweh faithfully kept his covenant promises and provided for all of his people, a number of individuals within the community were unfaithful. The apostle then lists several examples of how some of the Israelites set their hearts on evil, which is meant to serve as a warning to all the members of Christ's body.

A case could be made that water baptism represents the individual leaving the world just as Israel left Egypt. But this does not imply that the individual soul then goes through the same journey as Israel. Rather, it shows the individual has now publicly identified with the corporate people of God, who, together, are on pilgrimage. The individual is transformed, along with the rest of the community, as members grow in mutual affection and love in the progression the apostle Peter described above.

Another question is whether there is any scriptural support for the idea that individual believers are to turn inward to find their "true self"? This is something we need to consider carefully. For one thing, it's true that we are created in God's image and instructed to become like him (as we saw, this has a corporate connotation), and also that the Holy Spirit dwells within our hearts, communally and as individuals. It's also true that Christians are instructed to cultivate a rich interior life— scripture tells us to pray in secret, examine our hearts and practice "truth in the inner person" (which, by the way, is also a corporate concept). There is also a place for learning about our individual personalities, talents and gifts. So, on one level, we can personally experience God within ourselves.[136]

However, the concept of turning inward to find our "true self" is based on the Platonic idea that the highest part of the soul is innately divine, which the Bible does not teach. Also, we simply cannot experience all the Spirit has for us apart from the believing community.

As scripture teaches in 1 Corinthians 12-14, we find our true selves as we take our place in the body of Christ and begin using our unique, Spirit-given gifts to love, serve, and build up one another.[137]

## Two Spiritualties

Origen's individualistic ideas about the ascent of the soul and pursuit of personal perfection had an enormous impact on the course Christian spirituality took in the third century and beyond. As stated by McGinn, "Though it would be incorrect to ascribe the popularity of the ascent motif in Christian mysticism to Origen alone, there can be no doubt that his emphasis on itinerary had great influence on many later mystics."[138] Also, the personalized typology of the soul's journey based on Israel's corporate flight from Egypt is now such an integral part of the Christian tradition that it is rarely, if ever, questioned; to this day, the idea persists that Israel is a metaphor for the individual soul's journey.[139] In fact, as some see it, this is one of Origen's most creative and admirable contributions to the church.[140] On the other hand, Zizioulas observes that Origen's influence also "accounts for many serious deviations from the early biblical mentality."[141]

As a result of these events, from Origen's time forward two basic approaches or attitudes to spirituality have existed in the church: one is based on the Eucharistic community, in which, as Zizioulas points out, the "decisive factors of spirituality" involve the corporate body of Christ and its anticipation of Christ's return for his people.[142] Early fathers such as Ignatius of Antioch and Irenaeus, and later Calvin promoted a communal perspective of ascent. Irenaeus not only stressed Christ's descent and ascent in the flesh, one in which his people share, but, unlike Plato, he also emphasized "the involvement of the whole person, body and soul, in the scheme of salvation."[143]

The other type of spirituality introduced by Origen separates spirit and body. It is "based on the experience of the individual who struggles against passions and toward the achievement of moral perfection" that eventually culminates in the soul's mystical union with the Word (Logos) of God.[144] Again, this is not to say that Origen completely lost the corporate perspective, only that he layered Plato's framework over it, which inadvertently obscured the radically communal nature of Christian spirituality.

Zizioulas points out that "A study of the history of the church from the fourth century reveals that these two types of spirituality never ceased to coexist, *but at the same time they were not easily compatible with each other.*"[145] Commenting on the two approaches, Douglas Farrow contends, "that if we understand Irenaeus and Origen, and the alternative theological models they offer, we are in a position to understand the whole history of Christian thought."[146] Later writers sought to reconcile the differences and show how the spirituality of the community and the individual relate.[147] Nevertheless, as noted earlier, the individualistic form of spirituality introduced by Clement and Origen has had long-lasting effects.

## Testing the Premise

As you can see, this is a critical point in our family history so it's to our benefit to give thought to this turn of events. My intention is not to offer a critique of the Christian mystical tradition or sort through the complicated interaction of these two approaches throughout church history. Rather, I would like to focus on one main point. If what we have been discovering so far about scripture's corporate, Hebraic framework has merit, then we need to ask ourselves a fundamental question: is Clement and Origen's basic premise that Plato and Moses were describing the same realities true? This is one of those issues that will need to be explored in more depth later, but I would like to offer a few initial observations.

First, if we look at Moses's ascent on Mt. Sinai in its biblical context, what jumps out is that while the prophet may have gone up the mountain alone, it was clearly a corporate event. This is when Israel was formed as a nation. God had just collectively delivered the Hebrews from slavery in Egypt. In corporate solidarity with Moses, their God-chosen representative leader, Yahweh led his people across the Red Sea and to the foot of Mt. Sinai. In Exodus 19 Yahweh stated his purpose for this exodus: he wanted to set the Hebrews apart to be his "treasured possession . . . *a kingdom of priests and holy nation.*" And he planned to formalize this arrangement by entering into a covenant with them, which, as seen previously, later prophets described as being a type of marriage contract. As we also saw, the New Testament writers pulled these corporate Old Testament categories forward, applying them to the new covenant community in Christ.

Second, Moses did not enter into a spiritual, intelligible realm that could only be accessed by following the threefold contemplative path. Surely, we can agree that God is incomprehensible to our finite minds and that aspects of Moses's encounters with God on Mt. Sinai were mysterious and indescribable; we can only wonder what he experienced when he was in God's presence. And surely there were times of silence when no words would suffice.

However, there is no indication that Moses went "beyond thought" and into the "ignorance of unknowing" like the philosophical contemplatives. When the prophet met Yahweh on the Mount it was for the specific purpose of receiving the law and the terms of the covenant, which Moses wrote down and presented to the people to ratify. On subsequent visits, Yahweh also gave Moses detailed instructions for building the tabernacle, offering worship, and for practical living that he was to share with the people. Perhaps it could be said Yahweh showed him the pattern or, using Plato's language, the Form of the tabernacle. But even if this is granted, while Moses was in the "thick cloud of darkness" Yahweh's communications with the prophet had *substantial content that could be clearly expressed to others*—a notion that would not fit into Plato's framework.

Third, Moses did not turn inward, away from the material world, so that he could ascend to the spiritual realm using his intellect. Unlike the philosophical Forms or the One or the Unmoved Mover, Yahweh *descended* to meet with Moses in the material realm. And Moses was embodied and climbed up a real, physical mountain when he *ascended* to meet Yahweh. Furthermore, also unlike the philosophical First Cause, Yahweh was *interactive* and *relational*. At the same time that he was veiled in mystery, Yahweh chose to reveal himself, in part, through actions, sounds, visible manifestations, and by using *language* and *concepts*. Not only did the living God *dialogue* with Moses as a friend, but, at one point, Yahweh spoke so that *all* of the Israelites could hear. He also wrote the Ten Commandments on stone tablets so that *all* could read them.

Fourth, there is no indication in scripture that Moses's ascent on Mt. Sinai was ever meant to serve as a pattern for the individual believer's contemplative life. For one thing, God instructed *all* of the people, not just Moses, to be consecrated and wash their garments in preparation for this corporate encounter with him. And when God summoned Moses to come up the Mount to meet with him alone, it was to fulfill his specific mission as Israel's representative head and receive instructions from God for the people. There are many things to learn from Moses that we can apply to our own lives such as his humility, his heart to intercede for the people, his obedience, and his passionate desire to know God. But no other human being was ever called to ascend Mt. Sinai to receive the law—it was a non-repeated event in the life of God's people.

In connection to this I want to speak to a practice that has caused great confusion in the body of Christ. Often a singular event that relates to a specific person's mission is held up as a pattern for all believers. Examples include Moses's ascent on the Mount; Paul's encounter on the road to Damascus; Peter and John's sighting of the "uncreated light" when Christ was transfigured; and Paul's trip to the third heavens. These events show that sometimes God reveals himself in supernatural ways and that some believers may have these types of encounters in connection to their mission. However, it does not mean that all Christians should necessarily expect to have them as well.

I realize this may be a controversial statement given how deeply embedded the concept of the soul's ascent and some of Clement and Origen's ideas are in Christian thought, but as a biblical theologian, I can only say there is good reason to question their basic premise. Not only did layering Plato's individualistic story of the soul's ascent over this text confuse the biblical picture, it also diminished Israel's role in salvation history and pushed the Jewish backdrop of scripture further into the background.

A number of other subjects warrant further discussion in connection to the material we have just covered that can't be addressed here. For one thing, if, upon further investigation, Clement and Origen's premises do not hold up, then how might this affect the way we approach spirituality, corporately and personally? In light of the corporate nature of our union with Christ and one another, what place, if any, does the concept of turning inward to find our true self have in Christian spirituality? How do the individualistic, dualistic assumptions introduced by fusing the two frameworks continue to affect the way we view scripture and the human person? Some of these questions have been addressed in different ways among various Christian groups throughout the ages so we have things to learn from one another, but I suggest there is room for further discussion.

Moreover, although we don't have space to discuss them here, the Alexandrians introduced three novel philosophically inspired methods for scripture reading and spiritual practice that, as we saw in part, had a significant impact on Christian thought. These include: 1) the allegorical method that Clement and Origen used in various ways. This became a source of controversy in that it was accepted by some fathers but resisted by others; 2) the apophatic method, which touches on what it means to say that God is incomprehensible, whether he can be named, or if anything can be said of him. Exploring this approach is important as it is a major point of difference between the East and the West. And 3) the philosophically-inspired "scientific" method with its emphasis on reason that Clement introduced in seed form and which became so influential in the Medieval ages with the discovery of Aristotle's more complete works.[148] Much has been written about these three methods, but I suggest it is important to revisit them now that we are in the process of recovering the corporate, Hebraic backdrop for scripture.

## The Fragmented Person

Influenced by a combination of Platonic ideas and what he believed were some of Paul's views, Origen generated one other innovation relevant to our conversation—he introduced a fragmented, dualistic view of the human person into Christian thought that is foreign to scripture. In addition to accepting the basic Platonic premise that the soul was superior to the body, Origen also embraced elements of Plato's teachings about divisions *within* the soul itself but modified them.

Like Plato, Origen believed that before the fall from the spiritual realm, the soul had a pure, undivided rational nature. After the fall, he taught that a lower, fleshly nature was added. Origen then depicted the soul with its higher and lower elements (or tendencies) as being engaged in an internal spiritual battle with itself. As Origen framed it, the free will, which is seated in the soul, can choose which tendency it will follow.[149] Echoing Plato's concept, he also equated the flesh with the lower part of the soul, positioning it as a permanent, *interior* part of the human person. In his framework the "flesh is the force that attracts the soul towards the body."[150] This was a significant shift away from biblical thinking. The idea that the soul has higher and lower elements is simply not found in scripture. Also, it does not reflect Paul's corporate view of the flesh as unredeemed humanity that we saw earlier in our discussion of Romans 5-8.

Origen further complicated the picture when he reasoned that because humans are conceived through a "hot sex act" and pass through the impurities of childbirth, which the Old Testament describes as unclean, they are "inevitably associated with a series of 'stains.'"[151] This, and other ideas, led him to conclude that "some deep, original 'taint' must surely lie at the very beginning of human existence."[152] Origen and other fathers did not believe the taint was permanent, but some, most notably Augustine who was influenced by this ideas, taught "the stain," which was passed on biologically through Adam and Eve, remains until death. We'll look at this further in the next section. [153]

Before leaving the discussion of Clement and Origen, I want to make a couple of additional points. First, it is important to be charitable. In all likelihood, they did not deliberately seek to separate individual and corporate spirituality. However, given their circumstances, it was almost impossible for this not to happen. A good deal of their work involved defending the faith from the attacks of critics who were steeped in Hellenistic thought, and they had to help educated Greek converts acclimate to the believing community, so it was inevitable they would use the framework that was known to both groups. Nevertheless, the emphasis on individual spirituality led to an unfortunate loss of the corporate perspective.

I also want to address the issue of contextualization. Some have suggested Clement and Origen were simply trying to adapt biblical truth to the social setting of their day, and claim this same process occurred in scripture, citing Paul's encounter with the philosophers at Athens and the book of Hebrews as supposed examples. Regarding Paul's message on Mars Hill, however, the apostle was not engaging the philosophers in a debate about the similarities between Christianity and their views, as some claim.[154] All he did was throw a well-known quote from a famous philosopher into the ring to gain attention. The interaction was of the briefest kind because as soon as Paul mentioned the resurrection, the philosophers packed their bags and left! This was anything but a mutual exploration of each other's positions to gain greater intellectual material to buttress their own arguments, as some claim. And there is certainly no suggestion that Paul came away with a Hellenized understanding that enriched his ministry and equipped him for more meaningful encounters in the future. As the text makes clear, he was just as distressed over the ignorance of the Athenians after the encounter as he was before it.

As for the argument some make about Philo's influences on the letter to the Hebrews, William Lane has shown that the supposed parallels between the writer and Philo do not exist.[155] Rather the author used typological exegesis throughout the letter to show how elements of the Old Testament pointed ahead to Christ. For instance, the writer of Hebrews argued that the temple was built according to the plan given to Moses by God, and that it was a type of the worship that would come when the covenant promises had been fulfilled. This approach carries *no traces* of Greek exegetical methods —it is entirely Hebraic and is used throughout both the Old and New Testament scriptures, as the various writers make their case for the authority of the message they preached. For those who would like to explore this further, Leonhard Goppelt has written an excellent study on the powerful influence of typology on both the Old and New Testaments.[156] Finally, I would like to point out I have dealt with many such claims in my book, *Tom Wright and the Search for Truth*.[157]

There is thus very little evidence, if any at all, to suggest that either of these biblical authors *altered the actual content of the biblical message* or attempted to integrate Hellenistic philosophy with scripture in an effort to be culturally relevant.[158] While, as we saw earlier, it is accepted that Clement and Origen *did* introduce ideas that were alien to scripture in an attempt to woo Hellenists, there is absolutely no evidence this is what the author of Hebrews did.

**AUGUSTINE'S VIEWS OF SPIRITUALITY AND SIN¶** In looking at ways the biblical storyline was blurred over time, we are moving now to the fourth century and from the East to the West. Our goal is to see, how individualistic, dualistic philosophical concepts shaped some of Augustine's thinking on spirituality and original sin. This controversial father is important because he is credited (or blamed depending on who is talking) for laying the foundations of Western Christianity and also for playing a critical role in the development of Western civilization. One of the major accomplishments he is often lauded for is that he merged "the Greek philosophical tradition" with "the Judeo-Christian religious and scriptural traditions." [1][159] As his biographer, Peter Brown, notes, "Augustine was always concerned to bring together the 'God of Abraham, Isaac and of Jacob', with the 'God of the Philosophers'." [160] In fact, some see this merger as one of his most laudable contributions to the Western world. [161]

The challenge in talking about Augustine is that he's a beloved and respected figure in the West. Because many Westerners—Catholics and Protestants alike—regard him as our father in the faith and base their teachings to one degree or another on his thought, it's not always easy to raise questions about his views. Not only can it feel like we are being disrespectful, but it may also require us to reconsider some of our own beliefs. This can be very challenging, even threatening at times. For some, it may even seem heretical. However, just as children grow up and need to re-evaluate some of the things their parents taught them, I would like to gently suggest we are at a point in history where it would be to our benefit to have a charitable, family-wide conversation about some of the ideas we inherited from our father, Augustine. And I believe it is possible to do so while still respecting his considerable contributions to the church.

To see how hidden philosophical assumptions shaped some of Augustine's views, we first need to look at his relationship with Platonism and scripture in the early stages of his Christian life.

## Mixed Influences

Augustine is known for being a brilliant thinker, philosopher, prolific writer and a complex man. He was introduced to the Christian faith and baptized as a child, but for various reasons found it difficult to understand scripture. In his younger years, Augustine studied to become a classically trained rhetorician, so he was familiar with Greek literature. He also spent several years with the Manichees, a religious sect that named Christ and esteemed Paul's letters, but rejected the Old Testament and read the New selectively. After a while, their teachings did not satisfy, and Augustine became spiritually restless.

Two things helped turn him back to the orthodox Christian tradition. First, exposure to Neoplatonist writings opened his eyes to the spiritual realm in a new way, and second, he had a profound personal experience while reading Paul's writings. For the rest of his life, he had an ongoing relationship with the Platonists and scripture, which is why he is sometimes referred to as a Christian Platonist.[162] In addition to reading Neoplatonist works himself, he also inherited a number of Platonic assumptions that were indirectly passed on through Origen and some of the Latin fathers. Like his forefathers, he christianized certain philosophical concepts and overtly rejected others. But at the same time, because he believed all truth was God's truth, he had no problem weaving philosophical ideas together with scripture or his own original thinking when he thought it was merited.

It's important to note that, according to Augustinian scholar, Phillip Cary, Platonism came first chronologically in Augustine's life. He points out that by the time Augustine began to wrestle with the apostle Paul's writings for himself in context of Catholic doctrine, he had already embraced certain Platonist assumptions. These included such things as the distinction between the superior realm of Ideas and the inferior sensible world, and the priority of the inner life. Cary observes that as a result of reading scripture through this pre-existing grid, Augustine's "Pauline convictions about grace and human nature were made to fit into an overarching Platonist framework. When the fit turned out to be imperfect, the result was a set of pastoral problems that are an integral part of Augustine's enduring legacy to the West." [163] According to Cary, even though he came to rely more on scripture as he aged, Augustine never really stopped being a Platonist on some level; he "just became an increasingly judicious one."[164]

By the time Augustine became a church leader, a few key shifts had already taken place. As we've seen, aspects of the Jewish context of scripture with its corporate mindset were no longer well known. Also, the premise that Plato's journey of the individual soul was described in scripture, along with dualistic views of the human person, had already seeped into many parts of the church.[165] Even so, it's important to stress that Augustine was no individualist; he was a churchman at heart and did not have the same view of the autonomous person we have in the West today. He also valued the role of community; he was the founder of a particular form of monasticism patterned after the earlier Christian community described in the book of Acts. As a result of these core beliefs, ecclesial and communal themes run throughout his writings. Nevertheless, in contrast to the more corporate form of spirituality practiced by the primitive church, Augustine's theology took a sharp, introspective, and individualistic turn inward.

## The Private, Inner Self

Summarizing briefly, Augustine was the first to frame the novel concept of the private, inner self. This was a hugely significant development. Like Plato's followers, Augustine believed the individual needed to turn inward to find one's "true self" and God. However, he amended the Platonist scheme to reflect the clear distinction in Catholic doctrine between God, the Creator, and the creature. First, he taught that after going *inward*, the soul had to go *upward* to find God. He also posited that when the individual turned inward rather than immediately encountering the divine in itself, the soul first enters a *private*, inner world. This was a shift from Platonism, which taught that by turning inward the soul first rediscovered its own divinity and its connection with the greater Intelligible world of which it was a part before ascending to the spiritual realm.

As Augustine envisioned it, this private world was an intricate, expansive realm of the inner psyche, the depths of which needed to be carefully investigated. Adopting the philosophers theme to "know thyself," Augustine taught that,

> A man cannot hope to find God unless he first finds himself: for this God is 'deeper than my inmost being', experience of Him becomes 'better' the more 'inward'. Above all, it is man's tragedy that he

should be driven to flee 'outwards', to lose touch with himself, to 'wander far' from his 'own heart.'[166]

Augustine's biographer, Peter Brown, states, "This emphasis on the fall of the soul as a turning outwards, as a loss of identity, as becoming 'a partial thing, isolated, full of cares, intent upon the fragment, severed from the whole' is a clear echo of the thought of Plotinus." In Plotinus, the soul is a cosmic archetype and its "Fall" mainly represents the shadowy condition of humankind. Transformed by Augustine, however, this "fall" is "intensely personal," showing "itself in a hundred precise incidents of his past life," and causing him to flee from himself.[167] In his framework, going inward to explore these realities was the way to return to himself and the place where God could be found.

Phil Cary notes that to Augustine, these ideas were not new or original. In his view, the Bible taught that God created the soul and "the notion that the intelligible Light shines on the soul from above is as old as [Plato's] Allegory of the Cave."[168] However, in his efforts to show how Platonic thought was compatible with Catholic teaching, Augustine downplayed a significant difference between the two. For the Platonists, the reason for turning inward is because *the inmost self is God*. [169] Although Augustine developed the concept of the private, inner self to correct this, he still embraced the Platonic idea that God could be found by going within, but into a place that was deeper than our inmost being. Influencing subsequent generations, the notion that self-knowledge is a pathway for discovering God became deeply entrenched in the Western mindset.[170]

Initially adopting this modified Platonic framework, Augustine imported a type of individualistic spirituality into the West earlier in his Christian life that he later rejected. In his version of the soul's journey, the individual believer needed to go inward and climb a seven-step ladder to ascend to God.[171] The pinnacle of the soul's journey was to have a personal, *intellectual vision* of God that was higher than faith. Augustine was not speaking of seeing God face-to-face—he didn't believe this could happen until the afterlife. And he too believed that God was ultimately incomprehensible to our limited, finite minds. Rather, similar to the Platonists, Augustine saw it as a flash of insight like an "aha" moment in which the illuminated soul catches a glimpse of the Divine with the mind's eye that, in turn, floods the individual with delight.[172]

Although Augustine emphasized that the reward for the arduous climb upward was to experience God's love to a greater degree, nevertheless, his emphasis on the mind also injected an intellectual tinge to Western spirituality. This clashed with the apophatic way introduced by Clement and later promoted by Pseudo-Dionysius and others, which teaches that the purified soul needs to go *beyond* the intellect and *beyond* knowing to have a personal encounter with God.

It is fascinating to note that as he matured in the faith, Augustine changed his views and sought to critique and subvert this Platonically inspired approach to spirituality. Nevertheless, as Julie Canlis states, "though he later abandoned this project, it is this seven-step ascent of the early Augustine that was to have the most enduring legacy in the Christian tradition: it was adopted almost wholesale by Bonaventure and quoted even by Calvin. This pattern was to remain an important literary device."[173] Not only did Augustine's mystic scheme have influence through the Middle Ages, it continues to do so even now as people look to literature of the past for spiritual direction, some of which reflects this model.[174] Canlis observes, "One may wonder whether the generations of Western Christians who patterned their theology on the literary motifs of the early Augustine realized the extent to which he later moved away from them."[175]

Apart from his mystic spirituality, Augustine's novel concept of the private, inner self affected the Western world in another way. Phil Cary notes that, "For centuries, Westerners have supposed that the inner space of the soul was just there waiting to be discovered" by a brilliant thinker like Augustine.[176] As this idea took root, Colin Morris observes that Westerners came to think of themselves as "people with frontiers, our personalities divided from each other as our bodies visibly are. Whatever ties of love or loyalty may bind us to other people, we are aware that there is an inner being of our own; that we are individuals."[177]

## Original Sin and the Divided Self

While some his views changed as he matured, Augustine retained critical aspects of Platonic thought that affected his thinking on original sin. This doctrine is one of the pastoral conundrums bequeathed to us by Augustine, as his teaching on this matter has not only been a source of tension among believers in the West, but also between the church in the East and West. Augustine's concept of original sin is based on a nuanced combination of philosophical ideas, scripture, and his own thinking that combined corporate, individualistic, and dualistic elements. Given this mix, we will need to sort through his perspective carefully.

Looking first at Augustine's views on the human person which undergirds his doctrine on sin, let me clearly say that contrary to what is sometimes written about him, he did not think the body was evil. And as we saw, neither did Plato—it was the Gnostics and his old sect, the Manichees who believed this. Augustine agreed with the general consensus that came to be held by most orthodox Christians that since God created the body, it was good.

But this is where his views take a bit of a twist and a turn. Augustine still held to a form of Platonic dualism in that he believed the body was *beneath* or *inferior* to the rational part of the soul. At best, Augustine saw the body as a passive instrument of the soul and at worst, as being a weight or an obstacle.[178] Regarding the soul's relationship to the body, he adopted a hierarchical view in which God was up above shining down inwardly into the person. The first level was the soul, which Augustine saw as being divided into a higher and a lower part and the body was beneath the soul at the lowest level. Like Plato and Origen, Augustine believed the higher, rational part of the soul was responsible for governing both the lower part of the soul and also the body.

In his thinking about the two parts of the soul, Augustine modified a Platonically-inspired model based on an allegorical interpretation of Genesis 1-3 that originated with Philo, Origen, and others. In Augustine's view, Adam represented *higher reason*, which was able to comprehend divine truths; Eve signified *lower reason*, which had the task of collecting information from the sensory world; and Satan symbolized *sensual pleasure*. Following Plato's lead, Augustine continued referring to higher reason (Adam) as the *rational* part of the soul, and the lower part of the soul (Eve) as being *irrational* because it could be disturbed by emotions and desires.[179] Contrary to Plato, Augustine did not think the body was the main source of corruption for the human person; rather, as we'll see, he came to believe that what troubled men and women was something *inside the soul*.[180] In his view, "it is not the bad body which causes the good soul to sin but the bad soul which causes the good body to sin."[181]

Gerard O'Daly cautions that not all of Augustine's thinking on the soul can be attributed to Platonist influences, noting that some ideas came from other philosophical sources.[182] Nevertheless, Daly observes that much of Augustine's thought "has broad affinities with Neoplatonist accounts of conversion and ascent."

As he went deeper into scripture, Augustine's thinking on the soul and the human person evolved. Influenced by the apostle Paul, Augustine developed a more expansive definition of the flesh. Rather than seeing the term as referring primarily to the physical body or even just the lower part of the soul, he came to believe that in scripture, *flesh* also describes the whole of a person's humanity—body and soul—of "man himself . . . the nature of man."[183] In essence, he saw it as describing the human being.

## Lower Reason Takes Control

Augustine came to believe the flesh and pride played a significant role in the primal sin. As he saw it, the first sin came about because Adam began "living according to man" (according to the flesh) instead of living in obedience to God.[184] Listening to the devil, whose downfall was pride, Adam bought into the lie that he could be like God and therefore, looked to himself as the basis for his own existence. In Augustine's view, it's not that the flesh is bad in and of itself—after all, it was created by God—rather it became corrupted because of a turn to self.[185] And as he saw it, *in turning to himself*, Adam created a permanent disorder in the soul that subsequently affected all of humanity.

To explain, in his dualistic thinking about the soul Augustine reasoned that as long as the lower part of the soul explores the external world to gather information for the sake of the common good, that's fine. However, if it is tempted to investigate "for the sake of the individual and selfish pleasure, *concupiscently*," meaning if it is motivated by self-interest, lust, or sexual desire, that's a transgression.[186] As Augustine framed it, the inclination to explore the world for selfish reasons is only a minor sin since it's merely flirting with the forbidden.[187] But if higher reason, which is in contact with divine truth, is enticed to go along with the lower part of the soul and *act* on that temptation then the soul is engaged in the far more serious sin of spiritual adultery.

Kent Hieatt observes this is exactly what Augustine believed happened at the fall. Relying on the allegorical method, as he saw it, the fact that lower reason (Eve) took the serpent's bait and ate the forbidden fruit was a minor offense since it didn't involve higher reason (Adam). However, when Adam went along with Eve the sin was complete—in taking this step, the superior part of the soul "surrendered its governance of lower reason" and became subject to it.[188] In Augustine's opinion, this major and grievous sin had a negative effect on all humankind because after the fall, the right order of the soul was *permanently reversed,* and the lower part of the soul began to rule over reason.[189]

## Going to the Dark Side

This entire line of thinking represented a critical shift in Augustine's perspective. In his earlier years, like many in other parts of the church, he had a more positive view of the human condition—he believed the baptized Christian's soul was free and could gradually overcome sexual lust and other sinful desires as it progressed up the seven-step mystical ladder. However, after observing the ongoing struggles with sexuality and compulsive habits that seemed to bind him and others like a "cruel chain," his thoughts took a more pessimistic turn. He eventually came to agree with the pagans and Christians in his day that some great, mysterious sin seemed to lie behind humanity's misery. Based on this, he concluded that complete freedom from sin, even for the faithful Christian, was not possible in this lifetime.[190]

Furthermore, he began to suspect that sexuality was somehow connected to this terrible sin. His thoughts turned in this direction after observing a troubling dynamic in his own life—while other sins could be controlled, even though he sincerely willed to put away sexual desire his body simply would not comply—it appeared to have a will of its own. In reading the account of the fall in Genesis, Augustine felt like he began to understand why. It seemed to him that before the fall, Adam and Eve's soul and body were in a harmonious union; from this he deduced that sexual desire was submitted to their wills.[191] He noticed, however, that after disobeying God, Adam and Eve were deeply ashamed and in response, covered their genitals with fig leaves.

This was a great revelation for Augustine. To him, it not only showed *why* sexuality continued to be so problematic—sex became impure after the fall—but to Augustine, it also revealed *how* Adam's sin infected all of humanity. As Peter Brown describes it, when Augustine read this part of the creation story he exclaimed "'*Ecce unde.* That's the place! That's the place from which the first sin is passed on'" to the rest of the human race.[192] He came to believe that original sin was transferred through the sex act. From this point, he went on to reason that since sexual activity involves a loss of rational control, it is best indulged in as little as possible, even between married couples.[193]

From the Genesis account, other scriptures, and certain views expressed by the fathers before him, Augustine reached several critical conclusions. First, based on his understanding of Romans 5:12-21, a corporate element grounded his thinking—he saw all of humankind as being in solidarity with Adam. In this text, Paul describes how sin and death entered the world through Adam's disobedience and that because of this one man's actions, "the many"—meaning the rest of humanity—were made sinners. Augustine took this to mean that our first ancestor's sin also became "our own sin" and that all of humankind not only shared in Adam's guilt, but also inherited an innate compulsion to alienate ourselves from God as he did.[194]

Second, he reasoned "the uncontrollable stirring of the genitals was the fitting punishment for the crime of disobedience . . . sexual feeling as men now experience it was a penalty" for sin.[195] And third, Augustine concluded that as an irrevocable consequence of Adam's original sin, "the sexual organs, uniquely, no longer responded to the will, either positively, or negatively;" rather they had come "under the control of *an evil agency.*"[196] This was evidenced by shameful, unwanted imaginations expressed in dreams, embarrassing night emissions, and a continual "pressing throng of desires."[197]

So, what exactly is this evil agency? Based on his interpretation of Paul's letters, Augustine concluded that it was *concupiscentia carnis,* a "permanent flaw in the soul that tilted it irrevocably towards the flesh."[198] And, as we saw earlier, by *flesh* he was not referring to "simply the body; it was all that led the self to prefer its own will to that of God."[199] In fact, as Peter Brown explains

> The *concupiscentia carnis* . . . was such a peculiarly tragic affliction
> to Augustine precisely because it had so little to do with the body. It
> originated in a lasting distortion of the soul itself . . . Concupiscence
> was a dark drive to control, to appropriate, and to turn to one's
> private ends, all the good things that had been created by God to be
> accepted with gratitude and shared with others. It lay at the root of
> the inescapable misery that afflicted mankind. [200]

Although concupiscence was not limited solely to sexual desire, in
Augustine's opinion, of all the appetites this was the only one that
clashed "inevitably and permanently with reason."[201]

Echoing Origen's language, Augustine concluded that as a result of
Adam's original sin, the dark stain of concupiscence "tainted" the souls
of all of humanity. However, unlike Origen, while he taught that
baptism removed original sin and the guilt for concupiscence, he came
to believe the stain could not be removed in anyone—not even baptized
Christians—until death. In his view, while God's grace is able to elevate
human nature, concupiscence permanently remains as "punishment for
Adam's sin" and though it is not sin itself, "it inclines persons to sin."[202]

## Augustine and Romans 7

Augustine's revised understanding of Romans 7:14-25 supported
this perspective. As we saw earlier, this passage portrays the agonizing
dilemma of the Wretched Man who loved the law but couldn't keep it
because he was in bondage to sin. Here is where we see the effect of
mixing corporate and individualistic readings of Romans 5-8. While
Augustine recognized elements of Paul's corporate thinking in Romans
5, like many of the other fathers he read Romans 7 as being about the
individual believer but offered his own novel interpretation of the text.

Initially, Augustine concurred with most of the fathers from the
second century to his day that the Wretched Man was a description of
the *unregenerate* believer, but later changed his mind.[203] For one thing,
he reasoned that it was impossible for anyone who was not yet under
grace to inwardly delight in the law; in his opinion, this meant Romans
7 could not be describing the unregenerate person. Furthermore, the
Wretched Man's conflicted statement— "What I want to do I do not do,
but what I hate I do"—seemed to reflect the tortuous, internal struggle
that he and other baptized Christians continued to experience,
especially in the area of sexuality.

In thinking about it more and in light of other scriptures, Augustine eventually concluded that Paul must have been speaking of himself when he wrote about the Wretched Man. Only rather than describing the unregenerate believer, Augustine decided the Apostle was voicing the "impassioned, tension-filled . . . cry" of the *regenerate individual* "who, despite the reception of grace, still suffers because of the concupiscence of the flesh.""[204] As he came to see it, Paul was using his own experience to represent the timeless, universal, internal, never-ending struggle with indwelling sin that is at the very heart of the believer's life. To him, this reading of Romans 7 confirmed that the tension was not primarily between the body and soul, but *within* the individual believer's divided and conflicted soul.

This helps explain why Romans 7 played such a critical role in Augustine's theology. It tied into his view of the fall, how the taint of concupiscence permanently corrupted the soul, and other pastoral concerns he addressed throughout his lifetime. Thomas Martin notes, "To judge by the sheer volume of writing and research dedicated to the central role of Romans 7 in Augustine's thought and development, its pivotal place is beyond question."[205] Unfortunately, it did not occur to Augustine that to be consistent with Paul's overall line of thought that like chapter 5, Romans 7 was also best read through a corporate lens.

Basing his reasoning about original sin on a corporate view of Romans 5, an individualistic reading of Romans 7, a dualistic view of the soul, other scriptures, and his own experience, Augustine concluded, "human beings are born fundamentally disoriented." Humanity is "harmed in its very constitution. Discord between flesh and spirit becomes our new nature, and our intellectual and physical faculties are weakened."[206] And in a novel twist, he determined this condition not only described unredeemed humanity, *but the redeemed as well.*[207] The main difference between the two groups is that sinful believers can stand before God because they are forgiven, justified, and infused with God's grace (the Catholic view) or credited with Christ's righteousness (the Protestant view). This line of thought became the basis for the idea that all of humanity, including baptized believers, is totally depraved.

## Divides and Departures

In the West, Augustine's views on original sin and the degree to which concupiscence continues to affect Christians is still a subject of debate between Catholics and Protestants, and also between various Protestant groups. Some believe concupiscence remains but is not sinful, while others contend that it is. This last belief, in fact, informed Luther's famous doctrine of *simul justus et peccator*, which describes the Christian as "at the same time justified and sinner."

Regarding the effect of concupiscence on the will, one view is that humanity has been corrupted by sin, but not completely in that some measure of free will remains, which gives men and women the capacity to respond to God. Others teach that "every person born in to the world is morally corrupt, enslaved to sin and is, apart from the grace of God, utterly unable to choose to follow God or choose to turn to Christ in our faith for salvation."[208] Additionally, to this day the church has never agreed on how to interpret Romans 7, which as we have seen, has contributed to conflicting views about the human person and sin's role in the believer's life.

Augustine's position on original sin is also a point of division between the Western and Orthodox Church. Although Augustine defended his thinking as coming from forefathers in the faith—which is partially true—it is also important to realize that some of his ideas were also new at this stage in church history.[209] In fact, in the Orthodox view, Augustine's doctrine of original sin is a departure from the teaching of the ancient church. As they see it, John Cassian, a peer and respected monk in the desert tradition who challenged Augustine's ideas, had a better understanding of the church's historic position.

Cassian was alarmed because he firmly believed that Augustine's teachings on original sin, grace, and predestination were "a dangerous denial of the freedom of the will."[210] While the Desert Fathers agreed the war with sexual temptation was "indeed a conflict 'woven into the very fibers of our being,'" unlike Augustine, they taught that God had implanted sexual desire not as a punishment, but for our benefit.[211] As they saw it, God used it to reveal aspects of our soul that still needed to be addressed in the transformation process. In contrast to Augustine who maintained the soul could not experience freedom from sin in this lifetime, the Old Desert Monks believed that in time and with God's help, these desires could be mastered.[212]

Commenting on these conflicting positions, Peter Brown observes, "It is seldom that two Latin writers, each as gifted in their different ways with such powers of introspection and each capable of such magnetic literary expression as Augustine and John Cassian, have reached such diametrically opposite conclusions as to what precisely they had seen in their own hearts."[213] I am mentioning this because it underscores the danger of basing doctrine on our personal experiences as they can often be interpreted in vastly different ways. When our sacred texts are read through these variable perspectives, it can lead to distortions and divisions.

In the West, Cassian's position was sometimes branded as "semi-Pelagian," a label with negative connotations, and largely overlooked. In the Orthodox view, applying this term to Cassian is unjust. Rather than seeing Augustine and Cassian as being opposed to one another, one theologian contends they were essentially on the same side in that both were arguing against Pelagianism.[214] However, Cassian is lauded in the East for offering a more correct view of the cooperative relationship between grace and free will. As the Orthodox see it, Augustine's fundamental error is that he *overstated* the place of grace in the Christian life and *understated* the place of free will.[215] In one theologian's opinion, Augustine was "forced to this exaggeration by his own experience of conversion, joined to the over-logicalness of his Latin mind which caused him to attempt to define this question too precisely."[216]

## Rethinking Sin

Of course, a number of other issues related to these matters are not covered here. The main point I want to make at the moment is that at this present stage in history, there is good reason to re-evaluate our view of sin in the West. From the second century on, the church fathers have differed about how Adam's sin affected humanity. Contrary to Augustine, not all of them believed that Adam's "sin was inherited by each [person] as an actual sin" or that original sin permanently warped human nature.[217] As others saw it, even though humans were alienated from God and came under Satan's rule because of Adam's disobedience, each person made their own choice to sin, which temporarily tarnished the divine image in humankind. These fathers placed far more emphasis on the idea that "Christ had overcome the *estrangement of humanity from God* caused by sin."[218] And they also believed that once reunited to the Father, it is possible for Christians to progressively overcome sin and become more like God.

As we saw in previous chapters, this emphasis on humankind's separation from God reflects Paul's teaching. From his corporate perspective, the apostle sees that behind humanity's alienation and conflict with our Creator there is a whole universal order of rebellion that began in the spirit world and spread to the human family. Because humans are made in God's image, they are at the center of the battle. In the apostle's framework, all of humanity was caught up in the rebellion when Satan enticed Adam, humanity's representative, to turn away from God and enter into a covenant alliance with him that was binding on subsequent generations.[219] Born under the prince of this world's dark influence, all have sinned, though as Paul points out, not necessarily in the same way as Adam.[220]

Seen in this light, there is no need to teach that humanity has a permanent, inherent sin nature as a result of being exiled from God; or that sin was passed on through the sex act; or that we inherited Adam's actual sin or guilt as each of us is held responsible for our own sin. I want to make it clear that in raising questions about some of Augustine's teachings, I am not minimizing the seriousness of sin or its distressing effects on humanity. To the contrary, the gravity of sin and the urgent need for a savior become even more apparent when realizing that Sin/Satan is holding unredeemed humanity captive in the kingdom of darkness, and that he also seeks to deceive and destroy those who are in Christ if possible.

Various groups are engaged in encouraging efforts to overcome our historic divides in this area but there is still a way to go before Christians reach consensus. What I want to suggest is that if we are to resolve our differences, we first need to read scripture through a common framework. And I believe the starting place for this is to view it consistently through a corporate lens with the holistic, Hebraic view of the human person and Christ's body in mind. Retrieving this larger context can help us gain a greater understanding of the biblical concept of corporate solidarity and how the individual relates to the whole, both of which are important for seeing God's view of sin. It will also allow us to detect how individualistic and dualistic assumptions that are foreign to scripture have shaped our thinking.

Additionally, the Western view of sin is often set within the forensic framework of a criminal law court, when in scripture it is primarily viewed within God's covenantal relationship with humankind and more specifically, with his people. Recovering this relational framework is a vital part of rethinking our view of sin in the West.

Once this contextual groundwork has been laid, our next step would be to revisit Augustine's scriptural rationale and those used by others who teach variations of his doctrine. Also, it is important to consider the biblical reasons why Christians sin after they come to saving faith so that we can put our personal experiences into proper perspective.

## Moving Forward

I can only say these examples of how developments beginning in the second century began to blur the biblical storyline and key texts are far more complex and nuanced than what I have been able to show here. Nevertheless, this can serve as a useful introduction to some of the issues that will need to be discussed if we are to recover a clear view of the biblical storyline and overcome old divisions.

# Endnotes

### Introduction Endnotes – Shifting Lens

[1] Thomas Friedman, *The World is Flat: A Brief History of the Twenty-First Century* (New York: Farrar, Straus and Giroux, 2007), 8.

[2] Timothy Keller, *The Reason for God: Belief in an Age of Skepticism* (New York: Penguin, 2008), x.

[3] Unless otherwise specified, the West is defined as Western Europe, U.S., and Canada.

[4] Stephen Prothero, Professor of Religion at Boston University in *USA Today*, March 2008.

[5] For examples, see: Caroline Wyatt, "Is the UK still a Christian Country," *BBC News*. [May 25, 2015], http://www.bbc.com/news /uk-32722155; David Kinnaman and Gabe Lyons, *UnChristian: What a New Generation Really Thinks about Christianity . . .and Why it Matters* (Grand Rapids: Baker, 2007); Phyllis Tickle, *The Great Emergence,* (Grand Rapids: Baker Books, 2008); Soong-Chan Rah, *The Next Evangelicalism: Freeing the Church from Western Cultural Captivity* (Downers Grove: InterVarsity Press, 2009).

[6] Deepak Chopra, *The Third Jesus: The Christ We Cannot Ignore* (New York: Three Rivers Press, 2008), 7.

[7] Collin Hansen "Why Johnny Can't Read the Bible," *Christianity Today*. [May 24, 2010], http://www.christianitytoday.com/ct/2010 /may/25.38.html.

[8] Stephen E. Fowl, *Theological Interpretation of Scripture* (Eugene: Cascade, 2009), x.

[9] Barna Group, "The State of the Bible: 6 trends for 2014," *Barna*. [April 8, 2014], https://www.barna.org/barna-update/culture/664-the-state-of-the-bible-6-trends-for-2014#.V20PXlcywkI; Alex Murashko, "State of the Bible Survey: Bible Skeptics on the Rise," *Christian Post.* [April 10, 2014], http://www.christianpost.com/news /state-of-the-bible-survey-bible-skeptics-on-the-rise-117696/.

[10] Andy Crouch, *Culture Making* (Downers Grove: InterVarsity, 2008),189.

[11] E. Randolph Richards and Brandon J. O'Brien, *Misreading Scripture with Western Eyes: Removing Cultural Blinders to Better Understand the Bible* (Downers Grove: IVP Books, 2012), 11.

[12] Richards and O'Brien, *Misreading Scripture*, 11.

[13] Jorn K. Bramann, "Descartes: The Solitary Self," *The Educating Rita Workbook* (Nightsun Books, 2004), http://faculty.frostburg.edu /phil/forum/Descartes.htm.

[14] For a history of how the phrase "know thyself" evolved, see Eliza Gregory Wilkins, *"'Know Thyself' in Greek and Latin Literature* (George Banta Publishing Company, 1917; Digitized 2008), Google Book Search. Evidence of

the cultural influence of this maxim can be seen in Pope John Paul II's address, *Fides Et Ratio Encyclical Letter* (Libreria Editrice Vaticana, September 14, 1998), http://w2.vatican.va/content/john-paul-ii/en/encyclicals/documents/hf_jp-ii_enc_14091998_fides-et-ratio.html.

[15] Colin Morris, *The Discovery of the Individual 1050-1200* (Toronto: University of Toronto Press, 2000), 64-70.

[16] Jean M. Twenge, *Generation Me* (New York: Free Press,2006); Jean M. Twenge and W. Keith Campbell, *The Narcissism Epidemic: Living in the Age of Entitlement* (New York: Free Press, 2009).

[17] James K.A. Smith, *Who's Afraid of Postmodernism?* (Grand Rapids: Baker Academic, 2006), 29.

[18] Soong-Chan Rah, "New Realities in World Christianity" *The Regent World* [September 9, 2013], (italics added), http://world.regent-college.edu/leading-ideas/soong-chan-rah.

[19] I Pet. 2: 9,10.

[20] John D. Zizioulas, "The Early Christian Community" in *Christian Spirituality: Origins to the Twelfth Century* eds., Bernard McGinn, John Meyendorff, in collaboration with Jean Leclercq (New York: Crossroad, 1985), 28 (italics added).

[21] Zizioulas, "The Early Christian Community," 27 (italics added).

[22] For examples of how this has shaped Christian teaching see Kris Lundgaard, *The Enemy Within* (Phillipsburg: P & R, 1998) and Larry Crabb, *Becoming a True Spiritual Community* (Nashville: Thomas Nelson, 1999), 95-103.

[23] Kinnaman, *UnChristian*, 48-52.

[24] Christian Smith with Patricia Snell, *Souls in Transition* (New York: Oxford Press, 2009), 290.

[25] Note: while Anglicanism is sometimes referred to as Protestant, others see it in a unique category in that it combines elements of both Catholicism and Protestantism, http://anglicancleric.blogspot.com/2013/01/anglicanism-protestant-or-catholic.html.

[26] Smith, Souls in Transition, 49.

[27] "Biblical theology," *Theopedia.com,* http://www.theopedia.com/biblical-theology.

[28] Exodus 3:14.

## Chapter 1 Endnotes – Cleaning Up the Canvas

[1] See Richards and O'Brien, *Misreading Scripture.*

[2] For example, Marcion, a leader in the second century rejected the Old Testament and most of the New, except for Luke's Gospel (minus the first two chapters because they were too "Jewish") and Paul's letters (minus the pastoral epistles). In his view, Jesus could not be a true man with a material body as this would compromise his divinity. Marcion went on to form his own church that during the second half of the second century "was a noteworthy rival to orthodox Christianity" in certain areas. See Jaroslav Pelikan, *The Christian*

*Tradition, Vol 1: A History of the Development of Doctrine—The Emergence of the Catholic Tradition (100-600),* (Chicago: University of Chicago Press, 1971), 68-81.

[3] For instance, see Craig A. Evans, *Fabricating Jesus: How Modern Scholars Distort the Gospels* (Downers Grove: InterVarsity, 2006); Christopher Hall, *Reading Scripture with the Church Fathers* (Downers Grove, IL: InterVarsity, 1998); Gordon D. Fee and Douglas Stuart, *How to Read the Bible for All It's Worth: A Guide to Understanding the Bible* (Grand Rapids, MI: Zondervan, 1982).

[4] To lend credibility to what I am saying, in a review of an earlier book I wrote, *Contours of Pauline Theology* (Fearn, Scotland: Christian Focus, 2004), Prof. Anthony Thiselton, a world-renowned scholar in the area of hermeneutics wrote: "It provides a fresh and useful treatment of Pauline theology, and many of its arguments offer corrections to widespread misunderstandings of Paul." *Expository Times,* Vol 116:12, 425.

[5] See Quentin Skinner, "Meaning and Understanding in the History of Ideas" *History and Theory* 8:1, (1969): 7, 43.

[6] Holland, *Contours,* 51-54.

[7] E.P. Sanders, *Jesus and Judaism* (London: SCM, 1985), 19. A literature review of material published in the last 100 years or so on the historical Jesus is contained in James H. Charlesworth, *The Historical Jesus* (Nashville: Abingdon, 2008), 6-12.

[8] Mark Nanos, *The Mystery of Romans* (Minneapolis: Fortress Press, 1997), 7.

[9] Acts 17:16-34.

[10] Luke 24:13-35, 44; Acts 1:3.

[11] Rom. 2: 28, 29; Eph. 2:11-18; Phil. 3:3.

[12] Acts 13:43-53.

[13] J. Neusner, W.S. Green and E.S. Frerichs, eds., *Judaisms and Their Messiahs at the Turn of the Christian Era* (Cambridge: Cambridge University Press, 1990) in Holland, *Contours,* 61.

[14] For a helpful survey of the various scholarly positions, see Jarvis J. Williams, *Maccabean Martyr Traditions in Paul's Theology of Atonement: Did Martyr Theology Shape Paul's Conception of Jesus's Death?* (Eugene: Wipf & Stock, 2010), 3-26.

[15] N.T. Wright, *Jesus and the Victory of God* (London: SPCK, 1996), 576-611.

[16] Jarvis, *Maccabean Martyr Traditions,* 2.

[17] Tom Holland, *Tom Wright and the Search for Truth: A Theological Evaluation* (London: Apiary Publishing Ltd., 2017), 201-242.

[18] Rom. 3:21f; 1 Cor. 15:3.

[19] Evans, *Fabricating Jesus;* Bruce M. Metzger, *The Text of the New Testament* (New York and Oxford: Oxford University Press, 1968); Daniel Wallace, "The Majority Text and the Original Text: Are They Identical?" *Bibliotheca Sacra,* April-June 1991; N.T Wright, "Christian Origins and the Question of God," *Jesus and the Victory of God* (London: SPCK, 1996), 28-78.

[20] Alister E. McGrath, *The Science of God* (Grand Rapids: Eerdmans, 2004), 3-4.

[21] John 5:37-40, 7:37-47.

[22] Matt. 7: 15-23; 24: 4, 5, 11, 24.

[23] 2 Pet. 3:16.

[24] 1 Tim. 4:16; 2 Tim. 3:14-15, 4:1-5. See Matt. 7:15, 16:6; Acts 8:9-24; 2 Cor. 11:13-15; Gal. 3:1-5; Col. 2:18-23; 2 Pet. 2; 1 John 4:1-6; Rev. 2:20-22.

[25] Eph. 2:20-22.

[26] Gal.1:8. According to Paul, he did not receive the gospel from any man, but it was a revelation from Jesus Christ. Note that later, however, when he "set his message" before the leaders of the Jerusalem church, James, Peter and John approved of Paul's work among the Gentiles and extended the right hand of fellowship to him. See Gal. 1 – 2:10.

[27] For instance, one of the reasons Gnostic teaching was regarded as heretical is because many forms taught that Jesus did not come in the flesh. This standard is set forth in I John 4:1-3.

[28] Acts 17: 11.

[29] F.E. Stallan, *Things Written Afore Time* (Kilmarnock, Scotland: John Ritchie Ltd.) x; see also Evans, *Fabricating Jesus,* 39.

[30] Luke 24:27.

[31] Luke 9:31.

[32] Holland, *Contours*, 31-33.

[33] 1 Cor. 1:23.

[34] Luke 4:21.

[35] Holland, *Contours*, FN 25, 48.

[36] For example, Bultmann's reliance on Gnostic documents as an interpretive tool was misplaced trust. Although he contended Christians borrowed from Gnosticism, it was the other way around—scholars demonstrated Gnosticism had borrowed from Christians. See Holland, *Contours*, 52. See also "Excursus: Scholarly Opinion Concerning Paul's use of the Scriptures." Holland, *Contours*, 44-49.

### Chapter 2 Endnotes – Gaps and Gaffes

[1] In fact, so many new terms are in play today that a new online help called the Urban Dictionary has been created to define terms that are not found in the standard lexicons. So far, there are millions of entries and two thousand new words are submitted for entry consideration every day! *Urban Dictionary,* http://www.
urbandictionary.com/.

[2] Martin Hengel, *Judaism and Hellenism: Studies in Their Encounter in Palestine during the Early Hellenistic Period,* 1st English ed. (London: SCM Press, 1974), passim.

[3] Troels Engberg-Pedersen, ed. *Paul Beyond the Judaism/Hellenism Divide* (Louisville, KY: Westminster John Knox Press, 2001), 3.

4 This same scholar has now been appointed to one of the world's leading theological departments in one of the top universities in the world. Thankfully, at the time of this incident, almost every scholar present in the seminar rose to defend the position presented above and urged him to rethink his claim.

5 For an example, see John K. Goodrich, *Paul as an Administrator of God in First Corinthians* (Cambridge: Cambridge University Press, 2012). Interpreting Paul's description of apostles in I Cor. 4 and 9 as divinely appointed administrators (*oikonomoi*) against a Hellenistic background, Goodrich claims Paul defined his apostolic role in light of ancient regal, municipal, and private administration. Goodrich ultimately situates the image in the private commercial context of Roman Corinth. Nothing is said about Paul seeing himself as standing in the long line of the Hebrew prophets and servants of old, a perspective that permeates his writings (see Rom. 15:14-22; 2 Cor. 2:1-4:18). To questions if Paul could be drawing from both backgrounds and what difference does it make, by putting Paul in a Hellenistic context, all of the Old Testament relational imagery of what it means to be in a covenant relationship with God and to be his servant is obscured in exchange for an impersonal, business-like model that simply does not do justice to Paul's mindset.

6 Diogenes Allen and Eric O. Springsted, *Philosophy for Understanding Theology*, 2nd ed. (Louisville: Westminster John Knox Press, 2007), xv.

7 Allen, *Philosophy for Understanding Theology*, xviii.

8 Allen, *Philosophy for Understanding Theology*, xvii (italics original).

9 John D. Caputo, *Philosophy and Theology* (Nashville: Abingdon Press, 2006).

10 See Etienne Gilson's view of why the God of Plato and Plotinus cannot be the Christian God in *God and Philosophy*, 2nd edition (New Haven: Yale University Press, 2002), 25-59.

11 Quoted in Pinchas E. Lapide, *Hebrew in the Church* (Grand Rapids: William B. Eerdmans, 1984), 202.

12 James Barr, *The Semantics of Biblical Language* (London: SCM-Canterbury Press, 1983), 108.

13 John MacArthur, *Slave: The Hidden Truth About Your Identity in Christ* (Nashville: Thomas Nelson), 15.

14 MacArthur, *Slave*, 16, 17.

15 MacArthur, *Slave*, 22. What is important to note is that 1 Cor. 6:20, the verse this statement is based on is at the end of a discussion which began in 1 Cor. 5:7 where Paul said that Christ our Passover has been sacrificed for us. The Jews saw the Passover as the time Yahweh married Israel; she became his bride. I have shown elsewhere (see Holland, *Contours*, 111-139) how this theme runs through chapters 6 and 7 until we come to the statement "you were bought at a price." This is not referring to the individual nor is it about slavery. It is about the church who has been bought as the bride by the death of Christ, as is seen in Eph. 5:25ff. It follows the theme of OT redemptive history perfectly. This is far more glorious than being a slave!

16 Isa. 53:11.

[17] Isa. 41:8-9.

[18] N.W. Porteous, "The Theology of the Old Testament" in *Peake's Commentary on the Bible* (Glasgow: Routledge, 1962), 151-159 (italics added).

[19] R. De Vaux, *Ancient Israel, It's Life and Institutions* (London: Darton, Longman & Todd, 1990), 80, as quoted in Holland, *Contours*, 71.

[20] Exod. 33:11; Isa. 41:8; Jer. 3:4.

[21] There are a few examples of slaves who were so gifted in a particular skill their owner entered into an agreement that if they took on a business and made their master an agreed amount of money, they would receive their freedom. But such cases were far from typical and Paul makes no suggestion that he has this in mind. In fact, it would be so untypical that Paul's readers would hardly think to relate this to his use of *doulos*.

[22] Rom. 6:16.

[23] Deut. 15:16-17.

[24] Isa. 11:1-2, 42:1; Matt. 3:16-17 and Exod. 4:22; Isa. 44:3-5, 49:3-6, 63:14.

[25] Holland, *Contours*, 75-67.

[26] I Cor.15:22.

[27] Isa. 65:17.

[28] Isa. 49:8; 52:11.

[29] 2 Cor. 6:1-2 cites Isa. 49:8 and 2 Cor. 6:17-18 cites Isa. 52:11.

[30] Acts 14:22.

[31] See I and II Peter.

[32] Col. 1:24-27; 2 Tim. 1:8-10.

[33] Acts 9:5.

[34] I Cor. 12:25-26.

[35] Isa. 40:1-10; 54:11-14.

[36] Rom. 8:17-18.

[37] John Goodrich, "From Slaves of Sin to Slaves of God: Reconsidering the Origin of Paul's Slavery Metaphor in Romans 6," *Bulletin for Biblical Research* 23.4 (2013), 509-30, protests that *doulos* has to mean slave in Romans 6 when speaking of the status of believers because that is what the Romans were familiar with. (I have acknowledged it means slave when speaking of the Christian's *pre-conversion status*.) Based on such reasoning, Goodrich also holds that the Romans could only think that when Paul referred to *flesh (sarx)*, it had to be a reference to the physical body because that is what they were used to from their own culture. I am sure he would not want to say this, especially in light of his fine article "Sold Under Sin: Echoes of Exile in Romans 7:14-25," *New Testament Studies* 59.4 (2013), 476-95, in which he teases out the OT exile motif in Romans 7. It would have been impossible for the Romans to follow the argument Goodrich claims Paul is making if they had not been taught OT theology. It is that same theology that helped them choose the correct contextually controlled meaning of *doulos*. Goodrich is an example of a scholar who is caught between two theological worldviews and seeks to be faithful to

both. In response to Goodrich's skepticism, consider Anthony Thiselton, *Hermeneutics of Doctrine* (Grand Rapids: Eerdmans, 2007) 1st edition, 480.

### Chapter 3 Endnotes – Our Family Story

[1] Bruce Falconer, "Ancestry.com's Genealogical Juggernaut," *Bloomberg.com,* [Sept. 20, 2012], http://www.bloomberg.com/news /articles/2012-09-20/ancestry-dot-coms-genealogical-juggernaut.

[2] "Why Genealogy is Important," *GeneologyInTime Magazine,* http://www.genealogyintime.com/GenealogyResources/Articles/why_genealo gy_is_important_page1.html.

[3] Gen. 12, 15, 17.

[4] Rom. 9:1-9.

[5] Rabbi Irving Greenburg, "The Exodus Effect," *MyJewishLearning. com,* http://www.myjewishlearning.com/holidays/Jewish_Holidays /Passover/Themes_and_Theology/Meaning_of_Exodus.shtml. For its importance to the Christian faith, see Marvin R. Wilson, *Our Father Abraham: Jewish Roots of the Christian Faith* (Grand Rapids: Eerdmans, 1989), 237-255.

[6] Florenc Mene, an Albanian PhD student offered this valuable comment on the above text: "Isaiah's vision of Israel's future restoration, after its coming exile, is described in the language of a New Exodus. However, ESV translators seem to have (unintentionally) obfuscated the second part of this vision: canopy in Hebrew is חֻפָּה. (huppah), bridal chamber, or the canopy that the Jews to this day put over the soon-to-be-married couple at their wedding ceremony." I am thankful to Florenc for this valuable observation and would add that what adds to this marvelous observation is that it is not only Israel who is welcome to this event and who will know God in this unique marital way, but the nations are welcome, if they repent, to be part of the new Bridal community. As we shall see this statement, at the very start of the proclamation of the prophet, is that the nations will also know God. This is at the heart of the prophet's message and becomes the heart of the gospel message proclaimed by the apostles.

[7] For examples see Holland, *Contours,* 22-26.

[8] Exod. 50:1, Jer. 6:8.

[9] Holland, *Contours,* 27.

[10] Mark 4:12; for the outworking of this hardness see Mark 4:13-20.

[11] Isaiah 6:9-10 cf. 7:10-17.

[12] Mark 1:1-3 is the prologue, telling us what the gospel of Jesus is about— it is the fulfillment of what Isaiah said about the coming New Exodus. Throughout the gospel the miracles bear witness that Jesus is the Servant who had been promised to achieve the New Exodus. This is exemplified in the healings in Mark 5:19, 5:21-42, and feeding in the desert (Mk. 5:34-44). Jesus himself claims to be the son of David, whom Isaiah said would achieve the New Exodus (Mk. 12:35-37). Jesus would die as the Suffering Servant (Mk. 8:31; 10:32-34). He cleansed the temple in fulfillment of Malachi 3:1, bringing judgment on unbelieving Israel. He is anointed as the true king who is about to be rejected and put to death as the suffering servant (Mk. 14:1-9). Jesus

restructures the Passover, giving it a new meaning that centers on his death and what it would achieve (Mk. 14:22-26).

[13] Matt. 3:3, Mark 1:3, Luke 3:4, John 1:23.

[14] Luke 7: 22, 23.

[15] Matt. 3:17 (NASB), Mark 1:11, Luke 3:22.

[16] Isa. 42:1ff.

[17] Luke 9:31.

[18] Holland, *Contours*, 28.

[19] See Acts 26:17-18; Gal. 1:3, 4; Col. 1:12-14; and Rev. 1:5-6. Also, Luke 1 and 2 reflect the expectations of a group of devout Jews at the time of the birth of Jesus. These men were aware of the same traditions regarding a new Exodus that are reflected in the Damascus Document found in the caves at Qumran. Holland, *Contours*, 27. For more, see Daniel Lynwood Smith, "The Uses of 'New Exodus' in New Testament Scholarship: Preparing a Way through the Wilderness." *Currents in Biblical Research* 2016, Vol. 14 (2), 207-243.

[20] John 18:33-39.

[21] John 18:36.

[22] Ezek. 45:25.

[23] Acts. 15:15-17.

[24] For a methodology for doing this, see Holland, *Contours*, 34, 35.

[25] Rom. 3:21ff; 8:1-4; 9:30-33; 11:25-27; 1 Cor. 10:1-13.

[26] Rom. 9:6-8.

[27] Rom. 11.

[28] Acts 15:1-2; 21:17-26.

[29] Rom. 10:9-15.

## Chapter 4 Endnotes – Salvation Incorporated

[1] Toby Tyrell, *On Gaia: A Critical Investigation of the Relationship between Life and Earth* (Princeton: Princeton University Press, 2013) 209.

[2] Martin Luther King, Jr., "Letter from Birmingham Jail," *The Martin Luther King, Jr. Research and Education Institute*, [April 16, 1963], http://mlkkpp01.stanford.edu/index.php/resources/article/annotated_letter_from_birmingham/.

[3] See 1 Cor. 12–14.

[4] 1 Cor. 12:13.

[5] Rom. 6:4.

[6] In the 2011 NIV, the language was changed from "the body of sin" to "so that the body *ruled by* sin might be done away with . . ."

[7] Rom. 7:21-24. In the 2011 version of the NIV, the language was changed from "this body of death" to "this body that is subject to death."

[8] In support of the view that Paul is referring to himself as a regenerate Christian, see J.I. Packer, *Keep in Step with the Spirit,* (Grand Rapids: Revell, 1984), 263-270. For other views, see Robert L. Reymond, "Whom does the Man

in Romans 7:14-25 Represent?" from A *New Systematic Theology of the Christian Faith*, Rev. 2nd ed. (Nashville, Thomas Nelson, Inc., 1998), 1127-1132, http://kevincraig.info /romans7.pdf.

9 Gerald Bray, ed. *The Ancient Christian Commentary: New Testament Vol. VI – Romans* (Downers Grove: InterVarsity, 1998), 189; Martyn Lloyd Jones, *Romans: Exposition of Chapter 7:1–8:4* (Edinburgh: Banner of Truth Trust, 1973), 177-178.

10 Tom Holland, *Romans: The Divine Marriage* (Eugene: Pickwick, 2011), 230.

11 Holland, *Contours,* 89–96.

12 Semitic is defined as "a member of any of a number of peoples of ancient southwestern Asia including the Akkadians, Phoenicians, Hebrews, and Arabs." *Merriam-Webster.com,* http://www.merriam-webster.com.

13 H. H. Rowley, *The Faith of Israel: Aspects of Old Testament Thought, Sprunt Lectures* (London: SCM Press, 1956), 118 in Holland, Romans, 233.

14 Wilson, *Our Father Abraham*, 187.

15 Jer. 10:19-22.

16 Holland, *Romans*, 232-233.

17 For other examples where a personal pronoun is used in reference to the nation, see Ps. 44:4-8; Mic. 7:6-10; and Lam 1:9-22; 2:20-22. It is worth noting the confessions in Ezra 9:7 and Neh. 9:2, 34, where the two reformers prayed and confessed as representatives of the nations.

18 F.F. Bruce, *The Epistle of Paul to the Romans: An Introduction and Commentary* (Carol Stream: Tyndale, 1971), 38.

19 T. W. Manson, "Romans" in *Peake's Commentary on the Bible* (Routledge Company Ltd., 1962), 945, (italics added).

20 For more on the various definitions of *flesh* and role it plays in Paul's theology, see Holland, "Excursus F: Sin in the Theology of Paul" in *Romans,* 203-225.

21 Ezek. 36:26.

22 Rom. 8:3 "For God has done what the law, weakened by the flesh, could not do. By sending his own Son in the likeness of sinful flesh and for sin, he condemned sin in the flesh." (ESV) Flesh in this context is described as sinful, whereas in Gal. 2:20 it is a neutral term and in Ezekiel 36:26 flesh is used in a positive sense.

23 A 2011 NIV footnote to Rom. 7:5 regarding "realm of the flesh" states, "in contexts like this, the Greek word for flesh (sarx) refers to the sinful state of human beings, often presented as a power in opposition to the Spirit." For insights into the dilemmas translators face regarding the term "flesh" see Douglas J. Moo, "'Flesh' in Romans: A Challenge for the Translator" as contained in Glen G. Scorgie, Mark L. Strauss, and Steven M. Voth, eds., *The Challenge of Bible Translation: Communicating God's Word to the World.* (Grand Rapids: Zondervan, 2003), 365-379.

[24] Rom. 7:14. Bible translations differ in the use of *sarx* (flesh) when describing the Wretched Man's current state in verse 14, with some translating the word as carnal or unspiritual, and others more literally as of the flesh or fleshly.

[25] I Cor. 2: 1-16.

[26] Martyn Lloyd Jones, *Romans 7*, 240-242.

[27] For a list of various views on Romans 7, see "Romans 7:21-25 Commentary," http://preceptaustin.org/romans_721-25.htm.

[28] Charles Spurgeon, "Indwelling Sin," *The Spurgeon Archive,* (sermon: New Park Street Pulpit, London, UK, June 1, 1856), (italics added), http://www.spurgeon.org/sermons/0083.php.

[29] Dwight Edwards, *Revolution Within: A Fresh Look at Supernatural Living* (Colorado Springs: WaterBrook, 2008), 111. See also A.W. Pink, *A.W. Pink's Studies in the Scriptures 1936-1937*, Vol. 8 (Lafayette: Sovereign Grace Publishers, 2003), 146.

[30] Tim Keller, "The War Between Your Selves: Part I," sermon: Redeemer Presbyterian Church, (New York: August 17, 1997), http://www.gospelinlife.com/war-between-your-selves-part-41.

[31] John McArthur, "Dealing with Habitual Sins," *Grace to You,* 1993, http://www.gty.org/products/audio-lessons/80-106/Dealing-with-Habitual-Sins (italics added). See also commentary on Romans 6 and 7 in *The MacArthur Study Bible, New International Version* (Grand Rapids: Zondervan), 1695–1699.

[32] Kelly Kapic, "Simul Justus Et Peccator." *Ligonier Ministries,* http://www.ligonier.org/learn/articles/simul-iustus-et-peccator/

[33] Tim Challies, *The Discipline of Spiritual Discernment* (Wheaton: Crossways, 2007), 40-41

[34] Kevin DeYoung and Ted Kluck, *Why We Love the Church* (Chicago: Moody, 2009), 208-211.

[35] Larry Crabb, *Becoming a True Spiritual Community: A Profound Vision of What the Church Can Be* (Nashville: Thomas Nelson, 1999).

[36] Exod. 35:21; Deut. 4:9, 29, 6:5, 11:3, 30:6; 1 Kgs. 8:18, 2 Kgs. 22:19, Ps. 57:7; Luke 6:45. See excursus, "The Heart" in Holland, *Divine Marriage*, 220-223.

[37] John Piper, "War Within: Flesh vs. Spirit," *Desiring God,* (sermon: June 19,1983), http://www.desiringgod.org/sermons/the-war-within-flesh-vs-spirit.

[38] I Tim. 1:15; I Cor. 9:24-27; I John 1:18.

[39] I Cor. 4:3,4 (NKJ); The NIV translation says: "My conscience is clear, but that does not make me innocent. It is the Lord who judges me."

[40] Rom. 15:14 (NASB).

[41] I Tim. 1:13.

[42] 1 Cor. 6:11; Eph. 5:25-27; Rom. 6:6, 22; Gal. 5:1; Rom. 8:15-17; Eph. 1–2; Col 1:3-23; Col. 3; Eph. 4–5.

[43] 2 Cor. 6:14-16.

[44] 1 Peter 1:16.

[45] James 1:5-8.

[46] Bob Deffinbaugh, "The Necessity of Sanctification (Romans 6)," *Bible.org*, http://bible.org/seriespage/necessity-sanctification-romans-6.

[47] Let me just say here that most of the passages about perfection are spoken to the community, not the individual. I won't go into detail now, but when viewed within a corporate context, perfection has to do with how we love others.

[48] Wilson, *Father Abraham*, 168.

[49] The 2011 NIV uses the term "new humanity" instead of "new man."

[50] Eph. 4:22-24 NIV, ESV, NASB, HCSB.

[51] I Cor. 10:1-4.

[52] I Cor. 5:7.

[53] I Cor. 15:45 – 49.

[54] Gen. 3:1-5; Luke 22:31; Jn. 8:44; 2 Cor. 11:3, 14; 2 Tim. 2:26; I Pet. 5:8; I Jn. 3:8; Rev. 12:9.

### Chapter 5 Endnotes – A Deadly Marriage

[1] Exod. 32:1,4, 8; Ezek. 16:26-58; Hos. 4:15-5:7.

[2] Isa. 50:1-8.

[3] Isa. 49:20-21, 62:4-5; Jer. 31:31-34; Ezek. 36:24-36; Hos. 2:14-23.

[4] Matt. 22:1-4, 25:1-13; Luke 14:15-24; John 3:27-30.

[5] Rev. 19:7-9.

[6] 2 Cor. 11:2; Eph. 5:25-33.

[7] Hos. 6:7, 10.

[8] See Holland, *Contours*, 102, 103.

[9] Hos. 2:14-20; Jer. 2:1-13; Ezek. 16:1-22.

[10] Exod. 23:32. See also Exod. 20:5, 34:14; Deut. 4:23-24, 5:7; Psalm 78:58.

[11] Deut. 32:21.

[12] Jer. 3:8-10, 20; Ezek.16.

[13] Prov. 6:32-35.

[14] Gen. 3:1-5; Luke 22:31; Jn. 8:44; 2 Cor. 11:3, 14; 2 Tim. 2:26; 1 Pet. 5:8; I Jn. 3:8; Rev. 12:9.

[15] Rom. 5:12.

[16] Rom. 6:14.

[17] Wright, N. T. "New Exodus, New Inheritance. The Narrative Structure of Romans 3-8," *Romans and the People of God, Essays in Honor of Gordon D. Fee on the Occasion of his 65th Birthday,* ed. Sven K. Soderlund and N.T. Wright (Grand Rapids: Eerdmans, 1997) 39.

[18] John 5:19; Eph. 2:2 (NASB).

[19] Eph. 2:2; 2 Cor. 4:4. For other scriptures that describe Satan's role, see John 12:31, 14:30, 16:11; Acts 26:18; 2 Cor. 4:4; Eph. 2:2; 6:11-16; Heb. 2:14.

[20] Heb. 2:14.

[21] Although we do not know for sure why Paul preferred to use Sin to denote Satan in Romans 5-8, it may be because the Jews avoided using Satan's name as much as possible lest it contaminate them. When they did have to use his name, they would spit afterwards in an attempt to clean their mouths of the perceived defilement.

[22] Matt 21:42; Mark 12:10; Luke 20:17; Acts 4:11; Rom. 9:32-33; I Peter 2:4-6.

[23] Isa. 28: 15, 18.

[24] For synonyms of Satan, see R.P Martin, *Colossians: The Church's Lord and the Christian's Liberty* (London: Paternoster, 1972) 51; James D.G. Dunn, *Romans* (Word, 1988)1:360; G.H.C. MacGregor, "Principalities and Powers: The Cosmic Background of Paul's Thought," *New Testament Studies,* Vol. 1 (1954-55):17-28; W. Sanday and A. Headlam, *A Critical and Exegetical Commentary on the Epistle to the Romans* (London: T & T Clark, 1902), 169.

[25] For more on the covenant with death, see Holland, *Contours,* 100-103.

[26] See Col. 2:11 for use of the body of flesh, and Rom. 7:24 for the body of death. For further discussion see H. Ridderbos, *Paul: An Outline of His Theology* (Grand Rapids: Eerdmans, 1975) 229f. See also FN 34 in Holland, *Divine Marriage,* 189.

[27] Read the full story in the Old Testament book of Ruth.

[28] See Gal. 4:5; Tit. 2:14.

[29] Gen. 1:27-28; 2:21-25.

[30] Rom. 7:22-23.

[31] Matt. 22:37-40.

[32] See Prov. 3.

[33] Gal. 3:25 (NIV 2011). The 1984 version says, "So the law was put in charge to lead us to Christ."

[34] Isa. 51:4 (ESV).

[35] For the blessings and cursings, see Deut. 28.

[36] Rabbi Boruch Clinton, "What Does the Word Torah Refer To?" *Torah.org,* http://torah.org.il/learning/basics/primer/torah/torah .html.

[37] "The Bereshith or Genesis Rabba," *Internet Sacred Text Archive,* http://www.sacred-texts.com/jud/mhl/mhl05.htm.

[38] Gal. 6:7; Matt. 7:2; 26:52.

[39] Rom. 1:20.

[40] Isa. 29:13.

[41] Matt. 15:1-9.

[42] Matt. 23:4.

[43] Matt. 12:1-13; Mark 3:1-5; Luke 6:1-10; John 9:14-16. 5:16-18.

[44] Matt. 23:13-14.

[45] John 8:42-46.

[46] Rom. 5:20.

[47] Col. 2:16-17.

[48] See the Sermon on the Mount, Matt. 5-7. Christians are also instructed to submit to the governing authorities established by God (Rom. 13: 1-6).

[49] I Cor. 15:56.

[50] I John 1:8-9.

[51] Rom. 6:1.

[52] Phil. 3:3-6; Gal. 1:14.

[53] Holland, *Divine Marriage*, 230.

[54] Rom. 7:9.

[55] Rom. 5:14.

[56] Rom. 5:20.

[57] Exod. 20:17.

[58] In *The Divine Marriage,* my commentary on Romans, I originally embraced view four, that the Wretched Man in Romans 7 represented unredeemed humanity in Adam. However, upon further reflection and study, I became convinced of the fifth view that I am presenting in this chapter.

[59] 2 Kings 19:30-31; Isa. 10:20-23, 28:5, 37:32,46:3; Joel 2:32; Micah 2:12; John 10: 14,16; Rom. 11:4-5.

[60] Heb. 11:10,16.

[61] Romans 2:14-15.

[62] 2 Cor. 11:15; John 8:44.

[63] James 1:13-15.

[64] John 4:24; 1 Cor. 2:14.

[65] Rom. 7:17.

[66] Tatha Wiley, Original Sin: Origins, Developments, Contemporary Meanings (New York: Paulist Press, 2002), 93.

[67] Rom. 7:17-18.

[68] Gal. 5:19-21.

[69] Eph. 6:10-12.

[70] Rom. 3:9; 5:19; 11:32; Gal. 3:22-23.

[71] Rom. 8:2 (NASB).

[72] Eph. 4:8.

[73] Ezek. 20 shows that Israel as well as the Egyptians were under condemnation for looking to Egypt's gods for protection before Passover took place. See Exod. 1:16 for how Pharaoh intended to crush Israel.

[74] Exod. 12:23-24.

[75] Rom. 3:21-26, 8:3; I Cor. 5:7.

[76] 2 Cor. 1:20.

[77] Matt. 22:1-14; 2 Cor. 11:2; Eph. 5:25-27; Rev. 19:7.

[78] 2 Cor. 11:2.

[79] Rom. 8:19-21.

[80] See Holland, *Divine Marriage*, 263-266 regarding Paul's understanding of a corporate resurrection based on Ezek. 37.

[81] Rev. 2:5.

[82] I Cor. 11:29-30.

[83] Eph. 4:22-24; Col. 3:9-10.

[84] Jer. 31:3.

[85] Rom. 8:39.

[86] Holland, *Divine Marriage* (Eugene: Pickwick, 2011).

### Chapter 6 Endnotes – The Universal Prostitute

[1] Barbara Kellerman, *Bad Leadership: What It Is, How It Happens, Why It Matters* (Boston: Harvard Business School Press, 2004), 167.

[2] "Employee Theft Statistics," *Statistics Brain,* http://www .statisticbrain.com/employee-theft-statistics/; "Thematic Debate of the 66th session of the United Nations General Assembly on Drugs and Crime as a Threat to Development On the occasion of the UN International Day against Drug Abuse and Illicit Trafficking," *General Assembly of the United Nations,* (New York, June 26, 2012), http://www.un.org/en/ga/president/66/Issues/drugs/drugs-crime.shtml; "The Blue Campaign: Human Trafficking," *Department of Homeland Security*, https://www.dhs.gov/blue-campaign.

[3] Bo Lane, "How Many Pastors Are Addicted to Porn? The Stats are Surprising," *Expastors.com.* http://www.expastors.com/how-many-pastors-are-addicted-to-porn-the-stats-are-surprising/; Naomi O'Leary, "Sex abuse: the scandal the Catholic Church cannot shake," *Reuters; United States Edition-Life,* (May 7, 2013), http://www.reuters.com/article/idUSBRE92611A20130307; Ron Sider interview by Stan Guthrie, "The Evangelical Scandal," *Christianity Today,* (April 13, 2005), http://www.christianitytoday.com/ct/2005 /april/32.70.html.

[4] Kellerman, *Bad Leadership*, 147.

[5] 1 Cor. 7:1-6; 15:12.

[6] 1 Cor. 5:1; 6:12-20.

[7] Deut. 27:20. See Holland, *Contours*, 123.

[8] That church discipline is meant to be redemptive and not simply punitive is seen in 2 Cor. 2:5-11.

[9] 1 Cor. 5:6-8; 1 Cor. 6:11.

[10] 1 Cor. 6:2.

[11] 1 Cor. 6:13-20 (1984 NIV). In translating the Greek word *tou* in the phrase "outside of the [*tou*] body," the 1984 version of the NIV replaces the neuter article "the" with the masculine pronoun "his." Most translations, however, including the newer 2011 NIV, retain the neuter article.

[12] Ibid (2011 NIV).

[13] Ibid (2011 NIV).

[14] R. Kempthorne, "Incest and the Body of Christ: A Study of 1 Corinthians V1. 12-20," *New Testament Studies* 14 (1967-680), 568-574.

[15] Acts 9:4.

[16] 1 Cor. 1:2, 10.

[17] 1 Cor. 3:9, 16.

[18] 2 Cor. 11:2.

[19] 1 Cor. 6:19 (1984 NIV).

[20] 1Co. 3:16, 1Co. 6:19; 2Co. 6:16; Eph. 2:20-22; Heb. 3:6; Rev. 3:12.

[21] John 2:19-22.

[22] John 2, I Cor. 6:15-20; Eph. 2:19-21; cf. 5:25-33; Rev 19:6-8; cf. 21:22.

[23] I Cor. 13:9-12.

[24] I Cor. 12-14.

[25] 2 Cor. 6:14-18.

[26] 2 Cor. 7:1.

[27] 1 Cor. 6:11.

[28] 1 Cor. 10:2-4.

[29] 1 Cor. 7:4.

[30] 1 Cor. 7:14.

[31] 1 Cor. 8: 1-13.

[32] I Corinthians 10: 5.

[33] See Holland, *Contours*, 128-129.

[34] See Anthony C. Thiselton, *The First Epistle to the Corinthians* from the New International Greek Testament Commentary, eds. I. Howard Marshall and Donald A. Hagner (Grand Rapids: Eerdmans, 2000), 477. See also the Pulpit Commentary which says, "When we unduly press the metaphor, and ask from whom we were purchased, and to whom the price was paid, we build up scholastic systems which have only led to error and respecting which the Church has never sanctioned by any exclusive opinion." H. D. M. Spence-Jones, editor. *The Pulpit Commentary* (New York: London: Anson D.F. Randolph; Kegan Paul, Trench, 1883).

[35] For the case that we are slaves to Christ, see McArthur, *Slave*.

[36] Herman Ridderbos, John Richard De Witt, *Paul: An Outline of His Theology,* (Grand Rapids: Eerdmans, 1997),193.

[37] Hayyim Schauss, "Ancient Jewish Marriage," *MyJewishLearning. com,* http://www.myjewishlearning.com/article/ancient-jewish-marriage/; "The Jewish Wedding Analogy," *Bible Study Tools,* http://www.biblestudytools.com/commentaries/revelation/related-topics/the-jewish-wedding-analogy.html.

[38] Glenn Kay, "Jewish Wedding Customs and the Bride of Messiah," *Congregation Netzar Torah Yeshua*, http://messianicfellowship .50webs.com/wedding.html.

[39] Schauss, "Ancient Jewish Marriage."

[40] Louis Ginzberg, Julius H. Greenstone, "Dowry (Aramaic, Nedunya)," http://www.jewishencyclopedia.com/articles/5297-dowry.

[41] Gen. 24:47-61.

[42] Gen. 29:15-30.

[43] Ephesians 5:22-27.

[44] Acts 20:28.

[45] Eph. 1:7.

[46] Eph. 5:22-27.

[47] Mark 10:45; Vincent Taylor, *The Atonement in the New Testament Teaching*, 2nd ed. (Norwich: Epworth, 1954), 23.

[48] I Cor. 5:7. M.D. Hooker, *Jesus and the Servant* (London: SPCK, 1959), 73.

[49] Thiselton, *First Epistle to the Corinthians*, 470.

[50] Thiselton, *First Epistle to the Corinthians*, 476-477. He includes a discussion of other scholars' points of view.

[51] S.M. Baugh, "Cult Prostitution in New Testament Ephesus: A Reappraisal," *Journal of the Evangelical Theological Society*, 42.3 (1999): 443-460. The author argues for the absence of temple prostitution in Ephesus, but extends his argument to cover the whole Roman Empire, http://biblicalstudies.org.uk/article_ephesus_baugh.html

See also, Vinciane Pierenne-Delforge's review of Stephanie Budin, *The Myth of Sacred Prostitution in Antiquity* (New York: Cambridge University Press, 2008), http://bmcr.brynmawr.edu/2009/2009-04-28.html.

[52] Rom. 8:4.

[53] Eph. 5:30.

[54] 1 Cor. 6:15 in the 2011 NIV omits the word "members" when referring to the prostitute: "Do you not know that your bodies are members of Christ himself? Shall I then take the members of Christ and unite them with a prostitute?" However, the corporate parallel is clearer in NKJV, which says, "Shall I take the members of Christ and make them members of a harlot?" The NASB also says, "Shall I then take away the members of Christ and make them members of a prostitute."

[55] In the same way I capitalized Sin in order to reflect the difference between the Sin that affected collective humanity and sin as an individual transgression, I am capitalizing Harlot or Prostitute when it refers to the collective society of unredeemed humanity to distinguish it from an individual prostitute.

[56] C.F.D. Moule, *The Origins of Christology* (Cambridge University Press, 1977) 73.

[57] I Tim. 1:20.

[58] Rev. 2:22.

[59] Eph. 5:30-32.

[60] See Colin Hamer, Marital imagery in the Bible: An Exploration of Genesis 2:24 and its Significance for the Understanding of New Testament Divorce and Remarriage Teaching (London: Apostolos, 2015).

[61] Rom. 8:11, 18-25; I Cor.15: 35-49; Phil. 3:20-22; I Thess. 4:13-18.

[62] Evald Lovestam, "Divorce and Remarriage in the New Testament," *Jewish Law Annual* (Leiden: E.J. Brill, 1981), 4:56.

[63] Jer. 3:1-13, 13:26-27; Ezek. 16:15-32, 23:27, 43:7-9; Hos. 4:11, 6:10.

[64] Hosea 4:12, 5:3-7.

[65] T.H. Robinson, *Prophecy and Prophets in Ancient Israel,* 2nd ed. (London: Duckworth, 1953), 81.

[66] Ezek. 16:27-30, 16:44-49, 23:1-4; Jer. 3:1-5; Lam. 1:1-7.

[67] Rev. 19:6-7.

[68] For additional details regarding these five views, see Holland, *Contours*, 130-132.

[69] George Eldon Ladd, *A Commentary on the Revelation of St. John* (Grand Rapids: Eerdmans, 1972), 221-2.

[70] Hermann Olshausen and J. H. A. Ebrard, *Biblical Commentary on the Revelation of St. John* (T & T Clark, 1860), 110.

[71] T.F. Torrance, *The Apocalypse Today* (London: James Clarke & Co., 1960), 141 (italics added).

[72] Paul wrote 1 and 2 Corinthians c. 54 and c. 56; estimates differ about Revelation. Traditionally, it has been dated c. 95-96, but others suggest it was written as early as c. 68.

[73] Other sections in Paul's writings could be related to John's vision of the great Harlot as well. Identifying the corporate nature of the Prostitute also provides insights into some of Paul's other teachings about fleeing idolatry and sharing the Lord's Table versus the table of demons in 1 Corinthians 10. See Holland, *Contours*, 133-137.

[74] Ben Witherington III, *The Paul Quest: The Renewed Search for the Jew of Tarsus* (Downers Grove: InterVarsity, 1998), 216-217.

## Chapter 7 Endnotes – Birthing the New Man

[1] Matt. 3:6; Acts 2:38; Acts 19:4.

[2] Luke 3:16; 1 Cor. 12:13.

[3] Matt. 3:11.

[4] Luke 12:50; Mark 10:38.

[5] Rom. 6:1-4.

[6] I Cor. 10:2.

[7] Acts 8:36.

[8] 1 Cor. 10:2.

[9] Dan.12:3; Ezek. 37; Hos. 13:14.

[10] I Cor. 10:1-4.

[11] Exod. 12:26.

[12] Exod.13:8.

[13] Luke 9:31.

[14] Rom 6:4.

[15] Or "in" the Spirit.

[16] Acts 20:28; Rom. 16:5, 16; 1 Cor. 1:2; 2 Cor. 8:1; Phil. 3:6; Col. 4:15.

[17] 1 Cor. 10:1-5.

[18] 1 Cor.14:24-25. For more details regarding the comparison between the Moses and Israel (type), and Christ and the church (antitype), see Holland, *Contours*, 145-146.

[19] Rudolf Schnackenburg, *Baptism in the Thought of St. Paul*, tr. by G.R. Beasley-Murray (Oxford: Blackwell, 1965), 24.

[20] Gal. 1:4; 3:14; 4:1-7.

[21] Rom. 8:14.

[22] Exod. 4:22-23; Hos. 11:1.

[23] Ernest Best, *One Body in Christ: A Study in the Relationship of the Church to Christ in the Epistles of the Apostle Paul* (London: SPCK, 1955), 62.

[24] Rom. 6:1-4; Eph. 2:4-10; Col. 2:11-13.

[25] Best, *One Body in Christ*, 57, who quotes F.J. Leenhardt, *Le Sacrament de la Sainte Cène* (Neuchatel and Paris: Delachaux et Niestlé, 1948), 18.

[26] Exod. 13:8.

[27] Eph. 2:1-10.

[28] Ezek. 16:9.

[29] Ezek. 37:1-14.

[30] John 3:5.

[31] John 1:14; Exod. 29:45.

[32] John 1:40-50.

[33] Phillip J. Long, *Jesus the Bridegroom: The Origin of the Eschatological Feast as a Wedding Banquet in the Synoptic Gospels* (Eugene, Oregon; Pickwick, 2013); Jocelyn McWhirter, *The Bridegroom Messiah and the People of God: Marriage in the Fourth Gospel.* Society for New Testament Studies Monograph Series (Cambridge: Cambridge University Press, 2006); Brant Pitre, *Jesus the Bridegroom: The Greatest Love Story Ever Told* (New York: Crown, 2014). Pitre demonstrates Jesus's whole exchange with Mary at the wedding in Cana is about his own ministry (pp. 35-39) and that the writer of the fourth Gospel is employing contemporary Jewish wedding customs to portray Jesus as the divine bridegroom self-consciously taking the role occupied by Yahweh in the Old Testament imagery (pp. 39-45). See also Amos 9:11-13.

[34] Long, *Jesus the Bridegroom*, 2.

[35] D.A. Carson, *The Gospel According to John* (Leicester: InterVarsity, 1991), 195.

[36] Carson, *The Gospel According to John*, 195.

[37] Rom. 7:1-6; 2 Cor. 11:2; Gal. 4:24-31; Eph.1:5.

[38] The NIV 1984 translation of Rom. 8:14 quoted here uses the more literal translation of the Greek *huioi* as *sons*. The NIV 2011 translates it as *children*.

[39] See Rom.4:11-12; I Cor.12:13; Gal. 3:17.

40 For Paul's view on the maturity level of Christians, see 1 Cor. 3:1-3.

41 Quoted from the 2011 NIV.

42 Holland, *Contours,* 153.

43 Deut. 10:16; Jer. 4:4; Ezek. 44: 7, 9.

44 Ezek. 36:26.

45 Exod. 12:43-49.

46 Matt. 28:16-20.

47 Acts 2:33.

48 Matt 3:16.

49 Joel 2:28.

50 See Rom. 5:5; 2 Cor. 1:22, 3:3, 5:5, 11:4. The Spirit you received, λαμβάνετε verb indicative present active 2nd person plural from λαμβάνω so making it clear that the reception of the Spirit was by the community. See also Eph. 1:14; Gal. 3:5.

51 Acts 11:15 cf. 1:5.

52 Acts 19:2.

53 1 Cor. 14:1.

54 Acts 2:4, 4:8, 9:17, 13:9.

55 1Cor. 1:14.

56 1Cor. 1:17.

57 Matt. 3:11; Mark 1:8, 10:38-39; Luke 3:16; John 1:26,33.

58 Depending on how it's read, it may sound like Jesus baptized in John 3:22 but the Gospel writer clarifies in 4:2 that it was his disciples who did the baptizing, not Jesus himself.

59 Luke 3:3.

60 Joel 2:28; Ezek. 36:27.

61 Acts 2:38-39. Another text that some use to prove salvation occurs through water baptism is 1 Pet. 3:21. This verse speaks of the eight people in Noah's ark who were saved through water and says, "this water symbolizes baptism that now saves you also." Read in its full context, this text says that the water that saved Noah and his family condemned the people in his day who were disobedient and is the symbol of a greater judgment, Christ bearing our sins. So, water itself does not save but is a symbol or representation of the true baptism that does save, Christ's baptism into death and our union with him created by the Spirit that made it possible for us to die to Sin/Satan and be resurrected with him, who now sits at God's right hand with angels, authorities and powers in submission to him.

62 Acts 19:4-7.

63 Rom. 10:8-10.

64 Rom. 4:11-12.

65 Gal. 3:28, see also 1Cor.12:13.

66 Eph. 2.

## Chapter 8 Endnotes – Redemptive Threads

[1] Thomas Campbell, "How Medieval and Renaissance Tapestries Were Made," The Met: Heilbrunn Timeline of Art History (February 2008), http://www.metmuseum.org/toah/hd/tapm/hd_tapm.htm.

[2] Joanne Soroka, "Unmarked Lives: the weaving of meaning," *American Tapestry Alliance* (April 2008), http://americantapestry alliance.org/education/educational-articles/inspiration-creativity /unmarked-lives-the-weaving-of-meaning-by-joanne-soroka/.

[3] Rom. 3:21-26.

[4] Matt. 26:27-29; Luke 22:15-22; John 1:29; 1 Cor. 5:7; 1 Cor. 11:23-28; Heb. 9:13-14; 1 Pet. 1:18-19.

[5] 1 Tim. 2:4; see also Ezek. 33:11; 2 Pet. 3:9.

[6] 1 Tim. 6:16.

[7] 2 Cor. 6:14-15.

[8] Luke 15:11-32; Matt. 18:21-35.

[9] 1 Pet. 1:12.

[10] Rom. 3:21.

[11] See "Righteousness," *Bakers Evangelical Dictionary,* http://www.biblestudytools.com/dictionaries/bakers-evangelical-dictionary /righteousness.html; B.F. Meyer, "The Pre-Pauline Formula in Rom. 3:25-26a." *NTS* 29 (1983), 198-208.

[12] Matt. 23. See also C.H. Talbert, "Paul, Judaism, and the Revisionists." *CBQ* 63 (2001), 1-22.

[13] R.B. Hays, "ΠΙΣΙΣ and Pauline Christology: What is at Stake?" in *SBL Seminar Papers*, ed. E.H. Lovering, Jr. (Atlanta: Scholars Press, 199), 714-29; D.A. Campbell, "Romans 1:17—A Crux Interpretation for the ΠΙΣΤΙΣ ΧΡΙΤΟΥ Debate." JBL113:2 (1994) 265-85. In the NIV, the phrase translated as "through faith in Jesus Christ" in Romans 3:22 implies salvation is dependent on our faith. Sensitive souls will always ask the question: "Do I have enough of the right kind of faith?" to be saved. Some scholars are now accepting this phrase is best translated as "by the faithfulness of Christ." In this rendering, Christ's faithfulness is the grounds for salvation. Of course, this doesn't remove the needs for personal faith, but it lays a much firmer foundation. God delivered us from sin/Sin because of the faithfulness of his Son who achieved—through obedience and death—the great work of salvation.

[14] Lev. 11:44; 1 Pet. 1:16.

[15] Ps. 71:15; 85:13; 98:2.

[16] Deut. 32:1-35.

[17] Jer. 3:8.

[18] Isa. 54:14; 62:1-2.

[19] Isa. 51:5; 61:3.

[20] Gen. 3:15, 12:1-3, 15:1-16, 17:1-8.

[21] 2 Cor. 5:21; Col. 1:18-20.

22 Col. 2:10 (NKJ). Speaking to the church, the 2011 NIV says, "In Christ, you have been brought to fullness." See also, Romans 15:14; Col. 1:9-14; Eph. 4:1-6.

23 Col. 1:10.

24 I Peter 1:18-19; Eph. 2:13; Col 1:20; 1 John 1:7; Rev 12:11

25 "Moral Influence theory of atonement," *Theopedia,* http://www. theopedia.com/moral-influence-theory-of-atonement.

26 Eph. 1:10.

27 Irenaeus, *Against Heresies (Book V, Preface).* Translated by Alexander Roberts and William Rambaut. From *Ante-Nicene Fathers, Vol. 1.* Edited by Alexander Roberts, James Donaldson, and A. Cleveland Coxe. (Buffalo, NY: Christian Literature Publishing Co., 1885.), http://www.newadvent.org/fathers/0103500.htm.

28 "Satisfaction theory of the atonement," *Theopedia,* http://www.theopedia.com/Satisfaction_theory_of_the_atonement.

29 Michael J. Vlach, "Penal Substitution in Church History," *TMS* 20:2 (Fall 2009) 199-214, https://www.tms.edu/m/tmsj20i.pdf.

30 Vlach, "Penal Substitution."

31 J.I. Packer "What Did the Cross Achieve? The Logic of Penal Substitution," The Tyndale Biblical Theology Lecture, July 17, 1973, http://www.the-highway.com/cross_Packer.html.

32 "Governmental theory of atonement," *Theopedia,* http://www. theopedia.com/governmental-theory-of-atonement.

33 "Atonement of Christ," *Theopedia,* http://www.theopedia.com /atonement-of-christ . See also J. Denny Weaver, *The Nonviolent Atonement* (Grand Rapids: Eerdmans, 2001); René Girard, "The Anthropology of Rene Girard and Traditional Doctrines of Atonement," *Girardian Lectionary,* http://girardianlectionary.net/res/atonement _webpage.htm.

34 Robin Collins, "Understanding Atonement: A New and Orthodox Theory," http://home.messiah.edu/~rcollins/Philosophical%20 Theology/Atonement/AT7.HTM.

35 Robin Collins, "Understanding Atonement."

36 Packer, "What Did the Cross Achieve?"; Vlach, "Penal Substitution." For objections to penal substitution, see Phyllis Tickle, *Emergence Christianity: What It Is Where it is Going, And Why It Matters* (Grand Rapids: Baker Books, 2012), 197; John Philip Newell, *The Rebirthing of God* (Woodstock: Skylight Paths, 2014), 107.

37 Tickle, Emergence Christianity, 198.

38 Kaufmann Kohler, "Atonement," *The Jewish Encyclopedia,* http://www.jewishencyclopedia.com/articles/2092-atonement.

39 "Atonement.'" *Easton's Bible Dictionary,* http://eastonsbible dictionary.org/362-Atonement.php.

40 Ezek. 18:4 (NASB).

[41] Ezek. 18:32.

[42] Lev. 4-5:13; Guilt offerings are described in Lev. 5:14-6:7.

[43] Lev. 17:11.

[44] Rom. 1:32, 6:23.

[45] Lev. 16:29-34.

[46] Isa. 1:11.

[47] "Sacrifice and Offering," *Holman Bible Dictionary*, http://www.studylight.org/dic/hbd/view.cgi?number=T5431.

[48] Matt. 26:28, Heb. 9:26.

[49] Holland, *Divine Marriage*, 85.

[50] Scott McKnight, "The Wrath of God Satisfied," *Jesus Creed,* June 22, 2012, http://www.patheos.com/blogs/jesuscreed/2012/06/22/the-wrath-of-god-satisfied/.

[51] Holland, *Divine Marriage*, 85.

[52] Lev. 16.

[53] 4 Macc. 17:22.

[54] Rom. 1:3; 3:21.

[55] Deut. 24:18.

[56] Matt 27:17; Mark 14:12-20; Luke 22:7-23; John 2:23-3:16, 6:4-70.

[57] Ezek. 45:15, 17, 20, 25.

[58] Ezek. 20:13-20; 23:20, 37-38.

[59] Ezek. 45:17-24.

[60] James D.G. Dunn, "Paul's Understanding of the Death of Jesus" in *Reconciliation and Hope, Essays presented to L. L. Morris on his 60th Birthday*, ed. R. Brooks, Paternoster, 132-2.

[61] John 1:29 (NASB).

[62] J.M. Howard, "Passover and Eucharist in the Fourth Gospel," *SJTh* 20 (1967), 331-2.

[63] There is a strong probability that Ezekiel's prophecy contributed to the description of the end times temple in Revelation. Interestingly, the sacrificial language of Revelation concentrates exclusively on the Passover. See Rev. 1:5-6, 5:6-9; 7:17.

[64] Heb. 9:12.

[65] Ezek. 43:14,17, 20.

[66] Holland, *Contours,* 162-163.

[67] Holland, *Contours,* 162-165.

[68] Ezek. 20:4-12.

[69] Col. 1:15.

[70] Rom. 5.

[71] Luke 22:14-23; 24:44-47; John 1:29.

72 Exod. 24:3-8; Jer. 31:31; Matt. 26:17-29; Mark 14:12-25; Luke 22: 7-22; 1 Cor. 11:23-26.

73 Lev. 23: 5-12. Note: the Jewish calendar is different than the standard calendar in the West and their days begin at sunset. According to this text, Passover began at twilight on the 14th day of the month (Nissan); the Feast of Unleavened Bread begins on Sabbath, the 15th day; and the firstfruits offering was to be given on the day *after* the Sabbath during this holy week.

74 Deut. 26:1-11.

75 Rom. 4:20-25.

76 See F.F. Bruce, *The New Century Bible Commentary: 1 & 2 Corinthians* (London: Marshall, Morgan & Scott, 1971), 140; Holland, *Contours,* 284; Joel White, "'He Was Raised the Third Day According to the Scriptures' (Corinthians 15:4): A Topological Interpretation based on the Cultic Calendar in Leviticus 23," *Tyndale Bulletin* 66.1 (2015) 1-17.

77 I Cor. 5:7; 2 Cor. 5:21.

78 Isa. 65:17.

79 Holland, *Contours*, 173-179.

80 Holland, *Contours,* 175-179.

81 Lev. 16:8-10 ESV. (The NIV does not mention Azazel.) For a Jewish understanding of Azazel, see *The Jewish Encyclopedia*, http://jewishencyclopedia.com/articles/2203-azazel.

82 See "Azazel" in the *International Standard Bible Encyclopedia,* http://www.internationalstandardbible.com/A/azazel.html.

83 Ed Stetzer, "The Atonement and the Scapegoat: Leviticus 16 by Dr. Kenneth Mathews," *Christianity Today,* April 15, 2014, http://www.christianitytoday.com/edstetzer/2014/april/atonement-and-scapegoat-leviticus-16-by-dr-kenneth-mathews.html

84 "Azazel," *International Standard Bible Encyclopedia,* http://www.biblestudytools.com/encyclopedias/isbe/azazel.html.

85 1 Cor.10:1-3.

### Chapter 9 Endnotes – Loving Wrath

1 Isa. 55: 8-9.

2 James 1:20.

3 Leon Morris, *The Apostolic Preaching of the Cross* (3rd ed.; Grand Rapids: Eerdmans, 1955), 180.

4 Rev. 14:8, 10, 19; 15:1,7; 18:3; 19:15.

5 Rev. 19:15.

6 This combination of *orge* and *thumos* is also the level of judgment Paul speaks of in Rom. 2. They appear together in v 8.

7 David's statement in Psalm 7:11 which, in most Bible translations, reads God "displays his wrath every day," appears to contradict this. However, Adam Clark provided a different perspective in his 1831 *Commentary on the Bible.* After observing contradictions between versions of the verse in ancient texts,

Clarke concluded "the mass of evidence" shows the proper reading is "God is Not angry every day." http://www.sacred-texts.com/bib/cmt/clarke/psa007.htm. This reading can be found in *Young's Literal Translation* (YLT), the *Aramaic Bible* and the *New English Translation of the Septuagint* (NETS).

[8] Hos. 11:8, 9; Ps. 78: 38, 39.

[9] Exod. 34:6-7 (ESV).

[10] Jer. 9:23-24.

[11] Num. 14:18; Neh. 9:17; Ps. 86:15; 103:8; 145:8; Joel 2:13; Jonah 4:2; Nah. 1:3.

[12] Deut. 27.

[13] Deut. 28:1-14.

[14] Deut. 28:15-68.

[15] Deut. 29:25-28.

[16] Isa. 54:7-8. See also Deut. 31:17-18; 32:20; Isa. 8:17. As mentioned in chapter 3, the Assyrians had taken ten of Israel's twelve tribes into exile earlier. Judah, carried into exile by the Babylonians, is also referred to as Israel.

[17] Ezek. 16; 39:23; Lev. 25:1-7; 26:33-35.

[18] Hos. 11:8.

[19] Deut. 30:17-18; 1 Cor. 11:32.

[20] Deut. 30:1-11.

[21] Ps. 103:8-9.

[22] Jonah 3:1-10.

[23] Rom. 1: 21-26

[24] Rom. 1: 28-32

[25] 1 Tim. 2:4.

[26] Eph. 2:2 (ESV).

[27] Eph. 2:3 (ESV).

[28] Eph. 2-3.

[29] 2 Pet. 3:9.

[30] Rom. 2:5; 5:9; 2 Pet. 3:10-11.

[31] Gen. 6-8; Gen. 18-19; Exod. 11-12.

[32] Rom. 2:5, 8; 5:9; 1. Thess. 1:10; 2 Pet. 3:10-11.

[33] Luke 10:11-16.

[34] Rom. 2:5-11.

[35] 2 Pet. 2:4, 11; 3:7.

[36] Rev. 16:19.

[37] Rev. 19:2.

[38] Rev. 19:2; 18:24.

[39] Rev.19:11-21.

[40] Rev. 20.

41 John 3:16-21 (NIV); Eph. 2:3 (NASB).

42 John 3:17.

43 1 Thess. 1:4-10.

44 Rev. 19: 1-2; 15-24.

45 Rom. 12:19-21.

46 R.C. Sproul, "The Suffering of Christ," *Ligonier Ministries,* http://www.ligonier.org/learn/devotionals/the-suffering-of-christ/ (italics added).

47 Isa. 53:4-5.

48 Isa. 53: 8, 10, 12.

49 See 1 Pet. 2:21-25.

50 Isa. 52:13-15.

51 2 Sam. 7:12-15; Ps. 2:7.

52 Isa. 52:12.

53 Isa. 51:3.

54 Isa. 52:15. The Hebrew word that is translated as *sprinkle*, can also mean *startle.* Although there is good reason to favor *sprinkle*, it would also certainly be appropriate to say the sight of the servant, who suffers such terrible violence and then is exalted will startle the nations.

55 Isa. 28:18.

56 Exod. 32:7-10.

57 Exod. 32:11-14.

58 Ezek. 37:1-14.

59 Lev. 5:14-19, Exod. 30:33,38; 31:14; Lev. 7:20,21,25,27; 17:4,9; 18:29; 19:8; 20:18; 23:29; Num. 9:13; 15:30; Acts 3:23.

60 Other versions that use *for* include: RSV, NRSV, NASB, ESV, NKJV.

61 In addition to the Holman and NET bible, English translations of the Hebrew Septuagint and word-for-word translations of the Greek LXX also use *because of* or *on account of.* See the *Apostolic Bible Polyglot,* the *1917 Jewish Bible,* the *Complete Jewish Bible,* and the *Brenton Septuagint.*

62 1 Cor. 15:3.

63 NIV.

64 See the ESV, NASB, YLT.

65 James Barr, *Semantics of Biblical Language,* (Oxford University Press,1961).

66 John Goldingay, *A Critical and Exegetical Commentary on Isaiah 56-66* (London: T&T Clark); G. Wenham, *The Book of Leviticus*: The New International Commentary on the Old Testament (Grand Rapids: Eerdmans, 1979) 102-112; J. Motyer, *The Prophecy of Isaiah* (Leicester: Inter Varsity Press, 1993) in commentary on Isaiah 53:10-12. See also the Net Bible, note #28 for Isaiah 53:10 at https://net.bible.org/#!bible /Isaiah+53:10.

[67] John Goldingay, Commentary on Isaiah 56-66, 500.

[68] Isa. 40:2.

[69] "Punishment" *Merriam-Webster Dictionary*, https://www.merriam-webster.com/dictionary/punishment.

[70] Spiros Zodhiates, 5060, 76.

[71] John 9:2, 3.

[72] Prov. 3:11-12, Heb. 12:5-6.

[73] Rev. 3:19.

[74] Heb. 12:10.

[75] Heb. 12:11-13.

[76] NASB.

[77] John Goldingay and David Payne, *Isaiah 40-55* (London: T&T Clark International, 2006), 308. See also, John D. Watts, *Word Biblical Commentary, Vol. 25: Isaiah 34-66* (Revised Edition) (Nashville: Thomas Nelson, 2005), 789.

[78] John Goldingay, *The Message of Isaiah 40-55: A Literary-Theological Commentary* (London: Bloomsbury T&T Clark, 2005), 509.

[79] Watts, *Isaiah 34-66*, 789.

[80] Watts, *Isaiah 34-66*, 789.

[81] Hos. 8:6.

[82] Rom. 7:1-6; 2 Cor. 11:2; Eph. 5:21-5.

[83] Rom. 1:32; 8:4.

[84] 1 John 2:2, 4:10.

[85] Deut. 28:39; Isa. 25:8, 43:2, 51:8, 66:24; Jer. 9:21, 15:14 Matt. 4:16, 10:15; Mark 9:48; Rom. 2:5, 5:16; 1 Cor. 3:13, 4:5; 1 Tim. 5:24; 2 Thess. 1:8, 9; Heb. 6:2, 9:15; 2 Pet. 2:9; Rev. 14:7, 20:14.

[86] Isa. 29:6, 33:12, 42:25, 43:2; Jer. 5:14-17, 11: 9-16; Joel 2:3.

[87] N.T. Wright, *Jesus and the Victory of God* (London: SPCK, 1996), 596.

[88] Rev. 19:20; 20:10, 14, 15.

[89] Rom. 5:8,9 (NASB).

[90] Acts 2:23, 3:13-15.

[91] John 3:16, Rom. 8:32; Heb. 5:5-9; 1 John 4:9-11 speak of God's unique, loving relationship with the Son.

[92] Rom. 3:23-26.

[93] Gal. 3:13.

[94] Rev. 21.27.

[95] 1 John 4:17-18.

[96] Heb. 12:2.

[97] Rom. 11:33-36.

[98] 2 Tim. 2:13.

[99] John 15:13.

[100] Dunn, *Theology of Paul*, 223 (italics original).

## Chapter 10 Endnotes – Making Things Right

[1] Jer. 3:8.

[2] Ezek. 16.

[3] Isa. 55:3ff; Jer. 31:31-33; 33:15; Ezek. 36: 22-28.

[4] Rom. 3:25.

[5] St. Augustine, *In Jo. ev.* 72,3:PL 35,1823 quoted in the *Catechism of the Catholic Church,* (Libreria Editrice Vaticana, Citta del Vaticano), 1994, http://www.vatican.va/archive/ccc_css/archive/catechism /p3s1c3a2.htm.

[6] Peter Kreeft, *Fundamentals of the Faith: Essays in Christian Apologetics* (Ignatius Press: San Francisco, 1988), 278.

[7] Selected passages from Martin Luther, *Commentary on Galatians* (1538) as translated in Herbert J.A. Bouman, "The Doctrine of Justification in the Lutheran Confessions," *Concordia Theological Monthly* 26 (November 1955) No. 11: 801, https://media.ctsfw.edu /Item/ViewDetails/98.

[8] Bouman, "Doctrine of Justification," 801.

[9] For a summary of the New Perspectives on Paul see N.T. Wright, "New Perspectives on Paul," *NT Wright Page,* http://ntwrightpage.com /Wright_New_Perspectives.htm.

[10] "Joint Declaration on The Doctrine of Justification by the Lutheran World Federation and the Catholic Church," *Vatican: the Holy See.* http://www.vatican.va/roman_curia/pontifical_councils/chrstuni /documents/rc_pc_chrstuni_doc_31101999_cath-luth-joint-declaration_en.html.

[11] United States Conference of Catholic Bishops, "Catholics and Lutherans Release 'Declaration on the Way' to Full Unity," Oct. 30, 2015, http://www.usccb.org/news/2015/15-147.cfm.

[12] See James S. Cutsinger, ed., Reclaiming the Great Tradition: Evangelicals, Catholics and Orthodox in Dialogue (Downers Grove: InterVarsity Press, 1997).

[13] *Catechism of the Catholic Church,* 2019.

[14] For an explanation of Justification from the Catholic perspective, see Kevin Knight, ed., "Justification," *The Catholic Encyclopedia*, New Advent, http://www.newadvent.org/cathen/08573a.htm; see also, Sal Ciresi, "Bible Says Faith and Works Needed for Salvation," *EWTN,* Eternal World Television Network. http://www.ewtn.com/library/ answers/faworks.htm.

[15] Gal. 5:6.

[16] "Justification," *The Catholic Encyclopedia.*

[17] Michael Horton, *The Christian Faith: A Systematic theology for Pilgrims on the Way* (Grand Rapids: Zondervan, 2011), 622.

[18] Horton, *The Christian Faith,* 623.

[19] Horton, *The Christian Faith*, 622 (italics added).

[20] Peter Kreeft, "Ecumenical Jihad" in Cutsinger, *Reclaiming,* 27.

[21] Avery Cardinal Dulles, "Two Languages of Salvation: The Lutheran-Catholic Joint Declaration," *First Things*, Institute on Religion and Public Life, (December 1999), http://www.firstthings.com/article/1999/12/two-languages-of-salvation-the-lutheran-catholic-joint-declaration; Merold Westphal, *Whose Community? Which Interpretation? Philosophical Hermeneutics for the Church* (Grand Rapids: Baker Academic, 2009), 136-137; Bishop Robert Barron and Roger E. Olson, "Grace First or Grace Alone? What Catholics and Protestants Now Agree on—and What Still Divides Us." *Christianity Today*, April 2017, 43-46.

[22] N.T. Wright, *What Paul Really Said* (Oxford: Lion Publishing, 1997), 122.

[23] Holland, *Contours*, 183-234.

[24] Patrick Collinson, "The Late Medieval Church and Its Reformation (1400-1600)" in *The Oxford Illustrated History of Christianity* (New York: Oxford 1990), 258-59 (italics added).

[25] *Westminster Confession of Faith* 11:1 (italics added).

[26] *Westminster Confession of Faith* 11:3-4 (italics added).

[27] *Bakers Dictionary* points out that, "we tend to distrust legalism and thus we dismiss anything that savors of a legalistic approach. We should be clear that our hesitation was not shared by the biblical writers . . ." See "Justification," *Bakers Evangelical Dictionary of Biblical Theology*, http://www.biblestudytools.com/dictionaries/bakers-evangelical-dictionary/justification.html.

[28] *Bakers*, "Justification," online (italics added).

[29] Hos. 9:17; Jer. 44:11.

[30] Isa. 40:1-2, 44:1-5, 54:1-8, 62:1-5; Ezek. 16:59-62, 36:24-28; Jer. 3:1-23; Hos. 2:14-20; Matt. 22:4, 25:10; Rev. 19:7.

[31] Isa. 2:2-5, 42:1,6, 56:3-8, 66:18; Acts 15:14-19.

[32] Hos. 2:16, 19; Isa. 54:1-8, 61:1-10, 62:4-5; Jer. 3:1-23; Ezek. 16:59-63.

[33] Job 11:2; 25:4; Ps 51:4; 143:2; Isa 43:26; 45:25.

[34] Matt 9:13; 10:41; Luke 18:9; Rom 3:10; 5:19. Matt. 12:37; Luke 10:29; Acts 13:39; Rom. 2:13; 3:20, 24; 4:2; 5:1,9; 8:30; Gal 2:16.

[35] Isa. 51:5.

[36] Isa. 32:1; 42:6; 51:5; 54:14; 58:8; 62:1-2.

[37] 2 Cor 1:10.

[38] Rom. 3:26.

[39] Isaiah 43:26-44:5, 45:25.

[40] Rom. 6:1-4; 1 Cor. 10:4, 12:13; Gal. 3:24ff; Eph. 4:6, 5:27.

[41] I Cor. 6:11.

[42] Eph. 5:22-30.

[43] 1 Cor. 10:1-4; 1 Cor. 12:13.

[44] Col. 1:12-13.

[45] See Gen.12:1-9.

[46] Gal. 3:1-5.

47 See the original account in Num. 25:10-13.

48 Holland, *Contours*, 220-225.

49 D.E.H. Whiteley, "St. Paul's Thought on the Atonement," *Journal of Theological Studies* V:9 (1957), 250.

50 Rom. 3:24-25 (ESV).

51 Herman Ridderbos, "The Earliest Confession of the Atonement in Paul (1 Cor. 15:3)," in *Reconciliation and Hope, Essays presented to L.L. Morris on his 60th Birthday*, ed. R. Brooks (Paternoster, 1974), 85.

52 1 Cor. 1:30-31, 3:21-23.

53 Eph. 1:3-14.

54 Lev. 7:18; Ps. 32:2; Rom. 4:4.

55 Gal 4:8-9; 5:1-6.

56 Gal. 2:20.

57 Phil. 3:9.

58 NIV 1984.

59 Heb. 9:27; cf. 2 Cor 5:10.

60 Rom 14:11-12; 2 Cor 5:10.

61 See Holland, *Contours*, 229, n. 12.

62 Collinson, "The Late Medieval Church and Its Reformation," 258-59.

63 E.P. Sanders, *Paul: A Very Short Introduction* (Oxford: Oxford Press, 2001), 93.

64 Col. 1:20; Rev. 19:16; I Cor. 15:28.

## Chapter 11 Endnotes – First of All

1 Col. 1:15.

2 Larry. R. Helyer, "Arius Revisited: The Firstborn Over all Creation (Col 1:15)," *JETS* 31:1 (March 1988), 59. https://www.galaxie.com /article/jets31-1-06.

3 Italics added.

4 Col. 1:13, 20

5 Exod. 12:2, 15.

6 Col. 1:15. For further discussion, see Holland, *Contours*, 271-272.

7 Gen. 4:14-15, 23f; Num. 35:22-29; Deut. 19:4-10.

8 Isa. 43:3-4, 14-15, 47:4, 49:25-26, 59:16-20.

9 Luke 1:68-79, 18:7-8; 2 Thess. 1:6 -9; Rev. 6:9-11.

10 Lev. 25:8-34.

11 Isa. 51:11, 52:8-10.

12 Col. 1:13-14; Heb. 9:15; Rev. 21:1-4.

13 Deut. 25:5-10; Ruth 3:13; 4:1-8.

14 Isa. 49:20-21, 50:1-2, 54:1-8, 62:4-5.

15 John 3:28-29; Rom, 7:1-4; I Cor. 6:20; Eph. 5:25-32; Rev. 19: 6-8.

[16] See the scholarly arguments in Holland, *Contours*, 241-242.

[17] R. Alan Cole, *Exodus (Tyndale Old Testament Commentaries) Volume 2* (London: Inter-Varsity Press, 1973), 85.

[18] The absence of any mention of this practice when Moses returned from Midian later in the narrative suggests that it had been abandoned, perhaps while Moses was young. While there is no firm evidence as to whether or not Pharaoh's order to kill the male children was rescinded, it is likely the practice did not continue for long as there was no lack of laborers for the ruler's building program.

[19] Exod. 13:1-2.

[20] Exod. 13:1-16.

[21] Exod. 13:13.

[22] Num. 18:15-16.

[23] Exod. 13:14-16.

[24] Lev. 19: 33-34.

[25] Num. 8:19.

[26] Num. 1:53.

[27] Louis Ginzberg, *The Legends of the Jews* (Philadelphia: Jewish Publication Society of America, 1925), 3:226.

[28] Holland, *Contours*, 247-251.

[29] Holland, *Contours*, 253-262.

[30] See story of Ruth and Boaz, Ruth 4:4.

[31] Ivan Engell, *A Rigid Scrutiny: Critical Essays on the Old Testament*, tr. by J.T. Willis (London: SPCK, 1970), 1.

[32] Rom. 5:9.

[33] J. Jeremias, "A) δάμ," *Theological Dictionary of the New Testament*, eds. Gerhard Kittel and Gerhard Friedrich, tr. Geoffrey. W. Bromiley (Grand Rapids: Eerdmans, 1964), 1:143.

[34] H. Ridderbos, *Paul, an Outline of His Theology* (Grand Rapids: Eerdmans 1975), 84.

[35] N. Perrin, *A Modern Pilgrimage in New Testament Christology* (Minneapolis: Fortress Press, 1974), 76.

[36] Rabbi Joseph Soloveitchik as quoted in Paul R. Carlson, *O Christian! O Jew!* (Elgin: David C. Cook, 1974),142-143.

[37] John 11:25; Col. 1:13-20; Heb. 1:1-6; Rev. 1:5-7.

[38] Holland, *Contours*, 279-280.

[39] N.T. Wright, 'Theology and Poetry in Colossians 1.15-20,' *NTS* 36 (1990), 452-54.

[40] Col. 1:19-20.

[41] Isa. 55:12-13, 65:17-25.

[42] Rom. 8:19-21.

[43] Stephen Bedale, 'The Meaning of κεφαλή in the Pauline Epistles,' *JTS* ns. 5 (1954), 211-15.

[44] Col. 2:10,15.

[45] Col. 2:11.

[46] Col. 2:14-15.

[47] Col. 2:15.

[48] Col. 2:16-17.

[49] Col. 3:1.

[50] Col. 3:2-17.

[51] Col. 3:10.

## Chapter 12 Endnotes – In Bold Relief

[1] John 14:30.

[2] Eph. 6:12.

[3] 2 Cor. 5:18-21, 6:17; Eph. 5:8; Acts 13:47; 1 Pet. 2:9; 2 Cor. 10:4.

[4] 2 Cor. 7:1; 1 Pet. 1:15; James 5;16.

[5] Merold Westphal, *Whose Community Which Interpretation? Philosophical Hermeneutics for the Church*, series ed., James K. A. Smith (Grand Rapids: Baker Academic, 2009), 137.

[6] For an example, see David Bradshaw, *Aristotle East and West: Metaphysics and the Division of Christendom*, (Cambridge: Cambridge University Press, 2004).

[7] For examples, see Tom Holland, *Contours of Pauline Theology* (Christian Focus, Fearn, 2004).

## Appendix B Endnotes – Blurring the Lines

[1] Timothy J. Keller, *The Reason for God: Belief in an Age of Skepticism* (NY: Penguin Group, 2008), 15.

[2] Brian Rosner, *Known By God: A Biblical Theology of Personal Identity*, (Grand Rapids: Zondervan, 2017), 172.

[3] Knut Lundby, ed., Digital Storytelling, Mediatized Stories: Self-representations in New Media, (New York: Peter Lang, 2008), 30.

[4] I Cor. 12-14.

[5] Walter F. Wagner, *After the Apostles: Christianity in the Second Century* (Minneapolis: Fortress Press, 1994), 1 quoted in Michael J. Kruger, Christianity at the Crossroads (London: SPCK, 2017), 1.

[6] Gerd Lüdemann, *Heretics: The Other Side of Christianity* (London SCM, 1996) 11-12 (italics his) quoted in Kruger, *Crossroads*, 8.

[7] See Wolfhart Pannenberg, *Basic Questions in Theology*, Vol. II (trans. George H. Kehm: Philadelphia: Westminster Press, 1971), 182-83; Vladimir Lossky, *The Vision of God* (Crestwood: St. Vladimir's Seminary Press, 1963) 67, 68; Pelikan, *The Emergence of the Catholic Tradition*, 67; Anthony N.S. Lane, *John Calvin: Student of the Church Fathers* (Edinburgh: T&T Clark, 1999), 43.

[8] Kruger, *Crossroads*, 135-136.

[9] Thomas C. Oden, *After Modernity... What?* (Grand Rapids: Zondervan, 1992), 180 (italics his).

[10] Oden, After Modernity,181.

[11] Wilson, *Our Father Abraham: Jewish Roots of the Christian Faith* (Grand Rapids: Eerdmans, 1989) 83-84; Oskar Skarsaune, *Shadow of the Temple: Jewish Influences on Early Christianity* (Downers Grove: IVP Academic, 2002), 259-274; Robert L. Wilken, *Judaism and the Early Christian Mind: A Study of Cyril of Alexandria's Exegesis and Theology* (Eugene: Wipf & Stock, 1971) 9-53.

[12] Skarsaune, *Shadow of the Temple*, 197-199, 260; Wilson, *Our Father Abraham*, 78, 88.

[13] Wilson, *Our Father Abraham*, 89. Skarsaune, *Shadow of the Temple*, 267.

[14] As Paul teaches in Romans 4:16, being grafted into the Jewish root does not mean Christians actually become Jewish; rather he says it in the sense that believers share the same faith and hope as Abraham. See Skarsaune, *Shadow of the Temple*, 268; Wilson, *Our Father Abraham*, 83, 84.

[15] Wilson, *Our Father Abraham*, 89.

[16] Skarsaune, *Shadow of the Temple*, 260-276; Wilson, *Our Father Abraham* 79, Wilken, *Judaism and the Early Christian Mind*, 27, 46.

[17] Wilson, "A History of the Contempt: Anti-Semitism and the Church" in *Our Father Abraham*, 87-103.

[18] "Marcion." Theopedia. http://www.theopedia.com/marcion; Skarsaune, *Shadow of the Temple*, 248.

[19] Wilken, *Judaism and the Early Christian Mind*, 16.

[20] Wilken, *Judaism and the Early Christian Mind*, 16

[21] J. Kendall Soulen, *The God of Israel and Christian Theology*, (Minneapolis: Fortress Press, 1996), ix; Wilken, *Judaism and the Early Christian Mind*, 76-84.

[22] Justin Martyr, Dialogue with Trypho, a Jew 29.2.

[23] Skarsaune, Shadow of the Temple, 266.

[24] Skarsaune, Shadow of the Temple, 266.

[25] Skarsaune, Shadow of the Temple, 217.

[26] Pelikan, *Emergence of the Catholic Tradition*, 21. Origen and Jerome are two exceptions in that they both consulted with Jewish leaders and learned Hebrew, but Pelikan notes that Hebrew was not used as a common study tool before the sixteenth century.

[27] Quoted with permission from private correspondence with the author.

[28] Skarsaune, In the Shadow of the Temple, 269.

[29] Pelikan, *Emergence of Catholic Tradition*, 21.

[30] Christopher Hall, *Reading Scripture with the Church Fathers* (Downers Grove: IVP Academic, 1998), passim.

[31] Soulen, *The God of Israel*, 28.

[32] N.T. Wright, "Jesus and the Identity of God," originally published in *Ex Auditu* 1998, 14, 42-56, http://ntwrightpage.com/2016/07/12/jesus-and-the-identity-of-god/

[33] Soulen, *The God of Israel*, 3.

[34] Exod. 3:14, 15. When God revealed himself to Moses, he said "I am who I am," a self-revelation which received notable attention in historic discussions of God's name, being, and nature. However, he also identified himself to Israel as "the God of Abraham, the God of Isaac and the God of Jacob," explaining that "this is my name forever, the name you shall call me from generation to generation." According to David Runia, while Exodus 3:14 is cited by the church fathers on numerous occasions, "the following verse receives almost no attention at all." David T. Runia, *Philo and the Church Fathers: A Collection of Papers* (New York: E.J. Brill, 1995), 3.

[35] Soulen, *The God of Israel*, 32.

[36] Soulen, *The God of Israel*, 3.

[37] Jean Daniélou, *Gospel Message and Hellenistic Culture*, (trans., ed., John Austin Baker: Philadelphia: Westminster Press, 1973), 39; Joseph W. Trigg, *Origen* (Routledge: New York, 1998), 9.

[38] Rowan Greer, *Origen: An Exhortation to Martyrdom, Prayer and Selected Works* (Mahwah: Paulist Press, 1979), 32-33.

[39] Nicholas Wolterstorff, *Inquiring About God: Volume 1, Selected Essays* (Cambridge University Press, 2010), 284.

[40] Wolterstorff, *Inquiring About God,* 284; Wolterstorff, "Tertullian's Enduring Question," *The Cresset Trinity,* 1999 Special Issue Lilly Fellows Program in Humanities and the Arts, 11. http://www.lillyfellows.org/media/1406/nicholas-wolterstorff-1998.pdf

[41] Douglas B. Farrow, "The Doctrine of the Ascension in Irenaeus and Origen," *ARC,* 26 (1998): 32.

[42] Vladimir Lossky, *The Vision of God* (trans. Asheleigh Moorhouse: Crestwood: St. Vladimir's Seminary Press, 1963), 67.

[43] Lossky, *Vision,* 67

[44] Pannenberg, *Basic Questions in Theology Vol. II,* 182.

[45] Robert P. Casey, "Clement of Alexandria and the Beginnings of Christian Platonism," *The Harvard Theological Review*, 18:1 (Jan. 1925): 101.

[46] Werner Jaeger, "The Greek Ideas of Immortality," *Harvard Theological Review,* 52 (July 1959): 146.

[47] Greer, *Origen,* 34.

[48] Wilson, *Our Father Abraham*, 168. For additional supporting evidence of the enduring influence of Platonism see Julie Canlis, *Calvin's Ladder: A Spiritual Theology of Ascent and Ascension* (Grand Rapids: Eerdmans, 2010), 29-31.

[49] "Clement of Alexandria," *New Advent Catholic Encyclopedia:* http://www.newadvent.org/cathen/04045a.htm; Henry Fiskå Hägg, *Clement of Alexandria and the Beginnings of Christian Apophaticism* (Oxford: Oxford University Press, 2006), 252-268.

[50] In the 11th century, Orthodox theologian, Michael Psellus said it this way: "the famous Origen . . .was the pioneer of all our theology and laid its foundations, but on the other hand, all heresies find their origin in him." Quoted in Jaroslav Pelikan, *The Spirit of Eastern Christendom* (600-1700), 244. See also "Origen and Origenism," *Coptic Orthodox Church Network*, http://www.copticchurch.net/topics/patrology /schoolofalex2/chapter04.html

[51] Mark Julian Edwards, *Origen Against Plato* (Oxford: Ashgate, 2002), passim.; Trigg, *Origen*, 36-61; Joseph T. Lienhard, ed., *Ancient Christian Commentary on Scripture, Old Testament III Exodus, Leviticus, Numbers, Deuteronomy*, General Editor, Thomas C. Oden. (Downers Grove, IL: InterVarsity Press 2001), xix; Greer, *Origen,* 32-34.

[52] Mark Moussa, "Clement of Alexandria: The Original Christian Philosopher," *The Christian Coptic Orthodox Church of Egypt,* http://www.coptic.net/articles/ClementOfAlexandria.txt.

[53] Hägg, *Clement of Alexandria,* 252-268.

[54] David T. Runia, *Philo of Alexandria and the "Timaeus" of Plato* (Leiden: E.J. Brill, 1986), 520.

[55] Hägg, *Clement of Alexandria,* 35.

[56] Andrew Erskine, "Culture and Power in Ptolemaic Egypt: The Museum and Library of Alexandria," *Greece and Rome*, Vol xliii:1, (April 1995), 45, 46.

[57] Hägg, *Clement of Alexandria,* 41.

[58] Runia, *Philo of Alexandria,* 57

[59] Wilken, *Judaism and the Early Christian Mind,* 40.

[60] Hägg, *Clement of Alexandria,* 27.

[61] David T. Runia, *Philo in Early Christian Literature* (Minneapolis: Fortress Press, 1993), 8. Runia notes that "Nearly ever introductory work on Philo ends with the statement that his works were preserved because they were taken up in the Christian tradition. If the matter had been left in the hands of his fellow Jews, these works would have been swept away by the effects of time and decay." 8.

[62] Runia, *Philo and the Church Fathers,* 7; passim.

[63] Runia, *Philo of Alexandria,* 519, 535-536 quoted in Deirdre Carabine, *The Unknown God: Negative Theology in the Platonic Tradition: Plato to Eriugena* (Eugene: Wipf and Stock Publishers, 2015), 196.

[64] Joseph W. Trigg, "Allegory," in *Encyclopedia of Early Christianity* (New York: Garland, 1990), 23 quoted in Hall, *Reading Scripture,* 137.

[65] Karlfried Froehlich, ed., *Biblical Interpretation in the Early Church* (Minneapolis: Fortress, 1980) 19.

[66] Gerd Van Riel, *Plato's Gods* (Burlington: Ashgate, 2013), 105.

[67] See Plato's Allegory of the Cave in *The Republic: Book VII, The Internet Classics Archive* by Daniel C. Stevenson, Web Atomics, trans. Benjamin Jowett, http://classics.mit.edu/Plato/republic.8.vii.html.

[68] Plato, *Timaeus,* 41 a-b. 47e, 53b, 28c, 28c, 29a; Plato's Gods, 81.

[69] Plato, Timaeus 34c; Allen, *Philosophy for Understanding Theology*, 10.

[70] Plato, *Phaedrus* 246d.

[71] Van Riel, *Plato's Gods,* 30, 33, 54, 57, 110.

[72] Van Riel, *Plato's Gods,* 50.

[73] Van Riel, *Plato's Gods*, 12-24.

[74] Donald Zeyl and Barbara Sattler, ed. Edward N. Zalta, "Plato's Timaeus," *The Stanford Encyclopedia of Philosophy* (Winter 2017 Edition), https://plato.stanford.edu/archives/win2017/entries/plato-timaeus/.

[75] Zeyl, "Plato's Timaeus." In Plato's *The Republic IV*, the three parts of the soul correspond to the three classes of a society—reason: those who rule through love of learning; spirited: those who obey the directions of the rulers and defend the whole from external invasion and internal disorder; the appetites, the function of which is to produce and seek pleasure.

[76] Plato, *Phaedo,* 82e.

[77] Carabine, *Unknown God*, 20

[78] See Plato's *Symposium* and *Phaedrus* for the role of beauty and love in awakening the soul.

[79] Plato, *The Republic,* 526e quoted in Carabine, *Unknown God*, 20.

[80] Allen, *Philosophy for Understanding Theology*, 33.

[81] Allen, *Philosophy for Understanding Theology,* 23, 32.

[82] Allen, *Philosophy for Understanding Theology,* 32.

[83] Bernard McGinn, The Foundations of Mysticism: Origins to the Fifth Century (New York: Crossroads, 2001), 30.

[84] McGinn, Foundations of Mysticism, 33.

[85] Plato, *Parmenides* 137b; 137d;142a.

[86] Plato, *Letters,* 7: 342 c, d.

[87] McGinn, *Foundations of Mysticism,* 33.

[88] McGinn, *Foundations of Mysticism,* 33; for Philo's view of ecstatic experiences see page 39; for Plotinus's perspective see 44-53. (italics added). Also, for Plotinus, see R.T. Wallis, *Neoplatonism*, 2nd ed. (Indianapolis: Hackett, 1995), 3.

[89] Allen, *Philosophy for Understanding Theology*, 27.

[90] Plato, *The Republic Book V*, 473d.

[91] Van Riel, *Plato's Gods*, 1.

[92] Allen, *Philosophy for Understanding Theology*, 34.

[93] "Aristotle," *The Stanford Encyclopedia of Philosophy* (July 29, 2015), https://plato.stanford.edu/entries/aristotle/.

[94] Allen, *Philosophy for Understanding Theology*, 89.

[95] Aristotle, EN 1096a28.

[96] Mark J. Nyvlt, *Aristotle and Plotinus on the Intellect: Monism and Dualism Revisited*, (Lanham: Lexington Books, 1969) 111.

[97] Carabine, *Unknown God*, 35-51; Runia, *Philo of Alexandria,* 49-52; Wallis, *Neoplatonism*, 28-36.

[98] Runia, *Philo of Alexandria,* 53.

[99] Carabine, *Unknown God,* 52.

[100] Wallis, *Neoplatonism,* 16-17.

[101] Eric D. Perl, *Theophany: The Neoplatonic Philosophy of Dionysius the Areopagite* (Albany: State University of N work Press, 2007), 10-12.

[102] Perl, *Theophany,* 12.

[103] Wallis, *Neoplatonism,* 86. (italics added)

[104] Perl, *Theophany*, 13-16.

[105] Etienne Gilson, *God and Philosophy* 2nd ed. (New Haven: Yale University Press, 2002), 49.

[106] Michael Wyschogrod, *Abraham's Promise: Judaism and Jewish-Christian Relations* (Grand Rapids: Eerdmans, 2004), 40-41.

[107] Wallis, *Neoplatonism*, 100-105.

[108] Lossky, *Vision,* 49, 50.

[109] Lossky, *Vision,* 49.

[110] Lossky, *Vision,* 50.

[111] Lossky, *Vision,* 48-50.

[112] See Bernard McGinn, *The Presence of God: A History of Western Christian Mysticism, Volumes I-IV* (New York: Crossroads, 1998-2005); Evelyn Underhill, *Mysticism: The Nature and Development of Spiritual Consciousness* (Boston: Oneworld Publications, 1993); Vladimir Lossky, *The Mystical Theology of the Eastern Church* (Crestwood: St Vladimir's Seminary Press, 1976).

[113] Evelyn Underhill, T*he Mystic Way* (Atlanta: Ariel Press, 1992), 232.

[114] Lossky, *Vision,* 53.

[115] Zizioulas, "The Early Christian Community," C*hristianity Spirituality,* 38.

[116] Lossky, *Vision,* 54, 55.

[117] McGinn, *Foundations*, 140-142; Pseudo Dionysius, *The Complete Works* (trans. Colm Luibheid: New York: Paulist Press, 1978), 1, 33-34.

[118] The *Cloud of Unknowing,* written by an anonymous author in the latter half of the 14th century, became a spiritual guide to contemplative prayer in the late Middle Ages. Subsequently, it has inspired contemporary contemplative practices such as Centering Prayer, a form of Christian meditation developed by Trappist monks William Meninger, Basil Pennington, and Thomas Keating in the 1970s. Echoes of Plato, Clement, and the apophatic way can be heard in the author's language when he says, "For He can well be loved, but he cannot be thought. By love he can be grasped and held, but by thought, neither grasped nor held. And therefore, though it may be good at times to think specifically of the kindness and excellence of God, and though this may be a light and a part of contemplation, all the same, in the work of contemplation itself, it must be cast down and covered with a cloud of forgetting. And you must step above it stoutly but deftly, with a devout and delightful stirring of love, and struggle to pierce that darkness above you; and beat on that thick cloud of unknowing with

a sharp dart of longing love, and do not give up, whatever happens." (The Cloud of Unknowing and other works. Penguin Classics, 2001. Translated by A.C. Spearing.

[119] See Carabine, *The Unknown God*, passim; Hägg, *Clement of Alexandria*, passim; Lossky, *Mystical Theology*, passim.

[120] Hägg, Clement of Alexandria, 2.

[121] Daniélou, *Gospel Message*, 278.

[122] Daniélou, *Gospel Message*, 278-279.

[123] Daniélou, *Gospel Message*, 278.

[124] Zizioulas, "The Early Christian Community," *Christian Spirituality*, 38.

[125] Daniélou, *Gospel Message*, 280. Other themes include "the wounds endured for love" or "the eyes like doves."

[126] Harvey D. Egan, *Soundings in the Christian Mystical Tradition* (Collegeville: Liturgical Press, 2010), 4.

[127] Egan, *Soundings*, 18-19.

[128] Greer, *Origen*, 18.

[129] Origen, Hom, Ex. V, 4 quoted in Daniélou, *Gospel Message*, 279.

[130] Zizioulas, "Early Christian Community," 39.

[131] Zizioulas, "Early Christian Community," 39. (italics added)

[132] Matthew 5:48.

[133] 1 Tim. 1:5.

[134] In the 2011 NIV, 2 Peter 1:4 states "Through these (his glory and goodness), he has given us his very great and precious promises, so that through them you may participate in *the divine nature*, having escaped the corruption in the world caused by evil desires." In this verse, the phrase that is often translated as "divine nature" can also mean "divine order," which has to do with life in God's kingdom. In the context of 2 Peter, the second meaning is to be preferred. This clarification is important because historically, the term *partakers in the divine nature* has often been often associated with an individualistic type of spirituality that seeks to have personal unitive experience with the divine, an approach which has much in common with Plato's scheme. However, this verse is set within a communal context and shows how the entire community has been delivered from the world and has now come into a new existence. As participants of this new divine order, the believing community, i.e. the church, God's temple, is filled the Spirit and experiences God's life together as they relate to one another in love.

[135] 2 Peter 1:3-11.

[136] Matt. 6:6; Ps. 51:6; Rom. 7:22; Luke 6:45.

[137] 1 Cor. 12-14.

[138] McGinn, Foundations of Mysticism, 116. See also, Julie Canlis, Calvin's Ladder: A Spiritual Theology of Ascent and Ascension (Grand Rapids: Eerdmans, 2010), 31-33.

[139] For instance, contemporary spiritual teacher, Richard Rohr, states that "Israel is, of course, the standing metaphor and symbol for the individual soul and all of history," in Breathing Underwater: Spirituality and the Twelve Steps

(Cincinnati: Franciscan Media, 2011), 43 (italics his). See Greer, Origen, 18 for the basis of this idea.

140 Daniélou, *Gospel Message,* 278.

141 Zizioulas, "Early Christian Community," 38.

142 Zizioulas, "Early Christian Community," 41.

143 Farrow, "Doctrine of the Ascension," 33.

144 Zizioulas, "Early Christian Community," 41.

145 Zizioulas, "Early Christian Community," 41. (italics added)

146 Farrow, "Doctrine of the Ascension," 32.

147 Zizoulas, "Early Christian Community," *Christian Spirituality*, 42-43.

148 Daniélou, Gospel Message, 304-320; Allen, *Philosophy for Understanding Theology*, 77-101.

149 Henri Crouzel, *Origen, 1st ed.* (trans. A.S. Worrall: Edinburgh: T.&T. Clark, 1989) 88-9, 92.

150 Crouzel, Origen, 89.

151 Peter Brown, *The Body and Society: Men, Women, and Sexual Renunciation in Early Christianity* (New York: Columbia University Press, 1988), 352.

152 Brown, *The Body and Society,* 352.

153 Brown, *The Body and Society,* 351-353.

154 See Tom Wright, *Paul and the Faithfulness of God,* (London: SPCK, 2013) 1366-7 who argues that the text in Acts is an edited version of a major critical analysis of the god's of Hellenism.

155 William Lane, *Hebrews,* Word Biblical Commentary (Dallas: Word Books, c1991), CXii-CXViii. See also Alan M. Fairhurst, "Hellenistic Influence in the Epistle to the Hebrews." *Tyndale Bulletin* 7-8 (July 1961), 17-27.

156 Leonhard Goppelt, *Typos: The Typological Interpretation of the Old Testament in the New* (Grand Rapids: Eerdmans, c1982).

157 Tom Holland, *Tom Wright and the Search for Truth* (London: Apiary Publishing, 2017), 79-157.

158 Regarding Philo's influence on Hebrews see Ronald Williamson, *Philo and the Epistle to the Hebrews* (Boston: Brill, 1970); Fairhurst, "Hellenistic Influence," 17-27.

159 "Saint Augustine," *The Stanford Encyclopedia of Philosophy* (November 12, 2010), http://plato.stanford.edu/entries/augustine/.

160 Peter Brown, *Augustine of Hippo: A Biography*, 2nd ed. (Berkley: University of California Press,2000), 168.

161 John D. Caputo, *Philosophy and Theology* (Nashville: Abingdon Press, 2006), 13.

162 See Phillip Cary, *Augustine's Invention of the Inner Self: The Legacy of a Christian Platonist* (Oxford: Oxford University Press, 2000).

163 Phillip Cary, *Inner Grace: Augustine in the Traditions of Plato and Paul* (Oxford: Oxford University Press, 2008), 4.

164 In private correspondence with the author; used with permission.

165 W.R. Ward, *Early Evangelicalism: A Global Intellectual History, 160-1789* (Cambridge: Cambridge University Press, 2006)14-15.

166 Brown, *Augustine of Hippo,* 162.

167 Brown, Augustine of Hippo, 162.

168 Cary, *Invention,* 40.

169 Cary, *Invention,* 40.

170 Colin Morris, *The Discovery of the Individual 1050-1200* (Toronto: University of Toronto Press, 1972), 65-66; Cary, *Invention,* 140-145.

171 Canlis, *Calvin's Ladder,* 33-34.

172 Cary, *Inner Grace,* 4.

173 Canlis, *Calvin's Ladder,* 34.

174 Canlis, *Calvin's Ladder,* 41, notes that those "who inherited Augustine's seven-grade ascent are many." They include Gregory the Great's *Seven Steps to Spiritual Perfection*, Bonaventure's *The Mind's Ascent to God*, Ruysbroeck's Seven *Steps on the Ladder of Spiritual Love,* Teresa's, *The Interior Castle*, with its seven mansions, Guigo's *Ladder of Monks*, Richard of St. Victor's *De gradibus caritatis*, Walter of Hilton's *Scale of Perfection*, Gerson's three-step *Mountain of Contemplation,* and even the twelfth-century Cistercian monastery entitled *Scala Dei.* She notes "these similarly bear the mark of Augustinian desire, inwardness, and individualism."

175 Canlis, *Calvin's Ladder,* 36.

176 Cary, *Invention,* 40.

177 Colin Morris, The Discovery of the Individual, 1

178 Dera Sipe, "Struggling with Flesh: Soul/Body Dualism in Porphyry and Augustine," 15, https://concept.journals.villanova .edu/article/viewFile/266/229; Augustine, *City of God* Book XIV:1.

179 Gerard J.P. O'Daly, *Augustine's Philosophy of Mind* (Berkeley: University of California Press, 1987), 12-13.

180 Brown, *Augustine of Hippo*, 75.

181 Reinhold Niebuhr, *Christian Realism and Political Problems* (New York: Charles Scribner's Sons, 1953), 123 quoted in Donald G. Bloesch, *Spirituality Old & New: Recovering Authentic Spiritual Life,* 46.

182 According to O'Daly in *Augustine's Philosophy of Mind*, "much of the detail of the first three levels at least is. . . common ground among philosophers since Aristotle: we cannot exclude the possibility of an Augustinian amalgam of Platonic, Peripatetic and Stoic views, with a strong Ciceronian influence," 15.

183 Augustine, *City of God,* Book XIV: 2.

184 Augustine, *City of God,* Book XIV: 2.

185 Augustine, *City of God*, Book XIV: 4.

186 A. Kent Hieatt, "Eve as Reason in a Tradition of Allegorical Interpretation of the Fall," *Journal of the Warburg and Cortauld Institutes,* Vol. 43 (1980): 221-226.

[187] Hieatt, "Eve as Reason," 221.

[188] Hieatt, "Eve as Reason," 221.

[189] Hieatt, "Eve as Reason," 221; See also Tatha Wiley, *Original Sin: Origins, Developments, Contemporary Meanings* (New York: Paulist Press, 1989), 63.

[190] Brown, *Body and Society*, 406-408; 418.

[191] Hieatt, "Eve as Reason," 221.

[192] Brown, *Augustine of Hippo*, 390-391.

[193] Brown, *Augustine of Hippo*, 392-393; Brown, Body and Society, 419.

[194] Alan Jacobs, *Original Sin: A Cultural History* (New York: Harper Collins, 2008), 32.

[195] Brown, *Augustine of Hippo*, 391.

[196] Hieatt, "Eve as Reason," 221.

[197] Brown, *Augustine of Hippo*, 391

[198] Brown, *Body and Society*, 418.

[199] Brown, *Body and Society*, 418.

[200] Brown, *Body and Society*, 418.

[201] Brown, *Augustine of Hippo*, 391.

[202] Wiley, *Original Sin*, 64

[203] Gerald Bray, ed. *The Ancient Christian Commentary: New Testament Vol. VI – Romans* (Downers Grove: InterVarsity, 1998), 189-190; Martyn Lloyd Jones, *Romans: Exposition of Chapter 7:1–8:4* (Edinburgh: Banner of Truth Trust, 1973), 177-178.

[204] Thomas F. Martin, *Rhetoric and Exegesis in Augustine's Interpretation of Romans 7:24-25a*, (Lewiston: Edwin Mellen Press, 2001), 39; Paula Fredriksen, "Paul and Augustine: Conversion Narratives, Orthodox Traditions, and the Retrospective Self." *Journal of Theological Studies* NS37/1 (1986)," 25 quoted in Martin, *Augustine's Interpretation of Romans 7*, 40.

[205] Martin, *Augustine's Interpretation of Romans 7*, 38. Martin notes that other concerns, not just controversies about concupiscence, the body and sexuality, also motivated Augustine's evolving analysis of Romans 7. See pages 39-41.

[206] Jesse Couenhoven, "St. Augustine's Doctrine of Original Sin," *Augustinian Studies* 36:2 (2005), 367, http://www.academia.edu /1958072/St._Augustines_Doctrine_of_Original_Sin.

[207] J.N.D. Kelly, *Early Christian Doctrines* (Peabody Mass.: Prince Press, 2007), 364-366; Brown, *Body and Society* 418; Martin, *Augustine's Interpretation of Romans 7,"* 38.

[208] "Total depravity," *Theopedia.com,* http://www.theopedia.com /total depravity. See also, Ligon Duncan, "Total Depravity and the Believer's Sanctification," December 1, 2012. http://fpcj.blogspot.com /2012/12/total-depravity-and-believers.html.

[209] Wiley, *Original Sin*, 60-63.

[210] Brown, *Body and Society*, 420.

[211] Cassian, *Collationes* 4.7, p.172 quoted in Brown, *Body and Society*, 420.

[212] Brown *Body and Society,* 421.

[213] Brown, *Body and Society,* 423.

[214] Seraphim Rose, *The Place of Blessed Augustine in the Orthodox Church,* 3rd ed. (Platina: St. Herman of Alaska Brotherhood, 2007), 34-35.

[215] Rose, *Blessed Augustine,* 36.

[216] Rose, *Blessed Augustine,* 36.

[217] Wiley, *Original Sin,* 55. Couenhoven, *Original Sin,* 387.

[218] Wiley, *Original Sin,* 37-55. See also John S. Romanides, *The Ancestral Sin,* (Ridgewood, NJ: Zephyr, 2008) 164-169 (italics added).

[219] Hos. 6:7.

[220] Rom. 5:14, 19.

# Other books by Tom Holland

- *Contours of Pauline Theology: A Radical New Survey of the Influences on Paul's Biblical Writings,* ISBN978-1857924695

- *Romans: The Divine Marriage: A Biblical and Theological Commentary, Volumes 1 & 2,* ISBN 9781912445202 & 9781912445226

- *Hope for the Nations: Paul's Letter to the Romans,* ISBN 978-1912445004

- *Tom Wright and the Search for Truth: A Theological Evaluation, Second Edition Revised and Expanded,* ISBN 9781912445103

- *God and His Children: Learning about prayer through Christians in discussion (Volume 1),* ISBN 9781912445059

From www.Apiarypublishing.com